Controversial

PSYCHIATRY

issues in

IN

thought and

DISSENT

practice

Controversial

PSYCHIATRY

Anthony Clare

issues in

IN

SECOND EDITION

FOREWORD BY
MICHAEL SHEPHERD

thought and

DISSENT

practice

ROUTLEDGE
London and New York

First published in 1976
by Tavistock Publications Ltd

Second edition 1980
Reprinted 1983

Reprinted 1989 by Routledge
11 New Fetter Lane, London EC4P 4EE
29 West 35th Street, New York, NY 10001

© *Anthony Clare 1976, 1980*

Printed in Great Britain at the University Press, Cambridge

British Library Cataloguing in Publication Data

Clare, Anthony
    Psychiatry in dissent. — 2nd edn
    1. Psychiatry
    I. Title
    616.8' 9   RC 454
ISBN 0-415-03942-8

Contents

Acknowledgements

ONE DEBT, impossible to repay, is that which I owe to
my many colleagues and friends at the Maudsley
Hospital, members of the senior and junior medical staff,
nurses, occupational therapists, and social workers. Their
combination of clinical involvement and sceptical questioning convinces me that eclecticism need not be equated with
nihilism nor uncertainty with indifference. I greatly appreciate the support provided by Professor Robert Cawley and
Dr James Birley which ensured that I had enough time to
finish the book and to Professor John Wing who gave of his
particular experience in the field of schizophrenia. A number
of people, including Patrick Cosgrave, Paul Medlicott, and
Mary James, not professionally involved in psychiatry, provided me with constant constructive criticism and advice.
Their curiosity concerning aspects of psychiatric theory and
practice greatly stimulated me in this attempt to render more
meaningful the assumptions, the achievements, and the
limitations of current knowledge in this area. Mrs Audrey
Pritchett, with typical devotion and good humour, typed
the various drafts while Wyn Clare skilfully adapted several
diagrams. One other person, who is in no way responsible
for the contents of this book and who may very well disagree
with its central argument, merits a mention. Professor
Norman Moore of the Department of Psychiatry, Trinity
College, Dublin, is primarily responsible for my being in
psychiatry and I welcome the opportunity to publicly

acknowledge my debt and appreciation. Finally, there is the incalculable debt I owe my wife, Jane, and my three children, Rachel, Simon, and Eleanor, who have borne the inordinate demands on their leisure with remarkable good will and tolerance. Without their constant enthusiasm and support, I have little doubt that this book would not have been completed.

October 1975   ANTHONY CLARE

The author and publishers are grateful to the various individuals and publishers who have given permission for material to be reproduced.

Figure 1 on page 23 is reprinted from 'Model for Life Changes and Illness Research', by R. Rahe *et al.*, *Archives of General Psychiatry* **31** (1974): 172–177, © 1974 American Medical Association. *Tables 2* and *3* on pages 170 and 171 are reprinted from 'Genetic Theorising and Schizophrenia', by I. I. Gottesman and J. Shields, *British Journal of Psychiatry* **122** (1973): 15–30. *Table 4* on page 201 is reprinted from 'A Review of Earlier Evidence of Genetic Factors in Schizophrenia', by E. Slater in *The Transmission of Schizophrenia* (1968) edited by D. Rosenthal and S. S. Kety with the permission of the publishers Pergamon Press Ltd. *Table 1* on page 242 is reprinted from 'Prognostic Factors in Electric-Convulsive Therapy', by R. F. Hobson, *Journal of Neurology, Neurosurgery and Psychiatry* **16** (1953): 278–81. *Table 2* on page 243 is reprinted from 'The Diagnosis of Depressive Syndromes and the Prediction of E.C.T. Response', by M. W. P. Carney, M. Roth, and R. F. Garside, *British Journal of Psychiatry* **111** (1965): 659. *Figure 1* on page 272 is reprinted from 'A Program for Prefrontal Lobotomy with Report of Effect on Intractable Pain' by H. Elliott, S. Albert, and W. Bremner, *Treatment Services Bulletin* **3** (1948): 26–35. *Figure 2* on page 275 is reprinted from *Manter's Essentials of Clinical Neuroanatomy and Neurophysiology* (1970) edited by Arthur J. Gatz with the permission of the publishers F. A. Davis Company. *Figure 3* on page 278 is reprinted from P. D. MacLean, *American Journal of Medicine* **25** (1958): 62. *Figure 4* on page 283 is reprinted from 'The Brain in Relation to Empathy and Medial Education', by P. D. MacLean, *Journal of Nervous and Mental Diseases* **144** (1967): 374–382. *Figure 5* on page 287 is reprinted from 'Additional Stereotactic Lesions in the Cingulum Following Failed Tractotomy in the Subcaudate Region', by G. C. Knight in *Surgical Approaches to Psychiatry* (1973) edited by L. V. Laitinen and K. E. Livingstone with the permission of the publishers Medical and Technical Publishing Co. *Table 6* on page 399 is reprinted from 'Will There Be Enough Psychiatrists to Run the Psychiatric Service Based on District General Hospitals?', by G. F. M. Russell in *Policy for Action* (1973) edited by R. Cawley and G. McLachlan with the permission of the publishers Oxford University Press.

Foreword

O VER THE past two generations most developed countries have witnessed a growing interest in psychological medicine. In principle this is a trend to be welcomed. By acknowledging that the scientific study of abnormal behaviour need not be confined to the inmates of mental institutions and prisons, society has sanctioned a new set of attitudes which have led to the metamorphosis of the alienist into the psychiatrist, the asylum into the mental hospital, and the lunatic into the psychiatric patient. The change in names reflects the rising status of the subject.

At the same time it has become apparent that, however much it may accord with the vociferous assertions of some professionals and some influential sections of the lay public, this social process calls for continuous critical assessment. It is one thing to demarcate an area for development, another to build prematurely on uncertain foundations. And it is indisputable that while the gap between established knowledge and much psychiatric theory and practice remains uncomfortably wide, there has been an understandable but nonetheless mistaken tendency on the part of some psychiatrists to traffic in uncertain assumptions, unfounded speculations, and unproven hypotheses, which in some quarters have invested their role with the mystique of a priest or shaman equipped with the qualifications of an emotional engineer. Not the least of the disadvantages associated with an over-sell of this type is the inevitable disillusion and resentment that follow on unmet claims and promises and that can exercise an adverse influence on development of the less spectacular but more solid work in progress.

One numerically small but potentially important group of individuals to whom these issues are of particular importance is the body of undergraduate and postgraduate students of medicine. Thanks to the careful observations of medical sociologists we now know something about the sub-culture of the medical school, where career-choice is as dependent on example and emulation as in most centres of higher education. In most of the traditional branches of medicine stereotypes are well established: the successors of Sir Ralph Bloomfield-Bonington, Mr Cutler Walpole, and Dr Blenkinsop can be readily detected as guides or warnings to aspirant physicians, surgeons, and general practitioners in contemporary medical schools. But with psychiatry it is different. Here the student is more likely to encounter a heterogeneous collection of teachers propounding a bewildering variety of incompatible dogmas and precepts. Small wonder that there is concern about the quality of recruitment into the specialty.

The same problems apply *a fortiori* to the young man or woman who has opted for a career in psychiatry. In all postgraduate centres psychiatrists in training are currently bombarded with the same set of blandishments and exhortations that beset the medical undergraduate but few of them have taken as much trouble as Dr Clare to examine the underlying issues and their implications for students with a professional interest in psychiatry. In his analysis of current views on such controversial topics as the concepts of mental illness, schizophrenia, the notion of responsibility, physical treatments in psychiatry, and the mental health services he points out with acumen and tact many of the logical difficulties that must be tackled if psychiatry is to be given a scientific underpinning. In so doing he has rendered a service not only to all students of the subject, lay and professional alike, but also to those of its teachers who are open-minded and self-critical enough to follow his arguments.

September 1975   MICHAEL SHEPHERD
Professor of Epidemiological Psychiatry
Institute of Psychiatry
University of London

Foreword

... but also in those of his teachers and of experimental
... and will compel them to follow the arguments.

September 1972   MICHAEL RUTTER
                                  Professor of Developmental Psychiatry
                                  Institute of Psychiatry
                                  University of London

Introduction

PSYCHIATRY down through the ages has provided a fertile soil for the genesis and growth of explanatory theories of mental functioning and malfunctioning but an impoverished atmosphere for their survival. Astrology, phrenology, mesmerism, galvanism, orgone therapy, hydrotherapy, are but some of the speculative fancies that have masqueraded as scientific truths and that have commanded immense intellectual status together with the assent and patronage of the established scientific figures of their day. It might be anticipated, with some legitimacy, that such a historical foundation would induce a certain degree of hardheadedness and a strong seam of scepticism in contemporary psychiatrists, yet who would declare with unbridled confidence that today we lack our astrologists and our phrenologists or that we can always discern the genuine from the spurious, the valuable from the fake.

This book evolved out of discussions I have had during my psychiatric training with my colleagues, both teachers and peers, my fellow-professionals in social work, psychiatric nursing, clinical psychology, and general medicine, and with those who, while not immediately involved in the theory or practice of psychiatry, nonetheless were interested in the scope, pretensions, and wider implications of the subject. I have been impressed by the diversity of views advocated by these various professionals in the course of their collective task of defining and treating psychiatric disorders. It has been my experience that, for example, the idea of the family as a begetter of psychopathology, the stereotype of the 'schizophrenogenic' parent, and the conviction that all mental illness is environmentally determined, are all theories of causality of special appeal to social workers confronted in their day-to-day work by an awesome catalogue of economic hardship, fragmented personal relationships, and social stress. In contrast, such evidence as there is to support genetic and constitutional factors tends to command much less support from this quarter than from among medical and para-medical personnel, who are more accustomed to securing the foundations of the subject in a biological matrix, and less respectful of the causal claims of social factors. Clinical psychologists, understandably heartened by the modest success achieved by certain behavioural techniques in the management of a number of psychiatric conditions, and often out of sympathy with the theoretical approaches of their medical and social-work colleagues, are tempted to embrace an explanatory model rooted in behaviourist principles. In the midst of this ideological din, caught in a no man's land between psychiatrists, psychologists, and social workers, are the psychiatric nurses, whose main hope of professional survival is somehow to harness into a benevolent therapeutic force the contrary winds that blow around them.

There may be those, especially among my colleagues, who will be irritated at the amount of space and attention that I devote to the arguments of those who do not merely propagate idiosyncratic views on the nature of mental disorder but who actually challenge the reality of its existence. Whatever the ultimate worth of such ideas, they have proven to be remarkably influential within and outside the psychiatric arena. Many appear to perceive within them a sensitivity and a compassion believed to be absent from more orthodox approaches.

It is for such reasons that I open my book with two chapters devoted to a consideration of the concept of mental illness and the various ideological positions adopted by psychiatrists in the course of their professional work. Chapter 3 is concerned with the diagnostic process as it is applied in psychiatry. The formulation of a psychiatric diagnosis is often depicted as a sterile exercise in reductionism, an academic exercise of little practical value. In fact, every diagnosis in general medicine and in psychiatry is a hypothesis to be tested and refined. The practising psychiatrist is a clinician, that is to say someone who, in Feinstein's memorable phrase 'depends not on a knowledge of causes, mechanisms or names for diseases but on a knowledge of patients'. The clinician, at his best, is a superb observer and organizer of clinical data, and these skills, which to a regrettable extent have been overshadowed in general medicine by technological achievements, retain their primacy and their force in the everyday practice of psychiatry.

The most serious mental illness is schizophrenia. Confusion about what is meant by the term is not limited to the widespread abuse in everyday parlance of the adjective 'schizophrenic' but extends to its every aspect and facet. Chapter 4 considers what psychiatrists in Britain mean when they arrive at a diagnosis of schizophrenia, while Chapter 5 reviews the evidence for and against the various causal theories that have been advanced to explain the appearance of this most malignant of psychiatric disorders. These two chapters, taken together with the opening three, have running through them the common theme of the disease concept in psychiatry, its nature, its value, and its limitations.

The remaining chapters share only the common characteristic of being controversial. Electrical treatment is a widely used treatment of some forty years' standing. Psychosurgical procedures, at the present time, are used more sparingly, but recent advances in the physiology of the brain, coupled with the development of highly specialized surgical techniques, have stimulated interest, and an increase in the number of such operations performed each year can be anticipated. It is important to be able to assess as coldly as possible such evidence as exists to support the use of these two empirical treatments, but it is not easy to preserve an unbiased and sceptical approach in the midst of the intense and acrimonious discussion that they provoke.

Chapter 8 is concerned with the issue of responsibility and its relationship with the thorny problem of compulsory hospitalization. I do not pretend to deal adequately with the profound philosophical issues involved here. Other and better-qualified commentators have done so elsewhere. What I have tried to do is to indicate the guidelines that the clinical psychiatrist employs when he comes to decide when it is appropriate to certify a mentally ill person and when it is not. The reader is free to form his own opinion as to the adequacy of the legal controls protecting the individual against the abuse of such clinical power and the restraint, or lack of it, with which such power is implemented in clinical practice.

Finally, it is not possible to comprehend fully the forces at work in psychiatry in Britain without having some knowledge of the structure of the psychiatric services, their manpower, facilities, and resources. My analysis in Chapter 9, of the state of the psychiatric services may well be considered to be unnecessarily pessimistic and excessively preoccupied with shortcomings and inadequacies while somewhat dismissive of the immense and progressive changes that have taken place over the past two decades. Anticipating such a criticism, I content myself with Hardy's observation, 'If way to the Better there be, it exacts a full look at the worst', and I feel confident that it is in the long-term interest of psychiatry, its practitioners, as well as its patients, if those who are entrusted with the growth and development of psychiatric knowledge do that which they constantly exhort their patients to do and look reality steadily and straight in the eye. It can be argued, and a knowledge of psychiatric history does nothing to diminish such a view, that nothing does more to obstruct the progress of psychiatry and obscure its way forward than the readiness to adopt as established truth the frills, the fads, and the fancies of passing intellectual fashion. Changes in the organization of the psychiatric services, in common with new treatments and new theories, must be rigorously evaluated if they are not to fade into oblivion with the passage of time.

Psychiatry does not lack controversial topics and I have had to restrict my discussions to only a handful. Psycho-analysis and psychotherapy are among the most contentious issues which I have referred to only in passing. The strident claims of the behaviourists and the current vogue for group-centred therapy, both worthy of some detailed consideration, have had to be neglected. The growth of family and marital therapy, the status of alcoholism as a disease or deviant behaviour, the role of the psychiatrist as forensic expert – these all deserve an evaluation which space and time have not permitted. My final choice is a personal one and reflects my judgement as to what constitutes the crucial philosophical and practical issues in contemporary psychiatry.

References

FEINSTEIN, A.R. (1967) *Clinical Judgement*. Baltimore: Williams and Wilkins.

The concept of mental illness

Anyone who has reflected on the many definitions of health, and of mental health in particular, will, I think, conclude that there is no consensus, and he will see that when moral or social values are invoked there are scarcely any limits to the behaviour which might be called morbid. Medical criteria are safer; that is, criteria essentially concerned with the integrity of physiological and psychological functions.

SIR AUBREY LEWIS 1963: 1550

To the intelligent, sympathetic observer, intent on reaching a balanced and informed understanding of its content and its possibilities, the present fragmented state of psychiatry presents a formidable picture. The concept of mental illness appears to permit a bewildering number of interpretations. Is it a label for socially unacceptable behaviour behind which the deviant is permitted to take refuge and thereby evade the consequences of his antisocial activities? Is it an arbitrary concept which only serves to mislead people, by virtue of its medical connotations, into believing in 'mental sickness' when, more often than not, what it describes consists of disordered, interpersonal relationships wherein one person is scapegoated to carry the responsibility for the disturbances of the group? Is it merely a political expedient which enables those who hold power within society to devalue and degrade the dissenter and, by defining him as mentally ill, to violate his freedom and destroy his dignity? Or is it a concept, analogous to physical illness, which is applied to a patient who manifests not physical pathology but 'psychopathology', who experiences psychic rather than physical suffering, exhibits disturbances in his psychological rather than his physical functioning, and who, in some instances at least, suffers a serious impairment of his judgemental capabilities and his personal responsibility?

Given the fractious and acrimonious debate which rages over its legitimacy, it is hardly surprising that there have even been attempts to abolish the concept of mental illness altogether and replace it by some alternative, non-medical construct such as deviance, maladaption, social disturbance, problems of living, or community disorder. The object of the whole elaborate psychiatric exercise is variously labelled 'patient', 'client', 'deviant', 'dissident', 'analysand', or 'consumer', and his difficulties handled in accordingly different ways. Psychiatrists and psychiatric nurses may emphasize their professional links with their colleagues in physical medicine, but the majority of psychiatrists do not wear white coats nor the nurses uniforms and both tend to expect their patients to take more responsibility for their psychological disturbances than general physicians expect of those who are physically ill. There is confusion, too, over the criteria whereby an individual is deemed to be in need of psychiatric treatment. It is not an uncommon experience for a social worker or a probation officer to bring a seriously disturbed person to a psychiatrist only to be told that he is not suffering from a mental illness, or for someone who has not himself complained of anything at all to be compulsorily admitted to a psychiatric hospital and treated against his wishes.

Over the past decade, an 'anti-psychiatry' movement has sprung up, the main principle of which appears to be that mental illness is a reductive smear that obscures and defiles the despairing cries of the downtrodden and exploited against an alienating and dehumanized society. Psychiatric intervention is portrayed as a violent assault perpetrated under the guise of treatment, and the psychiatrist is deemed to be an agent of the dominant political order, and an agent of repression and of power. Anti-psychiatrists demand the abolition of existing psychiatric institutions and insist that psychiatrists either acknowledge their true role as society's thought police or become agents of personal and social change.

The public, bewildered by the apparent ideological chaos within psychiatry, is ready prey indeed for any spokesman who peddles a simple answer to the difficult philosophical and practical questions facing psychiatry in its present poorly developed state. The subject being largely a semantic one and the participants drawn in the main from medicine, sociology, psychology, and anthropology, disciplines that mix uneasily at the best of times, it is not easy for those who are not familiar with the general theory of disease to appreciate fully the complex, often subtle arguments over its applicability to psychiatric disorders. They are not helped by having the issue put before them in a deceptive and meretricious fashion. For example, one celebrated and widely read critic of clinical psychiatry, Thomas Szasz, himself a professor of psychiatry at the State University of New York in Syracuse, NY, declares:

> 'Disease means bodily disease. Gould's Medical Dictionary defines disease as a disturbance of the function or structure of an organ or a part of the *body*. [Italics in original] The mind (whatever it is) is not an organ or part of the body. Hence it cannot be diseased in the same sense as the body can.'   (Szasz 1974: 97)

This sort of semantic gymnastics only encourages one to reach for another dictionary, such as *The Concise Oxford Dictionary*, to find an alternative and opposing view to that of Thomas Szasz. Here we find, among the various definitions of disease, 'Deranged or depraved state of mind or morals' (fourth edition, 1950). So the problem promptly returns and lo! mental disease exists again! The concept of disease, in physical medicine as in psychiatry, is a complicated one, however, and any conclusion as to its relevance in psychiatry is hardly resolved by resorting to English language dictionaries.

One of the earliest ideas of disease, indeed it was held by

Hippocrates and his disciples, was that of a combination of signs and symptoms observed to occur together so frequently and so characteristically as to constitute a recognizable and typical clinical picture. This has been termed the clinical-descriptive or syndromal definition of disease. It was Thomas Sydenham, an English physician of the late seventeenth century, who drew particular attention to the importance of differentiating illnesses from each other and who pioneered the idea of a specific pathology underlying each disease. He argued that physical disease could be reduced to 'certain and determinate kinds with the same exactness as we see it done by botanic writers in their treatises on plants' (Taylor 1972: 11) and he believed that as one plant differs from another in some crucial manner so do diseases differ. He himself successfully dissected out on clinical grounds, from the existing morass of pathological signs and symptoms, such conditions as scarlet fever, measles, gout, smallpox, and malaria, and in the years that followed his disciples distinguished such conditions as heart disease, cerebral haemorrhage, tumours, and diabetes. At that time, diseases were envisaged as having some form of autonomous existence with natural histories of their own, as beings invading the body from without or as parasites growing within it.

However, the remarkable technical advances of seventeenth-century medicine, such as van Leeuwenhoek's discovery of the microscope, Harvey's triumphant demonstration of the circulation of the blood, and Malpighi's detailed anatomical dissections, contributed to a subtle and gradual change of emphasis in thinking about disease. From being preoccupied about the exact anatomical structure of the various parts of the body, physicians became absorbed in an attempt to understand how such parts worked. At about the same time, the concept of disease as extraneous pathology attacking normal life from outside began to yield to the concept of *pathological life* itself. Almost two centuries after Sydenham, Rudolf Virchow, the precociously brilliant Ger-

man pathologist, challenged the 'botanical' view of diseases
and relocated the source of disease *inside* the body:

> 'If the cells are the elementary constituents of the organism
> – its ultimate basic organised units in which the healthy
> signs of life occur – then the diseased pathological pro-
> cesses must also have their seat in the same cells.'
>
> (Venzmer 1972: 279)

Virchow clarified the definitions of thrombosis and em-
bolism and established the clinical picture of leukaemia long
before the neoplastic nature of the condition was understood.
Diseased organs became the focus for serious study and as a
consequence pathological anatomy flourished. Michel Foucault, in a provocative and fertile analysis of the historical
origins of modern clinical medicine, has drawn attention to
the development of what he terms the 'medical gaze' and the
manner in which, over the centuries, it has shifted from a
one-dimensional scrutiny alone to a two-dimensional one of
tissues and symptoms:

> 'Disease is no longer a bundle of characters dissociated
> here and there over the surface of the body and linked
> together by statistically observable concomitances and
> successions; it is a set of forms and deformations, figures
> and accidents, and of displaced, destroyed or modified
> elements bound together in sequence according to a geo-
> graphy which can be followed step by step. It is no longer
> a pathological species inserting itself into the body when-
> ever possible; it is the body itself which has become ill.'
>
> (Foucault 1973: 136)

Attention in the early nineteenth century began to turn to
the analysis of the various stages involved in the diagnosis
of sick organs. Diagnosis now became a matter of deciding
which organ of the body was affected and explaining how it
might be returned to normal functioning. The relationship
between the sick organ and the other, apparently normal
organs of the body, came under increasing scrutiny. Thus
did the 'medical gaze' focus with an ever-increasing intensity

on microscopic abnormalities of structure and function in the smallest cells of the organism. Virchow stated the new perspective with a characteristically polemical flourish: 'Diseases are neither self-subsistent, circumscribed autonomous organisms, nor entities which have forced their way into the body, nor parasites rooted on it . . . they represent only the course of physiological phenomena under altered conditions.' (Virchow 1847).

He later amended this somewhat uncompromising view and conceded that disease might indeed exist but only *inside* the body of the patient. Disease, in this schema, becomes something concrete, 'an altered part of the body' (Taylor 1972: 12)

Such a view of disease, with some modifications, quickly came to dominate medical thinking and its enthusiastic implementation led to a number of quite spectacular triumphs. The advantages of such a formulation are obvious, not least the fact that the presence of disease does not depend on this or that subjective clinical judgement. As we shall see, however, the dramatic technologically inspired successes of physical medicines have tended to obscure the disadvantages of such a formulation and have tended to obscure also the extent to which physical medicine still rests on a foundation of sound *clinical judgement* and still lacks a firm physico-pathological basis for many of the conditions it recognizes and treats.

One of the consequences of the 'disease as a lesion' approach has been the tendency amongst some psychiatrists to ground mental phenomena, normal and abnormal, on a physical foundation, namely on a foundation of cerebral anatomy, physiology, biochemistry, and pathology. Such attempts have not, however, been particularly successful. Elaborate anatomical constructions have been formulated ('brain mythologies') and unrelated phenomena, physical and psychological, forcibly associated. Specific brain cells have been identified as the source of memory and groups of nerve fibres have been linked in a highly simplified fashion to the association of thoughts and ideas. Nonetheless, the search for exact physiological parallels to psychic events, triggered by the astonishing achievement of physical medicine in integrating many normal and abnormal functions, has intensified over the years and the successful localization of various sensory and motor areas in the brain and of the sites of certain types of speech disorders in the left cerebral hemisphere have been amongst the achievements which have spurred on such an approach.

However, such a search also contributed to the growth of the naive belief that psychic disease is brain disease, a belief that serves to obscure rather than clarify the issues involved. Investigation of the somatic functions of the brain is clearly bound up with the investigation of psychic factors, yet the analogy that springs to mind is of an exploration of an unknown continent from opposite directions. Only the end links in the chain of causation from soma to psyche and vice versa are known and from these vantage points, the psychopathologist and the neuropathologist, the psychiatrist and the neurologist, the psychologist and the psychophysiologist, attempt to cross the enormous and uncharted terrain that lies between.

In practice, a parallelism is conceptualized between psychic and somatic phenomena. In practice, likewise, it is possible to convert the one set of terms, constructs, and concepts into the other. There are, however, serious dangers. On the one hand, there is the tendency to develop the somatic prejudice which assumes that man is only comprehensible in somatic terms and that the actual reality of human existence is itself a somatic event. Such a tendency is reflected in the commonly declared belief that all psychological interest in schizophrenia will quite properly cease once the underlying morbid biological process is uncovered.

On the other hand, there is the tendency to conclude that since the somatic analogy has led foolish and simplistic theorists, usually physicians, into fallacious anatomical constructions of psychic experiences and events, it would be better to avoid any direct analogy between somatic and psychic phenomena altogether. Such a view rejects the idea of an ideal unity of soma-psychic reality approached from opposite perspectives and argues instead that the somatic approach (medicine and its associated physical sciences) and the psychic approach (psychology and its associated behavioural sciences) involve two different and unrelated continents of exploration.

In actual clinical practice how are such differences resolved? Is the practice of medicine so distinct and different from that of psychiatry that the concept of disease, elaborated within the former, has no relevance to the latter? Or is it helpful in arriving at an understanding of the concept of mental illness to examine in more detail the concept of illness itself?

In contemporary clinical practice, the criteria of physical illness depend on the patient's own account of how he feels, on the manifest signs of impaired structure and function, and on any occult signs of such impairment, detected by special investigative instruments and procedures. Each of these three stages presupposes a norm. It is worth noting here that those critics of the alleged subjectivity of psychiatric diagnoses tend to emphasize the objectivity or 'hardness' of the norms used in physical medicine compared with those used in psychiatry. However, when one takes more than a cursory look at the implementation of these norms in practice it becomes clear that the situation is not as simple and polarized as these critics suggest.

In the *first* stage of the diagnostic process, the patient, in making a subjective complaint of physical ill-health, reports some change in what he has come to perceive as his normal state of physical well-being. There is an impressive and developing literature testifying to the extraordinary variability between what various individuals acknowledge as the norm of physical health. This is reflected in the considerable difficulty inherent in formulating a clear, concise, and acceptable definition of what constitutes *physical* health. At its inauguration, the World Health Organisation adopted a definition of health of such idealistic ambition that it prompted one critic to compare it with that state of perfection 'such as was enjoyed perhaps by archangels and by Adam before the Fall' (A. J. Lewis 1955: 180). The relevant passage in the WHO charter declares:

'Health is a state of complete physical, mental and social well-being and not merely the absence of disease and infirmity.'

If we were to apply such criteria of physical health, it would be difficult if not impossible to find a healthy person in any contemporary society. People differ in their conception of physical well-being and in their willingness to tolerate discomfort and worse as part of life's natural cycle rather than perceive it as evidence of sickness and disease. Zborowski (1952), in a series of celebrated studies, explored the reactions to physical pain of patients from various ethnic groups in a New York City hospital. He noted that whereas Jewish and Italian patients responded to pain in an emotional fashion, 'Old Americans' were more stoical and 'objective' and Irish patients more frequently denied pain altogether. He also drew attention to a difference in underlying attitudes in the Italian and Jewish patients towards pain; whereas the Italian patients in the main sought relief from pain and were relatively satisfied when such relief was obtained, the Jewish patients appeared more concerned about discovering its cause and possible consequences. In his description of the typical 'Old American family', Zborowski stressed the tendency of the mother to exhort her child to take pain 'like a man' and not to be a 'cissy', and while he refrained from drawing any such conclusion on the basis of this study, he did wonder how far such personal and cultural differences in coping with physical distress modified the tendency of ill persons to adopt publicly the mantle of the sick patient.

In his book *The Health of Regionsville: What the People Thought and Did about It*, Koos noted that upper-class persons were more likely than lower-class persons to view themselves as ill when they experienced particular symptoms and, when questioned about specific symptoms, reported more frequently than lower-class persons that they would seek medical advice. Twaddle (1969), studied the differences in behaviour of ethnical groups of sick patients and found Jewish patients to be more oriented towards the use of physicians than Italian-American Catholics or American Protestants. The Protestants in this study were the most resistant to the idea of making their illnesses public by way of contacting doctors and more readily turned to non-medical agents and agencies for help and relief.

The American sociologist, Professor David Mechanic, points out that how a person perceives his physical discomfort or disability can affect the way such discomfort or disability manifests itself and subsequently develops (Mechanic 1972). He refers to numerous reports, of an anthropological nature and in the experimental literature, indicating how a person's definition of a painful experience can condition how much or how little pain he is willing to tolerate without protest. He draws attention to those studies that have shown how emotional stress concomitant with the course of a physical disease, such as influenza or chronic brucellosis, can become so intermingled with the physical symptoms of the disease that the end-point of the disease easily becomes confused with the continuing emotional stress.

Different kinds of complaint result in different kinds of emotional response. Such responses are in turn affected by social factors. Rosenblatt and Suchman (1965) studied the attitudes towards and knowledge of health and illness in blue-collar workers and concluded that such workers had a greater tendency to lack confidence in medical advice and care than did white-collar and other professional workers. They noted that blue-collar workers ignored minor symptoms whereas white-collar subjects often took seriously conditions which, while far from incapacitating, simply by their existence called for medical attention.

Despite widespread misconceptions to the contrary, no objective norms of physical well-being exist and what one

man defines as personal malaise or ill-health another toler-
ates as one of the slings and arrows that flesh is heir to. The
need to establish normal standards of physical health for
relevant populations has been noted by a number of observers, in particular Scadding (1967). The latter has argued
that any disease implies a statistical deviation from a norm
which places the individual so deviating 'at a biological
disadvantage'.

'The rather vague term "biological disadvantage" is as
precise a statement as can be made about the criteria on
which it is generally decided whether deviation from norm
is to be regarded as associated with disease or not.'

(Scadding 1967: 877)

Scadding goes on to point out that the common characteristic which defines the group upon the study of which the
description of a named disease is founded may be of several
different types. It may be founded on no more than a combination of clinical symptoms and signs, observed to cluster
together frequently and distinctively as a syndrome. Some
diseases, particularly in psychiatry, are still definable only in
these terms. It may be founded on morbid pathological
changes, measurable disorders of function, biochemical
abnormalities, or specific deficiencies. It may even be defined on the basis of some chromosomal abnormality or
change. Depending on the stage to which a disease has
evolved, the formulation of a diagnosis can end in very different sorts of conclusions:

'The "diagnosis" . . . may state no more than a resemblance of the symptoms and signs to a previously recognized pattern; but more usually it makes a statement about
aetiology, about a microscopic or macroscopic anatomical
abnormality, about a disorder of function, about a specific deficiency or about a biochemical or chromosomal
abnormality.'   (Scadding 1967: 879)

In psychiatry, many diagnostic formulations state little
more than the recognition that a given set of symptoms and

signs resembles a previously recognized pattern. Nevertheless, the careful formulation of a diagnosis, based on an equally scrupulous and skilled eliciting of symptoms and signs (see Chapter 3) holds out the hope, realized in the evolution of many physical syndromes, that a fundamental abnormality or abnormalities may eventually be uncovered in psychiatric disease.

The second stage in this diagnostic process, it will be recalled, involved the eliciting of objective and manifest signs of impaired function and structure by the physician. The physician's training enables him to refer signs of disturbed structure and function to the norm. For some organs and systems he has more detailed and reliable information than he has for others. He can, for example, make more confident statements concerning the function of the patient's heart (he can gauge its size by palpation, its pumping integrity by listening via the stethoscope to its sounds, its rate by taking a pulse, and the volume of its output by examining the veins of the neck) than he can with regard to the structural and functional status of the patient's gallbladder. By and large, however, he does have a body of knowledge concerning each organ and system which permits him to make a judgement that is reasonably informed and that would for the most part be accepted by his professional colleagues, concerning the physical state of his patient. However, it is important not to exaggerate the simplicity of physical diagnosis. Let us take as an example the syndrome known as *dyspepsia*. For a start, there seems to be little agreement as to how common a condition it is. Reported prevalence rates in the United Kingdom range from 11·5 to 154 per 1,000 adults. There is confusion, too, over the clinical picture. Morris, in a thorough and informative review of the various causes of the condition, concludes with a paragraph of consummate honesty:

'Dyspepsia is a common and important symptom of gastrointestinal disease. Often the pathophysiological disturbances leading to dyspepsia are obscure. The patterns of clinical symptoms, such as pain, flatulence, nausea and weight loss, are of little value in distinguishing between its various causes. Radiological investigations are not always successful in diagnosing the origin of dyspepsia but endoscopy is proving a useful tool.' (Morris 1973: 147)

The existence of categories such as 'x-ray negative dyspepsia' and 'functional dyspepsia' bears witness to the inherent difficulties involved in delineating the physiochemical pathology of this 'common' symptom. A patient intermittently troubled by severe gastric pain and nausea would hardly be reassured by a physician who told him that since there is considerable doubt as to the precise cause, pathology, and prevalence of his condition it had been concluded that it does not exist! It is important to note that instead of drawing such a conclusion, physicians devote enormous energy and resources to developing more sophisticated tools of exploration. To uncover the cause of dyspepsia, the physician may take a sample of gastric juice through a tube passed into the stomach by way of the patient's nose or mouth, may take an x-ray of the stomach when empty and when full of barium (an opaque medium which shows up the outlines of the stomach on x-ray) and may pass an endoscope (an instrument which enables the hollow cavity of the stomach to be examined by direct visual inspection) down the throat and oesophagus of the patient. Even after all of this, according to Morris, it may not be possible to be certain as to the cause of the patient's subjective complaints.

Critics of psychiatric diagnoses tend to ignore the complicated evaluative process that is often involved in physical medicine and tend to portray the diagnostic procedure in physical medicine as smooth, detached, and efficient. They contrast such an idealized situation in physical medicine with the allegedly subjective and arbitrary state of diagnostic procedures in clinical psychiatry. Yet the lesson of dyspepsia appears to be that failure to clarify a diagnosis should result in a more intensive diagnostic search for clues and pathology. In psychiatry, failure to clarify the clinical picture is too often the signal for abdicating from making any diagnosis at all and for denigrating the whole concept of diagnosis as a futile and pointless academic exercise. The much-publicized Rosenhan study, discussed in more detail in Chapter 3, revealed that in some American psychiatric hospitals doctors diagnosed schizophrenia on the single symptom of hearing voices without making any further investigations of a physical, psychological, or social nature whatsoever. To complain of hearing voices is to complain of a symptom not a disease, in the sense that to complain of nausea, flatulence, pain, and indigestion is to complain of a collection of symptoms, a syndrome, and not a disease. In the latter situation, the complaint provokes the examining doctor into seeking a possible cause. In the former situation, a similar search is required if the various possible causes of auditory hallucinations (drug intoxication, alcohol abuse, depression, manic excitement, schizophrenia, organic illness, and malingering being just some of the possible explanations) are to be considered. Yet the deduction drawn from Rosenhan's study (1973) was not that the diagnostic skills of the doctors involved were abysmally deficient but rather that the diagnostic process in psychiatry is useless and 'we cannot distinguish the sane from the insane in psychiatric hospitals' (Rosenhan 1973: 257).

But has the psychiatrist any norms of mental structure and function, to which he can appeal, that can compare with the norms of physical structure and function available to the medical specialist? Consideration of the available definitions of what constitutes mental health does not at first glance hold out much hope for arriving at such psychiatric norms. The definitions of madness remain, as a certain Dr Good remarked over a century ago, 'so narrow as to set at liberty half the patients at Bethlem or the Bicetre . . . [or] so loose and capacious as to give a strait waistcoat to half the world'. In her characteristically trenchant discussion of the concept of mental illness, Baroness Wootton provided a number of quotations derived from a survey of the psychiatric literature, several of which are printed below. The definitions tend to share that quality of earnest, almost mawkish moral righteousness and sense of order that appears to be some psychiatrists' phantasy of what mental health, if they were ever to meet it, would be like.

'Let us define mental health as an adjustment of human beings to the world and to each other with a maximum of effectiveness and happiness. Not just efficiency, or just contentment – or the grace of obeying the rules of the game cheerfully. It is all of these together. It is the ability to maintain an even temper, an alert intelligence, socially considerate behaviour and a happy disposition.'

'Mental health consists of the ability to live . . . happily, productively, without being a nuisance.'

'In my work in other fields, my co-workers and I have settled for some such criteria as these: the ability to hold a job, have a family, keep out of trouble with the law, and enjoy the usual opportunities for pleasure. Industrial unrest to a large degree means bad mental hygiene, and is to be corrected by good mental hygiene.'

(Wootton 1959)

The above definitions embody a strong social value within the definition of mental health. The mentally healthy person is not a nuisance, does not challenge the rules, lose his temper, kick the cat, or park his car on a double yellow line. He makes no demands, passes his life quietly and productively and does not fiddle the social security, live with a mistress, or wear placards warning that the end of the world is nigh. Such attempts are typical of what is presented when a social definition of mental illness is requested. How such definitions might be applied in practice can best be judged by the remarks of Dr M. M. Kabanov, Director of the

Leningrad Psychoneurological Institute, speaking to an audience of American and Russian psychiatrists at a Social Psychiatry seminar at the Bekhterev Institute in Moscow, on the subject of psychiatric rehabilitation. He declared that the Russian aim in rehabilitation (i.e., the process whereby patients are returned from *mental ill-health* to *health*)

'. . . can be distinguished from the Anglo-American concepts of "re-socialisation" in that the former employs every socio-economic as well as medical means not only to make the individual more content but also to restore his capacity to serve his country through creative and consistent work. Progressive steps are (1) reparative, to correct the patient's somatic and psychic complaints . . . (2) re-adaptive to prevent isolation and "hospitalism" . . . (3) environmental, to furnish the best available cultural and occupational milieu for the patient's redirected efforts and (4) doctrinal, directed toward assuring a desirable improvement in his political philosophy and value systems.'   (Masserman 1971: 201–2)

The Conference Report is somewhat reticent concerning what, if anything, the American listeners made of the above. If they were listening, they must have experienced the, for them, unusual experience of hearing themselves diagnosed mentally ill by a fellow-psychiatrist! Dr Kabanov, doubtless, would be of the opinion that Dr John Schwab, Professor of Medicine and Psychiatry at the University of Florida, and the next speaker at the Conference, required a 'desirable improvement in his political philosophy and value systems' unless of course Professor Schwab turned out to be a card-carrying member of the Communist Party.

Psychoanalytical concepts of mental health and mental illness require somewhat different consideration. Since the majority of analysts concentrate on intrapsychic criteria and use terms that by definition render it impossible to consider whether someone is mentally healthy unless he has been psychoanalysed, it is difficult to translate the analytical jargon of normality and abnormality into non-technical language. In so far as it can be so translated, the analytical view of mental health appears to include an internal confidence of feeling and knowing, an ability to make the fullest use of mental powers and abilities, and a capacity for enjoyment and self-content. Aubrey Lewis, commenting on the fact that such language leaves room for absurdly wide differences of opinion about whether a psychoanalysed patient or indeed anybody at all is mentally well, observes:

'The inherent difficulty of the concept of mental health is underlined when we find the psychoanalyst, so expert in the microscopy of mental happenings, unable to dispense with equivocal and cloudy terms in stating his criteria of recovery.'   (Lewis 1955: 192)

Confronted by the sinister implications of a socially defined concept of mental illness and the impractical implications of the analytical definitions, it is worth turning for further clarification of the whole question to Lewis's seminal paper, entitled 'Health as a Social Concept', which he delivered to the British Sociological Association in 1953. In this paper, Lewis side-steps the intractable problem inherent in attempting a definition of mental health and declares that the most serviceable criterion of mental health is the *absence* of mental illness. What, then, does he believe mental illness to be?

He is quick to point out what, in his view, it is not. Failure or refusal to adapt to a social or political situation need not betoken mental illness. 'One can', he insists 'be *sociopathic* without being *psychopathic*' (Lewis 1955: 186). Though psychiatric illness may result in social non-conformity, there are many forms of social deviation that are not illness and many forms of illness that are not social deviation. At this stage it is worth noting that for the Russian communist psychiatrist, Dr Kabanov, social deviation and psychiatric illness mean much the same thing. For the American private practice psychiatrist, Dr Ronald Leifer, they mean the same thing too, but whereas Dr Kabanov is more than happy to set about 'doctrinal' rehabilitation with a will (perhaps even extending his efforts to 'rehabilitate' visiting troops of American capitalist colleagues) Dr Leifer is equally emphatic but in the opposite direction:

'To abandon the medical model and view mentally ill persons as social deviators instead of diseased would expose the structure and quality of our social life to criticism. To say that so-called mental illness is one of the most important public health problems today ... means that there are many more deviating persons in our society than we have publicly acknowledged and it means that there are many more unhappy people than we have admitted.'

(Leifer 1971: 18)

Well, if Dr Kabanov and Dr Leifer are wrong and mental illness can be distinguished from deviation, how does Professor Lewis suggest that such a distinction might be drawn? He points out that there have always been physicians who believed in such a distinction. What principle, for example, led such doctors to bring insanity and physical disease under one heading while leaving crime, for example, apart? The common feature between the first two, in Lewis's view, is an 'evident disturbance of part-functions as well as of general efficiency'. In physical disease, as we have noted, the development of an organ-based disease model led to the idea of disease as a disturbance in part-function. Environmental factors, including social and cultural ones, play an often crucial role, but the diagnosis of physical disease *rests* on a demonstration of a disturbance in an organ or bodily system. In mental disorders such a part-function disturbance is shown by a disturbance in one or more of the recognized mental functions; mental functions such as perception, learning, thinking, remembering, feeling, emotion, motivation, etc. Disturbances in perception or memory are the psychiatric equivalent of disturbances in, say the liver or the lymphatic system. Deviant, maladapted, non-conformist behaviour is pathological only if it is accompanied by a manifest disturbance of one or more such functions. For mental illness to be inferred, in Lewis's view,

'. . . disorder of function must be detectable at a discrete or differentiated level that is hardly conceivable when mental activity as a whole is taken as the irreducible datum. If non-conformity can be detected only in total behaviour, while all the particular psychological functions seem unimpaired, health will be presumed not illness.'

(Lewis 1955: 188)

Lewis is too wise a psychiatrist to believe that this is *the* answer to the thorny problem of what constitutes the essential difference between illness and deviance and, in his lecture, he drew attention to certain areas, such as sexual perversions, in which the presence or absence of a disturbance in, for example, motivation is not at present clear. But the crucial difficulty arises with psychopathic personality, a person so categorized being classically regarded as neither mentally ill nor defective but who manifests a persistent inability to adapt to social requirements on account of quantitative peculiarities of impulse, temperament, and character. The author of a recently published short textbook for postgraduate psychiatric students (Price 1972) provided a useful example of such a person, which I have summarized:

The case is that of a youth aged 16 who attacked his father viciously, uttered continuous obscenities and bullied his siblings. On examination he was described as aggressive, sullen and full of hate. He showed little interest in what he was doing and no remorse for what he had done. He showed no disturbance in any established psychological part-function, i.e., no disturbance of perception (e.g., he was not hallucinated), no disturbance of thinking (e.g., he was not deluded), no memory disturbance, no learning problem, no disturbance of mood (e.g., he was not depressed, excited, or suicidal), no disturbance of motivation (e.g., he could control his own actions, when it suited him), in short, no disturbance in his mental functions.

The author drew attention to a possible brain injury at birth, his parents' marital disagreements, his sibling rivalry, and his inability to form relationships as important factors in shaping his personality. However, his intelligence was above average and his electroencephalogram (EEG), while showing a wave tracing consistent with delayed maturation of brain function, did not provide clear-cut evidence of brain pathology. (Such wave tracings are seen in about 10 per cent of 'psychopaths' but are also seen, albeit less frequently, in otherwise normal individuals.) The author's diagnosis was one of 'personality disorder'.

Most psychiatrists practising in Britain would probably concur. Where disagreement would appear would be over the question of whether such a person is actually *ill*. Disturbed he may be, unhappy even, but is he ill? Some psychiatrists base their decision therapeutically to intervene or not on whether they consider such behaviour to be evidence of psychiatric illness. If they do not, they refrain from any further intervention and send him back whence he came or send him to someone who may provide support on a non-psychiatric, non-medical basis, such as a social worker, probation officer, or youth counsellor. Other psychiatrists may likewise believe that such a youth is *not* psychiatrically ill but, concluding that they are as well equipped to help him as anyone else, may decide to offer advice, assistance, and support.

This difference in the manner in which psychiatrists approach personality disorders is of course well known to those agencies who regularly refer clients to psychiatrists for clinical assessment. Many a social worker has referred to a psychiatrist an especially disturbed and socially disorganized client with a history of repeated acts of self-destruction, including drug abuse, overdoses and wrist slashing, superficial and brief emotional relationships, characterized by friction, separation, and violence, and difficulties in almost all areas of social living, such as housing, employment, and finances only to be informed that as the client is not deemed to be suffering from 'overt psychiatric illness' he is not thought suitable for psychiatric intervention. Such disturbed people may show transient and mild mood changes, such as depression, in response to their often deplorable social circumstances, but for the clinical psychiatrist, implementing the principles laid down by Lewis, such mood changes do not constitute sufficient evidence of a disturbance in psychological part-function and hence of mental illness.

Because the psychiatrist learns a good deal about normal psychological functioning as well as abnormal functioning he may well involve himself in the management of those who, by such pure criteria, are not truly mentally ill. Many people with sexual problems, marital unhappiness, drug dependence, or social difficulties are seen and advised by psychiatrists although it would be difficult to classify such patients as suffering from mental diseases. Doctors in general medicine, it is worth remembering, do not confine themselves to the physically ill either: the pregnant woman, the woman in labour, the person undergoing an examination for a life assurance policy, the airline pilot having his yearly check-up are not necessarily suffering from physical disease yet are properly considered as falling within the physician's area of interest and competence.

Lewis, therefore, insists that, where mental illness is concerned, the criterion of abnormality should be firmly rooted in a disturbance of psychological function in the same way as the criterion of physical abnormality is rooted in a disturbance of physiological function. However, Kendell (1975: 16) has pointed out that we know much less about psychological functions at the present time than we do about physiological ones. The course recommended by Lewis, in Kendell's view, is little more than an aspiration. 'In many areas, if we are determined not to resort to social criteria, all we can do is defer judgement.'

Kendell appears unhappy that psychiatrists might do just that and refrain from deciding one way or another about certain forms of behaviour in the absence of clear-cut disturbance in psychological functioning. In practice, however, I suspect that deferring judgement is what many psychiatrists do. In those conditions, such as some of the psychotic states, in which there is clear-cut evidence of disturbed psychological functioning, psychiatrists appear reasonably agreed as to their status as diseases. In those conditions, such as the so-called personality disorders, in which evidence of psychological disturbance is as conspicuously lacking as evidence of social disturbance is present, psychiatrists are clearly uncertain and the more cautious amongst them refrain from committing themselves one way or the other.

While Lewis denies a social content to the idea of mental ill-health, he is at pains to point out that he does not deny it a social *context*. To do so would be foolish given the remarkable body of knowledge testifying to the role played by social and cultural factors in the genesis and content of many psychiatric disorders. For example, much interest has been aroused concerning the nature of the relationship between certain kinds of life-events in a person's history and the subsequent onset of mental, or indeed physical, disease. A group of American workers, in an attempt to quantify the possible physical and psychological impact of various types of life-change, have developed a scale which ranges from major events, such as the death of a spouse (rated as worth 100 Life Change Units or LCU), to minor occurrences, such as a spell of leave for a serviceman (13 LCU). In an elaborate study of fifty US Navy and Marine Corps personnel, discharged on psychiatric grounds, they found that years of greater than average life-change uniformly preceded illnesses or illness clusters (Rahe *et al.* 1974). On the basis of this, and other similar studies, they have suggested an ingenious life-stress/illness model which utilizes the principles of optics (*Figure 1*).

A series of lenses and filters is employed to indicate the various steps along the pathway between a subject's exposure to recent life stress and his subsequent illness symptoms and illness report. The subject's recent life stress exposure is indicated in *Figure 2* by dark, solid lines which represent highly significant events and thinner lines representing less significant events. A subject's past

Figure 1 *Life stress and illness model*

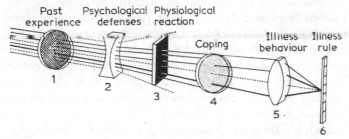

(Rahe *et al.* 1974: 173)

experience may alter his perceptions of the various significances of his recent life changes, a possibility which is shown by the 'polarising filter' in *step 1*. He may employ certain ego defence mechanisms, such as denial, that 'diffract away' the impact of certain life-stresses and this possibility is shown in *step 2*, by the use of a negative lens. Life changes not so diffracted away are thought to stimulate a multitude of physiological processes (a view supported by the growing literature on psychophysiology) and this assumption is symbolised by a 'physiological' black box, *step 3*. Lines emerging from the black box now cease to represent recent life events and now represent various psychophysiological reactions (e.g. elevated blood pressure). The 'colour filter' in *step 4* represents how he may or may not cope with ('absorb') some of these reactions and the model goes on to assume that prolonged ('unabsorbed') psychophysiological activations will eventually lead to organ system dysfunction and *bodily disease, steps 5 and 6.* (Rahe *et al.* 1974)

The significance of certain life events for the subsequent appearance of physical and psychiatric dysfunction is most dramatically shown by those studies of the mortality of bereavement. Several of these have pointed to the significantly higher suicide rates and the increase in the death rate due to coronary thrombosis and other arteriosclerotic and degenerative heart diseases in recently bereaved subjects. Linford Rees and S. G. Lutkins (1967), in a study of the first-degree relatives of 371 men and women who had died in a small Welsh semi-rural community, showed that there was a very much higher death rate amongst the bereaved than amongst a matched control group. This was so particularly for those who had lost a spouse and more marked again in the case of widowers.

Such has been the mushrooming of interest in and reports about the role of social factors in physical and mental disorders that some commentators, and in this country most notably Peter Sedgwick (1973), have questioned whether all diseases, *physical as well as mental*, might not be accurately described as 'social constructions'. Sedgwick has argued that the notion of disease is a human notion – the blight that affects corn or potatoes could as easily be conceptualized as a form of competition between two species as disease – and he suggests that man applies the disease concept on the basis of personal and social values that can and do change. He marshals as evidence a variety of disparate phenomena, such as that hookworm was regarded as part of normal health in parts of Northern Africa, that a South American tribe regarded with such favour the coloured skin spots seen in the disease of dyschromic spirochetosis that those who did not have them were regarded as 'pathological' and were ex-

cluded from marriage, and that 'among millions of British
working-class families it is taken for granted that children
will lose their teeth and require artificial dentures', to
support his thesis that what is described as 'disease' crucially
depends on the social values and personal mores of a particular society or culture. His conclusion to the effect that
mental illnesses can be conceptualized just as easily within
the disease framework as physical maladies such as TB is
similar to that of Lewis, but whereas the latter insists that
social factors, while important, are not and, by definition,
cannot be enough to justify a diagnosis of mental disease,
Sedgwick appears to believe the exact opposite.

Sedgwick also comments on the degree of relativity
implicit in any diagnosis of pathology. The septuagenarian's
fractured femur, he declares, has, within the world of
nature, 'no more significance than the snapping of an autumn
leaf from its twig', infection by cholera 'carries with it no
more the stamp of "illness" than does the souring of milk
by other forms of bacteria'. Disease, in short, is not pathological in the sense of being 'unnatural' at all but is as normal
and inevitable as the fermentation of a compost-heap or the
maturing of a cheese. The analogies drawn are deceptive in
that Sedgwick does not compare like with like. All milk left
to curdle will naturally do so whilst all trees cyclically flower
and die. By no means do all septuagenarians break their
legs nor is infection by cholera a 'natural', i.e., inevitable,
outcome of daily living. Additionally, he confuses declara-
tions of ill-health with disease and, as a result, gets himself
into a terrible muddle with his insistence that because a
tiger 'does not present itself as being ill' when it becomes
infected by a germ, trodden by an elephant, or scratched by
another tiger, it cannot be regarded as diseased.

However, Sedgwick is right to draw attention to the fact
that the concepts of physical health and disease are not as
neatly and objectively definable as some critics of psychiatry
would have us believe. Definitions of physical health, while
lacking the somewhat prissy quality that imbues mental

health definitions, are vague, woolly, and hopelessly impractical. Yet the very technological virtuosity of contemporary medicine only tends to emphasize the need for some pragmatic concept of health. As medical control over many of the acute physical disorders develops and attention is turned to the field of chronic physical ill-health, the planners and the politicians are being forced by the painful realities of cost and available resources to define the limits of medical intervention and to ask their medical colleagues to provide an operational definition of what constitutes physical health and malaise. Yet the techniques for measuring health and disease are as numerous and controversial as the working definitions. For example, Fanshel (1972) allocates the individual to one of eleven 'dysfunction' states, each of which is supposed to be a little worse than its predecessor, and he is given one of the following descriptive titles: Well-being, Dissatisfaction, Discomfort, Disability – Minor, Disability – Major, Confined and Bedridden, Isolated, Coma, and Death. However, such an index of health is based, as its author makes plain, almost entirely on social value-judgements. He points out that the concept of health, like any such concept, has a different meaning 'depending upon the perspective chosen', i.e., on whether a microcosmic or a macrocosmic view is taken. This qualification affects similar attempts to arrive at a meaningful measure of health. Grogono (1973) allocates a score of 0, 0·05, or 0·1 for each of the following aspects of life: work, recreation, pain, worry, communication, sleep, dependency on others, excretion, and sex. The scores are added to give the health index with normal health scoring 1·0. George Maddox (1972) scores five aspects of life: physical health, mental health, social resources, economic resources, and the capacity for carrying out activities of daily living; he employs a six-point scale for each aspect although this can be reduced to a two-point scale to obtain a manageable number of equivalency classes. Rachel Rosser and Vincent Watts (1972) score only two aspects of life – disability on an eight-point scale, ranging from none to loss of consciousness, and distress on a four-point scale, ranging from none to severe.

Lester Breslow, commenting upon these and other attempts to quantify health, argues that it does appear possible to measure health status through questions that only individuals can answer about themselves and through testing by physical means the extent of what he terms 'functional reserves' as in multiphasic screening.

> 'Medicine would then focus on improving health in the sense of (1) moving people toward the favourable end of the health spectrum, as determined subjectively by responses to questions, and (2) enhancing the bodily reserves, as determined by screening tests.'
>
> (Breslow 1972)

It is clear from these attempts that the idea of positive health, a state of not just being 'disease-free' but of wellness beyond the norm, has gradually emerged, at least in those communities that have significantly benefited from the improvements in physical health and social conditions that have been a feature of the past fifty years. The workers named above have deliberately cast aside familiar notions of specific diseases and have tried to measure health in the generic sense implied by the words in the WHO definition of health, 'physical, mental and social well-being'.

I mention these trends to illustrate the distance that has been travelled from Sydenham's primitive 'botanical' concept of disease and Virchow's cellular model. It is clear that Szasz and those other critics of the applicability of the so-called disease concept are unaware of such developments. Thus we find Szasz announcing that the concept of illness, whether bodily or mental, implies 'deviation from some clearly defined norm'.

> 'In the case of physical illness, the norm is the structural and functional integrity of the human body. Thus although the desirability of physical health, as such, is an ethical value, what health is can be stated in anatomical

and physiological terms. What is the norm deviation from which is regarded as mental illness?'

(Szasz 1960: 114)

Now I am nothing like as sure as Szasz that 'what health is can be stated in anatomical and physiological terms' and having reviewed some of the attempts by epidemiologists and health service planners to arrive at some pragmatic definition of the concept I am bound to admit that not merely the 'desirability' of health but health itself, physical or mental, appears very largely to be an ethical or social value. But I would agree with Szasz, that theoretically at least disease is best conceptualized in terms of a 'deviation from some clearly defined norm'. Szasz disputes the existence of such norms by drawing attention to the fluidity and subjectivity of some, such as the desirability of love, kindness, and a stable marriage relationship, not to mention certain psychoanalytical concepts such as 'ego strength' and 'maturity'. In effect, what he illustrates is that such social and analytic norms just will not do. But are they all psychiatrists have got? Szasz appears to feel so, arguing that any deviation from physical norms evident in a psychiatric disorder necessitates the disorder being reclassified as a physical disease. For him, the division between physical disease and mental disorders is simple. But is it?

Let us take phobic anxiety states. In such a state, the person experiences 'an irresistible and terrifying fear of perfectly natural situations and performances' (Jaspers 1923), 'a strong unreasonable fear of specific situations inhibiting the person from entering or remaining in them' (Terhune 1949) or a 'persisting fear of an object or of an idea which does not ordinarily justify fear' (Errera 1962). As Isaac Marks points out in his excellent account of these states (1969), phobic patients usually recognize that their fears are unrealistic and excessive but are unable to quell them. Confronted by their phobic situation, whether it be open spaces (so-called 'agoraphobia'), closed spaces ('claustro-phobia'), heights, animals, germs, people, strangers, thunder, lightning, or whatever, such patients experience overwhelming anxiety. They sweat, shake, feel sick, and experience a profound sense of dread. They breathe rapidly, have 'butterflies' in their stomachs, vomit, defaecate, and urinate with fright. To escape such anxiety, patients try to avoid their phobic situations and may, as a result, greatly restrict their activities and daily functions. The 'agoraphobic' housewife may become totally housebound, venturing forth only when accompanied or 'relaxed' by large doses of anxiety-relieving drugs or alcohol.

How does one classify such a state? There is a deviation from a reasonably clearly defined norm, albeit a statistical one, in that if one were to measure individual subjective appreciation of anxiety, it is likely that such patients would be found at one end of a continuum, at the other end of which would be those showing no functional limitation whatsoever as a consequence of anxiety. But there is evidence of a deviation from the norm of 'structural and functional integrity' too. It has been shown, for example, that the electric conductivity of the skin increases with increasing emotion. Using such a measure, Glenn Wilson successfully discriminated between phobic and non-phobic students.

'Twenty undergraduate students were chosen – 10 who reported intense fears of spiders and 10 who admitted to no such or other fears. Subjects sat in a dark booth facing a translucent screen onto which coloured slides were projected for 1 second at 15-second intervals. Eight pictures of spiders and eight of landscapes in alternating order were presented twice to each subject and the electric conductivity of the skin of the palms was measured. Response to landscapes did not differ for the two groups but there was a significant increase in skin conductivity in the phobic group compared with the non-phobic group when the spider pictures were presented.' (Wilson 1966: 25)

Other physiological measures, such as the blood flow through the arms and the concentration of steroids in the blood, have been shown to accompany anxiety and have been used not merely to aid in diagnosis but to monitor response to various methods of treatment. It is to be expected that with an increase in the number and applicability of such sophisticated physiological and biochemical measures, many such 'deviations' will be found to accompany the various psychiatric disorders currently recognized. The recognition of such changes does not of itself cast any light on possible causes; it does not logically follow because there is an increase in skin conductivity in anxiety states that this change must be the cause any more than the alteration in blood sugar levels is the cause of diabetes, but in both cases such alterations serve as relatively objective identification markers of abnormality.

The housewife who is unwilling to leave her house is not *necessarily* mentally ill. She may have decided that shopping for her husband and family is a slavish and degrading activity, that her role as a housewife is no more than ritualized prostitution, and that as a protest against the persistent devaluation of women in contemporary capitalist society she has decided to withdraw her labour. Such behaviour might well be dubbed deviant. It cannot be termed mental illness. However, if she is unwilling to leave her house not because of such reasons (or not primarily so) but because she is *unable* to do so without being overwhelmed by terror and panic, then her condition is viewed as a mental disturbance. The psychological part-function which is disturbed in this case is the housewife's affect or mood state. The 'deviant, maladapted, non-conformist behaviour' of refusing to shop is psychiatrically pathological *only* if it is accompanied by the manifest disturbance of some such psychological function. The fact that in phobic anxiety states such psychological disturbance is accompanied by a disturbance in physiological functions merely serves to emphasize the fallaciousness of Szasz's attempts to draw a simple and absolute distinction between bodily and mental dysfunctions.

It is a common belief that we are all a little mad. The nineteenth-century British psychiatrist John Connolly averred that 'the slightest irregularities, the most trifling uneasiness, the most minute imperfection in the performance of a bodily function is in itself a disease but we distinguish between these and severe disorder' and he attacked those medical men who

'. . . have sought a strong and definable boundary between sanity and insanity which has not only been imaginary and arbitrarily placed but, by being supposed to separate all who were of unsound mind from the rest of men, has unfortunately been considered a justification of certain measures against the portion condemned which, in the case of the majority, were unnecessary and afflicting.'

(Connolly 1830: 295)

A more spirited version of such a view is that provided by R. D. Laing in *The Politics of Experience*. 'The madness we encounter in "patients" ', he insists, 'is a gross travesty, a mockery, a grotesque caricature of what the natural healing of that estranged integration we call sanity might be' (1967: 119). A number of epidemiological studies would seem to bear out such a vision of widespread madness. Professor Neil Kessel in a study of a single general practice (1960) reported that when the definition of psychiatric morbidity was based on the International Classification of Diseases, fifty patients per 1,000 per year manifested psychiatric symptoms. However, when patients with 'Conspicuous psychiatric morbidity', i.e., conspicuous to the general practitioner, were included, the annual prevalence rate rose to ninety per 1,000. The inclusion of those patients who presented with physical complaints that did not have any detectable organic basis, i.e., 'psychosomatic disorder', caused the rate to reach 520 per 1,000. Thus, depending on the definition of psychiatric ill-health employed, the rate varied from one patient in twenty to one in two! A more conservative estimate has been suggested by Professor Michael Shepherd and his colleagues at the Institute of Psychiatry; a review of the available data indicates the presence of a large sub-group of emotionally disturbed patients 'amounting to between one-fifth and one-tenth of the total population' (Shepherd *et al.* 1966).

It is probably a mistake to conceptualize normality and madness as dichotomous, that is to say as states of mind, inhabitation of one necessarily mitigating against the other. Rather they are best thought of as opposite ends of a continuum, a continuum on which most of us find ourselves positioned in that grey and shady area between the two opposing poles. Many of the commonest medical conditions merge imperceptibly with normal physiological states, e.g., disorders of blood pressure, cervical cancer, and arteriosclerosis. The ubiquity of minor physical complaints also casts doubts on a simple health–disease model of functioning. The study by Professor Butterfield and his colleagues (Wadsworth, Butterfield and Blaney 1971) at Guy's Hospital, for example, reveals the extent to which ordinary people experience a wide variety of physical complaints on what is virtually a daily basis. Of the total population of 2,153 adults studied by these workers, less than 5 per cent reported themselves free of physical or mental complaints during the fourteen days prior to interview. Nineteen per cent reported complaints but had taken no action and just over 76 per cent were taking action for current complaints. Over half the persons screened were judged by the investigators to require further investigation and possibly treatment.

Few of us, apparently, can boast lives of absolute physical or mental health. Few of us refrain from regularly self-medicating ourselves. Few of us are not known to some health-care agency, be it the local pharmacy, the GP, or the hospital out-patient department. Few of us expect our bodies to function with scarcely a flaw or falter, and when they do not, few of us react with embarrassment or shame. Why should we expect the quality of our psychological health to be significantly different? For Allen Gregg there is no mystery:

'The three most powerful traditions of psychiatry are still, as they have been from time immemorial, the horror which mental disease inspires, the power and subtlety with which psychiatric symptoms influence human relations and the tendency of man to think of spirit as not only separable, but already separate from body. These are the inherent, the inveterate, the inevitable handicaps of psychiatry.'

(Gregg 1944: 285)

Such a dualistic philosophy is implicit in concepts like 'psychosomatic illness', in the desperate attempts by Szasz to split apart physical complaints (authentic disease, in his view) from mental ones (relabelled 'problems of living'), and in the anti-psychiatrists' scornful and hostile assaults on the application of the 'medical model' to the understanding of psychological dysfunction. If such a dualism is repudiated, then the areas of medicine and psychiatry become co-extensive and complementary. It is no longer possible to identify a state, reaction, or disease as physical *or* psychological. An emotion, such as phobic anxiety discussed earlier, can be described in psychological terms as a 'fear' or a 'terror' or in the physiological language of autonomic nervous system function and hormonal secretion. Forced by considerations of pragmatism and convenience to opt for one or other of the two languages, somatic and psychological, with which to describe psychiatric phenomena, psychiatrists create the unfortunate impression that there are two distinct kinds of disease – organic and functional. As Akiskal and McKinney have pointed out, the classification of psychiatric disorders into organic brain conditions and the so-called functional disorders

'. . . has unfortunately contributed to the belief that psychosocial factors are not operative in the former and that physiochemical factors are absent in the latter.'

(Akiskal and McKinney 1973: 369)

If the contemporary critical assault on the medical model in psychiatry can claim any achievement it is perhaps the somewhat ironic one of having forced a consideration not so much of psychiatry's claim to be a medical discipline as of medicine's claim to be a *social* science. Avoiding the dualism inherent in the dichotomous formulation of organic versus functional leads not merely to an acknowledgement of the role of physiochemical alterations in psychiatric states but of psychosocial factors in medical conditions, conditions as varied as leukaemia, arteriosclerosis, peptic ulcer, cancer, and myocardial infarction. Such a monistic understanding of physical and mental functioning in man underpins the best of clinical psychiatry in Britain. It is a model of psychiatry that has helped to clarify the psychological bases not alone of mental health and mental sickness but of physical health and sickness too.

References

AKISKAL, H.S. and MCKINNEY, W.T. (1973) Psychiatry and Pseudopsychiatry. *Archives of General Psychiatry* **28**: 368–73.

BRESLOW, L. (1972) A Quantitative Approach to the World Health Organization Definition of Health: Physical, Mental and Social Well-Being. *International Journal of Epidemiology* **1** (4): 347–55.

CONNOLLY, J. (1830) The Indications of Insanity. *Psychiatric Monograph Series* No. 4: 295. London: Dawsons of Pall Mall.

ELLENBERGER, H. F. (1970) The Discovery of the Unconscious. *The History and Evolution of Dynamic Psychiatry*. London: Allen Lane.

ERRERA, P. (1962) Some Historical Aspects of the Concept of Phobia. *The Psychiatric Quarterly* **36**: 325–36.

FANSHEL, S. (1972) A Meaningful Measure of Health for Epidemiology. *International Journal of Epidemiology* **1** (4): 318–19.

FOUCAULT, M. (1973) *The Birth of the Clinic*. London: Tavistock.

GREGG, A. (1944) A Critique of Psychiatry. *American Journal of Psychiatry* **101**: 285.

GROGONO, A.W. (1973) Symposium on the Measurement of Ill Health. *International Journal of Epidemiology* **2** (1): 5-6.

JASPERS, K. (1923) *General Psychopathology*. Berlin: Springer Verlag. (Trans. from German; 7th edition, 1963. Manchester University Press.)

KENDELL, R.E. (1975) *The Role of Diagnosis in Psychiatry*. Oxford: Blackwells Scientific Publications.

KESSEL, W.I.N. (1960) The Psychiatric Morbidity in a London General Practice. *British Journal of Preventive and Social Medicine* **14**: 16.

KOOS, E. (1954) *The Health of Regionsville: What the People Thought and Did about It*. New York: Columbia University Press.

LAING, R.D. (1967) *The Politics of Experience*. Harmondsworth: Penguin.

LEIFER, R. (1971) The Medical Model as Ideology. *International Journal of Psychiatry* **9**: 13-21.

LEWIS, A.J. (1955) Health as a Social Concept. *British Journal of Sociology* **4**: 109-24.

—— (1963) Medicine and the Affections of the Mind. *British Medical Journal* **2**: 1549-57.

MADDOX, G.L. (1972) Interventions and Outcomes: Notes on Designing and Implementing an Experiment in Health Care. *International Journal of Epidemiology* **1** (4): 339-45.

MARKS, I.M. (1969) *Fears and Phobias*. London: Heinemann Medical.

MASSERMAN, J. (ed.) (1971) *Current Psychiatric Therapies*. New York: Grune & Stratton.

MECHANIC, D. (1972) Social Psychologic Factors Affecting the Presentation of Bodily Complaints. *New England Journal of Medicine* **286** (21): 105-15.

MORRIS, J.S. (1973) Dyspepsia and Its Investigations. *British Journal of Hospital Medicine* **10** (2): 144-47.

PRICE, J.H. (1972) *Psychiatric Investigations*. London: Butterworth.

RAHE, R.H., FLEISTAD, I., BERGAN, R., RINGDALE, R., GERHARDT, R., GUNDERSON, E.K., and ARTHUR, R.J. (1974) A Model for Life Changes and Illness Research. *Archives of General Psychiatry* **31**: 172–77.

RAHE, R.H., MCKEAN, J.D., and ARTHUR, R.J. (1967) A Longitudinal Study of Life Change and Illness-Patterns. *Journal of Psychosomatic Research* **10**: 355.

REES, W.D. and LUTKINS, S.G. (1967) Mortality of Bereavement. *British Medical Journal* **4**: 13–16.

ROSEN, G. (1972) Freud and Medicine in Vienna. In J. Miller (ed.), *Freud: The Man, His World, His Influence*. London: Weidenfeld & Nicolson.

ROSENBLATT, D. and SUCHMAN, E.A. (1965) Blue Collar Attitudes and Information towards Health and Illness. In A. B. Shostak and W. Comberg (eds.), *Blue Collar World*. Englewood Cliffs, N. Jersey: Prentice-Hall.

ROSENHAN, D.L. (1973) On Being Sane in Insane Places. *Science* **179**: 250–58.

ROSSER, R.M. and WATTS, V.C. (1972) The Measurement of Hospital Output. *International Journal of Epidemiology* **1** (4): 361–68.

SCADDING, J.E. (1967) Diagnosis: The Clinician and The Computer. *Lancet* **ii**: 877–82.

SEDGWICK, P. (1973) Illness – Mental and Otherwise. *The Hastings Center* **1** (3): 19–40. Hastings-on-Hudson, New York: Institute of Society, Ethics and the Life Sciences.

SHEPHERD, M., COOPER, B., BROWN, A.C., and KALTON, G.W. (1966) *Psychiatric Illness in General Practice*. London: Oxford University Press.

SZASZ, T.S. (1960) The Myth of Mental Illness. *American Psychologist* **15**: 113–18.

—— (1974) *The Second Sin*. London: Routledge & Kegan Paul.

TAYLOR, F.K. (1972) A Logical Analysis of the Medico-Psychological Concept of Disease. *Psychological Medicine* **2** (1): 11.

TERHUNE, W. (1949) The Phobic Syndrome. A Study of 86 Patients with Phobic Reactions. *Archives of Neurological Psychiatry* **62**: 162–72.

TWADDLE, A. (1969) Health Decisions and Sick Role Variations. *Journal of Health and Social Behaviour* **10** (2): 105–39.

VIRCHOW, R. (1847) Standpoints in scientific medicine. In: *Diseases, Life and Man. Selected Essays by Rudolf Virchow.* Translated by L. J. Rather, 1958. Palo Alto: Stanford University Press.

WADSWORTH, M.E.J., BUTTERFIELD, W.J.H., and BLANEY, R. (1971) *Health and Sickness: The Choice of Treatment.* London: Tavistock.

WILSON, G.D. (1966) An Electrodermal Technique for the Study of Phobias. *New Zealand Medical Journal* **65**: 696–98.

WOOTTON, B. (1959) *Social Science and Social Pathology.* London: George Allen & Unwin.

ZBOROWSKI, M. (1952) Cultural Components in Responses to Pain. *Journal of Social Issues* **8**: 16–30.

2

Models of mental illness

Successful psychiatrists necessarily correspond in their natures to the needs and desires of 'nervous patients', since the mass of patients decide who is to be the successful therapist, and not the actual value or correctness of the doctor's own views or behaviour. Obviously, therefore, the greatest successes of all have not belonged to psychiatrists but to the shamans, priests, leaders of sects, wonder-workers, confessors and spiritual guides of earlier times.

JASPERS 1923: 806

GIVEN THAT psychiatry is at a fairly primitive stage in its development, some psychiatrists, faced with what appears to be a conceptual chaos, seek the security of a simple operational faith, a pragmatic model to which they adhere with varying degrees of obstinacy and conviction. There are those who insist that all genuine psychiatric disorders rest upon a physical basis and they pin their hopes for ultimate clarification of the present confused situation on discoveries in the fields of neurochemistry, neurophysiology, and psychopharmacology. Other psychiatrists, sceptical about what they consider to be a futile search for non-existent physical pathology, call instead for a radical examination of the values and ethics of society, for a reassessment of personal and social behaviour, and for an attack on poverty, unemployment, inequality, discrimination, racialism, and other social problems which, in their view, not merely affect but cause what is termed mental illness. There are even those who declare that there is no such thing as mental illness at all, but that it is the twentieth-century equivalent of witchcraft and that psychiatrists, in their search for the signs and symptoms of psychopathology in their patients, are the direct descendants of those Inquisitors who vigorously examined their victims for the sinister signs of demoniacal possession.

It is hardly surprising, therefore, that outside the confines of the psychiatric specialty, the clamour of ideological battle is even more deafening. Unable to comprehend the framework within which the clinical psychiatrist performs his professional duties, the public falls back on expressing its forebodings over the potential misuse of psychiatric techniques, such as psychosurgery and electrical treatment, its irritation at the apparent lack of a rational link between such treatments and the disorders for which they are used, and its resentment at the yawning gap that exists between the promise of psychiatric, particularly psychoanalytic, theory and its fulfilment. Paradoxically, there still lingers a belief in the omnipotent therapist who, while rare and difficult to find within the complex inner reaches of the National Health Service, nonetheless can by virtue of his mysterious training uncover the emotional traumata at the root of every neurosis. Buffeted this way and that by the philosophical storm which rages within and outside of psychiatry, the public appears at the mercy of whim and fashion so that one day it calls for a more rigid approach to the care of potentially dangerous patients and for the forcible incarceration of anyone exhibiting the slightest sign of aggressive intent, yet the next day it is deploring the loss of liberty implicit in current mental health legislation and is demanding that compulsory certification of the mentally ill should cease forthwith.

The great mass of Britain's two thousand psychiatrists, junior and senior, go about their clinical activities without engaging in much public discussion of their attitudes concerning ideological issues within their specialty. However, attempts have been made, in this country and in the United States, to separate out and identify the different professional orientations within psychiatry and to estimate their relative popularity. Initially, two main approaches, allegedly independent and contrasting, were described (Hollinghead and Redlich 1958; Kreitman 1962). On the one hand, there is the so-called *'organic'* or biological approach in which particular emphasis is laid on the role of genetic, biochemical, physiological, and neuropsychological factors in the causation of psychiatric illnesses and in which there is often a marked preference for physical treatment methods, such as ECT, drugs, and psychosurgery. A reasonable knowledge of and experience in general medicine is regarded as an essential requirement for a clinical psychiatrist and the close historical and developmental relationship between psychiatry and medicine is stressed. In contrast, there is a '*psychotherapeutic*' orientation whose adherents believe in the primary importance of the therapist having a thorough knowledge of his own psychological state, even to the point of undergoing a lengthy and expensive personal analysis, if he is to be effective in helping his patients to acquire self-knowledge. Certain factors, such as early childhood disturbances and difficulties encountered during critical stages in personality development, are deemed to be of crucial importance in the genesis of mental ill-health. Treatment, within the psychotherapeutic model, lays particular emphasis on the nature of the patient's interpersonal relationships, and especially upon the relationship that develops between the patient and his therapist, and it is directed at unravelling unconscious motives and impulses, analysing feelings and communications, and identifying for the purposes of alteration those intrapsychic variables believed to have an important bearing on the patient's psychological state.

A third orientation has been described, which, it is claimed, can be clearly distinguished from the first two (Strauss *et al.* 1964; Caine and Smail 1969; Pallis and Stoffelmayr 1973). This has been termed the '*sociotherapeutic*' approach. Here the main emphasis is placed upon the social functioning, adequacy, and potential of the patient. Particular attention is paid to the patient's social circumstances, his occupational status, his family relationships, his friends, his place in society, and indeed the quality of that society itself. The 'socio-therapeutic' orientation emphasizes the relationship between disturbances in the patient's social adequacy and skills and the demands made upon him by the society in which he functions. Treatment is aimed at modifying the patient's ability to cope with the everyday demands of living and at altering his immediate social milieu.

Recently, a fourth orientation may be detected whose apologists advocate the division of psychiatry into two independent parts, one concerned with 'organic disorders' and their treatment, and the other concerned with *behavioural disorders*' (Eysenck 1975). The first part would be the prerogative of medically trained psychiatrists while the latter would be 'the prerogative of non-medical psychologists trained in special courses for posts as clinical psychologists'. This division reflects the fact that whereas a number of behavioural techniques have been developed, which have been found to be useful in the treatment of certain neurotic illnesses and maladaptive behaviour patterns, no such techniques have yet been found that have anything to offer in the treatment of the major psychotic illnesses, such as schizophrenia and manic-depressive psychosis, or in some of the more severe neurotic disorders. In those disorders in which behavioural methods of treatment are employed, such treatment is directed purely and simply at symptom removal. Behaviour therapists do not apologize for narrowly focusing on behaviour and its consequences and on conscious rather than unconscious processes but firmly insist that it is symptoms and only symptoms which require treatment. Britain's most assertive behaviourist, Professor Hans Eysenck, puts the issue squarely:

'It has always been emphasized that behaviour therapy is *purely symptomatic* [author's italics]; behaviour therapy is based on a theory which maintains that there is no neurosis underlying the symptom but merely the symptom itself.'
(Eysenck 1963: 12)

In practice, behavioural methods of treatment are undertaken by clinical psychologists working alongside psychiatrists in hospitals and out-patient clinics. Those psychiatrists who employ behavioural methods of treatment appear to do so within the context of one or more of the other main ideological orientations. While there would seem to be few psychiatrists at the present time willing to accept Eysenck's simple division, there would appear to be equally few who would contest the value of the contribution made by behaviour therapy to the practice of psychiatry.

Other models have been described (Siegler and Osmond 1974) including the *conspiratorial*, in which psychiatric illness exists only in the eye of the observer, the so-called patient being the victim of labelling; the *family interaction* model, wherein the entire family is deemed 'sick' and is brought for help by the 'index patient' who may well be the healthiest member; and the *moral* model which portrays mental illness as identical with deviance and the mentally ill as responsible, autonomous, self-willed individuals to be held responsible for their anti-social activities. There is also the *psychedelic model* in which mental illness is viewed as a metaphorical 'trip', the patient proceeding through a state of 'super-sanity' and, if properly guided, emerging on the far side in a more enlightened and sensitive condition. This last view, popularized by the imaginative writings of Ronald Laing (Laing 1967), bears remarkable similarities to the highly romanticized view of tuberculosis which held sway during parts of the last century and which has recently been examined by Sontag (1979). Those afflicted with TB were often portrayed as highly imaginative, sensitive, and artistic individuals, too cultured and cultivated to bear the horrors of a vulgar, coarse, and brutal world. The illness itself was often seen as a pretext for leisure, a way of retiring from the world without having to take responsibility for the decision. So well entrenched was the idea that TB and artistic creativity were connected, that at the end of the century one critic suggested that it was the progressive disappearance of TB which accounted for the current decline of literature and the arts (Dubos and Dubos 1952). It is worth noting that Sontag dates the destruction of the TB myth from the time when proper treatment for the condition was developed, with the discovery of streptomycin in 1944 and the introduction of isoniazid in 1952. The implications for the romantic metaphor of mental illness and its eventual decline are obvious.

1 The organic orientation

One of the staunchest and most extreme exponents of the 'organic' orientation in contemporary psychiatry is Dr Richard Hunter, a psychiatrist at the Institute of Neurology in London and co-author of a celebrated monograph on the mental disturbances of George III (Macalpine and Hunter 1966). (The monograph claims that the King was not 'mentally ill' but suffered from a physical condition known as porphyria.) For Hunter, mental symptoms and abnormal mental states do not constitute illnesses in themselves but are the 'epiphenomena' of underlying physical disturbances.

Hunter refers to the history books those critics who object that the two major psychiatric conditions, namely schizophrenia and manic-depressive psychosis, have been termed 'functional' (as distinct from 'organic') for the very reason that intense, indeed exhaustive examination of the physical status of patients suffering from them has hitherto revealed no evidence of any underlying physical pathology. In his opinion, we are in a position at the present time, *vis-à-vis* these 'functional' psychoses, comparable to that in which physicians of the last century found themselves with regard to general paralysis of the insane (GPI) prior to the discovery of the responsible organism, the syphilitic spirochaete. That condition, which is characterized by severe personality changes, social uncontrollability, impulsiveness, grandiosity, and serious mental deterioration, had been variously attributed to 'the struggle for existence', the 'ceaseless agitation and ambitious striving' of a competitive epoch, and the physical manifestations of 'a feverish and fidgety age in which an unappeasable restlessness pervades all ranks and classes' (Crichton Browne 1871). Noguchi's post-mortem demonstration of the spirochaete in the brains of patients dying from the disease put paid to such imaginative, analytical speculations.

In support of his view, Hunter draws attention to those patients in whom mental symptoms are most prominent and in whom the underlying physical pathology is as a consequence often neglected:

'An immigrant girl of 19 complained of frightened feelings. She was given anti-anxiety pills and a social worker to help her with the complexities of London life. She became dispirited and slow. Antidepressants were added to her medication. She began to have bizarre experiences and developed strange ideas to explain them. Finally she became socially incapacitated and was sent to a mental hospital as a "depressed and anxious schizophrenic unresponsive to drugs". Physical examination was negative, blood tests and EEG were normal. Skull X-Ray showed a flake of (suprasellar) calcification. Drainage of a cranio-pharyngioma (a type of brain tumour) followed by radiotherapy cured the "psychosyndrome" by relieving pressure on the floor of the third ventricle and surrounding basal structures.'

(Hunter 1973: 18)

Hunter observes that this whole illness 'was played out in mental symptoms' but argues that these same symptoms were epiphenomena superimposed on the more basic organic disorder. He deplores the fact that many psychiatrists appear to have become dispirited at their failure to find such physical pathology in more than a small proportion of psychiatric patients and points out that it is only comparatively recently that biochemists and physiologists have begun to explore the functioning of the brain at an appropriately sophisticated level.

In the example provided by Hunter, the cause of the girl's disturbance was a relatively gross one, though undetectable without an x-ray. In the days before radiology her condition might well have been dubbed 'functional' and much imaginative speculation might have taken place concerning her immigration, her family relationships, her attitudes towards sexuality, and her sense of cultural anomie as possible causes of her peculiar behaviour. He concludes that there are similar, if more complex, physical causes of those 'functional' illnesses, such as schizophrenia and manic depression, for which as yet we lack the appropriately sophisticated diagnostic tools. He states elsewhere the basic premise of the organic approach with some pungency:

'The lesson of the history of psychiatry is that progress is inevitable and irrevocable from psychology to neurology, from mind to brain, never the other way round. Every medical advance adds to the list of diseases which may cause mental derangement. The abnormal mental state is not the disease, nor its essence or determinent, but an epiphenomenon. This is why psychological theories and therapies, which held out such promise at the turn of the century when so much less was known of localisation of function in the brain, have added so little to the understanding and treatment of mental illness, despite all the time and effort devoted to them.'   (Macalpine and Hunter 1974: 256)

The biologically inclined psychiatrist takes some satisfaction in the fact that the list of conditions in which psychological disturbances appear to be symptomatic of underlying physical pathology continues to expand. Such a list includes the dementing conditions secondary to arteriosclerosis affecting the blood vessels in the brain, the acute toxic psychoses secondary to the use and abuse of certain drugs, such as alcohol, amphetamines, and LSD, a number of nutritional disorders with gross manifestations, of which pellagra is a typical example, and certain brain tumours and epileptogenic lesions which are often accompanied by numerous psychological symptoms.

Such conditions constitute impressive evidence in favour of the organic view of psychiatric illness. Many of them (though by no means all) embody the major practical advantage of the physical model, namely that the discovery of a physical abnormality offers the possibility of treatment *before* the abnormality can produce psychological disturbances. The physical abnormality, it is true, may be difficult to treat but, as Medawar (1972: 61) caustically observes, 'not so difficult and much more realistic than, say, to abolish all family life as one "existential psychiatrist" is alleged to have recommended because some families create an environment conducive to mental disorder'.

In the example provided by Richard Hunter, the immigrant girl was labelled 'schizophrenic'. Hunter objects to such labelling with as much vehemence as Ronald Laing but for the very opposite of reasons. To Hunter, such labelling is tantamount to subscribing to the notion that mental symptoms imply the existence of 'mind disease' and it is this concept of 'mind disease', independent of any underlying physical pathology, which he questions. Whereas Ronald Laing in this country, and Professor Thomas Szasz in the United States, object to the concept of mental illness because it implies the *presence* of some form of physical illness when, in their view, there is none, Hunter rejects the concept because it implies the *absence* of an underlying physical pathology when, in his view, that is precisely what is involved. Thomas Szasz insists that those who regard mental symptoms as signs of brain disease should say just that and not something else (Szasz 1960). Richard Hunter promptly obliges. Hunter's view is, understandably, very hostile to the idea of treating supposed 'mind diseases' with psychotherapy. Whereas psychotherapists do not, nowadays, treat mental conditions that are secondary to physical disorders, such as brain tumours or thyroid disease, Hunter asks to what extent are they being wise after the event? What will happen to the psychotherapy of schizophrenia when, as he is confident, a physical basis for that condition is eventually demonstrated?

2 The psychotherapeutic orientation

The psychotherapeutic orientation has historical roots as deeply embedded in antiquity as those of the biological standpoint. In the view of one eminent psychiatric historian, 'modern dynamic psychotherapy derives from primitive medicine and an uninterrupted continuity can be demonstrated between exorcism and magnetism, magnetism and hypnotism and hypnotism and the modern dynamic schools' (Ellenberger 1970). According to this model, adult neuroses and vulnerabilities to stress are the consequence of early childhood deprivation, developmental fixations at certain crucial stages of maturation, distortions in early relationships and confused communications between parent and child. Therapy consists in clarifying the meaning of events, feelings, impulses and behaviour in the context of past and often forgotten or repressed events and experiences. A crucial aspect of this model is the doctor–patient relationship, the therapeutic alliance, which enables the patient to work through the disturbance and abandon familiar but destructive methods of coping with reality. As Hunter might be taken as an extreme exponent of the organic view of psychiatry so Thomas Szasz might serve as a radical spokesman for psychotherapy. Whereas many psychotherapists appear ambivalent about the extent to which their orientation can be regarded as treatment in the *medical* sense Szasz has no doubts on this score (Szasz 1972). Psychotherapy, in his view, is a human relationship characterized by certain aims and rules. Its medical value is scant. Its main intellectual and scientific worth lies 'in the kind of model the analytic relationship provides for achieving a better understanding of ethics, politics and social relations generally'. As we will see later, most psychotherapists, while gently demurring from Szasz's more trenchant pronouncements, do in fact adhere to a model of psychotherapy strikingly similar to that he endorses.

In one of the opening paragraphs of his iconoclastic essay, 'The Myth of Mental Illness' (1960: 113) Szasz refers to those psychiatrists, such as Hunter, who assume that 'some neurological defect, perhaps a very subtle one, will ultimately be found to explain all the disorders of thinking and behaviour'. Such an assumption he regards as nonsense. A defect in a person's visual field, he points out, may be explained by correlating it with certain lesions in his nervous system whereas a person's belief, be it in Christianity or in the idea that his organs are rotting, cannot be so correlated.

'In medical practice, when we speak of physical disturbances, we mean either signs (for example a fever) or symptoms (for example pain). We speak of mental symptoms, on the other hand, when we refer to the patient's *communications about himself, others and the world about him.* He might state that he is Napoleon or that he is being persecuted by the Communists. These would be considered mental symptoms *only* if the observer believed that the patient was *not* Napoleon or that he was *not* being persecuted by the Communists. This makes it apparent that the statement that "X is a mental symptom" involves rendering a judgment. The judgment entails, moreover, a covert comparison or matching of the patient's ideas, concepts or beliefs with those of the observer and the society in which they live. The notion of mental symptoms is therefore inextricably tied to the *social* (including ethical) *context* in which it is made in much the same way as the notion of bodily symptom is tied to an *anatomical* and *genetic context.*'

(Szasz 1960: 114)

In Szasz's view, it is not logically acceptable to invoke the concept of physical illness, in the shape of disorders of what he terms 'the physico-chemical machinery of the human body', to explain unusual mental functioning as, for example, occurs in delusional beliefs. Underlying his assumption is the belief that it is the business of the physician to diagnose, treat, and occasionally cure medical, i.e., physical, conditions, whereas it is the business of the psychiatrist to concern himself with his client's 'problems of living'; problems which, by Szasz's definition, owe nothing to the client's physical state and are therefore in no sense 'diseases'.

'The term "mental illness" is a metaphor. Bodily illness stands in the same relation to mental illness as a defective television set stands to a bad television programme. Of course, the word "sick" is often used metaphorically. We call jokes "sick", economies "sick", sometimes even the whole world "sick", but only when we call minds "sick" do we systematically mistake and strategically misinterpret metaphor for fact – and send for the doctor to "cure" the "illness"! It is as if a television viewer were to send for a T.V. repairman because he dislikes the programme he sees on the screen.' (Szasz 1972: 84)

In a preamble to a collection of his essays, Szasz asks a series of questions which he believes poses fundamental choices about the nature, scope, methods and values of psychiatry (1973). Is the scope of psychiatry the study of medical conditions or the study of social performance? Is the aim of psychiatry the study of human behaviour or the control of human misbehaviour? Is psychiatric practice composed of listening and talking or 'prescribing drugs, operating on the brain and imprisoning persons labelled as "mentally ill"'? It is quite clear that for Szasz these pairs of choices represent incompatible options – choosing one of the pair discards the other.

The organic and psychotherapeutic approaches, dichotomously opposed by Hunter and Szasz, both have their roots buried deep in the historical development of psychiatric theory. The divine, immaterialist view of mental disorders was challenged by physicians as far back as Hippocrates:

'It ought to be generally known that the source of our pleasure, merriment, laughter and amusement, as of our grief, pain, anxiety and tears, is none other than the brain. It is specially the organ which enables us to think, see and hear, and to distinguish the ugly and the beautiful, the bad and the good, pleasant and unpleasant . . . It is the brain too which is the seat of madness and delirium, of the fears and frights which assail us, often by night, but sometimes even by day; it is there where lies the cause of insomnia and

sleep-walking, of thoughts that will not come, of forgotten
duties and eccentricities.'　　　　　　(Hippocrates 1950)

It is popularly believed that the Middle Ages ushered in a
period of superstition, magic, and demonology which displaced the 'medical' view of mental illness and replaced it
with a view of it as devilish possession and witchcraft. One
influential historian writes of this period:

'Psychiatric interests were surrendered to the professional
hunter of heretics or to the lonely contemplator of the
world who still dared to puzzle about the nature of the
human mind. Psychology and psychiatry became completely isolated toward the close of the 12th century and
actually disappeared as subjects of scientific consideration.'
　　　　　　　　　　　　　　　　　(Zilboorg 1941: 128)

Such a straightforward view of that period tends to ignore
the fact that the influence of Galen's remarkable anatomical
and physiological theories of mental illness persisted well into
the sixteenth century, that most medieval towns as a corpor-
ate body accepted responsibility for the mentally ill (Rosen
1968) and that two centuries before the appearance in 1484
of the notorious *Malleus Maleficarum*, a sort of plain man's
guide to spotting witches, there was published the *Encyclopaedia of Bartholomaeus the Englishman*, a Franciscan monk
and professor of theology, which dealt with mental illnesses
in terms of natural causes rather than supernatural ones.
The *Encyclopaedia* was widely used at medieval universities,
having been printed in 1470, translated into English in
1495, and reaching twenty editions by 1500. Bartholomaeus
tried to localize the causes of madness to the regions of the
brain around the lateral ventricles. Following a description
of the symptoms of mania and depression, he proceeds thus:

'The medicines of them [the ill] is that they be bounde –
that they hurt not them selfe and other men. And namely
suche shall be refreshed and comfortid – and withdrawn

from cause and mater of drede and besy thoughtes. And they muste be gladded with instrumentes of musike – and some deale be occupied. And at the last if purgations and electuaries suffisen not – they shall be holpe and crafte of surgery.' (Hunter and Macalpine 1963: 4)

Such essentially materialistic conceptions of mental illness were popular until the Inquisition, established to combat heresy, began to concern itself with demonology and witch-craft, and an obsessive and all-pervading concern with sorcery and devils came to dominate religious, secular, and scientific thought. Centuries later, psychiatrists were to argue that the demonology theory of psychiatric illness owed much to attitudes prevalent during the latter part of the Middle Ages concerning the body's relationship with the soul. Whereas the soul was envisaged as giving dignity, humanity, and a claim to divine consideration to man, the body was seen as bestial, des-picable, and vile, a potential temple of Satan and the home of fiendish lust and powerful impulses which warred against the spirit and required constant subjection. 'To have supposed that the innermost sanctuary of nature', wrote the British psychia-trist Henry Maudsley in 1906, 'could be so entered through the humble portals of bodily function would have been regarded as an unwarrantable and an unholy exaltation of the body.' As a consequence of this anti-materialist tendency, the source of mental disturbance was sought not in the innermost reaches of the brain but in the medieval equivalent of Szasz's 'problems of living'. It is a matter of some irony that it is Szasz who accuses biologically inclined psychiatrists, in their search for physical causes, of resembling their medieval pre-decessors who sought the signs of demoniacal possession with a similar single-mindedness and vigour. Yet, in a sense, it is Szasz himself, with his insistence on a non-physical causation and his denunciations of physical explanations as reductive, degrading, and an attack on the human spirit, who is the true inheritor of that philosophy which regarded physical expla-nations of mental events as heretical and, consequently, blamed such events on *spiritual* disturbances such as witch-craft, sorcery, and demons.

The scientific revolution which occurred within medicine during the seventeenth, eighteenth, and nineteenth centuries did not, of course, leave psychiatry untouched yet the super-natural theory of insanity took considerable shifting. For Maudsley, the turning-point came when men recognized insanity as a disease which, like any other, 'might be allevi-ated or cured by medical or moral means'. Thus the stand-point held by the ancient Greeks had been regained:

'Insanity is in fact disorder of brain producing disorder of mind; or to define its nature in greater detail, it is a dis-order of the supreme nerve-centres of the brain – the special organs of mind – producing derangement of thought, feeling and action, together or separately, of such degree or kind as to incapacitate the individual for the relations of life.'   (Maudsley 1906: 11–12)

Far from mental illness being a label affixed to spiritual possession or problems of living, it came to be seen, more often than not, as the cause of such problems. There are psychiatrists at the present time who enthusiastically endorse an even narrower somatic conception of mental illness. William Sargant, probably Britain's best-known organically oriented psychiatrist, declared in a dramatic piece in *The Times*:

'In the last thirty years, the "soul or spirit" of man, if we can call it that, has shown itself increasingly subject to chemical and other physical methods of control. Brain-washing with drugs can make black seem white to a patient; highly selective operations on the brain can remove feelings of anxiety and guilt and make the most worrying person again feel that "sufficient unto the day is the evil thereof".'   (Sargant 1974)

He went on to name the apparent triumphs of the organic approach: electric shock treatment working miracles with severely depressed and melancholic patients, continuous sleep treatment freeing people from mental torment, new drugs getting 80 per cent of schizophrenics better in 'a matter of weeks' instead of at best a third improving either spontaneously or following psychotherapy 'over a three-year period'. The message, according to Dr Sargant, is that organic psychiatry *works* and in medicine, as in so many things, one is ill-advised to argue with success.

Now many, if not most, of Britain's psychiatrists lack Sargant's charismatic optimism and Hunter's rhetorical power. Many shun making such emphatic claims on behalf of the organic model of mental illness and balk from drawing the conclusion that because physical treatments *affect* mental symptoms physical factors must therefore *cause* them. It is difficult to say the extent to which the average psychiatrist, working in his busy hospital and clinic, and relying on drugs and electrical treatment as his main therapeutic weapons, leans on such an unsophisticated model of the mind as that extolled by Hunter and Sargant. But it would not be especially surprising to learn that such a model, or some modification, was widely shared.

The psychotherapeutic approach rejects many of the central features of the organic model. Formulating a diagnosis is not regarded highly and a continuum of emotional disturbance, ranging from mild neurosis to severe psychosis, is preferred to a typological system made up of discrete disease states. The question of cause is an important one, but answers are sought not so much in terms of genetic constitution, biochemical status, or physiological balance as of early infantile and childhood experiences and successive stages of psychosexual development and growth.

In their extreme form, these two approaches are clearly incompatible. Szasz attacks with vigour the organic view of mental illness, accusing it of devaluing the experiences of the suffering, and he believes the mandate of the psychiatrist who employs such an approach is

'. . . to obscure and indeed to deny the ethical dilemmas of life and to transform them into medical and technicalised problems susceptible to "professional" solutions.'

(Szasz 1973: 11)

Richard Hunter (1973), in contrast, makes it plain that he pays as little or as much attention to the answers given by his patients to the question 'Why are you depressed?' as he would to the reasons which patients might advance if asked why they had pneumonia!

Those psychiatrists, and they may well constitute the majority of practising clinicians, who are pragmatically rather than ideologically inclined, occupy with some diffidence and unease the rocky ground between these two windswept and exposed positions. On the one hand, the importance of what is termed a 'predisposition' in some people to develop certain psychiatric illnesses is stressed, such a predisposition being usually stated in genetic and constitutional terms. On the other hand, increasing attention is being paid to the contribution made by psychosocial factors to the aetiology and development of such illnesses. The American psychiatrist Seymour Kety puts this 'middle' case with customary clarity:

'Those interested in exploring the biologic aspects of mental disorders cannot with impunity ignore the psychologic, social and other environmental factors that operate significantly at various stages of their development. Leaving aside etiologic considerations, in which specific sociologic hypotheses like biologic ones are still unproved, it is clear that exogenous factors may precipitate, intensify or ameliorate the symptoms and confuse the biologic picture. The extent to which the classic psychologic features of chronic schizophrenia are created by prolonged isolation and hospitalisation will become apparent with the increasing adoption of community-oriented treatment, and examples are readily found in which uncontrolled nutritional, infectious or pharmacologic variables may have accounted for specific biochemical abnormalities in populations of patients with chronic schizophrenia.'

(Kety 1973: 32)

Over the past thirty years, British psychiatry has prided itself on its freedom from a particular ideological bias. In addition, it has earned itself a distinguished record for its exploration of the aetiological role of social factors in psychiatric illness. The work of researchers in Britain showing that many of the psychological and behavioural features exhibited by chronic mental hospital inmates owed more to the manner whereby such patients were treated than to the actual illness resulted in greater attention being paid to the social and personal circumstances in which psychiatric patients lived and worked. The new watchwords for the mental hospitals became 'socialization', 'rehabilitation', and 'therapeutic milieu', while in the community the new approaches stressed 'after-care' and 'family therapy'. A central feature of post-war British psychiatry has been the emphasis placed on the mobilization and rehabilitation of chronic long-stay patients in the large mental institutions. The 1959 *Mental Health Act* required local authorities to make provision for mentally ill patients not requiring hospitalization but needing support in the community. Psychiatric day hospitals, hostels, half-way houses, and sheltered workshops have developed in a number of programmes, reflecting the influence of psychiatrists such as Douglas Bennett at Netherne, Maxwell Jones at Belmont, David Clark at Fulbourne, and Donald Early at Bristol, who helped focus attention on the way in which the manipulation of certain environmental factors could affect the shape and course of psychiatric illnesses both within and outside of hospital.

3 The sociotherapeutic approach

All of this, and more, could well have been encompassed within either of the first two psychiatric orientations. However, a '*sociotherapeutic*' orientation has become recognized. In so far as it has a discernible aetiological theory, it is one that causally relates the presence of mental illness to the general malfunctioning of society. The mind–body dichotomy is recognized as spurious and the organism tends to be viewed as a unit, the condition, form, and destiny of which are primarily moulded by environmental forces. Illnesses are seen as evolving processes, reactions to these environmental factors, such as poverty, overcrowding, stress, pollution, competitiveness, acquisitiveness, which so significantly determine the individual's personal success or failure and the degree to which he approximates to society's ideal of the 'mentally healthy' individual. Such a view has given rise to the pious hope that shifting community attitudes, so that frustration, conflict, and aggression are lessened, might thereby reduce mental illness. (Such a social view has been confused with what has been called 'community psychiatry', which is really a delivery system that organizes psychiatric facilities in a particular way.)

A British psychiatrist, Dr Malcolm Heron, in a chapter he contributed to *A Hospital Looks at Itself*, a book of essays describing Claybury Hospital in Essex, which is run on 'therapeutic community' lines, outlines some of the theoretical assumptions that underpin the sociotherapeutic approach:

'The family is conceived as the first group and the basis of subsequent social development. Distortion and fixation of this original group experience is a source of permanent personal and interpersonal stress which contributes, under unfavourable circumstances, to development of mental illness. Whatever the aetiology of specific mental disorders (this view does not exclude somatic factors) the sufferer lives in a social milieu which, in varying degrees, reinforces or ameliorates his illness. Mental health, in any community, should allow for a satisfactory social intercourse between members . . .'   (Heron 1972; 16)

Heron goes on to point out that in a 'sick group' there will be distorted, unrealistic expectations with limited control and anxiety-ridden and stereotyped reactions. The main form of treatment involves various forms of group therapy – ward groups, staff groups, patient–staff groups, groups within and outside of hospital. Having a mental illness is, in the words of another social psychiatrist, 'a social project' and it is seen to concern not only the patient himself but

'. . . his friends and relations, neighbours, work mates and employers. The local authority and the Department of Social Security and Health may be involved. If he goes to hospital, psychiatrists, nurses, social workers, psychologists, occupational therapists, and welfare organisations of various kinds all come into the situation. So something essentially very private and personal, something which may seem a very inferior affair, now becomes of obvious public concern.'   (Schoenberg 1972: 43)

One interesting feature of the social model is the manner in which it unashamedly widens the area of psychiatric involvement and expands the number of people involved in the diagnosis and management of psychopathology. In the organic model, the object of therapeutic concern is the individual physical organism, composed of genes, anatomy, biochemistry, physiology. It is a limited object and the area of therapeutic concern is accordingly limited. The major criticism of the organic model is that is appears impersonal, cold, and scientific, and it is often alleged that within it the patient is treated as if he were a socially isolated organism, uncontaminated and unaffected by social and environmental relationships involving his participation. One major advantage of such an approach, however, is that by drawing its area of competence narrowly it avoids spreading the mantle of 'sickness' over a variety of social phenomena such as poverty, injustice, political intolerance, and intellectual dissent, and it demands (usually) that certain rigid criteria be attained before such a mantle is applied to the individual patient.

The psychotherapeutic model likewise concerns itself with the individual, but in this case it is the individual's psychic life, his emotional feelings and experiences, and his inner fantasy world that merit closest scrutiny. One advantage of such an approach is that the patient's communications are treated not as meaningless and irrelevant gibberish, the product of a defective machine, but as attempts to make sense of an inner chaos, a psychic agony expressed in a fragmented and distorted manner, opaque to all but the most skilled, sensitive, and determined interpreters. One disadvantage, already discussed, is the much publicized one whereby symptoms resulting from a biological disturbance are attributed to psychodynamic causes (e.g., Hunter's immigrant girl with the brain tumour).

A further disadvantage is that it has proved difficult, indeed in many cases impossible, to test the veracity of psychoanalytical theories. Psychoanalysts continually insist that their theories are confirmed by their clinical observations and express disdain for more objective methods of verification. Popper (1972) has argued that every good scientific theory is a prohibition; it forbids certain things to happen. The more the theory forbids, the better it is. Psychoanalytical theory, its critics argue, forbids nothing. Everything that occurs can be explained by it; as a theory it is irrefutable. The orthodox clinical psychiatric view of psychoanalysis is summed up, somewhat tersely, in the major postgraduate textbook currently used in psychiatric training:

'It must be realised that, despite its claim of comprehensiveness, the whole of the existing body of doctrine is inadequate to cover all forms of human behaviour . . . On the methodological side, room must be made for scepticism, for the experimental test, and for the abandonment of what has proved fallacious. It is time that the subject should be taught as any other subject . . . it would be best to abandon altogether that process of indoctrination which is called a teaching analysis. There is but one truth; and in our asymptotic approach towards it the worker in the field of human psychology has to submit himself to the same discipline as obtains in every other science.'

(Mayer Gross, Slater and Roth 1969: 20)

The social model widens the area of psychiatric involvement quite considerably. Now it is no longer the individual himself but the individual plus his *social situation* that become the proper objects of the psychiatrist's professional concern. In its most extreme form, such a model rests heavily on certain assumptions drawn from what has been termed 'the societal reaction perspective' (Lemert 1951). During the 1960s this approach, more popularly identified as 'labelling theory', developed into one of the most influential and pervasive theories of deviance. Social action theorists drew attention to the distinction between *primary* and *secondary* deviance, a distinction neatly clarified by Lemert thus:

'Primary deviation is assumed to arise in a wide variety of social, cultural and psychological contexts, and at best has only marginal implication for the psychic structure of the individual; it does not lead to symbolic reorganization at the level of self-regarding attitudes and social roles. Secondary deviation is deviant behaviour, or social roles based upon it, which becomes a means of defense, attack or adaptation to the overt and covert problems created by the societal reaction to primary deviation.'

(Lemert 1967: 17)

The odd, eccentric, or unusual behaviour of those who become singled out by the community for labelling is the primary deviation. The American sociologist Thomas Scheff (1966) argues that most of us learn our expectations and stereotypes of mental illness behaviour during early childhood and whilst much of the imagery involved is spurious such expectations and stereotypes are continually reaffirmed and reinforced in ordinary social interactions. At some point in time, society becomes unable to tolerate the eccentric or odd behaviour of one of its members and the psychiatrist, acting on society's behalf, designates him 'ill'. Once labelled, the individual begins to manifest additional behavioural 'abnormalities', such as the posturing, social withdrawal, and apathy of the chronic and institutionalized schizophrenic, the 'secondary deviation' described above.

Social action theorists tend to pay more attention to the way in which society responds to the behaviour of the deviant than to the quality of the deviance itself. Deviance is conceptualized as a property attributed to certain forms of behaviour by those who witness them rather than as a property inherent in such behaviour. As one exponent, Kai Erikson (1964), puts it, 'The critical variable in the study of deviance, then, is the social audience rather than the individual actor', for the simple reason that it is the audience that determines which episodes of behaviour are to be regarded as deviant and which are not. Within the terms of the societal reaction perspective, mental illness is but a label applied to certain forms of behaviour and the 'patient' but an 'outsider', stigmatized, along with the convict, the dissident, and the disenfranchised, as a consequence of the application by others of rules, values, and standards to his behaviour rather than as a consequence of some inherently pathological quality of the behaviour itself.

Labelling theorists argue that the most crucial step in the development of deviant behaviour is the experience of being caught and publicly labelled deviant. Whether or not this happens to one 'depends not so much on what he does as on what others do' (Becker 1963). The popular writings of Erving Goffman (1961, 1963, 1964), together with the equally influential if less publicized writings of Howard Becker, Kai Erikson, and Thomas Scheff, have drawn attention to certain stages involved in labelling processes. The public's decision to act against an individual involves a distinct transitional ritual by which he is removed from his 'normal' position in society and placed in a specific deviant and 'abnormal' role. The ceremonies, accompanying such a change, have three phases: a formal, confrontation stage in which the suspected deviant and the accusing community face each other (in a courtroom criminal trial or a psychiatric case conference); a judgement stage, in which a decision is announced concerning the nature of the alleged deviancy (a judicial verdict, a psychiatric diagnosis); and a stage of 'social placement' in which the deviant is assigned to a special role (prisoner, patient) and is, as a direct consequence, dramatically redefined in the eyes of society.

Much of the momentum behind the enthusiastic endorsement of the labelling theory of mental illness by sociologists and some psychiatrists appears to be derived from an appreciation of the *negative* effects of the diagnostic process. Thomas Scheff, working with American data, argues that the findings of Allen Haney and Robert Michielutte (1968), which show a higher compulsory hospitalization rate for negroes compared to whites, Dennis Wanger and Richard Fletcher's (1969) demonstration of the dramatic way in which the presence of a lawyer representing the patient in admission hearings decreased the likelihood of admission, Maurice Termalin's illustrations (1968) of the suggestibility of psychiatrists when confronted by individuals already deemed mentally ill, and David Rosenhan's description (1973) of the 'stickiness' of psychiatric labels, can all be explained with a minimum of difficulty by labelling theory. A British psychiatrist, Dr Alexander Mitchell of Fulbourn Hospital, Cambridge, draw attention to the reductive quality, which he believes to be a serious shortcoming of the diagnostic approach in psychiatry:

'Putting a label on a patient can invalidate the patient – "You are an invalid, and what you say is therefore invalid. You are sick because your label says so." Diagnosis can therefore become a way of restraining people and of rendering them even more impotent than they were when they started. To say someone is neurotic, psychotic, psycho-pathic or schizophrenic is not just a scientific descriptive statement. It can become a way of making a value judgement about the patient and putting him down.'

(Mitchell 1973: 35)

The diagnostic approach in clinical psychiatry is discussed later. At this point, it is worth noting that it is not sufficient to show that psychiatric diagnoses are abused and have unde-sirable consequences to prove that they are mere value judge-ments. To diagnose venereal disease mistakenly can have catastrophic effects for the person concerned and a number of severe secondary impairments or 'deviations' can result, but nobody would argue that venereal disease is merely a label for undesirable social behaviour! As Professor John Wing points out:

'. . . the most serious shortcoming of labelling theory is that although it is relatively easy to conceive how a societal reaction might pressurise an individual (selected for scape-goating because of some minor eccentricity of behaviour) into becoming an outcast, delinquent or rebel, it is difficult to imagine how a similar reaction would force him to adopt the central schizophrenic syndrome since this would need special coaching from an expert!'   (Wing 1973)

However, and this is of crucial importance in the under-standing of the appeal of labelling theory, if one widens the concept of an illness such as schizophrenia so that the diag-nosis no longer depends on establishing the presence of a number of highly specific and precisely defined symptoms but on the 'feel' or the 'impression' of the examining psychiatrist, then the boundary between deviance and disease becomes hopelessly blurred and labelling theory's claims to 'explain' the behaviour of the psychiatrist as well as the patient become significantly enhanced.

The social model of psychiatric illness is not, however, identical with labelling theory. For the most part it is a de-scriptive term applied to that approach which takes account of the largest possible number of factors affecting the psychiatric patient, such as his family situation, personal relationships, occupational circumstances, social role, etc. His community, composed of his relatives, friends, neighbours, work colleagues, and employers, formerly construed as a social community, begins to take on the appearance of a *therapeutic community*, such a transformation being achieved under the supervision of the psychiatrist, who is now expected to bring to his skills as a physician and psychotherapist the additional expertise of social engineer and community adviser. As the boundary line which serves to define the limits of psychiatry's involvement extends, so the psychiatrist finds himself treating not alone the traditional problems of psychotic and serious neurotic disturbances but the 'no-man's land of everyday unhappiness' (Oppenheimer 1971) as well. This has led to 'the psychiatrization of life' (Cerrolaza 1973) whereby individual psychiatrists have been propelled into claiming special professional competence in the fields of international diplomacy, over-population, pollution, and the hazards of nuclear war! Nor has British psychiatry been spared such overweening grandiosity; it is almost a quarter of a century since Professor Desmond Curran called for the establishment of 'Psychiatry Limited', emphasized that '. . . a limited liability company is one in which the shareholders, should the company fail or go bankrupt, are not liable for more than they subscribe' and attacked those who 'undermine the reputation of the firm by using the name to float bogus companies with grandiose prospectuses, backed up by balance sheets that do not add up to make sense' (Curran 1951: 105). More recently, one of Britain's more outspoken critics of psychiatric expansionism put it even more bluntly:

'. . . most of the abuses of the psychiatrist arise from his reluctance to restrict his activities to the field in which he is genuinely qualified to operate. The Oxford Dictionary's definition of a psychiatrist is "one who treats mental disease". Not, you will observe, one who prevents wars, cures anti-semitism, offers to transform the normally abrasive relations between men into a tedium of stultifying harmony, is the ultimate authority on bringing up children or selecting directors, or misuses his jargon to confuse any and every topical issue in an incessant series of television appearances.' (Miller 1969: 44)

What constitutes 'mental disease' is considered elsewhere, but it is worth noting at this stage the professional dilemma of the average psychiatrist. As long as he operates as a specialist in psychopathology, he does so from the viewpoint of altering his patient rather than society. Some psychiatrists, perceiving such a role to be confined and constricted, have rejected it and have committed themselves instead to changing the nature of society itself, their efforts, on occasion, being designated somewhat optimistically 'preventive psychiatry'. In so moving from the patient to society, they have in effect argued that mental illness is the product of social forces and structures and that it is in the analysis and alteration of these that the psychiatrist finds his true role. As a result, such a psychiatrist places himself firmly within the political arena. Such a trend has prompted one observer to warn that the expanding role is outstripping the gains in established knowledge (Shepherd 1971) and Professor Michael Shepherd's caution appears vindicated by the claims of the Chairman of the American Psychiatric Association's Task Force on Psychiatry and Foreign Affairs:

'We do not need to question our competence or relevance . . . To heal in the modern context goes beyond the physical and the psychological. It enters into the very issue of world survival, into a world of conflicting ideologies and social systems . . . Has not the time come for international psychiatry to expand into those realms that are of such critical importance to all of us?' (Davidson 1975)

It is not my intention to argue that the psychiatrist should disqualify himself from taking a lively interest in the political and social issues of his times. Indeed, it is difficult for him to avoid doing so, particularly if he accepts as his view of psychiatry that summarized by one of its most distinguished professors as

'. . . the study of abnormal behaviour from the medical standpoint, irrespective of whether it arises wholly or partly from physical disease, environmental stress, disturbed up-bringing, inherited abnormality or cultural circumstances.'

(Lewis 1953: 109)

In practice, the great majority of psychiatrists, working within the National Health Service, are 'community psychiatrists', that is to say, responsible in each case for the mental health of catchment area populations of up to 60,000 people (see Chapter 9). Responsible for the organization of the in-patient and out-patient psychiatric services, providing the psychiatric cover of those physically ill patients exhibiting mental stress, and participating in the area mental health team composed of social workers, general practitioners, health visitors, occupational therapists, psychologists, etc., such a psychiatrist can be expected to apply some of the major principles of the sociotherapeutic approach in practice. By virtue of the immense public demand for psychiatric care, as much as by reason of a particular faith in the efficacy of such treatments, many psychiatrists do seem to rely quite heavily on physical methods of treatment, such as anti-depressant drugs and ECT, and do stress the genetic and organic factors operating in psychiatric illness. Psychiatrists, especially when they appear in public before a non-professional audience, tend to stress their freedom from prejudice and bias, their open-mindedness, their willingness to select what is best from a wide variety of possibilities, in short their shrewd and well-informed eclecticism. Yet, as Michael Polanyi once observed, ideologies are fighting creeds. Eclecticism, in psychiatry, as in so much else, is somewhat suspect, the soft option of the wishy-washy, gutless mind, lacking decisiveness and clarity. The average psychiatrist may not have read Eysenck's critical broadside against the tendency to employ a mixture of therapies, but he does seem intuitively aware that subscribing to 'a mish-mash of theories, a hugger-mugger of procedures, a gallimaufry of therapies and a chari-varia of activities having no proper rationale and incapable of being tested or evaluated' (Eysenck 1971), whilst apparently clinically defensible, does render him especially vulnerable to the relentless, logical objections of his more sceptical colleagues.

Not surprisingly, some psychiatrists do opt for one or other of the major orientations and appreciate the intellectual security such certainty can provide. With certainty comes the urge to control and it is an interesting feature of the various orientations that each tends to extend its area of competence so that it eventually takes over and dominates the entire psychiatric arena. This has been discussed briefly in the case of the sociotherapeutic orientation. However, it is also true of the psychotherapists. Heinz Wolff, a leading British psycho-therapist, has distinguished between what he calls 'specialized psychotherapy', i.e., intensive, formal psychotherapy with highly selected patients, and 'general psychotherapy'. The latter form of treatment remains somewhat vague but makes up for this by being, it would appear, indispensable:

'This general psychotherapeutic approach is applicable to every patient receiving psychiatric care as an in-patient, out-patient, or in the community, independent of his diag-nosis and of whatever form of treatment he may be re-ceiving. In in-patient and day-hospital units it finds expression especially in large group and therapeutic com-munity methods.'   (Wolff 1973: 118)

Now it may well be that Dr Wolff is giving vent to a state-ment of no greater significance than that it is important to talk to patients whatever their problems. However, in view of the fact that he delivered this opinion at a conference devoted to a consideration of resources and manpower and in support of an argument for specially trained psycho-therapists to be recruited into the NHS, it is reasonable to assume that these psychotherapists will be necessary to *teach* 'the general psychotherapeutic approach' to the various members of the psychiatric entourage who need it. By such a route does the psychotherapeutic ideology become elevated to a dominant position and established as that treatment modality without which no other form of psychiatric intervention can be meaningful or efficacious.

Some psychologists, as I mentioned earlier, are making their own bids for power but, being relatively pragmatic and hard-headed men in the main, they have expressed their intentions with more caution. Whereas the psychotherapists expressed a need for the whole arena to be under their jurisdiction, the psychologists appear content to settle for 50 per cent! Professor Eysenck's suggestions for a 'divorce' (1975) reflect his conviction that whereas physical treatments have much to offer in the management of psychotic illnesses, certain behavioural techniques are strikingly effective in some neurotic and behavioural disturbances. So what could be more simple, or more sensible, than having the psychologists look after the neurotic and the psychiatrists look after the psychotic?

Eysenck ignores the fact that the vast majority of neurotic disorders are currently being managed by *neither* the psychiatrists nor the psychologists but by the general practitioners. He ignores too the fact that the distinction between neuroses and psychoses, while often convenient, is without substance. 'To argue whether a dubious case is neurotic or psychotic is like arguing whether a man of medium size is thin or fat: he is both and neither' (Shepherd 1969: 1335). He also disregards the available evidence suggesting that for many forms of neurotic disorder behaviour therapy has not thus far proved particularly effective while at the same time there is more to the management of the severe psychotic illnesses than physical treatments.

There is no clear dividing line between somatic medicine and psychiatry nor between psychiatry and clinical psychology as applied to the study and treatment of certain forms of psychological disturbance. There is no mental disorder, mild, moderate, or severe, psychotic or neurotic, in the causation of which bodily disease may not play a crucial part. The absence of an established, scientific corpus of knowledge in this whole area means that certain factors can have a disproportionate effect on the individual psychiatrist's orientation. A number of studies in this country (Kreitman 1962; Walton, Drewery, and Carstairs 1963; Walton 1966) have suggested that an interest in the psychological aspects of psychiatry is strongly associated with so-called 'thinking introversion'. Those doctors especially interested in the physical aspects of mental illness tend to be less reflective, self-analytical, and interested in abstract ideas. An investigation of the social and treatment attitudes of forty-two British psychiatrists by Pallis and Stoffelmayer (1973), which employed a number of attitude inventories and a Conservative scale, claimed to show a positive association between conservative social attitudes and a preference for physical methods of treatment. Their study concludes with the observation that

'. . . statements which are frequently made with some ideological fervour about the value of different treatment methods should perhaps be viewed with extreme caution. It is likely that if treatment orientation is embedded in general social attitude, discussion about the advantages of the various treatments will not be guided by factual arguments alone.'   (Pallis and Stoffelmayer 1973: 79)

Thus, peculiarities of temperament and character may well be added to the variety of other pressures (professional advancement, peer recognition, sense of personal and group security, etc.) influencing the choice of this or that particular orientation. Chosen for such reasons, a model is often increasingly defended by a recourse to denigratory attacks on the alternatives. That psychiatry has not split itself asunder in the midst of such contentious and fractious disputes is surprising. Perhaps it is due to what sociologists term the

Simmel-Ross hypothesis which states:

> 'A society . . . which is riven by a dozen conflicts . . . along lines running in every direction, may actually be in less danger of being torn with violence, of falling to pieces than one split along just one line. For each new cleavage contributes to narrow the cross clefts, so that one might say that society is *sewn together* by its inner conflicts.'
>
> (R. Merton quoted in Storer 1973: 68)

Such a hypothesis receives some support from the way in which psychiatry in this country has developed. In the United States, in contrast, where one single conflict, that between psychoanalysis and a somatically based clinical psychiatry, has dominated the psychiatric arena, there has been considerable danger that psychiatry would split in two. When the American Board of Psychiatry and Neurology decreed that the traditional one-year experience in the care of the sick, as exemplified by the medical internship, would no longer be required of a doctor intending to take up psychiatry, one professor of psychiatry was moved to declare that academic psychiatry appeared to be 'in full retreat from its hard-won battle to be recognised as a major medical discipline', a trend whose ultimate outcome 'could be the discrediting, if not the destruction, of psychiatry as a discipline' (Engel 1972). Such a situation has been avoided in Britain where the development of social psychiatry, psychiatric epidemiology, psychopharmacology, behavioural psychology, and non-analytically based variants of psychotherapy, superimposed on the particular delivery system of health care evolved in this country since the war, has done much to ensure that the division in psychiatry resembles multiple small cracks rather than a single, deep, divisive cleft.

I have made no mention of the so-called 'medical model'. It is often erroneously believed that this model and the 'organic' orientation, which stresses a physical basis for psychiatric illness to the exclusion of other factors, are syn-onymous. The medical model is an evolving one in which scientific methods of observation, description, and differen-tiation are employed, in which an illness is conceptualized as 'a process that moves from the recognition and palliation of symptoms to the characterization of a specific disease in which the etiology and pathogenesis are known and the treat-ment is rational and specific' (Kety 1974: 9). Such a process may take years, centuries even, and while many medical conditions have moved to the final stages of such under-standing, others are still at various points along the way. In psychiatry, the major conditions, schizophrenia, manic-depressive illness, obsessional disorders, etc., are still con-ceptualized in the form of syndromes, symptom clusters which may turn out to represent several aetiologies and pathogenetic factors. In medicine, the situation is not dis-similar. Diseases such as Hodgkin's disease and multiple sclerosis are examples of conditions in which the diagnosis is based upon a recognizable pathology, even though their cause is obscure, whereas the condition known as Parkinson's disease has not one but at least two distinct causes. The medical model does not envisage disease as something which 'happens' to a person independently of any action he may take (which appears to be Hunter's view of pneumonia and schizophrenia). Medical diseases do not exist independently of the people who are sick. The medical model, in short, takes into account not merely the symptom, syndrome, or disease, but the person who suffers, his personal and social situation, his biological, psychological, and social status. The medical model, as applied to psychiatry, embodies the basic principle that every illness is the product of two factors – of environ-ment working on the organism. Sir Aubrey Lewis underlines the point:

'Whether the constitutional factor is the predominant or determining influence, or the environmental one, is never a question of kind, never a question to be dealt with as an "either/or" problem; there will be a great number of possible combinations according to the individually inherited endowment and training and the particular constellation of environmental forces.' (Lewis 1936)

In the last resort, it can be seen that the variety of ideological positions within psychiatry, the biological, the dynamic, the social, the behavioural, represent different emphases. Identifying the respective contributions of man, culture, and nature to the phenomenon of mental illness demands of psychiatrists, and of those who work alongside them, a willingness to avoid doctrinaire devotion to one or other of the ideologies competing for support and a determination to refrain from inflating the somewhat meagre items of genuine psychiatric knowledge into a programme of social reform and a political manifesto for the attainment of Utopia. If psychiatry is to progress, it is more likely to do so if psychiatrists continue to withhold their allegiance from any one theoretical model and avoid deception by dogmas, fanaticisms, or absolutisms. The ideal psychiatrist, in Jaspers' view, is one who combines 'scientific attitudes of the sceptic with a powerful impressive personality and a profound existential faith' (1923: 808). He is someone with a solid foundation in medicine, the biological and behavioural sciences, who is able to cope with the intellectual isolation implicit in such a critical eclecticism. It cannot be said that the intervening years since Jaspers made his observation have diminished the need for such a rare combination of abilities.

References

BECKER, H. (1963) *Outsider: Studies in the Sociology of Deviance*. New York: The Free Press.

CAINE, R.M. and SMAIL, D.J. (1969) *The Treatment of Mental Illness: Science, Faith and the Therapeutic Personality*. London: University of London Press.

CERROLAZA, M. (1973) The Nebulous Scope of Current Psychiatry. *Comprehensive Psychiatry* **14** (4): 299.

CRICHTON BROWNE, J. (1871) The Cause of G.P.I.
Address to 7th Meeting of Medico-Psychological
Association.

CURRAN, D. (1951) Psychiatry Limited. *Proceedings of the
Royal Society of Medicine* **45**: 105.

DAVIDSON, W. (1975) Quoted in *Psychiatric News*, official
newspaper of the American Psychiatric Association.
February 5.

DUBOS, R. and DUBOS, J. (1952) Consumption and the
Romantic Age. In: *The White Plague*. Boston: Little
Brown and Company.

ELLENBERGER, H. (1970) *The Discovery of the Unconscious*.
London: Allen Lane and Penguin.

ENGEL, G.L. (1972) Is Psychiatry Failing in its
Responsibilities to Medicine? (editorial). *American
Journal of Psychiatry* **128**: 1561–3.

ERIKSON, K. (1964) Notes on the Sociology of Deviance.
In H. Becker (ed.), *The Other Side*. New York: The
Free Press.

EYSENCK, H.J. (1963) Behaviour Therapy, Extinction
and Relapses in Neurosis. *British Journal of Psychiatry*
109: 12–18.

—— (1971) A Mish-Mash of Theories. *International
Journal of Psychiatry* **9**: 140–47.

—— (1975) *The Future of Psychiatry*. London: Methuen.

GOFFMAN, E. (1961) *Asylums: Essays on the Social Situation
of Mental Patients and Other Inmates*. Garden City, New
York: Anchor Books.

—— (1963) *Stigma: Notes on the Management of Spoiled
Identity*. Englewood Cliffs, New Jersey: Prentice-Hall.

—— (1964) *Behaviour in Public Places*. New York: The
Free Press.

HANEY, C. ALLEN and MICHIELUTTE, R. (1968)
Selective Factors Operating in the Adjudication of
Incompetency. *Journal of Health and Social Behaviour* **9**:
233–42.

HERON, M. (1972) Therapeutic Community Practice in

an Admission Unit. In E. Schoenberg (ed.), *A Hospital Looks at Itself: Essays from Claybury*. London: Cassirer.

HIPPOCRATES (1950) The Sacred Disease. In *The Medical Works of Hippocrates* (trans. Chadwick and Mann). Oxford: Blackwell.

HOLLINGSHEAD, A. and REDLICH, F. (1958) *Social Class and Mental Illness*. London: Chapman & Hall.

HUNTER, R. (1973) Psychiatry and Neurology: Psychosyndrome or Brain Disease. *Proceedings of the Royal Society of Medicine* **66**: 17–22.

HUNTER, R. and MACALPINE, I. (eds.) (1963) *Three Hundred Years of Psychiatry*. London: Oxford University Press.

JASPERS, K. (1923) *General Psychopathology* (trans. J. Hoenig and M. Hamilton, 1963). Manchester: Manchester University Press.

KETY, S.S. (1973) Problems in Biological Research in Psychiatry. In J. Mendels (ed.), *Biological Psychiatry*. London: Wiley & Sons.

KETY, S.S. (1974) From Rationalisation to Reason. *American Journal of Psychiatry* **131**: 9.

KREITMAN, N. (1962) Psychiatric Orientation: A Study of Attitudes among Psychiatrists. *Journal of Mental Science* **108**: 317–28.

LEMERT, E. (1951) *Social Pathology*. New York: McGraw-Hill.

—— (1967) *Human Deviance, Social Problems and Social Control*. Englewood Cliffs, New Jersey: Prentice-Hall.

LEWIS, A. (1936) Melancholia: Prognostic Study and Case Material. *Journal of Mental Science* **82**: 488–588.

—— (1953) Health as a Social Concept. *British Journal of Sociology* **4**: 109.

MACALPINE, I. and HUNTER, R. (1966) The 'Insanity' of King George III: A Classic Case of Porphyria. *British Medical Journal* **8** (1): 66.

—— (1974) The Pathography of the Past. *Times Literary Supplement*, March 15.

MAUDSLEY, H. (1906) *Responsibility in Mental Disease* (6th edition). London: Kegan Paul, Trench Trubner & Company.

MAYER-GROSS, W., SLATER, E. and ROTH, M. (eds.) (1969) *Clinical Psychiatry* (3rd edition). London: Baillière, Tindall & Cassell.

MEDAWAR, P. (1972) *The Hope of Progress*. London: Methuen.

MILLER, H.G. (1969) Psychiatry – Medicine or Magic? *World Medicine* 5 (6): 44.

MITCHELL, A. (1973) What's on your Label? *Mind and Mental Health Magazine*: 32–5.

OPPENHEIMER, H. (1971) *Clinical Psychiatry*. New York: Harper & Row.

PALLIS, D.J. and STOFFELMAYER, B.E. (1973) Social Attitudes and Treatment Orientation among Psychiatrists. *British Journal of Medical Psychiatry* 46 (i): 75–81.

POPPER, K. (1972) *Conjectures and Refutations* (4th edition). London: Routledge & Kegan Paul.

ROSEN, G. (1968) *Madness in Society*. Chicago: University of Chicago Press.

ROSENHAN, D. (1973) On Being Sane in Insane Places. *Science* 179: 250–58.

SARGANT, W. (1974) The Movement in Psychiatry away from the Philosophical. *The Times*, August 22.

SCHEFF, R. (1966) *Being Mentally Ill*. Chicago: Aldine.

SCHOENBERG, E. (ed.) (1972) The Anti-Therapeutic Team in Psychiatry. In E. Schoenberg (ed.), *A Hospital Looks at Itself; Essays from Claybury*.

SHEPHERD, M. (1969) Psychological Medicine. In F. W. Price (ed.), *Textbook of the Practice of Medicine*. London: Oxford University Press.

SHEPHERD, M. (1971) A Critical Appraisal of Contemporary Psychiatry. *Comprehensive Psychiatry* 12 (4): 302–20.

SIEGLER, M. and OSMOND, H. (1974) *Models of Madness, Models of Medicine*. London: Collier Macmillan.

SONTAG, S. (1979) *Illness as Metaphor*. London: Allen Lane.

STORER, N.W. (ed.) (1973) *The Sociology of Science. Theoretical and Empirical Investigations of Robert K. Merton.* Chicago: University of Chicago Press.

STRAUSS, A., SCHATZMAN, L., BUCHER, R., EHRLICH, D., and SABSHIN, M. (1964) *Psychiatric Ideologies and Institutions.* Glencoe, Illinois: Free Press.

SZASZ, T. (1960) The Myth of Mental Illness. *The American Psychologist* **15**: 113–18.

—— (1972) Bad Habits are not Diseases. *Lancet* **ii** (83–4): 128.

—— (1973) *Ideology and Insanity.* London: Calder Boyars.

TERMALIN, M.K. (1968) Suggestion Effects in Psychiatric Diagnosis. *Journal of Nervous and Mental Disease* **147** (4): 349–53.

WALTON, H.J. (1966) Differences between Physically-Minded and Psychologically-Minded Medical Practitioners. *British Journal of Psychiatry* **112**: 1097–102.

WALTON, H.J., DREWERY, J., and CARSTAIRS, G.M. (1963) Interest of Graduating Medical Students in Social and Emotional Aspects of Illness. *British Medical Journal* **ii**: 588–92.

WANGER, D. and FLETCHER, C.R. (1969) The Effect of Legal Counsel on Admissions to a State Mental Hospital: A Confrontation of Professions. *Journal of Health and Social Behaviour* **10**: 66–72.

WING, J.K. (1973) *Schizophrenia: Medical and Social Models.* Unpublished.

WOLFF, H.H. (1973) The Place of Psychotherapy in the District Psychiatric Services. In R. Cawley and G. McLachlan (eds.), *Policy for Action.* London: Nuffield Provincial Hospitals Trust and Oxford University Press.

ZILBOORG, G. (1941) *A History of Medical Psychology.* New York: W. W. Norton & Co.

3

The diagnostic process

It is a capital mistake to theorize before one has data. Insensibly one begins to twist facts to suit theories instead of theories to suit facts.

SHERLOCK HOLMES

IN A WIDELY publicized, much-quoted study published at the beginning of 1973, D. L. Rosenhan, Professor of Psychology at Stanford University, reported how he and seven colleagues managed to pass themselves off as 'schizophrenics' and get committed to twelve mental hospitals in the United States simply by declaring that they heard voices saying the single words 'empty', 'hollow', and 'thud' (Rosenhan 1973). Beyond complaining of this symptom and falsifying their names, vocations, and employment, the eight researchers made no further alterations of their personal histories or family relationships. Nonetheless, despite ceasing to simulate *any* psychiatric abnormality whatsoever once admitted to hospital, they were confined for periods ranging from seven to fifty-two days (the average length of stay being nineteen days) before being released, having been diagnosed, in the majority of cases, as schizophrenics whose symptoms had temporarily remitted.

It is a matter of some interest that a solitary complaint of a hallucinatory voice in the absence of any other unusual experience or personal discomfort should actually persuade certain American hospitals to open their doors. Such is the current demand for a psychiatric bed within the National Health Service and the prevailing emphasis on treating patients outside hospitals and in the community that the average admitting doctor in Britain is likely to find himself under strict instructions to avoid admitting any patient who can see, speak, and move, and do all of these things without bothering himself or others to any significant extent. One suspects that, in Britain, Professor Rosenhan might well be advised to go home like a good man, get a decent night's rest, and come back in the morning (when he and another doctor could start all over again!).

However, that, of course, is not the central point of Rosenhan's paper. Rather, it is the question with which he opens it: 'If sanity and insanity exist, how shall we know them?' It is not clear, because Rosenhan does not tell us, how the American psychiatrists, confronted with these 'pseudo-patients', attempted to make this somewhat crude if vital distinction. His study does underline the fact, however, that leaving aside the question about a psychiatrist being able to distinguish between a schizophrenic illness and a manic-depressive one, he should at least be able to tell a sick man from a healthy one, an unhappy man from a contented one, a sane man from one who is mentally ill, a genuine patient from a fraud. Or isn't it possible?

As a practising clinician, the psychiatrist is concerned with individuals, each of whom is in his own fashion 'unique'. Yet if he is to function as a competent clinician, he requires certain general concepts and laws as a basis for his work. The psychiatrist looks to psychology and psychopathology in much the same way as a general physician looks to physiology and pathology. Psychopathology has, as its subject-matter, actual conscious psychic events. Although primarily concerned with pathological phenomena, the psychopathologist needs to know what people experience in general and how they experience it, in short he needs to know the full range of psychic reality. Psychology, which in the main is concerned with what has been called normal psychic life, provides the psychiatrist with the insights and knowledge that help illuminate the abnormal psychic phenomena with which he is primarily concerned. It has to be acknowledged, however, that at the present time psychopathologists are concerned with much material of which the normal counterpart has not yet been studied by psychologists, but in general psychology and psychopathology complement each other just as in the somatic area physiology and pathology complement each other.

The term *psychopathology* is often used loosely as if synonymous with 'psychodynamic'. However, 'psychodynamic' more accurately refers to the study of normal and abnormal mental processes from a particular viewpoint, namely the dynamic viewpoint of the psychoanalytic and allied schools. Psychopathology is concerned with every psychic reality and involves different frames of reference, including the dynamic one.

It was the German psychiatrist-turned-philosopher, Karl Jaspers, who, in his massive book *Clinical Psychopathology* (1959), systematized the main methods of approach in psychopathology and greatly facilitated the construction of a common terminology. His book has had enormous impact on psychiatric theory and practice in Britain. Several of the major psychiatric texts used in this country, particularly those by Fish (1962, 1967), Kraupl Taylor (1966), Anderson and Trethowan (1967), and arguably the most influential of all, that by Mayer-Gross, Slater, and Roth (1969), all draw heavily on his ideas and place great emphasis on the importance of carefully selecting, differentiating, and describing the particular phenomena of abnormal psychic experience.

Such *descriptive psychopathology* involves the identification of particular phenomena of experience which then, through the use of a chosen term, become defined and capable of identification again and again. In this way such phenomena as delusions, hallucinations, compulsive phenomena, overvalued ideas, and the different modes of personal awareness, drives, etc., have been identified and described. In Jaspers' words, 'this representation of psychic experiences and psychic states, this delimitation and definition of them, so that we can be sure the same term means the same thing, is the express function of *phenomenology*' (1959). An obvious shortcoming of this phenomenological approach is that it depends on a patient's self-descriptions, which can only be grasped by way of analogy with an observer's own mode of experience. Such phenomena Jaspers calls *subjective*, as opposed to those *objective* phenomena which can be directly demonstrated as they occur, and which they do in a number of fundamentally different ways, e.g., as somatic accompaniments (an increase in pulse rate during excitement, sweating during fear), as expression (facial expressions of ecstasy and gloom), as measurable performance (memory span, work output, etc.). Subjective phenomena in contrast

'. . . include all those emotions and inner processes, such as fear, sorrow, joy, which we feel we can grasp immediately from their physical concomitants; these we thus take to "express" the underlying emotion. Then there are all those psychic experiences and phenomena which patients describe to us and which only become accessible to us through the patient's own judgement and presentation. Lastly, subjective symptoms also include those mental processes which we have to infer from fragments of the two previous kinds of data, manifested by the patient's actions and the way he conducts his life.'

(Jaspers 1968: 1313)

Such differentiation between *subjective* (the patient's immediate experience, which can only be indirectly grasped by the observer) and *objective* (that which can be directly demonstrated in the external world) is not unequivocal. For example, Jaspers applied the term *objective* to the rational content of a delusion in so far as this can be understood 'in a purely intellectual way' (1959). *Subjective* then is applied to those psychic events constituting the original delusional experience which can be grasped by 'sympathetic insight' on the part of the observer.

In addition to collecting individual phenomena, psychopathology is also concerned with an enquiry into the connections between them, i.e., with an understanding or perception of *meaning*. Phenomenology, as Jaspers admits, presents us with a series of isolated fragments broken out from a person's total psychological experience. Psychopathology, therefore, is not merely *descriptive*, it is *interpretive* as well. Some psychiatrists appear to believe that one is antipathetic to the other and they exhibit the tendency to emphasize the one at the other's cost. Purified of any subjective bias, the study of objective data has become transformed into a behaviourally orientated psychology. Concepts such as performance, intelligence, learning ability, fatigue, and sense perception, which lend themselves to objective description, measurement, and replication, and which appear to be relatively independent of whether the observer is concerned with a robot, a living but mindless organism, or a human person with feelings and emotions, have become the preferred objects of study by many psychologists (and, indeed, some psychiatrists). An obvious advantage of such an emphasis is that it produces results that do not depend on subjective introspection and empathy, that are convincing, that can be tested, and that are often easier to comprehend than any analysis of subjective psychological explanations.

Some psychiatrists, in full flight from the chaotic swamp that the subjective psychic life of their patients appears to resemble, retreat into an allegedly scientific approach and lay particular emphasis on psychological tests, statistical measures, and physiological factors while deriding the value of attempting to understand patients' internal feelings and states. Others pay as little attention to objective symptoms and enthusiastically immerse themselves in an exploration of their patients' inner world. The balance, as ever, is a difficult one to maintain, yet the distinction between the identification and description of abnormal psychic phenomena, *descriptive psychopathology*, and the interpretation and understanding of these, *interpretive psychopathology*, must be acknowledged and preserved.

The manifold diversity of psychic phenomena makes it impossible for them to be studied *in toto*. The diagnostician must identify specific phenomena with which to work and must establish their relationship with other phenomena with which they must not be confused. Such abnormal psychological phenomena, which are identified, have to be described, interpreted, and clustered into groups. Such a process is currently somewhat out of fashion and is attacked for its alleged sterility. The merits, and the shortcomings, of the descriptive approach, an approach which helped to lay the foundations of the most widely accepted classificatory system in contemporary psychiatry, is illustrated by Emil Kraepelin's account of a case presentation of a patient showing signs of catatonic excitement. The account is quoted by and commented upon by Ronald Laing in his book *The Divided Self*.

' "The patient I will show you today has almost to be carried into the room, as he walks in a straddling fashion on the outside of his feet. On coming in, he throws off his slippers, sings a hymn loudly, and then he cries twice (in English), 'My father, my real father!' He is eighteen years old, and a pupil of the Oberrealschule (higher-grade modern-side school), tall, and rather strongly built, but with a pale complexion, on which very often there is a transient flush. The patient sits with his eyes shut and pays no attention to his surroundings. He does not look up when he is spoken to, but he answers beginning in a low voice, and gradually screaming louder and louder. When asked where he is, he says 'You want to know that too? I tell you who is being measured and is measured and shall be measured. I know all that and could tell you but I do not want to.' When asked his name, he screams, 'What is your name? What does he shut? He shuts his eyes. What does he hear? He does not understand; he understands not. How? Who? Where? When? What does he mean? When I tell him to look, he does not look properly. You there, just look! What is it? What is the matter? Attend; he attends not. I say, what is it, then? Why do you give me no answer? Are you getting impudent again? How can you be so impudent?

I'm coming! I'll show you! You don't whore for me. You mustn't be smart either; you're an impudent lousy fellow, such an impudent, lousy fellow I've never met with. Is he beginning again? You understand nothing at all, nothing at all; nothing at all does he understand. If you follow now, he won't follow, will not follow. Are you getting still more impudent? Are you getting impudent still more? How they attend, they do attend' and so on. At the end he scolds in quite inarticulate sounds." '

(Laing 1965: 29–30)

'Now there is no question that this patient is showing the "signs" of catatonic excitement', remarks Laing; no question, because Kraepelin, the descriptive psychopathologist, patiently describes, or allows his subject to describe, the *form* of the patient's behaviour and experience. However, Laing does not produce this extract to lionize the descriptive approach but to support his belief that Kraepelin does not *understand* what he sees and hears but appears content merely to record and describe. Kraepelin continues (and this part is not quoted by Laing):

'The patient understands perfectly and has introduced many phrases he has heard before into his speech. without once looking up. He speaks in an affected way, now babbling like a child, now lisping and stammering, sings suddenly in the middle of what he is saying, and grimaces. He carries out orders in an extraordinary fashion, gives his hand with the fist clenched, goes to the blackboard when he is asked, but, instead of writing his name, suddenly knocks down a lamp, and throws the chalk among the audience. He makes all kinds of senseless movements, pushes the table away, crosses his arms, and turns around on his axis, chair and all, or sits balancing, with his legs crossed and his hands on his head. Catalepsy can also be made out. When he is to go away, he will not get up, has to be pushed, and calls out loudly "Good-morning, gentlemen; it has not pleased me". The only physical disturbance worth noticing is a considerable acceleration of the pulse to 160 beats.'   (Kraepelin 1905: 79–80)

Kraepelin goes on to draw the attention of his students to the patient's *'inaccessibility'*, the frequent *'repetition of the same phrases'*, the *'confused speech'*, the *'impulsive actions, grimacing and extraordinary affected behaviour'*. The combination in the patient of *'good comprehension'*, *'atrophy of the emotions'*, and *'various kinds of vitiations of the will'* coupled with the above symptoms and signs lead Kraepelin to diagnose 'dementia praecox' (the forerunner, terminologically speaking, of schizophrenia).

Now Laing's irritation with Kraepelin's preoccupation with description reflects the contemporary disillusion with apparently sterile observation and recording. Kraepelin is accused of being more interested in establishing the signs of a 'disease' than in understanding his patient's distress. If Kraepelin appears mainly concerned with establishing the *form* of the disorder, Laing embarks upon an interpretative analysis of its *content*:

'What does the patient seem to be doing? Surely he is carrying on a dialogue between his own parodied version of Kraepelin, and his own defiant, rebelling self. "You want to know that too? I tell you who is being measured and is measured and shall be measured. I know all that and I could tell you, but I do not want to." This seems to be plain enough talk. Presumably he deeply resents this form of interrogation which is being carried out before a lecture-room of students. He probably does not see what it has to do with the things that must be deeply distressing him.'

(Laing 1965: 29–30)

Now the difference between describing the *form* of a person's mental state and interpreting its *content*, the difference in the examples quoted between Kraepelin and Laing, is, in practice, the difference between the first and second stages of the average diagnostic assessment of a psychiatrically ill patient. It is the *form* taken by the illness which greatly determines the diagnostic category selected. In the case described above, it is not because the patient resents and does not understand what is happening (Laing's suggested 'explanation' for his behaviour) that he is diagnosed a schizophrenic. It is because he exhibits certain psychological and behavioural phenomena, which are thought to be of particular significance in terms of possible causes, course, response to treatment, and probable outcome, that his condition is so classified. Whether such a classificatory system has any point and purpose to it (with regard to the condition known as schizophrenia) is considered in the next chapter.

Currently, descriptive psychopathology and classification are under considerable attack. Psychiatric classification is seen as an utterly unproductive form of occupational therapy for those psychiatrists who have little inclination to delve into the deeper recesses of their patients' minds, less stomach for what they might find there, little aptitude for intuitive understanding, and no ability to empathize with or imagine themselves into their patients' predicaments. A preoccupation with description and classification is itself portrayed as a symptom, an abnormal psychological phenomenon whereby psychiatrists defend themselves against their own inadequacy and fear by emphasizing the 'objectivity' inherent in their arid statistical and classificatory approaches and by hiding behind a smokescreen of measurements and 'scientific' jargon.

However, while there is a new urgency in the feud between what Jaspers called the 'describers' and the 'analysers' (Jaspers 1959), the feud itself is rooted in the historical development of psychiatry. The describer tries to outline an objective, concrete, yet living picture using ordinary language and little conceptual elaboration. In so far as there is a conceptual basis, it is one that is difficult to take further in any systematic way. The analyser, on the other hand, is not interested in drawing a classical picture but prefers to explore the presenting one to gain some understanding of this individual case. This is yet another dichotomy best avoided in clinical practice. Yet it is difficult to be both a detached, relatively uninvolved observer, describing in a dispassionate fashion what the patient says and does, demonstrating any dissonance between thought and emotion, noting any disjunction with objective reality, and at the same time an empathic, insightful analyst, imagining oneself into the other's predicament, seeking the missing connection, making sense of incoherent and fragmented communications. Inevitably, some psychiatrists opt to do one or the other and having opted for one they devalue the other. The descriptive psychopathologist may deride the analyst's interpretations as 'speculative' and 'fanciful' whereas the analyst often scoffs at the describer for mistaking description for understanding and shape for substance.

The distinction between the *form* and the *content* of psychiatric illnesses is an important one. Perceptions, ideas, judgements, feelings, drives, self-awareness, are all forms of psychic phenomena and they denote the particular mode of existence in which content is presented. For the phenomenological investigator, the form of the phenomenon is all-important. For patients, however, the form seems largely irrelevant; whether they are hallucinated, pseudo-hallucinated, deluded, or perplexed seems of much less importance than the often disturbing content of such phenomena. Content, however, modifies the manner in which psychic phenomena are experienced and points to the way in which they are conceived and interpreted.

In order to clarify this distinction further and to provide an understanding of how the distinction is in practice implemented, it is necessary to examine in a little detail the manner in which abnormal psychic phenomena are described and organized. The late Professor Frank Fish, in a popular short text on psychopathology, grouped the signs and symptoms of psychiatric abnormality under a number of headings – i.e., disorders of perception, disorders of thought and speech, disorders of memory, disorders of emotion, disorders of the experience of the self, disorders of consciousness and motor disorders. A more detailed look at a number of these groupings will be taken to underline the way in which the descriptive psychopathological approach is applied in clinical practice.

1 Disorders of perception

These can be divided into *sensory distortions* and *sensory deceptions*. In the former, there is a real and constant perceptual object which, however, is perceived by the subject in a distorted fashion; e.g., sounds may be heard louder or softer, colours may be perceived as brighter or duller, smells may be more pungent or less sharp. Some particular forms of sensory distortion can occur as a consequence of retinal disease, disorders affecting the eye muscles and lesions in the temporal lobes of the brain. Objects may be perceived as smaller than they really are (micropsia), larger than they are (macropsia) or otherwise altered in shape. Sensory distortion can occur in a variety of conditions including psychoses, delirious states, and certain drug intoxications (e.g., LSD).

In a *sensory deception*, a perception occurs which may or may not be a response to an external stimulus. Jaspers (1959) distinguishes three types of *illusions* – illusions due to inattentiveness (e.g., overlooking a misprint in an article yet noting the illusion of correctness the moment attention is drawn to it), illusions due to emotion (e.g., mistaking shadows for potential assailants when out alone in a strange place at night), and illusions due to pareidolia (that ability of the imagination to create illusionary forms from poorly defined impressions such as clouds, shadows, etc.). Illusions are differentiated from *misinterpretations* whereby erroneous deductions are drawn from correct preceptions (e.g., mistaking brass for gold, a doctor for a priest) (Fish 1962).

Hallucinations, on the other hand, can be defined as perceptions without an external object. They are false perceptions which are not in any way distortions of real perceptions. They are not necessarily pathological. For example, if one looks fixedly at a bright object for a moment and then looks away, an after-image in the central field of vision will persist for some time despite the fact that there is no matching external object in the person's visual field. Other forms of 'normal' hallucinations include those which occur during the transitional states between waking and sleeping (hypnagogic hallucinations) and between sleeping and waking (hypnapompic hallucinations). Voices may be heard; the subject may hear his name called. Other more organized false perceptions may occur. Such 'normal' hallucinations are usually recognized for what they are, namely purely subjective experiences, both at the time they occur and retrospectively. This applies also to many 'pathological' hallucinations such as those occurring in certain toxic states (e.g., LSD psychosis, alcoholic delirium tremens). In contrast, those hallucinations that occur in the so-called 'functional' psychoses (schizophrenia and manic-depressive psychosis) are fortified by a delusional conviction of their objective reality. In these conditions patients do not lose the conviction that there are objective percepts that correspond to their subjective perceptions even when it is made clear to them that their perceptions are not shared by others. When the illness in question has remitted, the subject may realize that he had been hallucinated, although this does not invariably occur. Hallucinations can be the result of intense emotional arousal, suggestion, disorders of the nervous system, sensory deprivation, and of other disorders of the central nervous system. They can and do occur in any of the sensory systems. *Auditory hallucinations* can be elementary (e.g., noise), partly organized (e.g., snatches of ill-defined music), or completely organized (e.g., hallucinatory voices). They can occur in organic states, in severe depressive illnesses, and in schizophrenia. Hallucinatory voices may comment on the subject's activities and thoughts, may give orders, utter irrelevant comments, may be abusive, sexually offensive, threatening, or incomprehensible. Occasionally, the voices may be friendly and may not upset the subject in any way. There may only be a single voice which addresses the subject or several voices which address the patient direct or talk to each other about the subject. The effect of auditory hallucinations can be variable; the subject can be totally unconcerned or very frightened. He may follow hallucinatory commands which order him to kill himself and/or somebody else or he may be forced to stop whatever he may be doing through the direction of the hallucinations or as a result of his being distracted by them. One type of auditory hallucination, regarded as diagnostic of a schizophrenic illness, is hearing one's own thoughts being spoken aloud (*echo de pensées*; *Gedankenlautwerden*).

Mellor (1970), in an analysis of various symptoms believed by many psychiatrists to be diagnostic of schizophrenia, provides the following example of audible thoughts:

'A 35-year old painter heard a quiet voice with "an Oxford accent" which he attributed to the BBC. The volume was slightly lower than that of normal conversation and could be heard equally well with either ear. He could locate its source at the right mastoid process. The voice would say "I can't stand that man, the way he holds his brush he looks like a poof"! He immediately experienced whatever the voice was saying as his own thoughts, to the exclusion of all other thoughts. When he read the newspaper the voice would speak aloud whatever his eyes fell on. He had not time to think of what he was reading before it uttered aloud.'

(Mellor 1970: 16)

Patients may explain the origin of their hallucinations by attributing them to witchcraft, atomic rays, radio, television, or to some other form of communication. Some patients may deny hallucinations and may insist that people are talking about them. Careful analysis may subsequently reveal that such people are in fact auditorily hallucinated but are attributing what they hear to people in their immediate vicinity. Such patients may attack other patients, nurses, or doctors because of the obscene or abusive things they are alleged to be saying.

> 'A good example of this was a Greek patient who spoke little English and had been a patient in an English Mental Hospital for years. She always denied hearing phonemes (hallucinatory voices) and from time to time she made assaults on her fellow patients which appeared to be un-motivated. One day she was asked if she would like some Greek newspapers or visits from someone who spoke Greek. She said that this was not necessary because every-one in the hospital spoke pure Greek. It then became obvious that she heard continuous phonemes in Greek which she attributed to real people in her environment and that she attacked other patients who appeared to be saying abusive things about her.' (Fish 1967: 24–5)

Visual hallucinations are less common than auditory hallucin-ations in the so-called functional psychoses of schizophrenia and manic depression but are quite common in acute organic states. Again, such hallucinations may be elementary (e.g., flashes of light), partially organized (e.g., patterns of light and shade), or completely organized (e.g., visions of people, animals, or scenes). A wide variety of visual hallucinations may be found in organic states, but small animals and insects, such as rats, mice, spiders, beetles, are commonly seen in delirium states. So-called 'formication hallucinations' have been described in psychoses secondary to amphetamine intoxication whereby the subject perceives snakes or bugs crawling on or under the skin. Such hallucinations are often associated with fear and in some cases with extreme terror. Visual hallucinations may be accompanied by auditory ones, such a combination being frequently seen in epilepsy affecting the temporal lobe area of the brain. In acute organic states, visual hallucinations occur in the setting of a disturbance of consciousness; the subject is usually confused and disorientated and it is this feature that helps to differentiate the organic delirious state with visual and, less commonly, auditory hallucinations from schizophrenia or manic-depressive psychosis.

Hallucinations of *smell* may occur in a variety of conditions. For example, some people who become severely depressed insist that they emit an odour. It can at times be difficult to know whether they themselves smell the odour (i.e., are hallucinated) or whether they base their belief on the fact that other people in their immediate vicinity behave as if they were emitting a smell. Attacks of temporal lobe epilepsy can be ushered in by unpleasant odours being perceived by the subject, such as paint or burning rubber. In some patients suffering from temporal lobe epilepsy, there may not be any true fits but intermittent activity in the abnormal brain focus may result in the patient perceiving strange smells. Fish (1967: 26) describes how a patient with an active temporal lobe focus suffered no fits but from time to time complained of the smell of stale cabbage water in the house and would turn it upside down to find the offending object.

People who suffer from *gustatory hallucinations* may complain that their food tastes peculiar. *Tactile hallucinations* may cause patients to complain of being touched, especially in the anal or genital regions, of feeling insects crawling over them, of experiencing blasts of hot and cold air, currents of electricity, waves, or rays directed at their bodies.

Hallucinations can occur in a variety of brain diseases (e.g., tumours, epileptic foci), toxic states (e.g., alcohol, amphetamines, LSD, cocaine, infectious diseases), head injury, and psychiatric disorders. When presented with a patient who complains of hearing voices (as were the psychiatrists in the Rosenhan study quoted at the beginning of this chapter), the diagnostician should seek to delineate the type of hallucinatory experience, its content and the presence or absence of associated features such as confusion, evidence of drug intoxication, other symptoms suggestive of psychiatric disorder (changes in mood, delusional beliefs, extreme anxiety, etc.), or evidence of brain disease.

2 Disorders of thought and speech

Any classification of such disorders is bound to be somewhat arbitrary. It is customary nonetheless to divide them into disorders of the stream of thought, the content of thought, and the form of thought.

(a) *Disorders of the stream of thought*

In some psychiatric disorders thoughts follow each other rapidly and there is no general direction of thinking. The connection between successive thoughts appears to be due to chance factors which, however, can usually be understood. The person's speech appears easily diverted by external stimuli and by internal superficial associations. Fish (1967: 36) notes that the chance linkage of thoughts in this *flight of ideas* is such that one can often completely reverse the sequence of the record of a flight of ideas and the progression of thought can be understood just as well. Jaspers provides an example in the case of a patient who asked by her doctor whether she had changed at all in the previous year replied:

> ' "Yes, I was dumb and numb then but not deaf, I know Mrs Ida Teff, she is dead, probably an appendicitis; I don't know whether she lost her sight, sightless Hesse, His Highness of Hesse, sister Louise, His Highness of Baden, buried and dead on September, the twenty-eighth, 1907, when I get back, red-gold-red . . ." '

> (Jaspers 1959: 209)

The trend of thought here is haphazardly interrupted; one topic is taken up, quickly displaced by another, and it, in turn, by another. In a classical flight of ideas, the point is continually lost amidst a web of jumbled thoughts associated together by similarly sounding words ('clang' associations), alliteration, proverbs, and clichés. There is often a massive flow of content into consciousness and the stream of thought is overwhelmed by ideas, images, distractions which prevent the formation of a coherent and comprehensible flow. It is typically seen in manic illnesses. In the less severe form of mania, so-called hypomania, a more ordered flight of ideas occurs in which, despite many irrelevances, distractions, and tangential journeys, the patient is able to return again and again to the central theme of his communication.

Retardation of thought and speech, the opposite of flight of ideas, may occur in a variety of psychiatric states. The train of thought is slowed down and there is a poverty of ideas and mental imagery. Such retardation is usually accompanied by a loss of concentration. Retardation of thought may be seen in severe depression. The patient may be mute or even stuporous. Other disorders affecting the stream of thought include circumstantiality, in which thinking proceeds slowly and is characterized by many trivial unnecessary details before the central point is reached, and *perseveration*, a common symptom in certain generalized and localized brain disorders, whereby the patient 'perseveres' with a particular response long after a change in his immediate environment has demanded a different reaction. Perseveration can often be quite obvious on clinical examination because the patient, after answering one question, goes on repeating this reply to different questions. It can be regarded as symptomatic of an inability to think clearly, which leads the patient to grope about for successive ideas; while he is doing this, the gap, which otherwise would occur, is covered up by the perseveration.

In the phenomenon known as *thought blocking* there is a sudden arrest of the train of thought and the commencement of an entirely new one. The sequence of ideas is suddenly interrupted and leaves a mental void. When clearly present this symptom is believed by some to be diagnostic of schizophrenia. Some exhausted and anxious people can, however, easily lose the thread of their conversations and may appear to block. Similarly, attacks of petit mal (a form of epilepsy in which consciousness is lost for a matter of seconds and the patient goes 'blank') may produce a picture in which the patient's thoughts appear to block. Whereas such thought block usually causes considerable embarrassment to the average person a schizophrenic patient whose thoughts block may stop, in the middle of a sentence, in a bland and un-embarrassed fashion. In early cases, the combination of retardation and thought blocking results in a 'woolly' vagueness. The patient's thought stream appears to be directed by alliterations, analogies, symbolic meanings, and condensation into one of several, perhaps contradictory, ideas.

'A young patient said "I feel that everything is sort of related to everybody and that some people are far more susceptible to this theory of relativity than others be-cause of either having previous ancestors connected in some way or other with places or things, or because of believing, or of leaving a trail behind might leave a dif-ferent trail and all sorts of things go like that".'

(Mayer-Gross, Slater, and Roth 1969: 267)

Apparently, the patient claimed that the above statement was a clear one and became quite angry when asked if he could explain it further. The authors point out that the gaps, the poverty, the indefiniteness, and the vagueness of thought block is difficult to capture in such examples. None-theless what is clear in the one above is that the patient's central theme has been almost lost amidst a woolliness of associations and symbolic meanings.

(b) *Disorders of the possession of thought*

The normal person experiences his thinking as his own. He also believes himself to be in control of his thought processes. In some psychopathological states, however, there is a loss of control or sense of possession of thinking.

In *obsessive-compulsive disorders*, the essential feature of the obsession (or compulsion) is that it appears against the patient's will. Schneider defined a compulsion thus:

'Compulsion may be said to occur when an individual is haunted by conscious contents although at the same time he judges them as senseless or at any rate senselessly insistent.' (Schneider 1958: 104)

Compulsions are obsessional motor acts. Lady Macbeth's obsessional fear of contamination underlay her compulsive hand washing. Obsessional ideas may take the form of rumination over a whole range of subjects. The obsessional may, for example, be terrified by the fear that he will shout obscenities in church, take his clothes off in public, injure himself or others, make indecent suggestions to strangers, or throw himself off high buildings or in front of moving vehicles. Taylor (1966) points out that those external objects and situations that provide such worrying thoughts in an obsessive-compulsive patient become *phobic objects* for him; i.e., their presence produces attacks of phobic anxiety in him and causes him to avoid them at almost any cost. Taylor illustrates very neatly the distinction and the similarities between the phobically anxious patient and the obsessive-compulsive patient who has become phobic to the situation that evokes his obsessional ruminations.

'An anxiety neurotic patient with a phobia about pins is forced by his fears to keep away from any pin he happens to notice but an obsessive-compulsive patient has to go to greater pains because after accidentally seeing a pin he is beset by the fear of somehow having used it to injure others. An anxiety neurotic patient with a phobia of dirt takes good care to keep away from anything dirty and if he has been in touch with a dirty object is driven by his panic to cleanse himself immediately and thoroughly. An obsessive-compulsive person with a similar phobia has to keep away even from objects that look scrupulously clean because the mere thought that they are dirty may magically make them dirty and also contaminate him even if he cannot remember having touched them. His magic fears also make his cleansing procedures more prolonged and vigorous.'

(Taylor 1966: 168)

Such obsessive-compulsive phenomena may occur in obsessional states, in depressive and schizophrenic illnesses, and occasionally in certain organic states, particularly post-encephalitic ones.

The obsessed patient recognizes that he is compelled to think about certain things despite his every effort to rid his mind of them, but he does not regard such thoughts as being alien. In *thought alienation*, on the other hand, the patient experiences his thoughts as being under the control of some outside agency. He may believe that others are participating in his thinking, that thoughts are being inserted into his mind from outside (thought insertion), or he may find that as he is thinking his thoughts suddenly vanish and he may attribute this to the belief that they are being taken out of his mind (thought withdrawal) by some foreign influence. *Thought broadcasting* is the phenomenon whereby the patient knows that as he is thinking so everyone else is thinking his thoughts in unison with him and is aware of his most intimate contemplations. Schneider (1958) argues that these various experiences of thought alienation, in which the boundary between the patient's ego and the surrounding world has dissolved, are diagnostic of schizophrenia when they occur in a non-toxic state and in clear consciousness.

3 Disorders of the content of thinking

In so far as there is a single mark of madness popularly conceived, such a mark is surely the *delusion*. The widely accepted definition of a delusion is that it is a *false belief*. However, one immediate difficulty with such a concept of delusion is that, like madness, it has a common parlance. Any idea held by others with which we disagree tends to be dismissed as 'delusional'. Enthusiastic supports of somewhat grandiose national enterprises, such as Concorde and the Channel Tunnel, research workers who claim that the American negro performs poorly on a certain IQ tests, terrorists who throw grenades into parked planes and bombs into public houses, can all be labelled 'delusional' by those who disagree with them (and often are).

There are, however, several characteristics in addition to the falsity of a belief, the presence of which determines the delusional status of the belief in question. A delusion is not simply a false belief but is rather an absolute and incontrovertible *conviction* about the truth of a proposition. Belief is too mild a word these days, used as it is to cover everything from a mercurial devotion to a local football team to a mildly expressed acknowledgement of the possibility of the existence of eternal life. A conviction is something more intense again. The deluded person does not merely believe with the mildness of the average Christian apologist on a Sunday religious chat show or indeed with the public sincerity of the party politician; he believes with an unshakable conviction that, for example, he is being spied upon, his food is being poisoned, his water contaminated, his skin damaged by powerful x-ray machines located in the local post office, his brain read by the News at Ten announcer. He does not profess to believe this to be the truth; he is absolutely convinced that it is so. Such persecutory delusions may appear absurd and irrational to the non-deluded. They appear likewise to others who may possess the same or different delusions, a fact which lies at the heart of the traditional joke of the two deluded Napoleons meeting and each deriding the other's belief as mad.

The criterion of *irrationality* must be used with caution. Today's delusion might after all be tomorrow's scientific breakthrough. As Taylor (1966) emphasizes, irrationality means little more than our inability to see how certain propositions can be correct. Such an inability may be due merely to the fact that such propositions are derived from convictions that are culturally conditioned and happen to differ from our own. Before deciding that a conviction is delusional, i.e., false and irrational, one has to decide whether such a conviction is shared by people of the same religious, social, educational, ethnic, or cultural background. For example, if the English-born husband of a woman in labour insists that she must be excluded from her immediate family and social environment, that she must deliver her child attended only by her mother and that after delivery an animal must be laid upon her abdomen, that for a full month afterwards she must live apart lest her uncleanliness pollutes and poisons those coming into contact with her, and that she must not for the same reason handle food, but must be fed on the end of a long pole, then such a man will be regarded as deluded, given the contemporary cultural values of British society. However, should such views be held by a Bribri Indian, we would have to refrain from classifying them as delusional in the absence of further information, for such beliefs are part of the common culture and mythology of this tribe and are held not individually or idiosyncratically but collectively.

A further qualifying characteristic of psychotic delusions is that they are *ego-involved*, that is to say, they are infused with a sense of immense personal significance, and refer to realities in which the patient's ego is centrally concerned. The combination of idiosyncrasy and *ego*-involvement is necessary for any conviction to be deemed delusional, but even this is not sufficient. All of us hold intense, usually private, views of ourselves, our potential, our deficiencies, and attributes, which if shared, as might occur during a therapeutic or encounter group, might be viewed as absurd, irrational, idiosyncratic, and ego-involved. Indeed Taylor (1961) has attempted to measure the extent to which a patient's ego-involved estimate of his own social popularity idiosyncratically deviates from the reality of his status as evaluated by other group members. Exposed to a different view of what constitutes a realistic assessment of ourselves, we may be jolted into a reappraisal or cling tenaciously to our original ideas. In non-psychiatrically ill people, convictions that are central and held with intense faith can be modified by contradictory evidence or indeed turned on their head by techniques of persuasion commonly referred to as 'brain-washing'. However, there appears to be no form of persuasion so effective, no method of reasoning so persuasive, that it can convince psychotic patients of the absurdity of their beliefs; no indoctrination, however brutal, ruthless, or destructive, can manipulate a psychotic person into acknowledging that his beliefs *might* be in error. Psychotic persons chose to burn at the Inquisitorial stake rather than renounce delusional convictions. Mentally ill patients, over the past two centuries, have been exposed to the most extraordinary physical and mental humiliations, to bleedings, purgings, beatings, freezings, boilings, neglect, torture, and death itself, yet their stubborn adherence to the content of their clearly delusional beliefs was not affected.

One other characteristic of a delusion, often though not always present, is that it *preoccupies*. During an acute psychotic episode, the patient is characteristically preoccupied with his delusions to the exclusion of all else. During more chronic phases of many psychotic illnesses, patients are able to concentrate on other activities although their delusions continue to smoulder at the back of their minds and retain the force of absolute conviction. Anderson (1971) describes a patient of his, a young doctor, who was somewhat addicted to benzedrine and alcohol and who continued his medical practice for some months during which time he believed that his car was followed by the police, carried on conversations with hallucinatory friends on his bedside radio, believed his room was wired and his thoughts read. He, nonetheless, presented no obvious outward anomaly yet on careful examination was found to be grossly disorientated and ultimately had to be admitted to hospital.

In summary, a delusion is not merely a false belief of morbid origin but is (a) an absolute conviction, (b) idiosyncratic, i.e., not culturally shared, (c) incorrigible, i.e., unamenable to reason, persuasion, contradiction, or even the possiblity of being in error, (d) often preoccupying, and (e) usually absurd or impossible.

Delusions are usually divided on phenomenological grounds into primary and secondary delusions.

(a) *Primary delusions*

Primary delusions, also known as autochthonous, delusions, delusions proper or true delusions, are generally held in the absence of coarse brain disease to be diagnostic of schizophrenia, at least as that condition is diagnosed in Britain. The essence of the primary delusional experience is that a new meaning arises in connection with some other psychological event. There is no disturbance in sensory perception in that the patient does not feel that there is any alteration in the colour, shape, size, texture, etc., of external objects. Nor is there a disturbance in apperception in that the patient is aware of what it is he perceives. Finally, it is not a disturbance of intelligence. The patient does not arrive at his delusional belief because he is stupid or ignorant of what is involved. The disturbance at the core of the primary delusion is one of symbolic meaning. The experience is immediate and appears out of the blue without warning or explanation. It may puzzle the subject yet it carries with it its own sense of conviction. Fish (1967:40) has likened such experiences to the 'brain waves' of normal individuals whereby an idea suddenly presents itself in consciousness.

'A young Irishman was at breakfast with two fellow-lodgers. He felt a sense of unease, that something frightening was going to happen. One of the lodgers pushed the salt cellar towards him (he appreciated at the time that this was an ordinary salt cellar and his friend's intention was innocent). Almost before the salt cellar reached him he knew that he must return home "to greet the Pope, who is visiting Ireland to see his family and to reward them . . . because our Lord is going to be born again to one of the women . . . And because of this they [all the women] are all born different with their private parts back to front".'

(Fish 1967 : 18)

A primary delusion may be preceded by what has been termed a delusional mood (*Wahnstimmung*). In such a mood, the patient vaguely and apprehensively feels that something unpleasant is about to happen or is happening around him, but he has no idea what it is until the delusion crystallizes out of the blue. In the example given above, the Irishman felt 'a sense of unease' just before the perception. After recovering from a psychotic episode, a young girl wrote the following description of the beginning of her illness:

' "We got off the bus and entered the cinema. I don't quite know how to say this but it seemed like a place for prostitutes. Inside were people and as they went through the doors I know they were there to judge me and would give their verdict. At first I enjoyed the film then it became disjointed and I realised that the actors were not who they were supposed to be and that it was all there to fool me in some way. We went into the car afterwards and a switch like an electric switch seemed to be moved across my mind and suddenly I was laughing and everything was fine, then I heard someone say 'She knows' and I suddenly thought 'Perhaps I'll only get a light sentence'. Once more it was like being judged. Then my cousin said, 'Oh, you've woken up, have you?' with a double meaning it seemed, as if I had suddenly woken up to the meaning of life." '

(Mayer-Gross, Slater, and Roth 1969 : 272)

Jaspers (1959) provides the example of a woman who on seeing a stranger in the street *knew* instantly that he was a former lover who had disguised himself, while Fish (1967: 41) describes how an Englishman, on being given a biscuit by his

American brother-in-law in a New York town, immediately *realized* that his brother-in-law was accusing him of being a homosexual and was organizing a gang to spy on him.

(b) *Secondary delusions*

Secondary delusions, which occur in many forms of serious mental disorders, can be understood as arising from some other morbid experience and in this way they differ from primary delusions. For example, a person who believes that he is being spied upon may interpret a creak on the stairs as the sounds of a detective coming to arrest him. (The perception in this example is more accurately termed a *delusional misinterpretation*.) Again, a severely depressed man may explain his guilt feelings and feelings of self-reproach by deciding that he must have committed a crime for which he is being hunted by the police. He may begin to believe that people are watching him, spying on him, or about to arrest him. A person walking across the street may be perceived as a plain-clothes policeman. Such a perception is a secondary delusion in that it arises out of the primary disturbance in the patient's mood state. As a mood disorder, such as a depression or an elation, can give rise to delusional perceptions so a primary delusional perception can lead to a change in mood state; e.g., in the example given earlier, the Englishman may well have complained of feeling seriously depressed because his brother-in-law believed him to be homosexual. For this reason, in cases where a mood disturbance and delusions coexist, it is necessary to distinguish if possible the temporal relationship between them, i.e., which came first.

Delusions are commonly categorized according to the predominant theme contained within them. Thus there are delusions of persecution, jealousy, love, grandiosity, physical illness, guilt, nihilism, hypochondriasis, etc.

(c) *Disorders of the form of thinking*

In a proportion of psychiatrically ill patients, disorders of conceptual or abstract thinking (formal thought disorder) are seen. Such disorders can be seen in organic brain disease and in schizophrenic illnesses. Cameron (1944) in an analysis of the different types of thought disorganization, grouped the symptoms into four main categories. In the first category, the thought disorder is characterized by a lack of causal links between successive thoughts or statements; there is a snapping off or unintentional breaking of the chain of thought, sometimes termed '*asyndetic thinking*'. In the second category, there is a use of related but imprecise approximations ('metonyms') whereby some substitute word or phrase is used instead of a more usual or expected one. Cameron points out that the patient may develop his own mode of speech full of personal idioms. In a third type of thought disorder, the patient shows an inability to maintain the boundaries of a concept and to restrict conceptual operations within a manageable framework. The patient shows a remarkable ability to generalize ('overinclusion') so that peripheral and vaguely related material is incorporated in to a concept to such an extent that the central idea in the communication in question is often buried completely. Finally, there is the phenomenon known as 'interpenetration of themes'. The speech may show elements related to the task in hand intermingled with heterogeneous elements derived from his fantasy life, from external happenings, related or remote preoccupations, and total unrelated factors. The patient appears to be unable to differentiate clearly between the streams which appear fused together.

An example of such thought disorder has been provided earlier (of 'thought blocking'). Bannister (1960) suggested that the clinical features of thought disorder might result from a loosening of a person's construct system. He employed a Reportory Grid technique based on Kelly's Personal Construct Theory, which asserts that an individual, on the basis of his personal experience, develops a personal repertoire of concepts and of relationships between such concepts. By means of these he is able to comprehend his environment and interrelate with it in a meaningful and consistent fashion. Thus if our construct of honest–dishonest is interlinked with other constructs such as punctual–unpunctual, trustworthy–untrustworthy, affectionate–cold, we will assume certain expectations of a person construed by us as honest. Bannister and Fransella (1966) published the details of a test whereby a subject is shown eight photographs of persons unknown to him and is asked to rate them according to how *kind* each person seems. This having been done, he is then asked to rank the photographs using the following constructs in turn: *stupid, selfish, sincere, mean,* and *honest.* Normal subjects show high correlations (either positive or negative) between the rank orders, i.e., a person who ranks a particular photograph as regards *kind* may give similar rankings in respect of *sincere* and *honest* and reverse ones for *stupid* and *selfish.* The higher these correlations, the greater the *intensity* of the interrelationships between the constructs. Thought-disordered schizophrenics have been shown to produce low *intensity* scores and when asked to repeat the test over again show low *consistency* scores as well (this latter score is obtained by comparing the rank-order correlations between results of tests performed on two occasions). Bannister (1965) has suggested that schizophrenics may show thought disorder as a result of being repeatedly invalidated in the construction of their personal construct system. Repeatedly exposed to a situation in which constructs such as sincere, honest, kind, selfish, stupid, unkind, etc., have no meaningful and consistent relationship (a situation such as might exist in certain emotionally chaotic and unstable families), a person may find himself unable to construct a personal system of coherence and order. To date evidence in support of such a theory is conflicting but more sophisticated studies are under way.

The phenomenological characteristics of hallucinatory and delusional experiences and disorders of thought have been briefly discussed. The manner in which these abnormal psychic phenomena are characteristically defined and described reflects the descriptive psychopathological approach in action. Such signs and symptoms are amongst those which, grouped in certain clusters or syndromes, constitute some of the main psychiatric disorders. The manner whereby one such disorder, schizophrenia, is categorized and defined will be discussed further in the next chapter. But for the moment, it might be appropriate to return to the Laing–Kraepelin discussion referred to earlier.

As we have seen, using the descriptive approach, signs and symptoms are painstakingly defined and described. The *form* of the phenomena is carefully delineated, without too much regard to their symbolic meaning or the 'understandability' of their *content*. Yet straight away there are difficulties. If the 'psychotic' quality of certain symptoms, e.g., thought disorder, depends on the 'understandability' (or lack of it) of the content of the symptom in question, then such an essentially descriptive approach, in neglecting the content, misses the point. Laing, in the example quoted earlier, claimed to provide an intelligent 'explanation' of what Kraepelin's patient was saying. 'You don't whore for me' – to Laing, this means that the patient believes Kraepelin is objecting because he, the patient, is not prepared to prostitute himself before the whole class of students; 'What is your name? What does he shut? He shuts his eyes...' – here, in Laing's view, the patient is expressing his resentment of Kraepelin's detached, impersonal, questioning approach to him. The patient is understandable but only if the observer ceases to see his behaviour as 'signs of a disease' and instead sees it as expressive of his existence.

Now Laing's criticism nourishes at its heart one of the major doubts about the whole diagnostic approach in orthodox clinical psychiatry. What is the point of a psychiatry that is less interested in making sense of irrationality than with obsessionally recording every minor manifestation with the dedicated application of a stamp collector? The very approach that the descriptive psychopathological style demands, which is that of a cool, detached, recorder of events, and discoverer of facts, results, it is alleged, in the psychiatrist placing himself alongside all those others who have treated the patient as an object, reduced his innermost experiences to the level of discrete, atomistic factors, and walled him off from genuine human relationships.

It is a valid criticism. If the collection of the primary data becomes the *raison d'être* of the psychiatrist's task and the interpretation of such data is dismissed as a derided and despised 'speculative' activity, the role of a psychiatrist is reduced to that of a categorizer, a labeller of unusual and deviant behaviour. Yet without the data, interpretation does indeed become speculative. Without a clear statement of the *form* of the behaviour, the comprehension of its meaning becomes an arbitrary work of imaginative fancy (an approach much loved by some psychotherapists who, given a couple of facts from a patient's history, will construct a fascinating interpretation of his psychopathology which, whatever subsequent facts emerge, will 'fit' the bill – if not, the bill will be fitted to the facts). Psychohistorians are particularly prone to construct such interpretative schemata. Darwin's disabling illness, for example, is diagnosed confidently by one analyst, on the basis of a 'wealth of evidence', as a crippling neurotic disorder resulting from 'the distorted expression of the aggression, hate and resentment felt, at the unconscious level, by Darwin towards his tyrannical father' (Good 1954). In this example, however, the interpretation loses a considerable amount of its magnetism, colour, and truth when a genuine attempt is made to *describe* the psychopathology, i.e., that 'wealth of evidence' which supposedly points so certainly towards such a diagnosis but which does no such thing. It must not be thought that only analysts are guilty of twisting the data to suit their theories; the highly publicized 'explanation' of George III's madness as being due to porphyria in the face of contradictory evidence (Macalpine and Hunter 1969) is another example of the same tendency.

Yet such historial diagnoses, whilst diverting and stimulating in their own way, are hardly of crucial importance. For a more worrying example of theorizing in the absence of appropriate data, one returns to Rosenhan's study (1973). According to this account, Rosenhan and his seven colleagues do not appear to have been psychiatrically assessed in any detail. In so far as their doctors attempted to elicit and describe the presenting psychopathological phenomena, this appears to have taken as long or as short as it takes to write down the words 'thud', 'empty', and 'hollow'! The auditory hallucinations of which they actually complained, even had they existed and not been the fabrication of the researchers, fail to constitute a symptom of schizophrenia. There is more to a hallucination than the hearing of a voice and more to the diagnosis of schizophrenia than experiencing hallucinations. Rosenhan's group appear unaware that the symptom they mimicked amounts to very little diagnostically. However, as Wing (1973) points out acidly, what is more worrying (and more important) is that the psychiatrists involved in assessing them appeared to be every bit as ill-informed!

The Rosenhan study raises some additional questions. The author points out that any diagnostic exercise which lends itself to such a massive error (diagnosing the sane as ill and the ill as sane) cannot be a very reliable one. Unfortunately, amidst a considerable amount of detail about how they were treated in hospital, what the other patients thought of them and how they felt, we are given remarkably little data on how the 'diagnostic exercise' was in fact carried out! If the message of the Rosenhan study is to the effect that doctors should not assign patients to diagnostic categories unless they know how to make a diagnosis – i.e., collect, organize, and categorize basic data – one can only nod one's head vigorously and agree. But Rosenhan and those many critics of psychiatry who have greeted his paper with enthusiasm seem in fact to be saying that, since the doctors did not appear to have the faintest idea as to what constitutes the operational concept 'schizophrenia' and yet applied it with haste to people showing virtually no signs nor symptoms whatsoever, the whole diagnostic approach should be scrapped! Well, one way of avoiding the diagnosis of diabetes mellitus is to ensure that as many doctors as possible do not learn the most elementary facts about blood sugar levels, the symptoms of hyperglycaemia, and the role of insulin, yet it is not immediately clear as to how such a revolutionary approach significantly alters the fact that the signs and symptoms of what is known as diabetes mellitus exist, independently of whether they are correctly elicited or not.

Rosenhan observes that once a patient is labelled 'schizophrenic' much of his so-called 'normal behaviour' is entirely overlooked or profoundly misinterpreted. As an example, he quotes a case summary prepared after one of his own researchers was discharged from hospital in 'remission'.

'This white 39-year old male . . . manifests a long history of considerable ambivalence in close relationships which begins in early childhood. A warm relationship with his mother cools during his adolescence. A distant relationship to his father is described as becoming very intense. Affective stability is absent. His attempts to control emotionality, with his wife and children, are punctuated by angry outbursts and, in the case of the children, spankings. And while he says that he has several good friends, one senses considerable ambivalence embedded in those relationships also . . .'   (Rosenhan 1973 : 253)

Rosenhan comments that 'the facts of the case were unintentionally distorted by the staff to achieve consistency with a popular theory of the dynamics of a schizophrenic reaction'. The similarities with Good's analysis of Charles Darwin are remarkable. Despite the fact that Darwin regarded his father with obvious reverence and described him as the kindest man he ever knew, he is declared guilty of an 'unconscious parricide' and, as in the case of Oedipus, his punishment is severe (he is sentenced to almost forty years of severe and crippling neurotic suffering) (Goode 1954). His father is described as 'tyrannical' on the somewhat slight basis of his disapproval of some of the young Darwin's friends and his reservations about Charles' desire to join the Beagle.

In both these examples, those of Rosenhan and Good, one is struck by the paucity of data coupled with the imaginative richness of the theoretically based interpretations. Rosenhan clearly believes that his study establishes the pointlessness of making a psychiatric diagnosis and underlines the utter arbitrariness of such procedures. In fact, the very deviation from the norm of diagnostic practice which he describes presupposes the existence of a norm. For diagnostic incompetence is opprobrious only if judged in terms of the standard of diagnostic accuracy; within another institutional context, such incompetence is defined as a positive virtue, being a firm rejection of a pedantic, semantic, obsessive pursuit of phenomenological minutiae (Fish 1967). In the process of condemning the doctors' violation of diagnostic mores, the mores are themselves affirmed.

An observation regularly made in clinical practice suggests that those psychiatrists most scrupulous about making a diagnosis rarely commit themselves unequivocally to one. Again, one finds a perfect example in another, this time phenomenological, analysis of a historical figure's psychopathological status. Johan August Strindberg suffered five episodes of severe mental illness after the age of forty-five. A variety of psychiatrists, including Jaspers, have speculated on the nature of the illness and the majority have diagnosed schizophrenia. Professor E. W. Anderson (1971), a phenomenologically inclined British psychiatrist, provides a fascinating account not merely of the illness but of the manner in which the various historical diagnoses account for some but not all of the symptoms manifested by the stricken writer:

> 'No question seriously arises as to the schizophrenic character of the symptomatology in the "crises" episodes but this is not the same as a diagnosis of schizophrenia. There are also symptoms in Strindberg's illness which are not characteristic of schizophrenia.'

> (Anderson 1971 : 114)

Anderson draws attention to the marked visual hallucinations, the exacerbation of symptoms at night, the panic and the mortal terror, skilfully sketches in Strindberg's dependence on alcohol and in particular absinthe (in its impure form, well known for its toxic effects), and suggests that one possible diagnosis is that of a toxic confusional state secondary to alcohol dependence. But, being the cautious diagnostician *par excellence*, he emphasizes the lack of data, the alternative possibilities, and the failure of his *own* explanation to account for all the evidence that is available.

There can be no doubt that Anderson's retrospective diagnostic assessment of Johan Strindberg could teach Professor Rosenhan's assessors something about the diagnostic process. In the end it will be objected that, regardless of correct and incorrect ways in which a diagnosis is made, the diagnostic exercise is in essence a futile exercise – *but that is a quite different objection.* It is one thing to say there is no point in a diagnostic assessment however conscientiously and professionally attempted; it is quite another to insist, as Rosenhan appears to do, that a study, which demonstrates how incompetently the average American psychiatrist assesses a patient who presents for professional help, proves the pointlessness of diagnoses. All it proves, I suggest, is that a diagnosis incompetently arrived at is more damaging and more destructive than no diagnosis at all.

A more telling criticism of psychiatric practice in this country is that psychiatrists are preoccupied with diagnostic detail and the *form* of abnormal psychic phenomena to the virtual exclusion of considerations of what such symptomatology might mean, of what is represented by the *content*. Academic and clinical case conferences tend to be monopolized by earnest clinicians haggling over whether this idea is a delusional preoccupation, a primary delusional experience, or an over-valued concept whilst social workers, seduced from the turbulent world of leaky roofs, family deprivation, alcoholic fathers, and battering mothers to see the 'experts' in action, watch with disbelief, wonder when someone is going to say something about what it all *means* and affirm to their harassed team leaders on their return that verily Emil Kraepelin is alive and well and lives at the British Institute of Psychiatry!

In his account of the paranoid illness of the German judge Daniel Paul Schreber (1842–1911), Dr Morton Schatzman (1973) explores this split between the analysis of the *form* and the *content* in some detail. He notes how Eugen Bleuler (who first used the term 'schizophrenia') 'classified Schreber's statements' but did not try to understand them as 'valid messages'. Schatzman points to the similarities between lunatic ideas held by Schreber's father with regard to the importance of eye exercises in children and his son's subsequent delusions about little men opening and closing his eyelids; between the father's devilish contraptions devised to ensure that little German children always sat straight, stiffened their backs, and kept their heads high and the son's conviction that persecutory agents manipulated his body into various postures; between the father's ideological penetration of the son's mind and the latter's conviction that rays emanated from God the Father, harming his own mental faculties. Schatzman dissects the *content* of Schreber's delusional system in a manner that reflects the influence of his colleague and mentor, Ronald Laing. His attack, however, is not only directed against those, like Bleuler (in this instance at any rate), who show scant interest in what the symptoms mean, but also against those who do focus on the content but interpret it in a preconceived fashion, in terms of the closed, pseudo-scientific, technical system that is Freudian analysis.

Now Schatzman clearly does not favour any old interpretation of the *content* of a particular illness, hence his attack on one such interpretative approach. The analysis of content, he agrees, is based on an accumulation of data. He is unhappy with the way in which phenomenologists appear to restrict such data collection to the abnormal, psychic phenomena manifested by the patient. He is alarmed at the way in which many analysts formulate their complex and imaginative interpretations in the absence of any significant information about the patient's family and social situation, other than that provided by the patient himself. (Moreover, as he shows in the Schreber case, in so far as information is provided by relatives it tends to be accepted at face value.) In effect, what Schatzman is saying is that it is not enough to establish the *form* of a psychiatric disturbance and that for a proper understanding of a patient's situation the psychiatrist must explore his immediate environment, his family, his social situation, the cultural influences affecting his development, his life-style, etc. Or as Fish puts it:

'The psychiatrist who is treating the psychologically ill cannot be satisfied with the simple empathic psychology of the intelligent sympathetic layman, since he is obliged to organise the knowledge he acquires in a way that can be used to help similar patients in the future. This leads to the creation of an interpretative psychology in which the ideas which have been obtained by empathising with the patient are formulated in terms of some general theory which has been derived from neurosphysiology, neurology, philosophy or mythology.' (Fish 1967 : 31)

It is worth noting that Fish distinguished between such an 'interpretative psychology' and 'scientific psychology' which investigates animal and human behaviour in 'a scientific way' and establishes rules and laws. Clinical psychiatrists use both varieties even though at times they do not seem aware of it and for most of the time they do not know the difference between the two. But it is important for them that they should. Schatzman may, as a result of his interpretative model of Schreber's paranoid state, end up with an understandable model of the illness. How far such a model approximates to some objective reality underpinning the illness can only be known if Schatzman, on the basis of his formulation in this particular case, were to construct a hypothesis explaining the genesis of paranoid delusions in general, a hypothesis which could then be tested. The elements of such a hypothesis can be perceived in his account of Schreber's illness. For example, do all paranoid schizophrenic patients exhibit the family interaction pattern evident in this particular case? How crucial for the development of such a condition is the mental health of the father? Of the mother? How applicable to other cases is Schatzman's suggestion that, in paranoia, what is often repressed is not a homosexual attraction towards the father but an homicidal hatred? But to even begin to provide answers to such questions demands an operational definition of the condition in question. If the *form* of the phenomena is irrelevant, we are but a short step away from saying that a Schreber, convinced that his body is being 'tortured and his mind destroyed', and a Rosenhan, declaring that he hears a voice saying 'thud', are experiencing psychic phenomena that phenomenologically differ but that the difference is of little consequence. Such a classifying system (if that is what one can call an approach that subsumes a complex systematized delusional state and a simple mono-hallucinatory one under the same category, be it schizophrenia, paranoia, mental illness, or whatever) would inevitably diminish the likelihood of clarifying any questions in any study in which it was employed. Define the concept of schizophrenia loosely enough and everybody will qualify for it – an interesting if novel way of confirming the hypothesis that we are all mad!

But don't define the concept at all, say the critics. It is reductive, destructive, and dehumanizing. Such a view is implicit in much of Laing's writings and indeed is explicitly stated in the introduction to the study of eleven families conducted by himself and Esterson (1964). Each of these families contained a person diagnosed by some other psychiatrist as 'schizophrenic', Laing and Esterson making it clear that they viewed such clinical terminology with distaste. Yet their study is a clear case of having your classifying cake and eating it; they disagree with the whole idea of the concept of schizophrenia yet one crucial factor that is common to the families in question is that such a diagnosis has been applied to a family member. 'We are concerned with persons, the relations between persons and the characteristics of the family as a system composed of a multiplicity of persons.'

This declaration appears to suggest that the deductions they make can be applied to family life *in general*, that they are not *specific* to families containing schizophrenic members. In which case, of course, any psychopathology they unearth in the family dynamics does not cast any helpful light on why some of the family members manifest their disturbance in the *form* of hallucinations, persecutory delusions, obsessive-compulsive rituals, and ruminations, etc. If Schatzman believes that the weird and formidable ideas of Schreber senior *caused* the paranoid delusional system to appear in his son, and, furthermore, believes that this is a common dynamic in such conditions, then he must look for and demonstrate such a causal relationship in other paranoid schizophrenic patients. But to do that demands some model, some operational definition of what constitutes paranoid schizophrenia itself.

Laing and Esterson avoided this binding situation by using other people's classifications whilst at the same time making clear their doubts concerning their validity. The explanation for this distaste for contemporary psychiatric nomenclature is provided by one of Laing's many American advocates:

'The crux of Laing's opposition to psychiatric diagnosis and much psychiatric practice has been that it is repressive, coercive, political rather than psychological in that it is really a means of controlling people and putting those who make nuisances of themselves out of the way or destroying their capacity to be their own obnoxious selves. Psychiatrists use insights derived from personality theory and data about the subject's psyche in order to do a more devastating job but they are basically unconcerned with his being and quite willing to sacrifice his selfhood for political ends.' (Friedenberg 1973 : 44)

If Friedenberg's analysis is correct, then all the above amounts to is that Laing dislikes psychiatric diagnoses because they can be abused. I am not at all sure that it is as simple as this. At times, Laing and other self-styled anti-psychiatrists appear to be denying *any* valid basis to the diagnostic process in psychiatry. But if Friendenberg is right then the problem we are left with, given the usefulness of an operational definition of a process such as 'schizophrenia', is how can we minimize the socio-political abuses to which it can give rise?

Clearly it would seem imperative that a psychiatric diagnosis be seen to rest on secure psychopathological data, competently collected and competently assessed. Such a diagnostic procedure should not depend on whether the examining psychiatrist is a Russian or an Indian, is paid for by the State or by the patient, works in a NHS out-patient department or in a Harley Street clinic. A diagnosis thus arrived at should carry some implications in terms of course, response to treatment, and prognosis. It should also be possible for two psychiatrists, acting independently, to arrive at and agree upon a diagnosis in a given patient.

But, the critics declare, no agreed objective clinical criteria for the diagnosis of psychiatric illnesses such as schizophrenia have been discovered, no consistency in premorbid personality, course, duration, and outcome demonstrated, no generally accepted view held as to whether, for example, schizophrenia constitutes a single disease or a group, an organic condition or a purely psychological one, a genetically transmitted disorder or one secondary to pathological interpersonal dynamics. In short, the diagnosis of mental illness, and particularly schizophrenia, as enacted by the average psychiatrist is as hard, objective, and detached as the average man's estimation of the political perspicacity of his local MP. It is almost entirely subjective in both cases and the judgement, when made, tells one more about the diagnostician than about the diagnosed.

Widely publicized as such a critical view of psychiatric diagnosis undoubtedly is, it is nonetheless false. It has served the critics well to exaggerate the amount of diagnostic dissent in psychiatry whilst comparing it unfavourably with an equally exaggerated view of the objectivity and scientific detachment of diagnostic practice in medicine in general. The formulation of a psychiatric diagnosis is often depicted as a sterile exercise in reductionism, an academic exercise of little practical value. In fact, every diagnosis in general medicine and in psychiatry is a hypothesis to be tested and refined. In September 1973 a new Task Force on Nomenclature and Statistics of the American Psychiatric Association was established to develop the Third Edition of the American Psychiatric Association's *Diagnostic and Statistical Manual* (DSM–111). The Task Force's goal has been to develop a classification system that will reflect the current state of knowledge regarding mental disorders. Spitzer and his colleagues explained the basis for the new edition in the course of a special conference held in St Louis, Missouri in June 1976. From the outset, the Task Force had assumed that in medicine an effective classification has many purposes. It is first a means by which the profession communicates effectively, clearly, and briefly within itself about clinically recognisable conditions for which it has professional responsibilities for diagnosis, care, or research. Secondly, the classification should be a useful guide to current differentiated treatments. A third purpose is to provide information about the likely outcome of psychiatric disorders, treated or untreated. Finally, the classification should reflect what is known about the causes or processes involved in the disorders. At the heart, therefore, of the attempts to provide a widely acceptable yet effective DSM–111 is the desire to provide criteria for operational identification of diagnosis.

The problems involved are formidable. Even if a reasonable level of agreement can be reached among psychiatrists concerning the major diagnostic categories, there is still the immense problem of bringing consistence and uniformity to the basic elements themselves. As Feinstein emphasises in a recent review, such terms as *anxiety*, *tension*, and *hostility* are really miniature diagnoses. 'In the absence of operational criteria', he points out, 'we have no idea whether anxiety in Toronto means the same thing as anxiety in New York, and whether New York's anxiety is the same as New Haven's'. (Feinstein 1977: 204).

Many diagnostic terms have aetiological implications, and the theoretical objections of different schools to each other's aetiological assumptions thwart attempts to arrive at an agreed classification. Such assumptions are quite explicit with diagnostic terms such as 'psychogenic psychosis' or 'reactive depression'. However, other diagnoses are often taken to *imply* certain kinds of causation, the polarizing of endogenous **versus** neurotic depression being just one example. One solution to this problem is that all diagnoses be shorn of their aetiological implications and be regarded simply as 'operational' definitions. Another solution is the use of a classification with separate axes for such things as symptomatology, aetiology, premorbid personality, physical and psychosocial factors. It is worth noting that the proposed DSM–III makes use of a multiaxial approach 'to insure that certain information of value in predicting outcome and planning treatment (is) recorded for each patient' (Spitzer *et al.* 1975). The first and second axes are used to record the mental disorders with the second axis reserved for *Personality Disorders* in adults and *Specific Developmental Disorders* in children. The third axis is reserved for listing non-psychiatric medical disorders adjudged to be pertinent in the aetiology or management of the psychiatric disorder listed on the first two axes. The fourth axis permits the clinician to indicate the severity of one or more psychosocial stressors which are judged likely to have contributed to the development or the exacerbation of the current episode of mental disorder, while the fifth axis allows the clinician to indicate the highest level of adaptive functioning by the patient during the past year. Such multiaxial diagnoses are seen by their advocates as an improvement over traditional psychiatric diagnoses in providing breadth and flexibility. Whether its use is feasible in varied clinical settings, however, remains to be established.

However, it is fair to say that when the three stages of the diagnostic process (data accumulation, data interpretation, and data categorization) are approached in a rational and competent way, the results in terms of diagnostic agreement and all that follows it compare favourably with those in a comparable field of medicine. This chapter has concentrated on considering the data, the abnormal psychic phenomena, the signs, and symptoms of psychiatric disturbance. It has not been possible to discuss more than a small proportion of such phenomena. I hope, however, that enough of the general phenomenological approach and of the specific symptoms have been described to make the next stages of the process, the interpretation and classification of the data, particularly the data relating to schizophrenia, more easily understood.

References

ANDERSON, E.W. (1971) Strindberg's Illness. *Psychological Medicine* **1** (2): 104–17.

ANDERSON, E.W. and TRETHOWAN, W.H. (1967) *Psychiatry*. London: Baillière, Tindall & Cox.

BANNISTER, D. (1960) Conceptual Structure in Thought Disordered Schizophrenics. *British Journal of Psychiatry* **106**: 1230.

—— (1965) The Genesis of Schizophrenic Thought Disorder. A Serial Invalidation Hypothesis. *British Journal of Psychiatry* **111**: 377–82.

BANNISTER, D. and FRANSELLA, F. (1966) A Grid Test of Schizophrenic Thought Disorder. *British Journal of Social and Clinical Psychology* **5**: 95–102.

CAMERSON, N. (1944) Experimental Analysis of Schizophrenic Thinking. In J. Kasanin (ed.), *Language and Thought in Schizophrenia*. Berkeley: University of California Press.

FEINSTEIN, A. (1977) A Critical Overview of Diagnosis in Psychiatry. In: *Psychiatric Diagnosis* (Eds V. M. Rakoff, H. C. Stancer, and H. B. Kedward). New York: Mazel.

FISH, F.J. (1962) *Schizophrenia*. Bristol: Wright.

—— (1967) *Clinical Psychopathology*. Bristol: Wright.

FRIEDENBERG, E.Z. (1973) *Laing. Fontana Modern Masters* (ed. F. Kermode). London: Fontana/Collins.

GOODE, R. (1954) The Life of the Shawl. *Lancet* 1: 106–7.

JASPERS, K. (1959) *General Psychopathology* (7th edition; trans. J. Hoenig and M. W. Hamilton). Manchester: Manchester University Press.

—— (1968) The Phenomenological Approach in Psychopathology. *British Journal of Psychiatry* 114: 1313–23. (Originally published in *Zeitschrift für die gesamte Neurologie under Psychiatrie*, 1912.)

KRAEPELIN, E. (1906) *Lectures on Clinical Psychiatry* (2nd revised edition). London: Baillière, Tindall & Cox.

LAING, R.D. (1965) *The Divided Self.* Hardmondsworth: Pelican.

LAING, R.D. and ESTERSON, A. (1964) *Sanity, Madness and the Family* (2nd edition). London: Tavistock.

MACALPINE, I. and HUNTER, R. (1969) *George III and the Mad-Business.* London: Allen Lane, The Penguin Press.

MAYER-GROSS, W., SLATER, E., and ROTH, M. (1969) *Clinical Psychiatry* (3rd edition). London: Baillière, Tindall & Cox.

MELLOR, D.S. (1970) First Rank Symptoms of Schizophrenia. *British Journal of Psychiatry* 117: 15–23.

ROSENHAN, D.I. (1973) On Being Sane in Insane Places. *Science* 179: 250–58.

SHATZMAN, M. (1973) *Soul Murder.* London: Allen Lane.

SCHNEIDER, K. (1959) *Clinical Psychopathology* (trans. M. W. Hamilton). New York: Grune & Stratton.

SPITZER, R.L., ENDICOTT, J. and ROBBINS, E. (1975) Clinical Criteria for Psychiatric Diagnosis and DSM-III. *American Journal of Psychiatry* 132: 1187–92.

TAYLOR, F. KRAUPL (1961) *The Analysis of Therapeutic Groups.* Maudsley Monographs, No. 8. London: Oxford University Press.

—— (1966) *Psychopathology: Its Causes and Symptoms.* London: Butterworth.

WING, J.K. (1973) Social and Familial Factors in the Causation and Treatment of Schizophrenia. In L. L. Iversen and S. P. R. Rose (eds.), *Biochemistry and Mental Illness*. London: The Biochemical Society.

4

What is schizophrenia?

A name can act as a myth . . . as the declaration and charter of a readiness to act. Lots of subjects in natural science, as well as social science, begin as names, claims on areas and methods of which we are in fact yet ignorant, promises and programmes to which credence can be attached. And names, too, are fences – devices by which people can be excluded as illegitimate, trespassers on a territory staked out as private property, even if not, in fact, explored and tested for ore.

MACRAE 1970 : 783

BEFORE THE Munich psychiatrist Emil Kraepelin first outlined his concept of *dementia praecox* to the University Psychiatric Clinic in November 1898, there had been no clear or useful classification of mental disorders. Other German psychiatrists (Neumann 1883; Zeller 1844; Griesinger 1845) had argued against the existence of discrete and distinct illnesses and in favour of one comprehensive mental disorder, manifesting different forms. Such a disorder was believed to begin with depression, which could turn to elation and excitement, become a delusional illness, and eventually terminate as a dementing process. Such a view reflected the very real difficulties encountered by those specialists who were attempting to discern some pattern and order operating within the mass of undifferentiated clinical symptoms that could be recognized.

Nonetheless, the efforts to delineate specific clusters of symptoms, showing particular patterns of onset, development, and outcome, gathered impetus during the second half of the last century. In 1851, the French psychiatrist Jules Falret (1853), using the two criteria of specific symptomatology and course, identified manic-depressive illness ('folie circulaire') as a condition characterized by a marked disturbance of mood, either of a depressive or elated nature, and showing an episodic course. Between these episodes, the patient's basic personality appeared to be relatively unimpaired. A compatriot of Falret, Benedict Morel, insisted that a true classificatory system in psychiatry should be based empirically on the cause, the symptomatology, the course, and outcome of a disease and in 1852 he employed the term 'démence précoce' to describe a debilitating mental disorder beginning in adolescence and characterized by withdrawal, bizarre mannerisms, and personal neglect, and ending, sooner or later, in severe intellectual deterioration (Morel 1852). The term 'démence précoce' actually meant 'rapid mental impairment' and subsequently came to be interpreted as meaning 'dementia at an early age'.

Different variations on Morel's theme appeared; the term 'hebephrenia' was applied to a similar clinical picture to 'démence précoce', whilst the label 'catatonia' was employed to describe an apparently separate condition characterized by stereotyped movements, mannerisms, and occasional outbursts of intense excitement, automatic obedience, negativism and stupor. Earlier, in 1818, the German psychiatrist Johann Heinroth had described a paranoid illness in which a single false idea resulted in a gross distortion of the person's relation with the outside world; included in this state were delusions about the supernatural, grandiose delusions, and a mixture of emotional, intellectual, and volitional disturbances.

But it was Kraepelin who was to bring together these different concepts of hebephrenia, catatonia, and paranoia into a single disease entity and who developed and extended the concept of dementia praeox (démence précoce') based on the possible cause, symptomatology, course, and outcome of the psychosis. In his 1898 lecture he stressed the necessity of distinguishing dementia praecox from manic-depressive disorder because, in his view, the symptomatology and the course were quite different in these two psychotic conditions. He recognized that the breakdown in dementia praecox was not an intellectual or a cognitive one nor was it necessarily precocious (i.e., it did not always begin in adolescence). He did not argue, as he is often now accused of doing, that the condition always resulted in severe dementia or that it always had a miserable prognosis. (Statistics had suggested to him that no fewer than 13 per cent of his cases seemed to recover completely, although he tended to believe that there might, nonetheless, be some traces of the condition in these recovered cases.) Kraepelin argued that the characteristic symptoms of dementia praceox included hallucinations, usually of an auditory or tactile nature, a decrease in attention towards the outside world, a disorder affecting the organization of the thinking process, an incoherence of speech secondary to the thought disorder, an impairment of understanding and judgement, delusional beliefs, emotional blunting, negativistic behaviour, and stereotyped movements. He stressed the fact that these symptoms occurred in a state of clear consciousness and unimpaired perception and memory. Such a phenomenological formulation said nothing about the possible cause of this condition, although Kraepelin himself appears to have favoured a physical, probably metabolic, cause.

It was the Swiss psychiatrist Eugen Bleuler (1911) who in 1908 first used the term 'schizophrenia' with reference to Kraepelin's 'dementia praecox'. He chose the term that, despite all the assaults of the semantic purists and the anti-psychiatrists, has stayed with us to the present day because, as he put it, '. . . the rending (disconnection) or splitting of the psychic functions is an outstanding symptom of the whole group'.

He retained the concept of a disturbance in the coherent integration of ideas and emotions as an essential feature of schizophrenia, but he did not speak of a discrete disease *per se*. He envisaged hereditary transmission as playing a part in the genesis of the condition and he speculated on the possibility that certain psychological factors might *evoke* the symptoms, although he was uncertain whether they were sufficient to *cause* the illness. His major innovation was his attempt to divide the symptomatology of schizophrenia into so-called 'primary' and 'secondary' symptoms. Primary symptoms were thought to be directly due to the underlying cause (whatever that might be), whereas the secondary symptoms represented the particular psychological reactions of the individual's personality to the illness proper. The primary symptoms were thought to be characteristic of the condition and believed to be present to some degree during all the stages. They included a disturbance in the logical and meaningful association of ideas, changes in emotional reactions, a withdrawal from reality, and a tendency to resort to phantasy.

A further development in Bleuler's formulation was his emphasis on understanding the possible psychodynamics of the disorder. Whereas Kraepelin maintained a formal, descriptive, and somewhat nihilistic (psychodynamically speaking) approach to the problem, Bleuler added impetus to the trend towards the exploration of individual life experiences and stresses for clues regarding the cause and the particular structure of the disorder. Bleuler eventually conceptualized schizophrenia as a group of disorders (the schizophrenias) in which some schizophrenics suffer from an *endogenous* or inborn disorder aggravated and made manifest by psychological stress factors, whereas others undergo a *reactive* form, due almost entirely to overwhelming external difficulties and pressures. The former 'organic' type he believed carried a worse prognosis compared to the latter 'psychological' variant.

Bleuler thus did more than merely alter Kraepelin's label for the syndrome. He extended very considerably the boundaries of the condition and loosened the diagnostic criteria. In Britain, psychiatric practice in the main favoured the Kraepelinian approach with its emphasis on possible biological causation, its use of relatively stringent and narrow diagnostic criteria, and its somewhat modest acknowledgement of the role of psychodynamic aspects in the condition. The greater influence of psychoanalytical theory in the United States meant that Bleuler's looser conceptual concept

and his insistence on the importance of psychological understanding and psychodynamic factors found more fertile
ground in which to develop. The current efforts by psychiatrists in both countries to agree upon an acceptable
operational definition of schizophrenia reflects this diver-
gence in the way in which the concept of schizophrenia
historically developed. These efforts have attained a new
sophistication in an international pilot study of schizophrenia
being conducted under the auspices of the World Health
Organisation and discussed later in this chapter.

But, has this struggle to achieve an accepted definition any
practical meaning? Is it necessary to have a diagnostic
category of schizophrenia at all? How important or relevant
to the practice of psychiatry is this apparently academic and
sterile collecting, naming, and classifying of arbitrarily
defined psychological phenomena? At the present time this is
one of the most controversial questions in contemporary
psychiatry. As one psychiatrist has put it, the emotions
surrounding the whole subject of psychiatric nomenclature
reach the fanatic proportions 'which in earlier times sur-
rounded debates as to how the deity should be named'
(Gruenberg 1969). Another has termed the process of
diagnosis 'character assassination' (Leifer 1970) and others
have made it plain that they regard it as analogous to
identifying witches (Szasz 1971), as a form of scientific
name-calling (Menninger 1969), or as a method whereby
the personal, usual, and valid experiences of others are
denigrated and ridiculed (Laing 1965).

For the average British psychiatrist, working in his busy
out-patient clinic, such discussions appear academic. This is
not to say that he is unaware of the serious limitations and
shortcomings of the 'disease-entity' approach at the present
stage of psychiatric theory. Robert Kendell's declaration on
the matter is probably closest to the view of the clinician:

'Although few contemporary psychiatrists are content with
this framework and even fewer would regard either manic-

depressive illness or schizophrenia as disease entities in the traditional sense, we continue to use this Kraepelinian edifice if only because it is familiar and we have nothing better to put in its place.' (Kendell 1972 : 383)

But if this is the best we have got, to what does it amount? If schizophrenia is not regarded as a disease entity 'in the traditional sense', in what sense is it regarded? What does it mean when a psychiatrist in this country formulates a diagnosis of schizophrenia in a given case? At first glance the situation appears somewhat chaotic. The term appears to be used in widely differing ways so that there appears to be little agreement, even among clinicians within the same hospital, as to what precisely is meant by the term. Some appear to reserve the diagnosis for those patients whose disturbance results in permanent damage to their personality structure whereas others apply it to patients regardless of the outcome. Some appear to restrict it to illnesses appearing in adolescence or in early adult life whereas others employ it in the case of illnesses appearing at any age. It is worth noting Kendell's view again:

'The problem, which in fact is common to all functional illnesses, is that as we know little of the aetiology of the condition and have failed to identify any consistent structural or physiological abnormalities in those possessing the familiar symptoms, the only defining characteristic available to us is the syndrome itself. In our present state of knowledge, our criterion for a diagnosis of schizophrenia can only be the presence of the typical clinical features of schizophrenia.' (Kendell 1972 : 383)

In Britain a diagnosis of schizophrenia, in practice, is usually based on 'typical clincial features'. If there is any evidence that certain symptoms are present or have been present at some time during the course of the illness, the diagnosis is made with confidence (Granville-Grossman 1971). As virtually all psychiatric symptoms can occur in schizophrenia, what is required is a description of those symptoms that *must* be present if a diagnosis is to be made.

In 1959 Kurt Schneider, a German psychiatrist especially versed in descriptive psychopathology, identified a number of symptoms which he regarded as of *first rank importance* in differentiating schizophrenia from other conditions. If any person experiences any one of these symptoms in the absence of physical disease, the diagnosis, in Schneider's view, is schizophrenia. Schneider's 'first-rank' symptoms are listed in *Table 1*.

These symptoms were evolved in the light of clinical experience. Schneider did not derive them from nor attempt to relate them to theoretical concepts of the underlying psychological mechanisms in schizophrenia. Such first-rank symptoms are of considerable importance in British psychiatry. For example, the Registrar-General's (1968) *Glossary of Mental Disorders* advises psychiatrists to base their diagnoses of schizophrenia on the presence of certain symptoms in a setting of clear consciousness, the majority of which are in effect the first-rank symptoms of Schneider (WHO 1967).

Schneider's operational definition has been popular in Britain, mainly as a consequence of the emphasis placed upon it by phenomenologically inclined psychiatrists at centres like the Maudsley Hospital in London, at Manchester, Liverpool, and Newcastle, and its popularization in certain textbooks (Mayer-Gross, Slater, and Roth 1969; Anderson and Trethowan 1967). The World Health Organisation's *International Pilot Study of Schizophrenia* (1973) has shown that the presence of any of the most common of Schneider's symptoms is highly discriminating for a diagnosis of schizophrenia. For example, of 227 patients exhibiting delusions of being controlled, 94 per cent were diagnosed as suffering from schizophrenia by local psychiatrists in each of the nine countries involved and the corresponding percentage for thought broadcasting, voices heard discussing the patient, and voices commenting on the patient's thoughts or actions were all comparably high.

Table 1 *First-rank symptoms of schizophrenia*

passivity experiences:	thoughts, emotions, impulses, or actions experienced by the individual as under external, alien control; these include the so-called 'made' experiences which the individual believes to be imposed upon him or in which his will seems taken away. Certain disturbances of thought control are included: *thought insertion* (the experience of thoughts being inserted into one's mind from outside and under external influence); *thought withdrawal* (the experience of thoughts being taken out of one's mind under external control); *thought broadcasting* (the experience of one's thoughts being broadcast to or otherwise made known to others).
auditory hallucinations in the third person:	hallucinatory voices heard discussing one's thoughts or behaviour as they occur (voices may maintain a 'running commentary'); heard discussing or arguing about one in the third person (i.e., referring to one as 'he' or by name) or heard repeating one's thoughts out loud or anticipating one's thoughts. To be 'true' hallucinations, the hallucinated voices must be experienced by the person as alien and under the influence of some external source.
primary delusions:	delusions in which the primary meaning arises from perceptions which in themselves are normal. Also known as 'autochthonous' delusions, these cannot be understood in terms of preceding morbid experiences. (See Chapter 3.)

Whereas Bleuler's so-called primary symptoms are loose, difficult to define operationally, and, as a consequence, permit a much wider selection of abnormal behaviour and experience to be classified as 'schizophrenic', Schneider's criteria have been criticized for being too narrow (Kendell 1972). In one sample of 166 chronic patients in an English mental hospital, originally diagnosed as schizophrenic, only 72 per cent showed one or more first-rank symptoms at the time they were studied and only in a further 7 per cent were one or more symptoms shown to have been present at some time in the past (Mellor 1970). It has also been shown that the presence of first-rank symptoms is associated with a poor short-term response to treatment and with the absence of other clinical features believed to predict a good prognosis. This suggests that Schneider's first-rank symptoms may delineate a *nuclear* or *core group* of schizophrenics, while missing those patients who exhibit less distinctive symptomatology but who otherwise justify such a diagnosis by virtue of the similarity of their clinical picture and of the onset, course, and outcome of their disturbance to that of the 'nuclear' type.

Schneider was aware of the problem. 'In my view', he wrote, 'the presence of first-rank symptoms always signifies schizophrenia, but first-rank symptoms need not always be present in schizophrenia' (1957). He also described 'second-rank' symptoms which could occur in other psychotic states and to some extent in non-psychotic states and on which one would not ordinarily rest a diagnosis of schizophrenia. However, in some cases, by virtue of the combination and the accumulation of these second-rank symptoms, they could be sufficient for a diagnosis of schizophrenia to be made.

Schneider's first-rank symptoms constitute symptom complexes; the links between these are obscure and any underlying theory of explanation speculative. Such symptom complexes, however, have provided the matrix of an operational concept which currently links together a large number of investigatory efforts and which has become a nodal-point for present-day knowledge.

In summary, the current diagnostic practice in Britain relies greatly on Schneider's operational formulation and when clinicians find one or more of his first-rank symptoms present, in the presence of clear consciousness and in the absence of coarse brain disease or toxic factors (e.g., ingestion of amphetamines or LSD), they diagnose schizophrenia. In the absence of first-rank symptoms, a diagnosis of schizophrenia may still be made, for it is recognized that in the very early and acute stages of the schizophrenic illness and in the chronic 'defect' state of the severely handicapped patient, first-rank symptoms are often absent.

Two fundamental objections to this phenomenological approach to the diagnosis of schizophrenia tend to be raised. First, how reliable is the diagnosis when it is made? Do psychiatrists, in practice, agree on what is and is not evidence of a schizophrenic illness? If the chances of being diagnosed as a schizophrenic in the United States are four times greater than in the United Kingdom (suggesting to one ironic critic that the best cure for an American schizophrenic would be to cross the Atlantic!), surely the whole elaborate diagnostic exercise is a waste of time? Second, even if there is reasonable agreement between psychiatrists, both within and outside Britain, as to what constitutes the syndrome of schizophrenia, does such a diagnosis have any significance for patients and their relatives apart from the reductive and derogatory one whereby patients' experiences are labelled mad, insane, and irrational?

1 Diagnostic agreement

In the majority of published studies concerning the incidence and prevalence of various mental disorders in countries throughout the world, little attention tends to be paid to the quality of the diagnostic judgements they contain. Yet there is disquieting evidence that suggests that under ordinary clinical conditions psychiatric diagnoses can be extremely unreliable. For example, in one American study (Katz, Cole, and Lowry 1969), a short cine film of psychiatric interviews was shown to audiences of psychiatrists. The psychiatrists made significantly varied ratings of the extent to which a symptom such as 'apathy' was present in two of the patients, in spite of their employing a common standard rating method

(Lorr and Klatt 1967). One of these films was later shown in both the United States and Britain and it was found that the American psychiatrists tended to perceive symptoms and behaviour as abnormal to a greater extent than did their British colleagues.

Passamanick and his co-workers (1959) showed that within one hospital the amount of diagnostic variation can be remarkable. Five hundred and thirty-eight female patients were arbitrarily divided among three wards. The resulting groups of patients did not differ with regard to a wide variety of personality characteristics and there was no reason to suppose that the final diagnostic breakdown of each group would be very different. In fact marked differences were found and were traced to the differing diagnostic conceptions of the three psychiatrists in charge of the three wards. For example, one psychiatrist made a diagnosis of schizophrenia in two-thirds of his patients whereas the other two psychiatrists only diagnosed schizophrenia in 22 per cent and 29 per cent of their respective patients! This study is of importance in that the authors were able to show that such variations in diagnostic practice were not of academic interest alone but were associated with differences in treatment as well. They concluded that 'despite protestations that their point of reference is always the individual patient, clinicians in fact may be so committed to a particular psychiatric school of thought that the patient's diagnosis and treatment is largely predetermined'.

The possibility that a diagnosis made at one point in time could be changed some time later has also been examined. In one well-known study (Masserman and Carmichael 1938) 100 patients were assessed one year after they had received their initial diagnosis. Forty-one of the patients required a revision of the diagnosis. However, it has been pointed out (Cooper et al. 1972) that it is not possible from this study to tell whether such diagnostic revisions resulted from a real change in the condition of the patients or a change in the diagnostic habits of the clinicians themselves. There is evidence from a British study that changes in doctors produce most changes in diagnosis over time. Dr (now Professor) John Cooper (1967) looked at a group of 200 mental hospital patients who had four admissions to hospital within two years of their first. In view of the fact that all the admissions came within a short period of each other, it might have been expected that in the majority of the patients the diagnosis would not change. Using the somewhat detailed International Classification of Diseases, Professor Cooper found that only 37 per cent retained the same diagnosis throughout. However using somewhat broader diagnostic groupings (schizophrenia, affective disorder, neuroses, personality disorder, drug dependence, etc.) and subjecting the case notes of each admission to a uniform assessment by one psychiatrist, he found that the proportion of patients retaining the first diagnosis rose to 81 per cent.

In another study (Ward *et al.* 1962) the final stage in the diagnostic process, namely that of choosing a term from a nomenclature, was scrutinized. Each of a series of 153 patients was seen and diagnosed separately by two different psychiatrists who then met to discuss and identify the sources of the disagreement that occurred in forty cases. In twenty-five of these cases it was found that the description of the diagnostic categories being used overlapped and the categories were not mutually exclusive. There also had been inadequate guidance and instructions about how to give precedence to one disorder when two or more were adjudged to be present. Inconsistency on the part of the diagnostician was responsible for disagreement in thirteen of the cases and inconsistency on the part of the patient (the patient presented quite different psychiatric symptoms to each of the two psychiatrists) was responsible for disagreement in two cases.

Impressed by these diagnostic discrepancies, a variety of experts have suggested that the conventional descriptive diagnoses are so unreliable that they should be discarded (Masserman and Carmichael 1938; Colby 1960; Menninger 1963; Laing 1967; Mannoni 1973). However, Professor

Cooper and his co-workers (1972) disagree. They point out that most of the diagnosticians working on the above studies were working under ordinary clinical conditions, had not undergone any special training, and at the most had only a brief acquaintance with an agreed rating scale or with a glossary of terms. They show that one study, despite being performed under fairly minimal conditions of standardization did achieve diagnostic consistency mainly because the diagnosticians involved had a similar psychiatric training. This study (Wilson and Meyer 1962) compared the distributions of different diagnoses in a psychiatric liaison service in a general hospital over two consecutive years and found them to be very similar in spite of a different set of patients and a different set of diagnosticians being involved. For example, the proportion of patients diagnosed as schizophrenic remained at 15 per cent, all types of depression marginally changed from 23 to 25 per cent, and personality disorders only changed from 38 to 34 per cent.

Two recent large-scale international studies have been mounted with the standardization of diagnoses of schizophrenia as their aim. Both studies are based on a special technique of interviewing patients known as the *Present State Examination (PSE)*. In essence, this is a standardized form of the psychiatric diagnostic interview ordinarily used in this country and in other Western European countries. One of the early reports on the development and use of the PSE (Wing *et al.* 1967) demonstrated that a high degree of reliability could be achieved when diagnoses were made under optimal conditions. For example, during work primarily directed at establishing the reliability of symptom scores between raters, a provisional diagnosis was made by each of two pairs of interviewers independently of each other at the end of each interview. The interviewers had all been trained at the same Institute and all used a set of instructions geared to the interview and specially prepared for the purpose of making this categorization. Over a series of 172 patients, of whom half had schizophrenia, just under half had some type of mood disorder, and the remainder had a variety of other conditions, there was complete agreement with regard to the primary diagnosis in 84 per cent, partial disagreement in 7 per cent, and serious disagreement in only 9 per cent. A large proportion of the disagreement involved the notoriously difficult diagnostic category of personality disorder. Professor Cooper and his colleagues (1972) emphasize that this high level of agreement shows what can be expected when a special effort is made to control known sources of inter-observer variation. Such results suggest the need for a more systematic examination of the diagnostic process in psychiatry.

The first of the international studies which made use of the PSE, the US–UK Diagnostic Project (Cooper *et al.* 1972), was concerned with patients admitted to hospital in New York and London. An American psychiatrist (Kramer 1961) had earlier drawn attention to the large and persistent differences between the diagnostic statistics generated by American and British psychiatric hospitals. Although overall admission rates are similar for the two countries, the admission rate for arteriosclerotic dementia and schizophrenia are considerably higher in the United States whereas the admission rate for manic-depressive illness is higher in England and Wales. Such differences could, of course, be due to genuine variations in the clinical characteristics of patients entering the hospitals, or to the differences in diagnostic criteria employed by psychiatrists in Britain and America, or to a combination of the two. The US–UK Diagnostic Project was established to find out which of these possibilities was operating and in what way.

Complementary research teams, based in London and New York, were set up. A series of two hundred and fifty (250) admissions to the Brooklyn State Hospital and to Netherne Hospital, south of London, were assessed. Each patient was examined by one of the project's psychiatrists as soon after admission as possible and independently of the hospital staff. Because of the overriding need to maintain a uniform procedure on both sides of the Atlantic, structured interviewing procedures were used throughout. A 'Project Diagnosis' based on the nomenclature of the International Classification of Diseases was made on the basis of the information obtained in these interviews. The 'Hospital Diagnosis' of these two series of patients was also obtained. The 'Hospital Diagnoses' showed the familiar national differences; there were far more schizophrenics and alcoholics at Brooklyn and far more psychotic depressives and personality disorders at Netherne. The differences between the two sets of 'Project Diagnoses' were far smaller however. There were still significantly more patients with depression at Netherne and more alcoholics at Brooklyn but the difference was reduced for every other major diagnostic category and for schizophrenia it ceased to be statistically significant. That is to say, *using a standardised psychiatric assessment, there was no significant difference* in the number of patients diagnosed as suffering from schizophrenia in the New York hospital compared with those diagnosed as schizophrenics in Netherne.

(Cooper *et al.* 1972)

An additional comparison was carried out between samples of patients drawn from all the public mental hospitals in New York and London. The hospital diagnoses of the two samples showed the same striking differences as before, with twice as many schizophrenics and six times as many alcoholics in the New York sample and five times as many psychotic depressives and twelve times as many manic-depressives in the London sample. But the majority of these differences failed to survive the transition from hospital diagnosis to project diagnosis. Comparison of the two sets of project diagnoses indicated that there were indeed more alcoholics in the New York sample and more patients with affective (i.e., manic-depressive and other depressive illnesses) disorders in the London sample, but again none of the differences for other diagnostic categories, including schizophrenia, were significant.

The second major project, the International Pilot Study of Schizophrenia (IPSS), is currently being carried out under the auspices of the World Health Organisation. The preliminary study involved over 1,200 patients in nine international centres (Aarhus, Denmark; Agra, India; Cali, Columbia; Ibadan, Nigeria; London, England; Moscow, USSR; Taipei, Taiwan; Washington, USA; Prague, Czechoslovakia). One of the preliminary conclusions which has emerged from this ambitious study is that similar groups of schizophrenics can be identified in each of the widely differing countries involved.

Each of the patients in the study received an intense initial examination by the research team at each centre. Three main interviewing schedules – the PSE, a psychiatric history schedule, and a social description schedule – were used (*Figure 1*). This study showed that two groups of patients, described as 'schizophrenic', could be distinguished. The first group, which we can call the 'nuclear' group, accounted for about two-thirds of all those given such a diagnosis and manifested symptoms that were highly discriminatory for a diagnosis of schizophrenia; that is to say, when a patient exhibited such symptoms there was more than a 90 per cent chance of his being diagnosed as suffering from schizophrenia whatever centre he found himself in. Most of these highly discriminatory symptoms are similar to the 'first-rank' symptoms of Kurt Schneider.

Of 227 patients manifesting delusions of control; 96 per cent were diagnosed as suffering from schizophrenia. 97 per cent of 328 patients exhibiting thought insertion, thought withdrawal and/or thought broadcasting received a diagnosis of schizophrenia as did 95 per cent of 172 patients reporting auditory hallucinations in the third person.

The second group, made up of the remaining third of the patients in the study, did not manifest such highly discriminatory symptoms. Two-thirds of these were patients with coherently expressed delusions of persecution, of self-reference, or of religious or other content not culturally based, and without auditory hallucinations or first-rank symptoms. The remaining one-third (i.e., approximately 10

Figure 1 *International pilot study of schizophrenia*

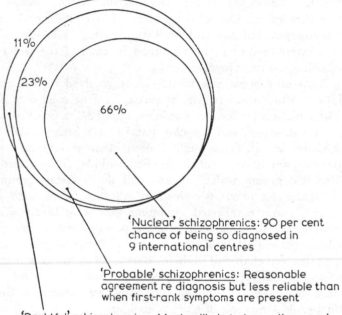

'Nuclear' schizophrenics: 90 per cent chance of being so diagnosed in 9 international centres

'Probable' schizophrenics: Reasonable agreement re diagnosis but less reliable than when first-rank symptoms are present

'Doubtful' schizophrenics: Most unlikely to be so diagnosed outside particular centre (two centres particularly prone to such idiosyncratic approach – Washington and Moscow)

(World Health Organisation 1972)

per cent of the entire sample) was in the main made up of patients diagnosed as suffering from schizophrenia in two centres – Washington and Moscow. In the United States, as was suggested by the US–UK Diagnostic Project, the prevailing concept of schizophrenia appears to be much broader and patients who, in the UK, might be diagnosed as suffering from depressive, manic-depressive, or neurotic disorders, appear to be diagnosed as schizophrenic. In the Soviet Union, the 'Moscow school' is also regarded as having a broader concept of schizophrenia than elsewhere and categories such as 'sluggish', 'periodic', 'and 'shift-like', not employed elsewhere, are used there.

Studies of European diagnostic practices *vis-à-vis* American ones (Overall and Gorham 1962; Engelsmann *et al.* 1970; Pichot, Bailly, and Overall 1967) have suggested that the broad diagnostic concepts of schizophrenia, mania, and depression used in the five countries studied (France, Germany, Italy, Czechoslovakia, and the United States) are all similar. However, it has been pointed out (Hordern *et al.* 1968) that there is not necessarily a correlation between the way diagnostic categories are constructed in theory and the way they are used in practice. For this reason, three psychiatrists (Kendell in London, Pichot in Paris, and Von Cranach in Munich) attempted to study in more detail the diagnostic practices of psychiatrists in these three cities.

Videotape recordings were made of brief diagnostic interviews with 227 newly admitted patients in a London hospital. These were then shown to groups of English-speaking psychiatrists in the three cities involved. Comparisons of the diagnoses suggested that English, French and German psychiatrists have similar concepts of schizophrenia, neurotic illness, personality disorder and alcoholism but differ quite markedly with regard to affective illness. (Kendell, Pichot, and von Cranach 1974)

These authors acknowledge the possibility that the English-speaking psychiatrists in Munich and Paris may not necessarily be representative of psychiatrists throughout their respective countries. John Copeland and his colleagues (1971) did establish that the diagnostic practices of the doctors in the London centre (the Maudsley Hospital) do not differ appreciably from those of their colleagues throughout Britain, but there is no comparable evidence concerning diagnostic reliability within France or Germany.

If it is possible to standardize psychiatric diagnoses in such a way that there can be 90 per cent agreement between psychiatrists about what does and does not constitute the central core diagnosis, how does this compare with the diagnostic reliability of non-psychiatric physicians? (The literature, critical of psychiatry, tends to disparage the allegedly low level of agreement amongst psychiatrists confronted by psychiatric disorders and compares the situation unfavourably with the state of affaris in general medicine.) In one interesting study of comparison (Butterworth and Reppert 1960) 933 physicians were tested for their ability to match fifteen diagnoses with the same number of taped heart sounds. The tape recordings were taken from a library of phonocardiograms and were felt to represent good examples of some of the main clinical entities such as complete heart block, mitral insufficiency, etc. This was a matching test in that each observer had a list of the fifteen diagnostic entities in his possession. Furthermore, the physician could watch an oscilloscopic representation of each sound as he listened. Certified cardiovascular specialists obtained an accuracy of 79·1 per cent but all other groups of physicians did less well.

Another study tested the reliability of three radiologists in diagnosing peptic ulcers by means of x-rays (Etter *et al.* 1960). They were given 116 gastrointestinal films and were asked to classify them into two categories. Each radiologist was scored on each occasion when he agreed with either of the other two – this occurred 74 per cent of the time. Each radiologist then read forty-six sets of film a second time and achieved an intra-observer consistency of 83 per cent. (In other words, he agreed with at least one of the other two raters three out of every four times and with himself five out of every six times.)

Derryberry (1938) assessed paediatricians' abilities to estimate the nutritional status of over 200 children. Either five or six paediatricians examined each child and were given as much time as they needed. Yet in only seven cases was there complete agreement between the raters! Even more noteworthy was the fact that four of the children were placed in every category – poor, fair, good, and excellent nutritional status – by the raters. Perhaps one of the most extraordinary findings is that of Belk and Sunderman (1947) who studied the performance of more than fifty clinical chemistry laboratories. The laboratories were asked to analyse several chemical 'unknowns' (the composition of these 'unknowns' was known to organizers of the study). Although a reasonable allowance was made for errors attributable to the techniques employed, only 42 per cent of the analyses fell within the acceptable range and not a single laboratory attained seven 'satisfactory' scores out of seven tests. So much for the 'hard' and 'objective' data of general medicine.

These findings are in line with those of Beck *et al.* (1962) who drew attention to the significant inter-observer errors reported in the assessment of such conditions as chest disorders and the degree of pathological inflammation of the tonsils. There are good grounds for believing that all varieties of the diagnostic process are at times subject to significant inter-observer (and, to a lesser extent, intra-observer) variation. It is because of the particularly vulnerable state of contemporary psychiatric classification that psychiatrists must be prepared and have recently been prepared to devote more attention than perhaps other diagnosticians to analysing inter-observer differences in diagnoses with a view to reducing these to an absolute minimum.

2 Diagnostic implications

If, as the above studies suggest, a respectable degree of agreement can be reached by psychiatrists with regard to what symptoms of psychological distress and behaviour constitute the syndrome of schizophrenia, what are the implications, if any, of such an agreement? In the field of general medicine a diagnosis supposedly says something about the likely course of a condition if left untreated, the sort of treatment it is likely to respond to, and the likely outcome or prognosis. (In addition a diagnosis in medicine usually, though not invariably, says something about the cause of the condition.) For example, the appearance of a lump in the breast which is hard, tethered to the underlying tissue, is painful and is accompanied by a bloody discharge from the nipple may lead to a diagnosis of breast cancer. The degree of malignancy can be established by biopsy of the lump and, as a result, some prediction can be made concerning the likely outcome, treated and untreated. Some assessment can be made of the most effective treatment, be it radiotherapy, conservative surgery (limited removal of the breast and adjacent lymph glands), or a radical mastectomy (involving breast, much of the chest wall, and almost the entire lymphatic drainage to the area). The patient can be given a reasonable idea of what suffering from such a malevolent disorder is going to mean for her, both in the short term and the long term. Most of us, when we fall ill, want to know what is wrong with us, i.e., what the *diagnosis* is, not because we are fascinated with the intricate workings of our physical bodies (though some of us are), nor because knowing the *diagnosis* provides us and others with a label which enables us to communicate our problem in an acceptable shorthand form (though it often does), but because, for the most part, a diagnosis enables a doctor to make a prediction for us and/or our relatives as to how long we are likely to suffer, what in the meantime can be done, and, as a result of any therapeutic intervention, whether our condition is likely to respond.

If a diagnosis is loosely applied, its predictive value will accordingly be limited. If we are all suffering from schizophrenia, then there is nothing specific, prognostically speaking, about being schizophrenic. In certain American studies, as we have seen, a wide spectrum of psychological disorders is encompassed under the diagnostic category of 'schizophrenia' with the result that any specific prognostic factor will be lost, diluted by the contaminating presence, methodologically speaking, of borderline or 'pseudo-schizophrenic' persons. If by 'diabetic' we mean those individuals whose blood sugar level cannot be maintained within normal limits without recourse to insulin injections, then 'diabetes' so diagnosed will manifest one sort of course and one sort of outcome. If, however, we broaden the diagnostic category to include those individuals who do not require insulin but need anti-diabetic drugs to maintain a normal blood sugar, then the course and outcome will be different. The diagnostic category can be broadened further by the inclusion of individuals who require neither drugs nor insulin but who must diet and avoid sugar and broadened again by the inclusion of individuals who show no signs or symptoms of illness but whose blood sugar levels are at the upper limit of normal. Each expansion of the diagnostic category alters the sorts of predictions that can be based upon it. So it is with the diagnostic category known as schizophrenia and it is for these reasons that prognostic predictions concerning schizophrenia must be treated with caution. The most that can be said is that a good prognosis is more likely in an illness that is of acute rather than insidious onset, that occurs in an otherwise stable and mature personality of average or above average intelligence, that shows signs of having been 'triggered' by some obvious precipitating factor(s) of a psychological nature (e.g., sudden bereavement) or physical nature (e.g., viral infection), and that affects an individual whose family history shows a tendency to develop schizophrenia no greater than that shown by the general population. In contrast a slowly developing illness, in a somewhat unstable person of limited intelligence, from a family particularly prone to such illnesses, which occurs in the absence of and obvious precipitating factor has a more grave prognosis (*Table 2*).

It has to be admitted, however, that almost all such and similar prognostic factors, favourable and unfavourable, remain controversial. Two studies illustrate this rather neatly. Hoenig and Hamilton (1966) studied sixty-two schizophrenic patients, most of whom had been treated with drugs and had spent some time, usually short, in hospital. At the end of a

Table 2 *Prognostic factors in schizophrenia*

	good	bad
pre-morbid:	no family history of schizophrenia	family history of schizophrenia
	stable personality	withdrawn, solitary, eccentric personality
	warm personal relationships	poor work record
	stable home relationships	poverty of relationships
		stormy domestic situation
features of illness:	identifiable precipitating factor or 'life event'	no obvious triggering factor or 'life event'
	acute onset	insidious onset
	few first-rank symptoms	many first-rank symptoms
	Disturbance of mood, i.e., evidence of depression or (rarely) elation	no mood disturbance blunting of emotional responses
	initiative, interest, and motivation retained	initiative, motivation, and interest impaired
	prompt treatment	treatment delayed

four-year follow-up period 27·5 per cent were generally symptom-free, a further 27·5 per cent were improved, and 16·5 per cent were not improved at all; 9·7 per cent had died and in the remaining 19 per cent no follow-up information could be obtained. During the four years, the majority of patients showed an improvement in social adjustment and at the time of follow-up almost one-third had been working for at least three years, while less than a third had been unemployed for the entire period.

As against this picture, Simon and his co-workers (1965) carried out a nine-year follow-up and reported an improvement rate of only 20 per cent. Fifty per cent of their sample were reportedly worse and the remaining 30 per cent were unchanged. They concluded that 'schizophrenia remains extremely resistant to treatment'.

So if the diagnosis of schizophrenia is somewhat confusing in terms of what it says of the outcome, does it have any predictive value concerning the course of the illness? Here a new problem arises. What are the criteria of outcome of a chronic illness such as schizophrenia? The rate of discharge from hospital, a commonly used criterion, is a measure vulnerable to social and administrative variables. A schizophrenic patient may be discharged into the community 'improved' or 'cured', but such terms become meaningless if, within several weeks, he is unable to support himself, maintain any relationships, is again deluded, and has swopped his long-stay ward for a bed in a reception centre. In a review of physical treatment methods in schizophrenia, Robert Cawley (1967) declares:

'... the adequate description of outcome of illness in patients suffering from schizophrenia is a formidable task if we take into account both the variability of the illness and the multiple criteria of full or partial recovery. It is in this kind of situation that we have to try to assess the impact of our treatment procedures.'   (Cawley 1967: 103)

The same reservations must be expressed then concerning the evaluation of the efficacy of treatment as were expressed about measuring prognosis. Define a cohort of 'schizophrenics' so that it includes on the one hand persons complaining of a voice saying 'thud', and little else, and, on the other hand, persons who believe their guts are rotting, their neighbours are Japanese spies poisoning the water, and their thoughts are being nationally broadcast via the Crystal Palace transmitter, and the response to treatment of such a group will necessarily be somewhat varied (and inconclusive). In so far as careful and well-defined studies have been performed, it seems clear that a certain group of drugs, developed during the 1950s, the phenothiazines, do exert an ameliorating effect on the psychotic symptoms of schizophrenia. The most convincing evidence (Grinspoon and Greenblatt 1961; Valliant, Semrad, and Ewalt 1964) suggests that for short-term treatment, particularly for acute episodes of illness, the phenothiazines are of prime importance whereas the longer the illness, the more important do social and environmental factors become in determining the degree of symptom relief and social adjustment. Recent studies (Leff and Wing 1971; Hirsch *et al.* 1973) have clearly established the value of phenothiazines as against the use of a placebo (i.e., an inert, non-active substance) in the management of more chronic schizophrenic illnesses and particularly in the maintenance of recovered schizophrenics in the community. These studies have shown that phenothiazine drugs, given by mouth or by injection, help to prevent further episodes of schizophrenia, and such drugs appear to be most useful for the group of patients who, when exposed to highly stimulating conditions, tend to relapse.

Such drug treatments appear to be specific. Schizophrenic symptoms do not improve with anti-depressant treatment (Fink *et al.* 1955; Overall *et al.* 1964) and indeed there is some evidence that they may actually get worse (Pollack *et al.* 1965). Some depressed patients do respond to phenothiazines (Paykel *et al.* 1968), but this is probably as a result of a non-specific sedative effect. Lithium, a substance that improves and prevents manic illness, does not have any effect on schizophrenic symptoms (Johnson *et al.* 1971) and ordinary so-called 'minor' tranquillizers such as diazepam ('Valium') and chlordiazepoxide ('Librium'), whilst effective tranquillizers in their own right, do not appear to affect the course of schizophrenic illnesses.

A diagnosis of schizophrenia then does appear to have some prognostic and therapeutic implications, even if currently they are somewhat crude. There are specific drugs to which the conditions respond, and specific sorts of events that 'trigger' the illness at the outset or aggravate or improve it once it has developed (see next chapter). Thus there would appear to be a somewhat more secure and respectable basis to the typological model of diagnosis (so-called because it describes the existence of discrete illness 'types' or disease) in the case of schizophrenia than is popularly assumed.

Yet there are problems with such a typological approach. Because it is a model that *implies* a cause, despite the fact that there is none immediately obvious, its use tends to stimulate those research programmes, therapeutic trials, and clinical attitudes that all *presume* the existence of a *cause* or *causes* and tends to suppress those approaches that may see schizophrenia as, for example, an exaggeration of normal experiences and responses (the 'dimensional' view). The typological model describes phenomena in such a way that one either has them or one does not. One either is hallucinated or one is not. Hempel (1967) points out that sciences early in their history tend to characterize variables *dichotomously*, i.e., as being either present or absent. As the science in question develops, it becomes possible to evaluate variables more precisely and this usually results in their being dimensionally rather than typologically defined. John Strauss (1973) believes that such a transition may be occurring in psychiatry at the present time. He points out that concepts previously considered dichotomous (either present or absent) are beginning to be seen as points on a continuum: e.g., hallucinations being represented at one end of a continuum with normal perceptions at the other end, psychotic depression on the same continuum as neurotic depression and also with 'normal' depression, and even poor outcome–good outcome (Strauss 1969; Kendell 1968; Astrup and Noreik 1966; Brown *et al.* 1965) sharing opposite ends of the same continuum.

A second problem, inherent in the 'typological' approach, is that it presupposes that schizophrenia can be clearly distinguished from other psychiatric disorders even though it may, in practice, share certain common characteristics with some of them. Current diagnostic practice, reflecting the influence of Kraepelin, postulates the existence of two major functional psychoses – schizophrenia and manic-depressive psychosis – which are regarded as separate and discrete.

Manic-depressive disorders constitute a large group of conditions which are characterized by disturbances of affect (i.e., feelings and emotions) but in which emotional and cognitive deterioration do not occur. The terms 'manic' and 'depressive' refer to the extremes of pathological affect which occur and to the often repetitious, alternating or cyclical attacks. Depression and elation are not the only symptoms of affective illnesses. Associated with depression are symptoms such as insomnia, anorexia, feelings of guilt and self-reproach and suicidal thoughts. Associated with elation may be hyper-activity, flight of ideas and marked pressure of thoughts. In serious manic-depressive illnesses, patients often manifest delusions and hallucinations, the content of which can be understood as arising out of the primary disturbance of the mood.

In practice, there is no clear demarcation between the two conditions of manic-depressive psychosis and schizophrenia. Various attempts have been made to account for those patients who exhibit symptoms common to both disorders, but to date the net effect has been the emergence of a confusing terminology which threatens further developments and hampers the achievement of consistent research results.

A more intriguing challenge to the typological approach is contained in the findings of a study by Carol Sheldrick and her colleagues at the Institute of Psychiatry and the World Health Organization's Division of Mental Health in Geneva (Sheldrick *et al.* 1977). Analysing follow-up data from the International Pilot Study of Schizophrenia they found that a proportion of patients originally diagnosed as suffering from schizophrenia subsequently developed clear-cut manic-depressive illnesses *after* a period of remission from the original psychotic episode. Such evidence of a change from one supposedly discrete psychotic illness to another carries significance for the disease entity theory and indeed for the classification of the functional psychoses as a whole. As these workers point out, the establishment of such a sequence argues against an absolute separation of the two major groupings, indicating as it does the possibility of a 'metamorphosis' of one disorder into another. It suggests that some at least of the categories within the syndromes of schizophrenia and affective psychosis are not mutually exclusive, thereby reviving the issue of the 'unitary psychosis' raised by Zeller (1837) and Griesinger (1845) and more recently discussed by Rennert (1965).

Another serious limitation in the 'typological' approach is that, with its sharp delineation of 'types' of illnesses, there is a tendency for clinicians to 'fit' individual patients into one or other of these types and to 'shape' the symptoms so as to match one with the other. Typological models of diagnosis are among the most simple methods of classification and, as a result, may lend themselves especially to use by those psychiatrists (the majority in Britain) who deal with large numbers of patients. Working in large hospitals with a patient-load that makes it difficult to get to know each patient to any significant extent, many psychiatrists focus more on the disease type than on the particular peculiarities of the individual's state (some may prefer to work this way). When individual differences are scrutinized with some care, it can turn out to be a more troublesome task to assign all but the most 'typical' patients to the prescribed categories. Symptom-clusters change with time (the catatonic variant of schizophrenia is seen relatively infrequently today; it figures prominently in the psychiatric textbooks at the turn of the century, however), a fact indirectly referred to by Ronald Laing in a passage in *The Divided Self*:

'I must confess to a certain personal difficulty I have in being a psychiatrist, which lies behind a great deal of this book. This is that except in the case of chronic schizophrenics I have great difficulty in actually discovering the "signs and symptoms" of psychosis in persons I am myself interviewing. I used to think that I was not clever enough to get at hallucinations and delusions and so on. If I compared my experience with psychotics with the accounts given of psychosis in the standard textbooks, I found that the authors were not giving a description of the way these people behaved with me.' (Laing 1965: 27–8)

Laing does not analyse his personal, though perhaps widely shared, experience further. (Strauss quotes as a clinical axiom, 'The better a clinician knows a patient, the harder it is to make a diagnosis.') Instead, he opts for one of the several possible explanations and attributes it to the artificial and detached manner in which the early descriptive psychopathologists assessed their patients and elicited psychiatric data; i.e., they 'examined' the patients in an artificial fashion and ended up with artificial symptoms. He does, however, refer, albeit obliquely, to an alternative possibility when he exempts 'chronic schizophrenics' from his reservations. The chronic schizophrenic patients seen by Laing resembled those seen by Kraepelin and his contemporaries whereas Laing's acutely ill patients did not match the textbook description. This may well be due to the fact that, as a consequence of current psychiatric approaches, both pharmacotherapeutic and psychotherapeutic, and of the more highly developed psychiatric and social services, people suffering from psychotic illnesses are identified and treated earlier than in the past and their conditions remit or stabilize without progressing to the more chronic and classic form. The older mental hospitals, such as the one in which Laing himself worked, all have their chronic patient populations, derived in the main from pre-treatment days, containing patients closely resembling those painstakingly documented by Kraepelin, Bleuler, and others, and described in the 'standard textbooks'. The newer patients, it may be argued, are rarely permitted to progress to the 'textbook' case.

The busy psychiatrist, faced with a patient exhibiting typical 'first-rank' symptoms, should have no problem. It is when he is presented with someone who shows a bewildering collection of symptoms and signs which change and change again, that he is tempted to allocate almost randomly by way of the most obvious symptom to one or other diagnostic category or fall back on using a multi-diagnostic label. However, the typological model tempts him to do more. Based as it is so clearly on a medical model of illness, this approach strongly reinforces the tendency to see simple explanations for the cause of the disorder in question. The pneumococcus 'causes' pneumonia, the treponema pallidum causes syphilis, nicotinamide deficiency results in pellagra, excess thyroxine leads to thyrotoxicosis – why not some equally straight-forward cause for schizophrenia? (That the question of *cause* is not as simple as this in general medicine has been discussed in Chapter 1, but the wrong lesson tends nonetheless to be applied in psychiatry.) Jules Henry (1973) recalls how, when he was studying in a psychiatric hospital, he became inter-ested in a patient and asked her doctor what was her diagnosis. 'Piss-poor protoplasm' was the elegant, scientific formulation he received. It is this simplistic, reductive, degrading approach, under-pinned by a naive conceptualiz-ation of what the disease model as applied to mental dis-orders actually means which, when employed by some psychiatrists, understandably enrages the critics of psychiatry and results in the following confident rejection of the entire approach:

'There's no condition called schizophrenia: it's a term of personal and social invalidation. This relates to how the word was coined. Originally, the word was "dementia praecox", an early invention applied to people whose behaviour seemed to show signs of progressive mental and physical deterioration. They then found that this deterior-ation doesn't necessarily occur. You see, there's no such thing as schizophrenia really. It's a hodge-podge term referring to certain symptoms which doctors can supposedly distinguish in other people during the course of an inter-view.'   (Berke 1974: 234)

Allowing for the historical inaccuracy (Kraepelin, who coined the term 'dementia praecox', accepted *from the beginning* that progressive deterioration did not necessarily occur), Joseph Berke puts the case against the existence of schizophrenia with characteristic simplicity. His colleague, Morton Schatzman, expresses a similar view of mental illness when he says:

> 'No-one has proven it to exist as a thing nor has anyone described its attributes with scientific precision and reliability.'   (Schatzman 1974: 208)

Yet herein is the central contradiction in the anti-psychiatry argument. The concept of mental illness, and of schizophrenia, it is argued, is hypothetical and as yet unproven. But when attempts are made to classify and organize these unusual types of behaviour and experience, which have been recognized long before Kraepelin's conceptualization, which have been and are described in every culture and throughout every civilization, when searches are made for relevant bio-chemical, physiological, social, and interpersonal factors, and when attempts are made to standardize approaches so that what mental illness and schizophrenia mean does *not* depend on this cultural view or that political view but on as objective a set of criteria as can be established, the anti-psychiatrists regard the entire enterprise as an elaborate and pseudo-scientific exercise in collective brainwashing.

> 'Official psychiatry trains the young psychiatrist not to see what is in front of his face when it teaches him to class patients' attempts to protest against their situations as signs and symptoms of illness. He learns to label patients as "ill" with "personality disorders" if they make problems for *others* by defying the authority of the hospital or society.'
> (Schatzman 1974: 209)

Here we see added to the familiar accusation that psychiatrists reduce the experiences of their patients to the level of irrational and mechanical symptoms a new criticism that psychiatrists see what the textbooks describe but not what their patients actually show. The psychiatrist appears hoist by his own petard; seeing what is not there, he and not his patient is hallucinated; believing what is demonstrably false, he and not the patient is deluded. (And, presumably because he is encouraged by the status and pay enjoyed by the contemporary NHS psychiatrist, he and not the patient is going to progressively deteriorate!)

Such discussions can appear somewhat academic given the enormous pressure on psychiatrists, whether they like it or not, to intervene in situations and diagnose this or that person as suffering from a mental illness. An alternative approach to understanding why the process of diagnosis, despite its obvious shortcomings given the present scientific status of psychiatry, may be often not merely desirable but necessary, is to consider its implementation in actual clinical practice. I have chosen three cases, each of which has already been discussed in public and each of which has been described from a different vantage point.

The first is an autobiographical account of how 'an affluent highly regarded Hollywood scriptwriter' named John Balt, one January day in 1963 savagely stabbed his wife to death in a frenzied assault. Arrested 'naked as the day he was born and covered with blood from the top of his head to his toes', he was asked why he had done it and replied, 'She had my balls. I had to get my prick back'. *By Reason of Insanity* (Balt 1972) describes how several years into his marriage, Balt began to lose interest in his work, stopped writing, and became uncontrollably and excessively anxious. He began to have psychoanalytic treatment from a doctor who, it turned out later, was quite inadequately qualified. During the course of his 'analysis', Balt became increasingly disturbed. He began to develop doubts about his writing abilities, complained of agonizing pains in his groin, and told his psychiatrist that he was hallucinating. (The psychiatrist insisted that Balt was not experiencing 'hallucinations' but 'sensations', although the distinction, which seems to have been an important one to the psychiatrist, was never adequately explained to Balt.) His marriage, which had begun promisingly and had developed into a satisfying and contented one, began to show signs of strain. His wife suffered a depressive mood swing following the birth of their third child, and began to see a psychologist. Balt disliked the idea, resenting his wife's dependence on someone other than himself, but kept his reservations to himself. Following the death of his father, his psychiatric state worsened. He was now unable to cope with his work, made several ineffectual attempts to change his job, experienced severe panic attacks, and on a number of occasions showed signs of violence. On his thirty-fifth birthday, he became acutely psychotic and was actively hallucinated, disorientated, and suicidal. Following this episode, which provoked one psychiatrist to quit the case and another to engage in ineffectual 'explanations' concerning the 'meaning' of what was happening, his wife became increasingly frightened by the transformation of her husband's mental state. Little professional help, of a practical nature, was forthcoming, however, and on the night of the murder, Balt, racked with stabbing sensations in his groin, accused his wife of castrating him and suddenly, savagely stabbed her to death.

He was arrested and charged with a capital crime. While in custody, he was flamboyantly psychotic. He held earnest and animated conversations with his dead wife, with the Deity, with President Kennedy. He heard voices talking engaged in running commentaries about him and accusing him of being a homosexual. He was convinced that the United States Navy would shell the prison, destroy it, and enable him to escape, that his brain cells were dissolving, and that his doctors were engaged in experimental dissections of his brain and mutilations of his body. On several occasions he tried to kill himself and he berated those who prevented him, calling them his 'executors' and 'torturers'. Throughout all this, and more, he insisted that he was perfectly sane.

He was initially treated with phenothiazines and then intensive psychotherapy was begun. Slowly, he began to recover. His delusions weakened and his hallucinations ceased. He was adjudged fit to plead and, on the testimony of his prison psychiatrists, he was eventually found not guilty by reason of insanity of the murder of his wife.

Several features are worthy of note in Balt's account of this frightful event. First, there is the slow insidious slide into illness. It begins innocuously enough – some loss of confidence, anxiety, lack of drive, and the development of a number of odd physical sensations. Then a number of events occur. His wife becomes depressed (as a consequence of her pregnancy? Of his illness? Of both?) and she seeks help. He becomes even more convinced of his weakness and of the way in which his wife advertised it by seeking help outside the marriage. The death of his father stirs memories in Balt of his parental marriage, of his father's passive and ineffectual posture in the face of his mother's assertive demands. He begins to suspect that it is his wife who is responsible for his condition; it is she who has drained him of his masculinity and rendered him impotent, unable to write, unable to think, unable to survive. As the 'sensations' in his groin worsen so an 'explanation' of them as the physical manifestations of his wife's sinister intentions towards him evolves and becomes elaborated into a systematized delusion, and the ghastly murder sets the seal on a full-blown psychotic state.

If the *content* of Balt's delusions and hallucinations can be understood, the *form* (i.e., the fact that his ideas of inferiority, inadequacy, impotence were expressed through elaborate delusions and hallucinations) proves more difficult to explain. It is the *form* his state took that led his doctors to diagnose him as suffering from schizophrenia and this in turn led the court to demand of these same doctors information concerning the prognosis in such a condition, the possibility of relapse, the prospects for treatment. It is difficult to argue that the diagnosis in this case reduced or demeaned the status of Balt. His psychiatrists still struggled to understand

and to provide him with an understanding of what had happened (not an easy thing to do – for long periods in prison, Balt believed his wife to be alive and well and waiting for him outside). But they also *diagnosed*, thereby drawing on their experience of other patients who, even if they did not act out their delusions in such a grim fashion, nonetheless showed a similar symptomatology to Balt.

The court, confronted by this man who killed the wife he had cherished for six years because on the night in question and for some time before he believed she had castrated him, asked his doctors a number of questions. Did he genuinely believe that he had been castrated? (After all, many men *feel as if* their wives are castrating them but don't stab them to death.) Would he become deluded again? What was the likely course in such a condition? Would he respond to treatment? Were there effective treatments for this condition? What could possibly have caused it?

Such questions relate to cause, course, outcome, and response to treatment. It is not easy to see how any one of them could begin to be answered without psychiatrists gathering together cases in which certain symptomatology is shared and observing over periods of time the course and the outcome in such cases. In the court, Balt's psychiatrist told the judge of the latest evidence concerning the outcome in schizophrenia. Without some operational definition, it is difficult to see how any useful information on such a factor could be provided. It is precisely because to date there has been a relative failure among psychiatrists to agree upon such definitions that information concerning the basic questions relating to psychotic states has been so lacking.

Diagnostic categories are commonly depicted as labelling devices that reduce and degrade the diagnosed. Compulsory hospitalization (see Chapter 8) is likewise portrayed as a flagrant violation of the rights of the individual. It is worth noting that Balt has publicly acknowledged that he owes his recovery and his liberty to those psychiatrists who were able and willing to formulate a diagnosis, interpret the form and content of his psychopathology, organize treatment, and provide, to the satisfaction of the court, an estimate of the possible response of his psychotic state to their therapeutic efforts.

The second case is that of Mary Barnes, one of the most publicized 'schizophrenic' patients of the past decade. In the account of her illness provided by herself and Dr Joseph Berke (Barnes and Berke 1971), it is described how she first came to Kingsley Hall, the therapeutic centre in the East End of London run by Ronald Laing, after she had already experienced several episodes of mental illness and been the recipient of more orthodox treatment in a large mental hospital. At Kingsley Hall, she was allowed to regress. She smeared faeces on the walls, refused to eat, had to be fed from a baby's bottle, would not wash, and exploded into aggressive and childlike behaviour from time to time. Gradually, her therapists, with remarkable forbearance and tolerance, managed to steer her through her psychotic condition and, by the end of the story, some five years after her first contact with Kingsley Hall, we are left with a portrait of a woman who appears to have developed some understanding of her own conflicts and difficulties.

Her co-author, Joseph Berke, is the same man who declared vehemently that 'there is no such thing as schizophrenia', thereby adding his voice to those who have argued that mental illness is the fabrication of deluded psychiatrists rather than the suffering of deluded patients. Yet nowhere in Mary Barnes's account of her self-described 'madness', nor in Berke's comments on it, is there any suggestion that her odd, bizarre, 'psychotic' behaviour is anything other than 'sick'. Indeed, it is her very 'madness' which leads her to state elsewhere:

> 'I was one of those people who just cannot be helped through spasmodic help, whilst living in an ordinary situation. I just had to be in a special place, a house for madness.' (Barnes 1970: 176)

Now 'madness' is her word and not that of some reductive, dehumanizing, detached doctor. It is her 'madness' that apparently entitles her to obtain what she wants – the freedom to smear faeces, shriek, curse, bite, beg, regress, become the enwombed foetus, suspended in an amniotic bag of care, warmth, succour, and affection, mothered, bathed, fed, clothed, and supported. It is her *sickness* that justified such demands, lifting them from the realm of a silly, selfish, importunate forty-five year old baby to that of a sick, confused, and suffering, psychotically ill woman. What has led her to such a state? If her account is to be believed, some remarkably common and mundane experiences.

Her family were 'abnormally' nice in that friends, relatives, and neighbours thought that they all lived happily together. they did not – 'deep down we were torn with hatred and strife' (very deep, it would seem, for little in the way of evidence is provided to support such an apocalyptic view). Her younger brother's birth led her to experience feelings of jealousy she would never acknowledge. Mother was often ill, would rest in bed while the children inwardly 'longed' for her 'weakness'. (Mary's brother, Peter, was to have a nervous breakdown in his teens and Mary, of course, did achieve ill status and become the cared for rather than the caring.) Although her story provides elaborate details of how difficult Mary was as a child, her resentments, her envies, her isolations, her rejections, it is free of the dark, savage traumas of popular psychology (there is nothing to match, for example, the incest 'causing' the schizophrenic breakdown of Scott Fitzgerald's Nicole, no childhood horror to compare with the witnessing of murder by Hitchcock's Marnie).

The experiences which she believes led to her 'madness' are so common (and the Laingian view of family life insists that such experiences are the daily stuff of close family relationships) that they raise the question, 'Why, then, did such common happenings do this to Mary Barnes?' To answer such a question, there are many things one needs to know. One would, for example, need to know how to

describe what has happened to Mary Barnes in language just
a little more distinctive and precise than 'sickness', 'madness',
'insanity', more precise even than Berke's 'rational intentionality' and 'psychotic intentionality', terms out of
which he makes a philosophical and phenomenological meal
when all they describe are Mary's 'consciously considered
moves and counter-moves' and her 'unconsciously considered
moves and counter-moves'. (In Balt's case, the court asked
whether he was responsible, i.e., in command of the 'moves
and counter-moves' which resulted in his wife's death, and
the fact that it concluded that he was not, rested on the
diagnosis of a symptom cluster, schizophrenia, in which so-
called 'unconscious moves and counter-moves' can occur with
often tragic results.) Berke, having thrown away the language,
albeit imperfect, of descriptive psychopathology has to create
another of his own, one which turns out to be if anything
less precise, less attractive, and less clear.

No one reading Mary Barnes's account would deny her
illness. Her therapists (and the patient) make certain striking
claims for the efficacy of a time-consuming, demanding,
indeed exhausting, therapeutic approach. They even use the
word 'healing'. We are told that Mary is better for her
journey which immediately raises the question of whether
such an approach was uniquely appropriate for her or
whether it would suit others *like* her. If it would, how similar
to her would they need to be? How would one describe
their experiences? If they showed a different dramatic
response to such an approach, would we deduce that their
'madness' was different or that the therapy only suited some
and not all who suffered as Mary suffered? In short, how can
we avoid formulating diagnoses if we wish to avail ourselves
of effective therapies in the battle against mental suffering?
How can we avoid formulating diagnoses if therapies are to
be judged effective or ineffective?

The third case illustrates how some psychiatrists avoid
making diagnoses altogether. It is less well known in this
country than that of Mary Barnes, being the account of the

illness of the son of the American journalist James Wechsler (The father wrote the account of his son's deterioration. and death in 1972.) Michael Wechsler died at the age of twenty-six years after an agonizing, episodic illness which lasted ten years. He was never subjected to the 'humiliation' of a diagnosis and his parents were never to have any idea of what was wrong with him, although he saw in all eight different doctors including private practitioners and State hospital physicians, analysts and organicists, male and female psychiatrists. When Michael first became depressed, suicidal, and obsessional, Dr First (Wechsler rather effectively preserves the anonymity of the doctors by referring to them in the order in which they 'treated' his son) refused to have anything to do with the parents 'on principle', although such a principle did not extend to the sending of a hefty monthly bill for Michael's 'therapy'. The next two doctors followed this approach and refrained from formulating any explanatory model, let alone a label, that might brighten the darkness. Dr Fourth did tentatively suggest 'depersonalization', but since he refrained from defining this perplexing term further (and Mr Wechsler's forays in the dictionaries served only to confuse since the definitions found there bore little resemblance to his son's state), all four Wechslers (Michael had a younger sister) were no better informed than before. His promising academic career now in ruins as a result of his recurrent attacks of profound despair and crippling obsessionality, Michael took some LSD and became alarmingly psychotic. Two more psychiatrists became involved; from one came the inevitable condemnation and scapegoating of the parents as the 'source' of all the trouble and from the other emerged the dreaded word 'schizophrenia' for no apparent reason other than that Michael was now dangerously suicidal! Dr Seventh, an 'inspirational', 'warm', 'appealing' man who believed in a family approach and symptom-relieving drugs, did appear to be making progress, but his arrival came after Michael and his parents had become somewhat disillusioned with psychiatry, orthodox and unorthodox, and his efforts were accordingly frustrated. Finally, in a mood of profound pessimism and nihilism, Michael killed himself, leaving his family guilt-ridden and desolate and his various therapists reaching for their professional defences and knowledgeable explanations.

Wechsler's moving account of his son's voyage through despair is all the more remarkable for its refusal to counter-scapegoat the doctors. It describes 'absurd, abysmal failures of communication' but bravely accepts that it takes two sides to communicate and that the Wechslers were not without fault in this regard. There are 'misgivings' about how everyone concerned handled Michael's oscillation in mood and there is a sad, despairing declaration that his parents 'are no wiser now than before about whether Michael's affliction, in the present state of medical knowledge, was hopeless or whether he was ultimately a victim of a fatal blindness on the part of parents and therapists alike'. In spite of these efforts to be non-judgemental, what emerges from this book is a picture of professional incompetence and an ignorance masquerading as omnipotence, a picture of eight different psychiatrists, not one of whom appeared to have the slightest idea of how to formulate Michael's chaotic symtomaptology into some order and sense, of how to communicate some possible understanding of his experiences in a relatively simple, informative way, of how to draw together the various strands – phenomenological, psychological, interpersonal, social, biological, physiological – which were waving in the wake of the unfortunate man's clear-cut mood swings. A diagnosis, in a case such as this, in itself means nothing, but without such a formulation it is difficult to believe that any therapist can do much for someone as tortured and self-destructive as the Michael Wechslers of this world unless he is in possession of a coherent and communicable idea of what constitutes the important operative factors and the probable order of their importance.

It might seem that this defence of the value of a diagnosis labours the obvious. Yet the attack on the diagnostic process in psychiatry is pressed home with vigour. In so far as it draws attention to the abuses which can follow an excessive zeal in categorizing illness-behaviour, such as the 'turning-off' of certain psychiatrists once they have elicited 'first-rank' symptoms and the dismissal of the *content* of what patients say because the *form* is judged to be abnormal, such criticisms have not been totally destructive. In so far as they have directed much-needed attention to the often arid, paternalistic, impersonal, and authoritarian qualities of some psychiatrists, the critics have performed and are performing a valuable service.

When Berke declares 'Insanity' to be 'a social and cultural fact', argues that what is 'normal' in one society may be deemed 'mad' in another, and concludes that one might as well not bother too much about diagnosis, he may well believe himself to be remarkably advanced and radical and on the side of the angels. In fact, he finds himself alongside such notable liberals as those Russian psychiatrists at the Serbsky Institute in Moscow (Working Group on Internment 1971) who, declaring Grigorenko mentally ill on the basis of 'reformist' ideas and 'an uncritical attitude to his own utterances and acts', and classifying the Red Square protester, Natalia Gorbanevskaya, 'schizophrenic' on the basis of 'no clear symptoms' and 'slowly increasing mental changes', showed that they too believe that to pay scrupulous attention to what constitutes accepted diagnostic criteria in mental illness in general, and schizophrenia in particular, is an academic exercise!

What protects the dissident, the deviant, and the outsider from being labelled 'mentally ill' is not the psychiatrist who does not believe in psychiatric classifications (for he is easily discredited when confronted by a John Balt or a Mary Barnes) but rather the psychiatrist who acknowledges that people can suffer from serious mental disturbances, that the symptoms of these can be grouped and defined in such a way as to produce a reasonable degree of agreement as to their validity and reliability, and that those people who do not show such symptoms cannot be classified as mentally ill, whatever society may say or do. It is no accident that in those countries where diagnostic criteria are loosest (the Soviet Union and the United States) most of the serious cases of psychiatric abuse have been reported.

Some of the crucial symptoms in schizophrenia appear to be the result of a breakdown in the mental processes by which we differentiate our own inner selves from the external world. There is a 'permeability' of the barrier between the individual and his environment (Schneider 1957), the so-called 'loss of ego boundaries'. The clear-cut distinctions between speaking, thinking, perceiving, readily apparent to the normal person, are blurred in schizophrenia so that, for example, thoughts originating within the patient's head are experienced as alien and outside his control. Many of the patient's most private phantasies, feelings, thoughts, and acts appear to him to be known to, shared with, or caused by, others. The disturbances of thought processes results in an idiosyncratic use of words, an impairment of logical organization, and a fragmentation in the orderly association of ideas. The environment may appear a hostile and a persecuting one or one that is changed in some strange fashion so that everyday objects, situations, and actions become charged with special, often sinister meanings for the affected individual.

Whether there is one condition, called schizophrenia, or several which are currently mixed up together under a common classificatory label is still an open question. So too is the controversial problem of the cause. There has been no lack of postulated causal agents for schizophrenia. As one might expect, in a field like psychiatry, they are plentiful and imaginative and reflect every model and ideology. In the last resort, however, the validity of the claims on behalf of a casual role for disordered family relationships or abnormal brain functioning or faulty genes or the other aetiological factors discussed in the following chapter can only be tested if there is some prior agreement as to what clinically constitutes the disorder in the first place.

References

ANDERSON, E.W. and TRETHOWAN, W.H. (1967)
Psychiatry (2nd edition). London: Baillière, Tindall
& Cassell.

ASTRUP, C. and NOREIK, K. (1966) *Functional Psychoses:
Diagnostic and Prognostic Models.* Springfield, Illinois:
Charles C. Thomas.

BALT, J. (1972) *By Reason of Insanity.* London: Panther.

BARNES, M. (1970) Flection/Reflection. *The Radical
Therapist* **1** (4).

BARNES, M. and BERKE, J. (1971) *Mary Barnes: Two
Accounts of a Journey through Madness.* London: MacGibbon
& Kee.

BECK, A.T., WARD, C.H., MENDELSON, M., MOCK, J.E.,
and ERBAUGH, J.K. (1962) Reliability of Psychiatric
Diagnoses: II. A Study of Consistency of Clinical
Judgement Ratings. *American Journal of Psychiatry* **119**:
351–7.

BELK, W.P. and SUNDERMAN, F.W. (1947) A Survey of
the Accuracy of Chemical Analyses in Clinical Labs.
American Journal of Clinical Pathology **19**: 853–61.

BERKE, J. (1974) Antipsychiatry, An Interview.
In Radical Therapist/Rough Times Collective
(ed.), *The Radical Therapist.* Harmondsworth:
Penguin.

BLEULER, E. (1911) *Dementia Praecox or the Group of
Schizophrenias* (trans. 1951 by J. Zinkin). London:
Allen & Unwin.

BROWN, G.W., BONE, M., DALISON, B., and
WING, J.K. (1965) *Schizophrenia and Social Care.*
London: Oxford University Press.

BUTTERWORTH, J.S. and REPPERT, E.H. (1960)
Auscultatory Acumen in the General Medical Population.
Journal of the American Medical Association **174**: 32–4.

CAWLEY, R.H. (1967) The Present Status of Physical
Methods of Treatment of Schizophrenia. In A. Coppen

and A. Walk (eds.), *Recent Developments in Schizophrenia.* Ashford, Kent: Headley Bros.

COLBY, K.M. (1960) *An Introduction to Psychoanalytic Research.* New York: Basic Books.

COOPER, J.E. (1967) Diagnostic Change in a Longitudinal Study of Psychiatric Patients. *British Journal of Psychiatry* **113**: 129–42.

COOPER, J.E., KENDELL, R.E., GURLAND, B.J., SHARPE, L., COPELAND, J.R.M., and SIMON, R. (1972) *Psychiatric Diagnosis in New York and London.* London: Oxford University Press.

COPELAND, J.R.M., COOPER, J.W., KENDELL, R.E., and GOURLEY, A.J. (1971) Differences in Usage of Diagnostic Labels amongst Psychiatrists in the British Isles. *British Journal of Psychiatry* **118**: 629–40.

DERRYBERRY, M. (1938) Reliability of Medical Judgments on Malnutrition. *Public Health Report* **53**: 263–8.

ENGELSMANN, F., VINER, O., PICHOT, P., HIPPIUS, H., GILBERTI, F., ROSSI, L., and OVERALL, J.E. (1970) International Comparison of Diagnostic Patterns. *Transcultural Psychiatric Research* **7**: 130–37.

ETTER, L.E., DUNN, J.P., KAMMER, A.G., OSMOND, L.A., and REESE, L.C. (1960) Gastroduodenal X-ray Diagnosis: A Comparison of Radiographic Techniques and Interpretations. *Radiology* **74**: 766–70.

FALRET, J.P. (1853) *Clinical Lectures on Mental Medicine: General Symptomology.* Paris: Baillière.

FINK, M., POLLACK, M., KLEIN, D.F., BLUMBERG, A.G., BELMONT, I., KARP, E., KRAMER, J.C., and WILLNER, A. (1964) Comparative Studies of Chlorpromazine and Imipramine. In P. B. Bradley, F. Fleuge, and P. H. Hoeh (eds.), *Neuropsychopharmacology* Vol. 3. Amsterdam: Elsevier.

GRANVILLE-GROSSMAN, K. (1971) *Recent Advances in Clinical Psychiatry.* London: J & A. Churchill.

GRIESINGER, W. (1845) *Die Pathologie under Therapie der Psychisen Krankheiten*. Berlin.

GRINSPOON, L. and GREENBLATT, M. (1961) Pharmacology Combined with Other Treatment Methods. *Proceedings of Third World Congress of Psychiatry*. Montreal: University of Toronto Press.

GRUENBERG, E.M. (1969) How Can the New Diagnostic Manual Help? *International Journal of Psychiatry* 7: 368–74.

HEINROTH, J.C.H. (1818) *Lehrbuch der Storungen des Seelenleben's oder der Seelenstorungen und ihrer Behandlung* (2 vols.). Leipzig: F. C. W. Vogel.

HEMPEL, C.G. (1967) Introduction to Problems in Taxonomy. In J. Zubin (ed.), *Field Studies in the Mental Disorders*. New York: Grune & Stratton.

HENRY, J. (1973) *Pathways to Madness*. New York: Vintage Books.

HIRSCH, S.R., GAIND, R., ROHDE, P.D., STEVENS, B.C., and WING, J.K. (1973) Outpatient Maintenance of Chronic Schizophrenic Patients with Long-Acting Fluphenazine: Double-Blind Trial. *British Medical Journal* 1: 633–7.

HOENIG, J. and HAMILTON, M.W. (1966) The Schizophrenia Patient under New Management. *Comparative Psychiatry* 7: 81–91.

HORDERN, A., SANDIFER, M.G., GREEN, L.M., and TIMBURY, G.C. (1968) Psychiatric Diagnosis: British and North American Concordance on Stereotypes of Mental Illness. *British Journal of Psychiatry* 114: 935–44.

JOHNSON, G., GERSHON, S., BURDOCK, E., FLOYD, A., and HEKIMIAN, L. (1971) Lithium and Chlorpromazine in the Treatment of Acute Manic States. *British Journal of Psychiatry* 119: 267–75.

KATZ, M., COLE, J.O., and LOWRY, H.A. (1969) Studies of the Diagnostic Process: the Influence of Symptom Perception, Past Experience and Ethnic

Background on Diagnostic Decisions. *American Journal of Psychiatry* **125**: 937–47.

KENDELL, R.E. (1968) *The Classification of Depressive Illness*. Maudsley Monograph, No. 18. London: Oxford University Press.

—— (1972) Schizophrenia: the Remedy for Diagnostic Confusion. *British Journal of Hospital Medicine* **8**: 383–90.

KENDELL, R.E., PICHOT, P., and VON CRANACH, M. (1974) Diagnostic Criteria of English, French and German Psychiatrists. *Psychological Medicine* **4** (2): 187–95.

KRAMER, M. (1961) Some Problems for International Research Suggested by Observations on Differences in First Admission Rates to the Mental Hospitals of England and Wales and of the United States. *Proceedings of Third World Congress of Psychiatry* **3**: 153–60. Montreal: University of Toronto Press.

LAING, R.D. (1965) *The Divided Self*. Harmondsworth: Penguin.

—— (1967) *The Politics of Experience*. Harmondsworth: Penguin.

LEFF, J.R. and WING, J.K. (1971) Trial of Maintenance Therapy in Schizophrenia. *British Medical Journal* **3**: 599–604.

LEIFER, R. (1970) The Medical Model as Ideology. *International Journal of Psychiatry* **9**: 13–19.

LORR, M. and KLETT, C.J. (1967) *Inpatient Multidimensional Psychiatric Scale*. Palo Alto: Consulting Psychologists' Press.

MACRAE, D. (1970) A Behavioural Scientist. *New Society* 398: 783.

MANNONI, O. (1973) The Antipsychiatric Movement(s). *International Social Science Journal* **XXV** (4): 489–503.

MASSERMAN, J. and CARMICHAEL, H.T. (1938) Diagnosis and Prognosis in Psychiatry. *Journal of Mental Science* **84**: 893–946.

MAYER-GROSS, W., SLATER, E., and ROTH, M. (1969)

Clinical Psychiatry (3rd edition). London: Baillière, Tindall & Cassell.

MELLOR, C.S. (1970) First Rank Symptoms of Schizophrenia. *British Journal of Psychiatry* **117**: 15–23.

MENNINGER, K. (1963) *The Vital Balance*. New York: Viking Press.

—— (1969) *The Crime of Punishment*. New York: Viking Press.

MOREL, B.A. (1852) *Endes Cliniques I*.

NEUMANN, H. (1883) *Leitfadan der Psychiatrie*. Breslau.

OVERALL, J.E. and GORHAM, D.R. (1962) The Brief Psychiatric Rating Scale. *Psychological Reports* **18**: 799–812.

OVERALL, J.E., MEYER, F., KIMBELL, I., and SHELTON, J. (1964) Imipramine and Thoridazine in Depressed and Schizophrenic Patients. Are there Specific Antidepressant Drugs? *Journal of American Medical Association* **189**: 605–8.

PASSAMANICK, B., DINITZ, S., and LEFTON, M. (1959) Psychiatric Orientation and its Relation to Diagnosis and Treatment in a Mental Hospital. *American Journal of Psychiatry* **116**: 127–32.

PAYKEL, E.S., PRICE, J.S., GILLAN, R.U., PALMAI, G., and CHESSER, E.S. (1968) A Comparative Trial of Imipramine and Chlorpromazine in Depressed Patients. *British Journal of Psychiatry* **114**: 1281–7.

PICHOT, P., BAILLY, R., and OVERALL, J.E. (1967) Les Stéréotypes diagnostiques des psychoses chez les psychiatres français. Comparison avec les stéréotypes américains. In *Neuro-Psycho-Pharmacology. Proceedings of the Fifth International Congress of the Collegium Internationale Neuropsychopharmacologicum, Washington, 1966. International Congress Series*, No. 129: 16–26. Amsterdam: Excerpta Medica.

POLLACK, M., KLEIN, D.F., WILLNER, A., BLUMBERG, A.G., and FINK, M. (1965) Imipramine-Induced

Behavioural Disorganisation in Schizophrenic Patients: Physiologic and Psychologic Correlates. In J. Wortis (ed.), *Recent Advances in Biological Psychiatry*. New York: Plenum Press.

RENNERT, H. (1965) Die Universalgenese der endogenen Psychose. *Fortschritte der Neurologie, Psychiatrie und ihrer Grenzgeniete* **33**: 251–72.

SCHATZMAN, M. (1974) Madness and Morals. In Radical Therapist/Rough Times Collective (eds.), *The Radical Therapist*. Harmondsworth: Penguin.

SCHNEIDER, K. (1957) Primary and Secondary Symptoms in Schizophrenia. In S. Hirsch and M. Shepherd (eds.), *Themes and Variations in European Psychiatry*. Bristol: John Wright.

—— (1959) *Clinical Psychopathology* (5th revised edition, translated by M. W. Hamilton). New York: Grune & Stratton.

SHELDRICK, C., JABLENSKY, A. SARTORIUS, N. and SHEPHERD, M. (1977) Schizophrenia succeeded by affective illness: catamnestic study and statistical enquiry. *Psychological Medicine* **7**: 619–24.

SIMON, W., WIRT, A.L., WIRT, R.D., and HALLORAN, A.V. (1965) Long-Term Follow-Up Study of Schizophrenic Patients. *Archives of General Psychiatry* **12**: 510–15.

STRAUSS, J.S. (1969) Hallucinations and Delusions as Points on Continua Function. *Archives of General Psychiatry* **21**: 581–6.

—— (1973) Diagnostic Models and the Nature of Psychiatric Disorder. *Archives of General Psychiatry* **29**: 445–9.

SZASZ, T. (1971) *The Manufacture of Madness*. London: Routledge & Kegan Paul.

VALLIANT, G.E., SEMRAD, E.V., and EWALT, J.R. (1964) Current Therapeutic Results in Schizophrenia. *New England Journal of Medicine* **271**: 280–83.

WARD, C.H., BECK, A.T., MENDELSON, M., MOCK, J.E., and ERBURGH, J.K. (1962) The Psychiatric

Nomenclature: Reasons for Diagnostic Disagreement. *Archives of General Psychiatry* **7**: 198–205.

WECHSLER, J.A. (1972) *In a Darkness*. New York: Norton.

WILSON, M.B. and MEYER, E. (1962) Diagnostic Consistency in a Psychiatric Liaison Service. *American Journal of Psychiatry* **119**: 207–9.

WING, J.K., BIRLEY, J.L.T., COOPER, J.C., GRAHAM, R., and ISAACS, A.D. (1967) Reliability of a Procedure for Measuring and Classifying 'Present Psychiatric State'. *British Journal of Psychiatry* **113**: 499–515.

Working Group on the Internment of Dissenters in Mental Hospitals (1970) *The Internment of Soviet Dissenters in Mental Hospitals*. Cambridge, England: Cornelia Mee.

World Health Organisation (1967) *Manual of the International Statistical Classification of Diseases, Injuries and Causes of Death* (8th revision). Geneva.

—— (1973) *The International Pilot Study of Schizophrenia*. Geneva.

ZELLER, E. (1837) Bericht über die Wirksamkeit der Heilanstalt Winnenthal von ihrer Eröffnung den 1 Marz bis zum 28 Februar 1837. *Medizinisches Correspondenzblatt des wurtembergischen ärztlischen Vereins* **7**: 321.

ZELLER, E. (1844) Bericht über die Wirksamkeit der Heilanstalt Winnenthal. *Allgemeine Zeitschrift für Psychiatrie* **1**: 79.

5

Causal
factors in
schizophrenia

I N DESCRIBING the concept 'dementia praecox', Kraepelin believed he had defined a unitary metabolic disorder.
In widening the concept so that the newly named 'schizophrenias' implied the existence of a group of disorders,
sharing certain pathological characteristics but having
different causes, Bleuler provided an impetus for research
into schizophrenia which was not limited to the identification of organic factors. Each in his own way gave rise to a
school of thought whose approach to and understanding of
schizophrenic illnesses contrasted sharply with the other.
Kraepelin invited Ernst Rudin to Switzerland to help set up
an intensive research study of the possible genetic basis of
schizophrenia, whereas Bleuler's approach was enthusiastically taken up by analysts and psychotherapists, convinced
that the key to understanding the disorder would be found
in a thorough exploration of intrapsychic and interpersonal
conflicts.

Such a division persists to this day. Though 'we are all
eclectics now' might appear to be the battle-cry of the
average clinical psychiatrist as he notes the genetic, psychological, phenomenological, interpersonal, and social
factors which are claimed to be of relevance to an understanding of schizophrenia, the hoary counter-posing of
genetic and experimental evidence, as though they are
necessarily opposed and dichotomous, continues to dominate
the arena and contaminate much of the research. Repre-

sentatives of each viewpoint castigate the claims of the other while insisting on the merits of their own approach. Fortunately, not all researchers behave thus. Many who deliberately restrict their research to a consideration of some narrow aspect of the problem, such as the question of genetic transmission or the communication patterns in schizophrenic families, readily acknowledge that theirs is but one approach from one vantage point and that information from a number of quite different research avenues must eventually be forthcoming if a valuable working model of what causes and constitutes the schizophrenic condition is to be described.

In this chapter, a sample of the immense research effort made and being made into the question of what *causes* schizophrenia is discussed. It represents only a tiny proportion of what is an enormous area of scientific endeavour. It is still not clear whether schizophrenia constitutes a single disorder with a single cause manifesting itself in a variety of ways or whether it is an 'umbrella' term which includes several conditions with different causes and deceptively similar clinical manifestations. Researchers distinguish between acute episodes of the condition and the chronic disorder, between illnesses apparently 'triggered' by obvious stress and those arising 'out of the blue', between attacks in families peculiarly predisposed to the disorder and those affecting a solitary family member. Running right through every research strategy, every study, every review is the thorny question, discussed earlier, of what constitutes a diagnosis of schizophrenia. Some may still feel that in the individual case the question 'is this schizophrenia?' is an academic question. It is difficult to believe that anyone who has taken more than a cursory glance at the enormous research effort devoted to this condition would continue to hold such a view. If Laing claims that certain types of family communications can *cause* schizophrenia then this can only be tested by having some operational definition of what 'schizophrenia' is and then looking for the allegedly pathological patterns in families with schizophrenic members and families without them. If, as geneticists claim, there is an increased risk of schizophrenia in biological (blood) relatives of affected individuals, then again to prove or disprove such an assertion one must have some idea of what this 'schizophrenia' is that is being talked about.

Regrettably, many studies in this area are reported in such a way that what the researcher believes to be schizophrenia is never stated. We have seen that schizophrenia is differently conceptualized in the United States, which means that particular caution has to be exercised in comparing claims about the condition made in that country with those made in Britain. Fortunately, the impetus behind the major international studies conducted over the past few years has pushed researchers into a greater awareness of the shortcomings of present diagnostic categories and has made it easier to compare studies performed in one part of the world with similar ones performed elsewhere. But such a trend can only continue if psychiatrists, far from discarding diagnostic categories, devote as much and more attention to refining such concepts as they do to other aspects of their particular studies.

Genetics and schizophrenia

'It seems reasonable to postulate that genetic factors are largely responsible for the specific nature of most of the schizophrenias and that these factors are necessary but not sufficient for the disorder to occur.'

(Gottesman and Shields 1966: 80)

It has been calculated (Slater 1968), on the basis of the Registrar-General's 1960 returns, that the expectation of a man being admitted to a Health Service hospital in Britain by the age of fifty-five, with a diagnosis of schizophrenia, is 1·13 per cent; the equivalent expectation of a woman is 1·08 per cent. The expectation of schizophrenia for relatives of people suffering from the condition is very much higher

(*Table 1*). Children, both of whose parents suffer or have suffered from schizophrenia, have a 46 per cent chance of experiencing a similar disturbance. Siblings of a person ill with schizophrenia show an expected risk of between 10 and 17 per cent, depending on whether, in addition, one parent suffers from the condition. The parental risk, to judge from a number of studies, appears low although Slater (1968) has

Table 1 *Expectation of schizophrenia for relatives of schizophrenics*

relationship	total relatives (age-corrected)	schizophrenic (%)	
		(a)	(b)
parents	7,676	4·4	5·5
sibs (all)	8,504·5	8·5	10·2
sibs (neither parent schizophrenic)	7,535	8·2	9·7
sibs (one parent schizophrenic)	674·5	13·8	17·2
children	1,226·5	12·3	13·9
children of mating schiz: × schiz:	134	36·6	46·3
half-sibs	311	3·2	3·5
uncles and aunts	3,376	2·0	3·6
nephews and nieces	2,315	2·2	2·6
grandchildren	713	2·8	3·5
first cousins	2,438·5	2·9	3·5

(a) Diagnostically certain cases only
(b) Also including probable schizophrenics

(After Slater and Cowrie 1971)

argued that this is a statistical artifact and has claimed an expectation rate in parents of schizophrenic children of around 11 per cent. Summarizing this data, it would seem that the risk of experiencing a schizophrenic illness is very much higher in first-degree relatives of people who suffer such a disturbance than in the general population; in the case of second-degree relatives (half-sibs, uncles, aunts, etc.) a definite risk is still demonstrable but is of a lower magnitude. As the degree of relatedness weakens, so the risk of schizophrenia diminishes to the point where it differs little from that of the general population.

Thus far, such findings are quite consistent with either a genetic interpretation of the transmission of the disorder or with some form of environmental transmission. Yet, these data do pose a number of problems for those who argue that, for example, the mode of parent–child communication is what determines the onset of schizophrenic behaviour. For example, why should only 46 per cent of the children of parents, both of whom suffer from schizophrenia, be affected by the disorder? The family atmosphere of such a home must be a particularly disturbed one, an emotionally chaotic one in fact, yet less than half the children growing up in such an atmosphere develop such a condition themselves. The environmentalist might counter that such a finding is not easy to explain genetically either. He would point out that if schizophrenia is due to a single *dominant* gene, that is to say a gene which, if present, automatically results in the appearance of schizophrenia in the individual carrying it, the expected risk of schizophrenia in children of two schizophrenics would be 75 per cent. If, on the other hand, the condition is due to a *recessive* gene (i.e., such a gene being needed on both chromosomes for the condition to appear), then there would be a 100 per cent risk of expectation of schizophrenia in the children of two schizophrenics.

Yet the risk is less than 50 per cent! The geneticist counters this by postulating that the condition is due either to a variety of genes of varying strength (*'the polygenic theory'*) or to a gene of *intermediate penetrance* (a gene that is not as dominant as a typically dominant gene but more dominant than a recessive one). Both concepts (the polygenetic theory and the theory of an intermediate gene) are well established in genetics and either could account for the findings in the offspring of schizophrenic parents.

Another interesting finding is that the risk of schizophrenia in children appears to be of the same order of magnitude whether the schizophrenic parent is its father or its mother (Slater 1968; Kallmann 1938). Such a finding is consonant with a genetic explanation (mothers being no closer genetically to their children than fathers), but it is not all that easy to explain on an environmentalist basis, in that most of the exponents of the latter, implicitly at least, suggest that mothers are psychologically closer and potentially more damaging to their children than fathers.

Another approach to the problem of teasing out the relative contributions of environment and genes to the development of schizophrenia makes use of what is known as '*the twin method*'. This method of studying genetic transmission was first described by Galton in 1875. It was not until half a century had passed that the principles of such investigations and some results were described (Newman 1923; Siemens 1924; Dahlberg 1926).

Twin studies

Twins can be *monozygotic* (MZ), i.e., derived by division of one fertilized egg cell and therefore genetically identical, or *dizygotic* (DZ), i.e., derived from two fertilized egg cells and therefore no more alike genetically than any pair of nontwin siblings. A number of environmental factors affect MZ and same-sexed DZ twins in a comparable fashion, and, as a result, can be regarded as constant in any study involving the two kinds of twins.

In identical (MZ) twins the genetic material in each twin is identical to that of the other. If there is an important genetic factor operating in schizophrenia, one would expect that in the case of one MZ twin manifesting the disorder the other twin would be affected as well, that there would be *concordance* between the twins for the disorder. In the case of fraternal, non-identical (DZ) twins, the genetic material is not identical; indeed the genetic material in each twin resembles the other only in as much as that of one sibling resembles that of another. In this case, again supposing that genetic factors are important in schizophrenia, one would expect to find that the risk of schizophrenia in a DZ co-twin of a twin who suffers from the condition to be no greater and no less than the risk in a non-twin sibling of an affected family member. Furthermore, if family interaction and communication are important aetiological factors in the disorder, one would expect to find rates of concordance (the extent to which twins share the same trait) in DZ twins similar to those found in MZ twins.

Concordance can be estimated in one of two ways. In the

Table 2 *The earlier twin series*

investigator	date	MZ pairs			DZ pairs*		
		N	C	%	N	C	%
Luxenburger	1928	19	11	58	13	0	0
Rosenoff *et al.*	1934	41	25	61	53	7	13
Essen-Moller	1941	11	7	64	27	4	15
Kallmann	1946	174	120	69	296	34	11
Slater	1953	37	24	65	58	8	14
Inouye	1961	55	33	60	11	2	18

* DZ pairs are same-sexed   (Gottesman and Shields 1973)

so-called *proband* method, the sick twins are collected and the percentage of the series showing a co-twin similarly affected is estimated. (If a co-twin has been independently found to be a schizophrenic, he becomes a proband in his own right and the twinship is regarded as yielding two probands each with an affected co-twin.) In the *pair-wise* method, the concordance rate represents the proportion of affected co-twins of previously defined index cases (or probands). Both approaches have certain specific advantages and disadvantages, but it is sufficient for our purposes merely to note that the proband method yields higher material values of concordance and can thereby convey to the genetically uninitiated the impression that genetic factors are more important than the evidence indicates.

Irving Gottesman and James Shields (1973) have summarized the evidence arising from twin studies in schizophrenia and have divided the results into two parts. The earlier twin studies (*Table 2*) are simple pair-wise rates. Concordance for schizophrenia ranged in MZ twins from 58 per cent (Luxenburger 1928) to 69 per cent (Kallmann 1946) and in DZ twins from 8 per cent (Luxenburger 1928) to 18 per cent (Inouye 1961). The recent twin studies (*Table 3*) have been reported by the authors themselves as showing a range of rate that are dependent on what conditions are included for discussion, i.e., on how narrowly

Table 3 *Concordance (proband method) in recent twin studies at a leve approximating to the consensus diagnosis of schizophrenia*

investigation	MZ		DZ	
Kringlen, Norway (1967)	31/69	45%	14/96	15%
Fischer *et al.*, Denmark (1969)	14/25	56%	12/45	26%
Tienari, Finland (1971)*	7/20	35%	3/23	13%
Allen *et al.*, USA (1972)*	52/121	43%	12/131	9%
Gottesman and Shields, UK (1972)	15/26	58%	4/34	12%
	119/261	46%	45/329	14%

* Male pairs exclusively   (Gottesman and Shields 1973)

or loosely schizophrenia has been defined. These recent studies have used the proband method, and concordance rates in MZ twins range from 35 per cent (Tienari 1971) to 58 per cent (Gottesman and Shields 1972), and in DZ twins from 9 per cent (Allen, Cohen, and Pollin 1972) to 26 per cent (Fischer, Harvald, and Hauge 1969).

In the Maudsley twin study (*Table 4*), Gottesman and Shields (1972) used an operational definition of schizophrenia based on a consensus of six diagnosticians from three different countries. These diagnosticians arrived at their conclusions re concordance from reading typed summaries on the state of each twin which did not refer to the diagnosis nor to the zygosity (i.e., whether the co-twin was mono- or di-zygotic). The authors claim that such a consensus provides a more accurate MZ/DZ discrimination than attempts to apply very strict or very broad criteria.

Leonard Heston (1972) summarized the data from twin studies and concluded that, first, some 40–45 per cent of MZ co-twins of schizophrenics are themselves schizophrenic. This compares with a correlation of around 10 per cent in DZ co-twins. 'The evidence', declares Heston, 'strongly supports the association of genes with schizophrenia.' Second, he concluded that another 40–45 per cent of MZ co-twins of schizophrenic twins show signs of significant psychiatric impairment but are not schizophrenic. Third, there is a positive association between the severity of the illness and concordance with MZ pairs. That is to say, the more severe the illness is in a member of a MZ twin pair, the more likely it is that the other member will suffer from schizophrenia as well.

There have been several methodological criticisms levelled at twin studies in schizophrenia. Most of these are included in a recent analysis of the concept of schizophrenia by a British sociologist, Jeff Coulter (1973). Coulter quotes Jackson (1960) to the effect that monozygotic twins show higher concordance rates of schizophrenia than dizygotic twins because they are more prone to such stresses as confusion of identity and weak ego formation. Parental perceptions of monozygotic and dizygotic twins (identical and non-identical) reportedly differ (Cohen *et al.* 1973), that is to say parents and other close relatives do confuse identical twins with each other. Such identity confusion is an environmental variable to which MZ twins are more exposed than DZ ones and which could therefore explain the higher rates. The assumption that underlies many genetic investigations comparing identical and non-identical twins, namely that the life experiences of both twins are comparable, is therefore questionable.

However, if such identity confusion with its alleged interference in ego formation is of causal significance in schizophrenia, monozygotic (identical) twins should show higher rates of the illness than in the general population. The extensive research into this very question has been reviewed (Rosenthal 1968) and no evidence of an increased rate of schizophrenia in identical (MZ) twins has been found.

A second objection raised by Coulter is that higher concordance rates in MZ twins might be due to a greater tendency on the part of a MZ twin to identify with its co-twin than might occur between a DZ twin pair. Yet such an identification should work in either direction. For example, a potential schizophrenic should be as likely to be prevented from becoming psychotic by strong ties with his normal twin as a healthy co-twin is of being driven into a psychosis by identifying with a sick co-twin.

A third way in which an environmental factor rather than a genetic one might explain the higher concordance rate in MZ twins arises from the possibility that such twins might be more likely to be exposed to a predisposing environment than DZ twins. The strongest argument against such an explanation is derived from studies of twins reared apart (see below).

Additional objections advanced by Coulter include the assertion that there has been a lack of dialogue between the geneticists and the biochemists: 'there are broad statements about heredity on the basis of statistical inference but rarely a mention of the sort of biochemical research that might presumably corroborate these at the organic level itself'. This is a most curious objection. The amount of biochemical research into schizophrenia is vast. True, the results to date are parsimonious. Yet several genetic-biochemical studies have raised hopes of progress. For example, in one project, several biochemical measures, supposedly able to distinguish schizophrenics from non-schizophrenics, were applied to sixteen pairs of monozygotic twins discordant for the condition (Stabenau 1969). It was hoped that these measures would distinguish those twins who were ill from those who were not. The study was double-blind (i.e., the research worker assessing the biochemical results did not know from which twin they were derived or which twin suffered from schizophrenia). Two biochemical measures did distinguish the ill from the well, although the authors concede that other possible explanations may exist and that anyway the sample is a small one. More extensive studies are under way.

A further objection is raised by Coulter when he points out that more MZ twins discordant for schizophrenia than concordant for it have been reported in the literature. However, this is quite a spurious objection. One is not concerned with numbers but rather with rates and to date not a single reputable study of genetic factors in schizophrenia has failed to uncover a significantly higher concordance rate for schizophrenia in MZ than in DZ twins. Coulter is perfectly right when he points out that there are MZ co-twins of sick twins who do not suffer from the condition, but, as has been mentioned earlier, this can be explained genetically (indeed, somewhat better than it can environmentally).

Finally, Coulter spends much time attacking certain geneticists for introducing the concept of 'schizophrenia spectrum disorders' into the discussion of genetic factors. Such a concept figures prominently in the work of Kety and his co-workers (1968), in which an attempt is made to construct a genetic model that would take account of the observation that many co-twins of schizophrenic twins, while not showing evidence of schizophrenia themselves, nonetheless manifest disturbances which bear a greater resemblance to true schizophrenia than to any other psychiatric condition. The introduction of such a concept does raise all sorts of methodological problems. It has proved difficult enough to arrive at an agreed definition of what constitutes schizophrenia. The mind boggles at what psychiatrists would make of borderline and indefinite variants. Coulter, in his criticism, however, implies that the introduction of such a concept casts doubt on the reliability of the results of twin studies *in general*. In fact Kety makes it clear that 'schizophrenic spectrum disorders are those which occur in MZ twins over and above the more narrowly defined schizophrenia'! The concept has no bearing on the results obtained in those major twin studies which have invoked a relatively narrow concept of schizophrenia.

I have briefly discussed some of Coulter's criticisms not because he is the only, or indeed the first, critic to point them out but because he is one of the few non-psychiatrists to take the trouble to look at the genetic evidence for the transmission of schizophrenia before rejecting it out of hand. It is therefore regrettable that in his discussion of the genetic basis of the condition, far from presenting the results of the multitude of studies performed in any detail he contents himself with identifying alleged shortcomings in their methodology. Indeed, there are times when he presents his criticisms as if they had never been thought of by those who have undertaken and reviewed much of the research in this area. The fact is, however, that the shortcomings of the twin method in schizophrenia are well known and have been acknowledged by researchers, the majority of whom have continually modified their results accordingly. In addition, an alternative approach, based on the study of twins adopted out from home early in life and separated from their co-twins, has been devised to supplement the twin method and to tease out further the relative contribution of gene and environment in the genesis of the condition.

One of the most difficult objections made against the genetic argument by environmentalists is that hereditary and environmental influences, which can equally explain a transmitted factor in the aetiology of schizophrenia, are almost always coincidental in a patient's home of rearing. By studying twins reared apart, schizophrenic patients reared away from their biological parents, and by studying schizophrenic rates in the biological and adoptive relatives of schizophrenics adopted from their biological parents, those obstacles have been largely removed.

There have been approximately 26 MZ pairs reported as having been reared apart where at least one of them was schizophrenic (Shields 1978). Many are not described in detail and several were not separated until relatively late. As Shields points out, they do not make a suitable group for estimating the 'true' concordance rate for schizophrenia in twins. But, as he emphasises, the fact that in about two-thirds of these pairs both twins had schizophrenia or a schizophrenic-like disorder strongly supports the notion of an important genetic factor in the condition.

Somewhat more sophisticated adoptive studies, which do not rely on considerations of twinning, have been undertaken. Heston (1966) followed up fifty-seven individuals born to hospitalized schizophrenic mothers. Separation occurred in the majority of cases at birth. Five of these offspring went on to develop schizophrenia whereas, in a control group of fifty children born to non-schizophrenic mothers and placed in matched foster-homes, there were no cases of schizophrenia. A similar study was carried out in Copenhagen of forty-four children born to schizophrenic patients, most of whom developed their psychosis some time *after* their illegitimate children had been placed in their adopted homes (Rosenthal 1972). Three of the forty-four were diagnosed as definitely schizophrenic whereas not one of the sixty-seven controls was so diagnosed. Jon Karlsson (1970) looked at a group of schizophrenic mothers who had given birth to their first child around the time when they were hospitalized and were detained in institutions for at least five years or until they died. (Such a design ensures the separation of the children to be studied from affected family members.) Fourteen children were discovered who, as far as could be ascertained from extensive hospital records, had grown up without significant contact with their psychotic mothers or relatives. Of the fourteen, three were found to have been hospitalized for schizophrenic illnesses. Karlsson (1974) concludes a review of foster studies with the following assertion:

'The above results appear to demonstrate that the very important family influence in schizophrenia is largely genetic in nature. No family connected factors have been detected which are not fully accounted for by the hereditary contribution. If the place of rearing has no effect on the risk of psychosis, the tendency must already be present at birth. Even intrauterine factors are excluded by the observation that the risk in children of schizophrenics is the same whether the ill parent is the mother or the father. The possibility still remains that environmental factors play a significant role in the induction of schizophrenic symptoms, but the above findings suggest that they can only be influences which are encountered in all ordinary settings rather than being specific to the families of psychotic patients.' (Karlsson 1974: 29)

A rather intriguing approach to the problem of teasing apart the roles of genetic and environmental factors in schizophrenia involves psychological assessments of the biological and adoptive relatives of adopted schizophrenics. Paul Wender and his colleagues examined the adoptive relatives of ten schizophrenics and employed as a control group schizophrenics reared by their biological parents. The biological parents were rated as being significantly more disturbed than the adoptive parents of the schizophrenics.

These workers also examined the relationship between the severity of illness in the parents and the severity of illness in the offspring. They postulated that if the condition is 'psychologically' transmitted one would expect the sicker *adopting* parents to have the sicker children. Likewise, if schizophrenia is 'genetically' transmitted one would expect that the sicker *biological* parents would have the sicker children. They found a positive correlation between the severity of pathology between parents and offspring in the 'biological' sample, consistent with the hypothesis of biological transmission, but a negative correlation in the adoptive sample, a finding the reverse of that predicted by the psychological transmission hypothesis.

Seymour Kety and his colleagues (1975) studied nearly five and a half thousand adoptions granted in the city of Copenhagen between 1924 and 1947 to adoptive parents not biologically related to the child. In thirty-three adoptees a diagnosis of schizophrenia had been made. The biological and adoptive relatives of these patients were psychiatrically assessed, as were the biological and adoptive relatives of a matched control group of adoptees who had not been admitted to a psychiatric hospital. (This study made use of the extensive information contained in Danish population registers.) A significantly increased rate of schizophrenia was found in the biological relatives of the thirty-three schizophrenics, compared with the biological relatives of the matched non-schizophrenic adoptee controls. The prevalence of schizophrenia in adoptive relatives of both groups was very much lower and the condition was randomly distributed. This study strongly supports the view that genetic factors are of considerable importance in the transmission of schizophrenia. If family interaction patterns were of crucial aetiological importance, one would expect high rates of the illness in the adoptive relatives of schizophrenics, but those studies which have made a serious attempt to establish such a finding have notably failed to do so. In contrast, such studies have invariably found a very much higher rate of schizophrenia in biologically (i.e., genetically) related relatives of schizophrenic patients even when these relatives were shown to have little or no close family contact with the patients.

Whereas the evidence derived from twin and adoptive studies serves to emphasize the role of genetic transmission it does not necessarily disprove the hypothesis that family communications are of fundamental importance. Theodore Lidz, a researcher in this area who favours the dysfunctional family view, believes that the above evidence does not rule out the possibility that certain types of family disorganization are crucial to the aetiology or transmission of schizophrenia. He accepts that the condition only occurs in clear-cut form in those individuals who have a genetic predisposition to it. To rule out a causal role for family factors, however, one must show, he argues, that schizophrenia appears in stable families. He believes that adoption studies should pay particular attention to those adoptive homes in which schizophrenic patients were raised (Lidz 1968), particularly as one study (that of Wender and his colleagues above) found the adoptive parents of the schizophrenics to be more disturbed than the adoptive parents of matched normal subjects. Though acceptance of a significant genetic factor in schizophrenia may appear unavoidable, the more recent twin studies, more rigorous in their methodology and more restrictive regarding the operational diagnosis of schizophrenia, do report lower concordance rates for monozygotic twins. Clearly environmental factors do need to be considered in any aetiological model of the condition.

Family life and schizophrenia

> 'The family's function is to repress Eros: to induce a false consciousness of security: to deny death by avoiding life: to cut off transcendence: to believe in God, not to experience the Void: to create, in short, one-dimensional man: to promote respect, conformity, obedience: to con children out of play: to induce a fear of failure: to promote a respect for work: to promote a respect for "respectability".'
> (Laing 1967: 55)

Laing's apocalyptic vision of the contemporary family encompasses in a typically sweeping fashion the breadth of the assault that has been mounted against the family as an institution. Psychiatry, through some of its more articulate spokesmen, has tended to reinforce a view of the family hearth as the nurturer not of healthy, mature, independent, and creative adults but of conformists, robots, dehumanized people lacking hope, sensitivity, and imagination. To such a gloomy view is added the conspiratorial one in which the bosom of the family is seen to nourish all that is twisted and pathological in the human condition – the child molester, the mass murderer, the baby-batterer, the sadistic torturer; all these, the family's critics remind us, emerge from the sanctity of the home.

In view of the family's track record in such matters, it is not surprising that some students of family relationships argue that it is in this area that the key to the development of schizophrenia is to be found. Schizophrenia is seen as a response, an intelligible and inevitable response by the child to overwhelming interpersonal and social stresses, the main source of which is located in the parents. There is no single theory of family psychopathology as such. Rather there is a constellation of theories, drawing its support from anthropological, sociological, and psychological data. Three main theoretical and interwoven strands may be distinguished however: the problem of 'binding', disturbances in parental relationships, and disturbances in family relationships.

1 Binding and family relationships

Transactional and analytical studies of parent–child relationships suggest that they are *transitive* and *reciprocal* (Stierlin 1974). They are transitive in that they denote parental moulding of their immature, dependent offspring and reciprocal in that a two-way exchange develops whereby the children mould and influence their parents as much as the latter mould and influence them. When so-called binding occurs, the parents (some theorists focus particularly on one parent, usually the mother) interact with their children in a way that appears destined to ensure that the children cannot escape, are unable to develop an identity outside the 'family ghetto', and are pathologically dependent on the parental presence. Gregory Bateson and his colleagues (1956) have elaborated on this view and have claimed that a particular type of pathological binding, the so-called 'double-bind', is seen in those parent–child relationships that lead to the onset of schizophrenia in some of the children. As these workers describe it, the necessary ingredients for the double-bind are:

1. *Two or more persons:* one they designate the 'victim', the other, not necessarily the mother alone but often some combination of mother, father, and/or siblings, inflicts the harm.

2. *Repeated experience:* the double-bind is assumed to be a recurrent theme; the hypothesis does not invoke a single traumatic experience but rather a repeated one which tends to become an habitual expectation.

3. *A primary negative injunction:* this may be in one of two forms –
   (a) 'Do not do so-and-so or I will punish you'
   or (b) 'If you do not do so-and-so I will punish you'.

4. *A secondary injunction:* this conflicts with the first at a more abstract level and, like the first, is enforced by punishments or signals which threaten security or survival.

Bateson and his colleagues illustrate their concept with an account of an incident occurring between a schizophrenic patient and his mother on the occasion of a visit by her to the hospital. The patient was glad to see his mother and put his arm around her. She stiffened, he withdrew his arm whereupon she asked, 'Don't you love me any more?' When he then blushed, she said, 'Dear, you must not be so easily embarrassed and afraid of your feelings.' Bateson and his colleagues comment that the mother's reaction of not accepting her son's affection is 'masterfully covered up' by her condemnation of him for withdrawing and the patient denies his perception of the situation by accepting her condemnation. The statement 'Don't you love me any more' appears to imply 'I am lovable', 'You should love me and if you don't, you are bad and at fault', and 'Whereas you did love me previously you don't any longer'. The focus is shifted from his expressing affection to his inability to be affectionate. He, for his part, is unable to point out her freezing response. To challenge her interpretation of the situation would result in his losing her affection and the impossible dilemma thus becomes: 'If I am to keep my tie to mother I must not show her that I love her (because she apparently cannot cope with this) but if I do not show her that I love her I will lose her.'

The double-bind essentially consists of a paradoxical communication passed from one person to another, the superficial or primary injunction of which suggests one message while the deeper and secondary injunction suggests another and contradictory one.

Bateson and his colleagues argue that the potential schizophrenic is especially exposed to such communications and learns to cope by either withdrawing from such an inter-action (often into a phantasy world of his own) or by be-having in a completely ambiguous and irrational fashion himself. In particular, he learns to disguise the meanings of his replies so that he cannot be held responsible for what he says or does in such circumstances. This theory suggests that the marked disorders of thinking and emotional behaviour seen in schizophrenic illnesses are in part derived from the patient adopting such a coping mechanism in an early chaotic double-binding family environment so that impossible demands can be handled.

2 *Disturbed parental relationships*

Whereas the Bateson school concentrates on the parent–child relationship, other workers, particularly Lidz and his colleagues (1965), have focused on the triadic relationships involving both parents and the child and have scrutinized parental interrelationships for clues concerning the genesis of schizophrenia. The entire family is regarded as 'pathological' and the 'schizophrenic' patient is merely the member selected to play the role of 'scapegoat'. Two interesting concepts are utilized in this approach, the concepts of 'skew' and 'schism'. The normal family involves the active participation of two adequate parental figures. If one is inadequate in his/her role (i.e., is passive, withdrawn, weak, or uninvolved) and/or the other is excessively dominant (i.e., demanding, possessive, manipulative, overwhelming) a 'skew' is set up. Relationships in a family in which the parental roles are skewed become distorted and there is a resultant stunting of personal and emotional growth in the children, the severity of such stunting in each case being dependent on such factors as the sex of the child and its age at the time of the development of the 'skew'. The notion of 'schism' refers to a type of personal relationship in which one of the two partners is cold, hostile, and even destructive towards the other, resulting in what has been termed 'emotional divorce'. Lidz summarizes the general approach as follows:

'They [one or both parents] seek to delimit the environment, particularly the family environment, to establish and maintain conditions that permit them to maintain the one limited role they can perform. Reality cannot alter nor new circumstances modify the conception of themselves and the family they hold and must hold to maintain their precarious emotional equilibrium. The parents' delimitation of the environment and their insistence on altering the family members' perceptions and meanings, create a strange family milieu filled with inconsistencies, contradictory meanings, and a denial of what should be obvious. Facts are constantly altered to suit emotionally determined needs. The children in such families subjugate their own needs to the parents' defences, and their conceptualisation of experiences are in the service of solving parental problems rather than in mastering events and feelings.'   (Lidz 1968: 179–80)

For Lidz and his colleagues, the 'transmission of irrationality' is crucially related to parental difficulties in communication which in turn appear to be derived from the parents' loose ego boundaries and precarious emotional balance.

3 Disturbed family relationships

Two American researchers, Wynne and Singer (1963, 1965), have suggested that the types of thought disorder seen in schizophrenia are functions of the mode of family transactions and particularly of the style of focusing attention and establishing communications. These authors studied family interaction patterns using taped interviews and a battery of psychological tests and compared families containing schizophrenic members with matched families containing members suffering from non-psychotic psychiatric conditions. They claim to have demonstrated that the *families* of schizophrenics tend to have forms of disorganization and communication which are similar to those found in the schizophrenic patients themselves. They claimed to be able to deduce which families contained schizophrenic members by a 'blind' study of the methods of communication used in the families themselves. From samples of conjoint family therapy sessions, they demonstrated, in the patients' parents' amorphous and fragmented styles of thought, inabilities to focus attention selectively and difficulties in sharing percepts or feelings. Meaningful communication, in their view, is virtually impossible in many families that produce one or more schizophrenic members. Wynne and his colleagues argue that within the families studied no independent expectations on the part of the children were tolerated. Communications involving conflicting needs and demands were consistently distorted. Mishler and Waxler (1965) have claimed that the parents of schizophrenic patients can be differentiated from parents of other individuals in terms of over-protectiveness, rejection, aloofness, thought disorder, and abnormalities of speech.

Clearly the three approaches overlap considerably and are only separate in the sense that each reflects a particular emphasis. Together, they support a view of the genesis and transmission of schizophrenia that places the problem squarely within the family context. It is a model that appears to have a ready public appeal. The stereotyped contemporary family with its bossy, dominant, castrating mother, its henpecked, cowardly, and inadequate father, and its adolescents fighting a rearguard action against parental emotional blackmail and subtle double-binds has become the thinking man's guide to schizophrenia. But on what is it based?

With regard to the double-bind concept, psychiatrists have used it to widen their understanding of family communications in general. However, the evidence does not support a possible aetiological role in schizophrenia. The double-bind theory itself has been developed into a much more complicated systems theory of communication, but to date there is no hard evidence that suggests that it is a form of communication particularly prevalent in schizophrenics' families.

The Lidz hypotheses have been the subject of a great many research projects. One study by Kohn and Klausen (1956) explored the attitude held by schizophrenics and normal controls towards their respective parents. The schizophrenics tended to see their mothers as strong, dominant figures whereas they perceived their fathers as weak, passive, and inadequate. However, they drew attention to the need to control for social class when they showed that normals of low social class tended to see their mothers similarly to schizophrenic patients, whereas non-schizophrenics of higher social class visualized their fathers playing the dominant, powerful family roles. Kohn and Klausen also noted that the pattern of relative maternal dominance is not specific to schizophrenia but has been reported in studies of manic-depressive illness, ulcers, anorexia nervosa, juvenile delinquency, and drug addiction.

Since this comparatively early study there has been an enormous volume of research into family relationships and schizophrenia, much of it inadequately designed. According to Kohn (1968), the majority of studies are flawed either as a result of being composed of highly selected patients from whom one could not validly generalize to schizophrenics at large or 'the samples were peculiarly selected not to test a hypothesis but to load the dice in favour of a hypothesis'. In many studies the control groups are quite inadequate or do not exist at all. To date, there has not been a single well-controlled study that demonstrates any substantial difference between the family relationships of schizophrenics and those of non-schizophrenics from similar backgrounds.

Wynne's work, in which it was claimed that up to 90 per cent of the parents of schizophrenics could be distinguished from the parents of people with other conditions on the basis of their responses on the Rorschach Test, however, looked so promising that attempts to replicate the findings were made in London (Hirsch and Leff 1971, 1975). The results obtained were far from convincing. Wing (1973) notes ruefully, that a possible explanation for this discrepancy is that the patients used in the USA and the UK studies were not suffering from the same conditions although both groups had been diagnosed as schizophrenic. 'Problems of this kind', he inisists, 'will continue to arise until standardised diagnoses are the rule in scientific work in psychiatry'.

One serious defect in most family studies, noted interestingly enough by Jules Henry (1973), himself an impressive analyst of family psychodynamics, is that these tend to classify as 'pathological' certain patterns of communication which, far from being specific to schizophrenic families, are in fact commonplace and found in many families. 'I wonder', he writes, 'whether family therapists would find any families lacking all the following "pathogenic" features:

a mother's great emotional dependence on her daughter, the need of mothers to feel superior, self-protection through acquiescence, "symbolic" attachments among members of the family, pressure ("excessive" pressure) to maintain the sub-culture of the family, "emotional divorce", i.e., husband and wife lead outwardly tranquil and conforming lives but do not give each other what they need, a parent cares largely for himself as reflected in his child, children are rewarded when they behave as the family wishes and are punished for being independent,

parents keep much of what goes on and their own motivations secret from the children,

two members of the family form an alignment,

etc., etc., etc.'

Perhaps, concludes Henry, what we have here is the discovery of the contemporary family rather than the pathological (or schizophrenic?) family.

Some analysts, such as Laing, do appear to hold the view that the contemporary family is a 'pathogenic' institution. Such a view hardly tells us much about what kind of family psychopathology '*specifically*' predisposes its members to develop schizophrenia. 'We are all prostitutes and murderers now', Laing once declared passionately (1967). Such a judgement, stressing as it does our common innate potentialities to self and mutual despair and destruction, does not provide us with any helpful discriminating information as to what it might be inside the family which provokes, of all possible responses, the schizophrenic response. The other question which remains to be resolved concerns the difficulty of separating *cause* from *effect*. Confronted by evidence of serious family psychopathology and a member manifesting schizophrenic symptoms, one may be tempted to opt for a cause-and-effect model and 'diagnose' the family disturbance as the *cause* of the schizophrenia. But confronted by any vicious cycle, the diagnostician has a thorny task in deciding which causes what! For example, William Pollin (1972) has noted that the schizophrenic twin in discordant monozygotic twin pairs is more often than not the one who was smaller at birth, shows more minor neurological signs, more episodes of disturbed sleep and feeding, certain biochemical and some slight endocrinological changes. He has also drawn attention to the fact that the weaker twin tends to be overprotected, develops a marked dependency relationship with its mother, and becomes submissive to its co-twin. Pollin's findings have been broadly confirmed by other researchers in this general area. What are we to make of them? Is it the submissiveness within the context of the twin relationship that produces the morbidity in the affected twin? Or is the submissiveness itself the result of a weaker constitution, which in itself is the predisposing factor in the genesis of the illness? Is the dependence on the mother provoked by the obvious physical and emotional 'inferiority' of the weaker twin – i.e., does the weaker twin provoke its mother into treating him in such a way that schizophrenia results?

Most family investigators acknowledge the possibility that the disturbed, chaotic, destructive behaviour seen in certain families of schizophrenics may reflect the same genetic factors that have led to a full-blown classical schizophrenic illness in one of the family members. They usually acknowledge likewise the possibility that such pathological behaviour on the part of the family members is itself a reaction to the behaviour of the schizophrenic person in their midst. Such questions remain to be further investigated.

Family therapy (and I use this term in its everyday usage to mean the study, diagnosis, and treatment of disordered family relationships) is a relatively new area of psychiatric involvement. As with every new theoretical sophistication, it has been greeted with enthusiasm, has spawned an impressive vocabulary, and produced an awesome catalogue of claims. Its more cautious exponents refrain from making causal connections at this early stage in its activities. Yet, as with every other psychiatric development, this one has many adherents who could scarcely be called cautious.

Thus Laing declares (my italics):

'*without exception* the experience and behaviour that gets labelled schizophrenic is a *special strategy that a person invents in order to live in an unliveable situation.*'

(Laing 1967: 95)

Now elsewhere Laing recognizes how easy it is to keep shifting the 'blame' for the condition from the patient to the patient's biochemistry, the patient's mother, the parental marriage, the nuclear family, the social environment, the capitalistic system, the Total World System. It is not, as he puts it, 'a matter of laying the blame at anyone's door'. But, unfortunately, such caveats as he and others enter live somewhat wanly and uneasily beside the gigantic insistence which emerges from his and his colleagues' writings that it *is* the family who has driven the schizophrenic mad, that the illness is that *only* 'intelligible' response that can be made in such a situation, and that psychiatrists, in seeking to alleviate the schizophrenic's sufferings, are merely furthering the family's destructive interests. So it is that Mary Barnes describes her 'abnormally nice family' (though it is never stated in what way they were abnormal) and the reader of that much-read book is left in no doubt that the colourful variety of Mary's family interactions and experiences *caused* her illness and that of her brother. Michael Wechsler's parents were placed by several therapists in the invidious position of having to prove their innocence of a crime, never established, indeed never even defined. (Some critics of psychiatry confuse the situation further in that they assert that schizophrenia does not exist and that parents are responsible for making their offspring suffer from it!) Of the British commentators, Professor John Wing (1973) has been the most critical of those who, while denying the existence of schizophrenia (or implying that it is manufactured by the doctors), nonetheless proceed as though there is a condition known as 'schizophrenia',

'. . . the cause of which is variously attributed to society, to psychiatrists or to the family. This scapegoat tendency is one of the least attractive aspects of the new doctrines and illustrates the harmful effects of labelling quite as well as the misuse of diagnosis does. In addition to these problems, the fact that no real alternative method of controlling disturbed behaviour is put forward means that the stigma is likely to build up disproportionately. Certainly if the police and the prison have to be regarded as alternatives to doctors and the hospital, the latter seem likely to adopt a less harsh attitude to deviants. Finally, none of the alternative explanations of "schizophrenic" behaviour is scientific – almost nothing can be predicted from them and they are therefore virtually untestable.'

(Wing 1973a)

It is a massive indictment and Wing's use of words beloved of psychiatry's critics, words like 'stigma', 'scapegoating', and 'labelling', is quite deliberate as he seeks to underline the fact that the family model of causation in schizophrenia labels, scapegoats, and stigmatizes every bit as much (and more?) as the much-maligned medical model. In the family model, however, the targets for blame tend to be the parents, the family, and to a lesser extent society whereas in the medical model the targets, in so far as there are any, are the largely impersonal ones of brain, biochemistry, and blood levels.

But the aim of this section is not to dismiss family approaches, for that way we return to ideological confrontation and polarization. Family studies have provided and are providing systematic insights into family communications and relationships which may yet have immense implications for psychiatry in the future. Not all psychiatrists would share Wing's irritation with the woolliness of current hypotheses (and Wing himself elsewhere generously acknowledges the worth of the family therapy approach). Most, I suspect, would agree with Henry that current formulations represent the necessary preliminary steps to discovering further and possibly vital information concerning the aetiology of emotional suffering in general. It is, as he acknowledges, a credit to psychiatry that it has taken such steps. But the family in contemporary life is an area every bit as sensitive as infantile sexuality was in Freud's day. Theorists would do well to exercise caution if we are not to be plunged into another sterile and split situation where psychiatrists align themselves according to the 'Family-as-an-instrument-of-terror', 'Family-as-an-instrument-of-social-good', or 'Family-is-totally-irrelevant' schools. Yet again, the problem facing psychiatrists is how to avoid making grandiose claims, being destructive and nihilistic, or ending up bemused, intellectual dilettantes admitting that anything is possible, everything is relevant, and nothing can be dismissed.

Biochemical factors and schizophrenia

'Biochemists in the field [psychiatry] seem to divide their time between disproving the research of their less rigorous colleagues and adding to an increasingly long catalogue of essentially negative results; everyone regrets the failure of research in the field to contribute anything of significance to the pathology of the major mental illnesses and thus facilitate their diagnosis and treatment. It is important to recognise the magnitude of this failure.'

(Rodnight 1971: 353)

To follow one of Britain's leading social psychiatrists declaring his pessimistic view of family studies in schizophrenia with the above statement from one of the country's leading researchers into the biochemistry of mental illness is to invite the charge that either this country produces some remarkably nihilistic scholars or that, to date, mental illness defies analysis. Yet Rodnight's assertion is a welcome douche of cold water in a field where some of the enthusiastic statements make the fiery cries of family therapists sound like modest murmurings of mild interest. The reasons for his reservations are not difficult to find. The study of biochemical function in the brain is at a relatively unsophisticated level.

Knowledge of fundamental neurochemistry is meagre. Durrell (1973) has pointed to the difficulties inherent in the interpretation of abnormal biological findings in psychiatrically ill patients. If, for example, one wishes to compare a group of patients with a group of controls with regard to some simple factor such as the level of a particular enzyme in the cerebro-spinal fluid, one has to be sure that the two groups are matched not merely for the usual factors of age, sex, and social class but for such factors as nutritional status, history of infectious disease, recent drug history, activity patterns, reactions to the test situations, and other equally subtle variables.

Kety (1973) has drawn attention to the fact that most biochemical research into schizophrenia has been carried out in patients with a long history of hospitalization in institutions where overcrowding is difficult to avoid and where hygienic standards are often difficult to maintain. It is easy to see how chronic infection, especially of the digestive tract, may spread among such patients and as a result contaminate biochemical findings. Again, in variety and quality, the institutionalized schizophrenic's diet is rarely comparable to that of a non-hospitalized 'normal' control. As a result, the demonstration of a dietary deficiency in a schizophrenic group compared to a non-schizophrenic group may merely indicate a difference in dietary intake rather than a true metabolic defect intrinsic to schizophrenia. Even when institutional diets are adequate they do not necessarily offer a free choice. Kety neatly illustrated this with the example of the thyroid dysfunction, which had been attributed to schizophrenia, being found to be associated with a dietary deficiency in iodine; the deficiency promptly disappeared when iodine was added to the institution's salt! Some aromatic amine metabolites, found in excessive amounts in some schizophrenics, and as a result regarded as possible causal agents or involved in a causal chain, were later found to be of external origin; such metabolites were closely related with chronic tea and coffee drinking!

This then has tended to be the pattern in biochemical research into schizophrenia. A group of workers report finding an unusual metabolite in the urine of schizophrenics or an unusual plasma factor in their blood. The study is scrutinized by other workers and attempts are made to replicate the findings. It is then discovered that the unusual metabolite or factor is due to some incidental aspect of the schizophrenia itself. Rodright's critical judgement, therefore, is amply justified.

But there are a number of areas in which, if breakthroughs are not exactly forthcoming, some clues concerning a possible biochemical substrate for illnesses such as schizophrenia are emerging. Two of these areas merit a mention.

1 Biogenic amines and schizophrenia

The biogenic amines include the catecholamines, dopamine, noradrenaline, tryptamine, and acetylcholine. These substances are found in various parts of the brain and appear to act as neurotransmitters, i.e., they facilitate the transmission of electrical impulses from one brain cell to another. Interest in the possible role of these substances in schizophrenia has been stimulated by the discovery of the role played by one of them, dopamine, in the pathogenesis of Parkinsonism. Parkinson's disease (named after the London physician who in 1817 published his *Essay on the Shaking Palsy* vividly describing the condition) is characterized by a shaking tremor, a curious plastic stiffness or rigidity, and disturbance in voluntary movements. In 1957, dopamine was identified as a normal constituent of the mammalian brain, and was found to occur in high concentration in two key areas of the so-called 'extra-pyramidal system' (a part of the central nervous system involved in the control and co-ordination of voluntary movement, the development of motor skills, and the elaboration of complex motor acts), namely the caudate nucleus and the putamen. In 1963, Hornykiewiez demonstrated that Parkinsonism is associated with a significantly *decreased* dopamine (DA) content in the caudate nucleus secondary to a degeneration of a tract of nerve fibres originating in a nearby area, the *substantia nigra*. These nerve fibres normally secrete dopamine at their nerve endings. Dopamine, or more accurately its precursor, L-Dopa (which unlike dopamine crosses with ease the 'barrier' existing between the blood-stream and the cells of the brain), has been found to be of benefit in the treatment of Parkinsonism. Given in massive doses, it causes a significant increase in dopamine levels in the caudate nucleus and produces in many cases a dramatic clinical improvement.

Now a number of drugs affect the concentration of dopamine in this area. Amphetamine potentiates dopamine at nerve endings and can produce frank psychotic episodes. LSD and certain anticholinergic drugs, such as atropine, appear to suppress anti-dopamine substances, and they can also produce psychoses. Finally, L-Dopa itself, which, as we have seen, increases dopamine concentration, has reportedly led to the development of psychotic states. The phenothiazines, on the other hand, the most powerful *anti-psychotic* drugs available, and a newer group of anti-psychotic agents, the butyopherones, *block* dopamine receptors and appear as a result to inhibit its effect. Such observations have given rise to the hypothesis that whereas Parkinsonian symptoms may result from a *decrease* in dopamine levels secondary to an *increase* in a dopamine antagonist or to a *blockage* of dopamine receptors (chlorpromazine and related dopamine-receptor blockers can in moderate doses give rise to side-effects which are indistinguishable from the signs and symptoms of Parkinsonism), psychosis, and particularly schizophrenia, may result from an *increase* in the level of available dopamine secondary to a *heightened sensitivity* of dopamine receptors or to a *decrease* in a dopamine antagonist.

The dopamine theory of schizophrenia is further complicated by the fact that dopamine appears to have a variety of facilitatory and inhibitory functions. Its effects, too, cannot be considered independent of the nature of the different types of dopamine receptors known to exist in the brain.

The catecholamines have been implicated in psychosis not only as neurotransmitters which for some reason are out of balance but also as precursors of compounds that provoke psychotic reactions (so-called 'psychotomimetic' compounds). The catecholamines, dopamine and noradrenaline, structurally resemble *mescaline*, a well-established hallucinogenic substance, and several of the major breakdown products of these two catecholamines possess an even more marked structural similarity. It has been suggested that some abnormality in the normal metabolic pathway of catecholamine breakdown may occur in schizophrenia, resulting in the production of hallucinogenic or 'schizophrenogenic' substances. A number of research projects are based on such a hypothesis.

Innumerable searches for abnormal breakdown products in the urine of schizophrenic patients have been conducted. In 1962, Friedhoff and Van Winkle claimed that an analogue of dopamine was excreted in the urine of 60 per cent of an acute schizophrenic group and was not excreted by a normal control group. The compound DMPEA (3,4-dimethoxyphenethylamine) was said to possess mescaline-effects in rats, but attempts to demonstrate similar effects in man have not proved successful. Despite a virtual epidemic of studies, further claims about the present DMPEA in schizophrenics' urine have been conflicting.

Another approach involves administering certain breakdown products to schizophrenics to see if symptoms are exacerbated as a result. Chronic schizophrenics given the amino-acid methionine tend to show an acute flare-up in their condition. (Pollin *et al.* 1961). This finding has since been replicated by other workers with other groups of patients leading Iversen (1978) to remark that 'hardly any other finding in this area of research has proved to be so reliable'.

The problem is to know what to make of it! One explanation, the so-called *transmethylation hypothesis* suggests that schizophrenia may be related to over-activity in one of the metabolic systems which involves methylation of the catecholamines. According to this theory, methionine may worsen schizophrenic symptoms by increasing the rate of methylation of the catecholamines leading to an excess of toxic by-products. However, evidence in favour of such an explanation is currently lacking.

Nevertheless, there is no sign that the search for such toxic metabolites is slowing up. N-dimethyltryptamine (DMT) and the related compound bufotenin are currently the compounds most scrutinized. Why might DMT be linked with psychosis? First, its immediate precursor, tryptamine, is present in the human brain. Second, tryptamine concentrations are allegedly raised in the urine of some schizophrenics. Third, the enzyme necessary for converting tryptamine to DMT is present in the human brain. Rodnight and his colleagues at the Institute of Psychiatry using a carefully diagnosed patient population detected urinary DMT in twenty of forty-two schizophrenics while a positive result was obtained in only one of twenty normals. However, the same workers detected the amine in the urine of a significant proportion of patients suffering from psychotic illnesses other than schizophrenia (Rodnight et al. 1977).

Another group of workers (Wyatt et al. 1973) have found that the activity of DMT-forming enzymes is higher in the blood of acute schizophrenics whereas normal subjects had significantly lower levels. Ingeniously, they extended their work to fourteen MZ twins discordant for schizophrenia and found the activity of DMT-forming enzymes to be significantly higher in the schizophrenic twins than in the non-schizophrenic co-twins. This finding suggests that the raised enzyme activity is unlikely to be genetically determined and must either be produced by some environmental factor before the onset of the psychosis or be associated with the psychosis itself. When these same workers looked at the levels of monoamine oxidase (the enzyme actively involved in breaking down DMT and thereby reducing its active concentration) they found striking reduction in thirty-three patients with schizophrenia. Using the same fourteen MZ twins, they found that this time both the schizophrenic and non-schizophrenic twins showed lower than normal levels of monoamine oxidase but there was a significant correlation between the severity of the schizophrenia and the monoamine oxidase decrease.

It would seem, therefore, that schizophrenics may have an *environmentally induced* increase in capacity to form DMT and a *genetically determined* decrease in capacity to degrade it (*Lancet* 1974). There is also the implication in these studies that a genetic marker, such as monoamine oxidase activity, may be identifiable, as an indicator of vulnerability to schizophrenia.

Despite Rodnight's pessimism, biochemists appear a resilient and a hardy lot, not given to throwing in the sponge. The variety and ingenuity of some studies defy description. There have been studies based on the hypothesis that the pineal gland hormone melatonin is improperly synthesized (McIsaac 1961), that schizophrenics have an abnormally high tolerance for histamine (Carlini, Santos, and Sampaio 1965), and that schizophrenia is related to wheat consumption, an excess of which precipitates in the predisposed the classical psychotic reaction (Dohan 1966). A treatment modality, enthusiastically supported by the Nobel Laureate Linus Pauling (and taken up with gusto by members of Schizophrenia Anonymous, an offshoot of Alcoholics Anonymous), is based on the claim that schizophrenics are low excretors of certain vitamins and that the condition responds to massive doses of ascorbic acid (vitamin C) and the two B vitamins, niacin and pyridoxine (Hawkins and Pauling 1973). The evidence for such a simple model is not strong, but, as we have seen with enthusiasts for other approaches, this does not prevent this particular hypothesis from being promulgated by its supporters as the *definitive* answer to the problem of schizophrenia.

So we find Friedhoff, whose own 'pink spot' theory languishes for lack of supporting evidence, optimistically reviewing the research to date on the role of the biogenic amines in the aetiology of schizophrenia and declaring with confidence that

'. . . a definite role for the extra-pyramidal system as a regulator of behavioural function involved in psychosis seems to be emerging. Also we can now design compounds with relative assurance that they will either produce psychotomimetic effects or be useful as therapeutic agents. This represents an impressive advance to knowledge.'

(Friedhoff 1973: 124)

Yet Rodnight is not so impressed and advises caution. Biochemical breakthroughs have been claimed before which have since proved worthless. Certain areas do seem as if they might yet yield useful information, but to date, despite Friedhoff's enthusiasm, the 'impressive advance' is still anxiously awaited.

2 *Plasma factors in schizophrenia*

The study of so-called toxic factors present in the serum of schizophrenics is another popular area for contemporary biological research into schizophrenia. Some of the studies read like projects out of Frankenstein's lab. For example, one researcher claimed that feeding serum from schizophrenic patients to certain spiders caused the latter to spin bizarre webs. Another reported that in rats reward learning was severely retarded following the administration to them of 'schizophrenic sera'. Subsequent studies suggest that the toxic factor involved is a protein, an alpha-2-globulin of high molecular weight. Charles Frohman and his colleagues (1971) isolated such a protein in the plasma of schizophrenics which they claimed could seriously affect the oxidation processes of cells as evidenced by an alteration in the ratio of lactic acid to pyruvic acid in cells after incubation (the L/P ratio). This abnormal protein was also found to affect the transport of vital amino-acids into cells.

To date, research into such a plasma factor has been conducted in two American centres and one Russian one. The three groups have employed two different isolation techniques, two different types of bio-assay, and a variety of ill-matching diagnostic criteria. Yet the researchers do not appear abashed. In a review of the research, Frohman (1973) concludes that investigators have isolated a common protein factor and several related substances in the blood of schizophrenics, although

> 'The relationship of these various substances to one another has still to be determined and their role in the pathophysiology and/or etiology of the disorder defined. The world-wide results to date are suggestive of significant progress and give encouragement that more definite answers may be found in the near future.'
>
> (Frohman 1973: 145)

So we have another active researcher, having reviewed the results of two hectic decades of biological investigations into schizophrenia and having come up with very little other than some interesting and possible signposts, nonetheless expressing satisfaction with what has gone before and a breezy optimism with regard to what has yet to come.

It is difficult reading the results from any of the major areas of research into the possible causes of schizophrenia (other than genetics) without being impressed, as is Rodnight, by the 'magnitude' of the failure. No doubt, the enthusiasm of the individual researcher is partly a defence against such a response. Volumes of urine have flowed through the research laboratories, 'pink spots' and 'mauve spots' have danced seductive patterns across the retinae of persistent workers, toxic factors have been identified, denied, and found again, yet still the search goes on for an elusive link.

Nevertheless, there is no shortage of biological theories of causation in schizophrenia. Indeed, Horrobin (1979) has even attempted to bring many of them together in one integrated and complicated explanatory theory. In addition to the dopamine, melatonin, and wheat sensitivity theories mentioned above, Horrobin includes a theory involving the recently discovered brain peptides, the endorphins and enkephalins. These substances are found in the human brain (Hughes and Kosterlitz 1977) and have similar properties to those of morphine which has raised speculation concerning their possible role in altering the individual's sensitivity to physical and psychological pain. There is some evidence that the brain contains a system which has as its transmitter an enkephalin or 'opioid' and which may well function as an inhibitor of other transmission systems. Horrobin's theory is that these various explanatory theories are all related to another complex collection of recently discovered substances, the prostaglandins, substances which exert a variety of actions on brain function.

However, despite the extraordinary richness and vitality of biological speculation in schizophrenia, it still remains to be demonstrated conclusively that this or that factor in the urine, serum, or cerebrospinal fluid of carefully and reliably chosen schizophrenic patients is indeed a causal factor and not simply a direct or indirect manifestation of the disorder. Durrell (1973) takes a rather sanguine view of the relationship between biological, psychological, and environmental factors than perhaps do many of the critics of clinical psychiatry when he states:

'The implications are that exceedingly complex inter-actions between genetics and other biological variables and experiential variables may be required to account for many of the patterns of disordered psychological behaviour of relevance to psychiatry'. (Durrell 1973: 9)

The only consistent change found in the postmortem schizophrenic brain is an increase in the numbers of dopamine receptors. Therapeutic benefit follows their blockade but only after an interval of two weeks, suggesting that some other change has to occur. Crow (1980) points out that the therapeutic effects of dopamine receptor blockade, and presumably of the anti-schizophrenic drugs in general, appear limited to so-called 'positive' symptoms (delusions, hallucinations, and thought disorder), symptoms characteristic of acute schizophrenic illnesses. Negative symptoms (flattening of affect, poverty of speech, and loss of drive), more commonly seen in chronic schizophrenia, benefit less from treatment. Crow argues that two syndromes may be involved – one, equivalent to 'acute schizophrenia', associated with changes in dopaminergic transmission, the other, more chronic, associated with structural brain changes. A possible underlying biological cause, Crow suggests, may be a slow virus infection, a suggestion currently the focus of much research (Crow *et al.* 1979).

Social and cultural factors in schizophrenia

Two broad types of epidemiological hypotheses can be distinguished with regard to the development of schizophrenia. The first suggests that the condition is associated with factors that vary in different cultures and/or with different levels of civilization. The second hypothesis suggests that it is linked with immediate social stresses and/or with stresses acting early in a person's life which may impair his constitution in such a way that the later development of schizophrenia is facilitated or made inevitable.

1 *Culture and civilization*

Eliot Slater (1968) noted that using the European definition of schizophrenia the condition appears to be equally frequent in all countries 'where adequate investigations have been made' (*Table 4*). Slater argues that it is difficult to explain this relative constancy from one country to another, particularly when such countries differ in terms of their social organization and their model patterns of intra-familial relationships, unless one hypothesizes a genetical predisposition fairly evenly distributed over Europe and very likely over the world. However, some markedly deviant estimates of schizophrenia expectation have been found in a number of regions. For example, Book (1953) estimated a schizo-

Table 4 *Expectation of schizophrenia for the general population*

date	country	N^*	expectation %
1931	Switzerland	899	1·23
1936	Germany	7,955·5	0·51
1942	Denmark	23,251	0·69
1942	Finland	194,000	0·91
1946	Sweden	10,705	0·81
1959	Japan	10,545	0·82
1964	Iceland	4,913	0·73

$*$ N = number of lives at risk   (After Slater 1968)

phrenic rate of 2·85 per cent (or three times the Scandinavian rate) for an isolated part of Sweden, north of the Arctic Circle. However, inbreeding in such an isolated community could contribute to a somewhat higher frequency of the genetic predisposition and hence to the higher rate of illness. Less easy to explain is Garron's (1963) estimate of a schizophrenic expectation rate of 2·4 per cent in Geneva, although it is possible that the diagnostic criteria used in this study differed from the general European pattern.

Murphy (1968) has pointed to significantly higher expectation rates in four groups: the Tamilians of Southern India and Ceylon, the people of North-West Croatia, the Southern Irish, and Roman Catholics in Canada. He has argued that such a finding is strong evidence in favour of the view that cultural factors can affect the genesis of schizophrenia. However, it is not easy to identify what these factors might be. In an earlier study, Murphy had focused on the marked and culturally produced difficulties that young Tamilians manifest in coping with authority. In the case of North-West Croatia, he notes that this area has been seriously affected by the conflict of loyalties and identities arising from the Croats being Roman Catholic yet caught up in a national and pan-slavic movement to which Rome was opposed. He believes that a 'long-standing socio-cultural ambivalence' concerning its links with Europe, as opposed to its links with the rest of Croatia, 'could offer a hypothetical link to schizophrenia'. With regard to the Southern Irish and the Catholics in Canada, he speculates on a possible link between the genesis of schizophrenia and the cultural traditions of the Catholic Church. However, the high schizophrenic rates in these two areas apply only to males; the rates in females are not significantly higher than the equivalent non-Catholic rate. If the common aetiological factor is religious affiliation, whereby the specific religious teaching of the Church is in some way 'schizophrenic', one has to ask why such an effect should show itself in men rather than women. Murphy, somewhat ingeniously, tried to get around this by suggesting that the celibacy of the priesthood, and the fact that in Catholic life an important adult model held before growing males is one that excludes marriage and sexuality, may in some way raise specific problems for the schizophrenic-prone male. However, the celibacy of nuns presents girls with similar problems. Another explanation which has been advanced is that Catholicism, by stressing communality, obedience, and a greater attention to intangibles than, say, Protestantism, is less geared to modern competitive capitalism and that, as a result, Catholics face a greater difficulty in reconciling various expectations (religious, material, commercial, social) than do Protestants.

However, the explanation may be much simpler, illustrating the hazards of drawing conclusions from alleged differences in schizophrenic rates. For example, in the South of Ireland those areas hit hardest by the severe emigration affecting that community show the highest rates of schizophrenia. It is possible that there has been a selective emigration from these parts, leaving a higher proportion of schizophrenia-prone people behind, thereby artificially swelling the rate. The large percentage of single males in those areas showing high schizophrenic rates is of particular significance in that, as Brenden and Dermot Walsh (1968) have shown, the unmarried state increases the first admission risk to a greater degree for the Irish male than the Irish female. My own study of Irish immigrants to London (1974) found a schizophrenic rate that is no higher than that found in Britain, a surprising finding in view of the fact that most studies of immigrant groups show higher rates of schizophrenia than are found in the indigenous population.

This raises the possibility that the Irish who emigrated were in the main those genetically less prone to develop schizophrenia. Those left at home may represent a highly selected sample particularly predisposed to develop the condition. Thus the high rate of schizophrenia in the Southern Irish may well be explained on a demographic basis without recourse to cultural or religious hypotheses.

2 *Present social stresses*

Most of the major epidemiological studies of schizophrenia can be viewed as attempts to resolve problems of interpretation posed by some pioneer studies such as those of Faris and Dunham (1939) in Chicago, Clark (1948) in the same city, and Ødegaard (1936) in Norway.

Faris and Dunham, in their classic study, found higher rates of first hospital admissions for schizophrenia in the central areas of lowest socio-economic status in Chicago and diminishing rates as one moved towards higher-status, peripheral areas. Clark found a positive correlation between high rates of schizophrenia and a low socio-economic status, measured by occupation; as one moved up the occupational ladder so the rates of illness fell. High rates of schizophrenia have been reported in central areas of low socio-economic status in a number of American cities and two studies performed in European cities, Edward Hare's in Bristol (1967) and that of Sundby and Nyhus in Oslo (1963), are in substantial agreement. Likewise, the concentration of mental illness, and particularly schizophrenia, in low-status occupations has been repeatedly confirmed.

High rates of schizophrenia have also been reported in the poorer areas of London. A report by the Psychiatric Rehabilitation Association (1973) showed mental hospital admission rates in Hackney and Tower Hamlets well above the national rates and estimated the prevalence of schizophrenia in the two boroughs to be between two and three times the national average.

The Norwegian epidemiologist Ødegaard pioneered research into rates of illness in migrants. Consistently higher rates of schizophrenic illness have been reported in a wide range of immigrant groups although it is still far from clear whether this is due to the fact that those people predisposed to schizophrenia tend to migrate or that the stresses of migration provoke schizophrenic illnesses.

Indeed a major problem concerning the data on social stresses concerns the direction of causality. For example, rates of schizophrenia in the lowest socio-economic groups may be high either because conditions of life for such groups are conducive in some way to the development of the condition or because those in the higher socio-economic groups who develop schizophrenia suffer a decline in status. Or it could be a combination of both trends. The first hypothesis is referred to as the 'stress' hypothesis; the second is the so-called 'drift' hypothesis. Srole and his colleagues (1962), in their mid-town Manhattan study, argued strongly in favour of the 'stress' hypothesis and claimed that the rates of mental disorder correlated almost as well with the socio-economic status of the patients' parents as with that of the patients. Goldberg and Morrison (1963), in a much-quoted and influential British study, found that although the occupations of male schizophrenic patients admitted to hospital in England and Wales showed the usual concentration of cases in the lower socio-economic class, their fathers' occupations did not. Some aspects of this study are questionable, e.g., the index of social class employed is debatable and data are lacking for 25 per cent of the originally drawn sample. Nonetheless within its limits it presents a strong argument in favour of the 'drift' hypothesis.

Turner and Wagonfeld (1967) in a study of Munro, a county in New York State, discovered that the rates of first treatment of schizophrenics are disproportionately high both for patients of low occupational status and for patients whose fathers had low occupational status, but they showed that these by and large are not the same patients but constitute two separate groups. This study provides evidence both for the proposition that the stresses inherent in lower-class life are conducive to schizophrenia and for the proposition that most lower-class schizophrenics drift downwards as a result of contracting the illness.

One intriguing study (Rogler and Hollingshead 1965), which suggests that stress may play a more important aetiological role than has been commonly accepted, involved an intensive investigation of the life-histories of a sample of lower-class schizophrenics in San Juan, Puerto Rico. These patients were matched with a group of non-schizophrenic individuals who were as intensively assessed. No substantial difference emerged between the early life-experiences of the schizophrenics and the controls. However, what did emerge was the finding that within the period of a year prior to the appearance of symptoms of schizophrenia, the schizophrenics had been subjected to a far greater amount of stressful experiences. The authors of this study point out that all lower-class slum dwellers of San Juan suffer continual and dreadful deprivations of one sort or another, yet the members of the schizophrenic sample were apparently exposed to even further and more intolerable difficulties which appeared to 'trigger' the illness.

Hare (1967) concluded from an examination of the evidence available up to 1965 that the 'drift' hypothesis seemed better supported as an explanation of the association between high schizophrenic rates and poor socio-economic conditions and his view commands widespread support throughout clinical psychiatry in this country. It can, however, be contrasted with that of David Mechanic (1973), an American medical sociologist, who points out that, whereas the association between schizophrenia and social class does not appear to be a causal one, nevertheless social class does seem to have a major effect on the course of the condition by exposing lower-class schizophrenics to conditions that exaggerate the debilitating effects of the disorder.

A different approach to the relationship between 'stress' and schizophrenia involves the study of what have been termed 'life-events'. A group of American workers (Rahe, McKean, and Arthur 1967) set about analysing various changes in the average person's life-pattern and scored a series of forty-one types of life-change according to their estimate of the extent of such changes and the amount of adjustment required of an individual in meeting them. A *Life-Change Scale* was constructed, ranging from major events, such as the death of a spouse, to minor events, such as a period of leave. These workers claimed that a year of greater than average life-change preceded illnesses or clusters of illnesses in a random sample of fifty US naval personnel discharged on psychiatric grounds (see Chapter 2).

Two British workers, George Brown and James Birley (1968), studied consecutively admitted psychiatric patients diagnosed as suffering from an acute onset of a schizophrenic illness. They used a somewhat refined version of this life-change approach and, to reduce the possibility of memory errors, they charted the occurrence of life-events for the preceding three months only. They found that the schizophrenic patients experienced a significantly higher frequency of such events during a twelve-week period prior to the onset of their illnesses than did a matched group of non-schizophrenic controls.

'50 schizophrenics, in whom the onset of illness had occurred within 3 months of admission and could be dated within 1 week, were studied. Each patient and at least one relative were interviewed about events such as moving house, death, birth and illness of family members, starting or leaving a job, interpersonal conflicts etc. These events were classified as "independent" (i.e. outside the patient's control) or "possibly independent". In the 3-

week period immediately preceding the onset of the illness 46% of the patients experienced at least one "independent" life event compared to 12% of the patients who had experienced such an event in each of the three earlier 3-week periods. When both types of life events were considered (i.e. "independent" and "possibly independent"), the corresponding figures were 60% for the 3-week period before the onset of illness and 23% for the three earlier 3-week periods. The percentage of a control group of 325 persons experiencing a life event remained the same for all four 3-week periods preceding the interview ("independent" events, 14%; "independent" and "possibly independent" events, 19%).' (Brown and Birley 1968: 203)

A number of studies have laid particular emphasis on the apparent sensitivity of the schizophrenic to 'stress'. Peter Venables (1966) has drawn attention to a heightened physiological arousal in schizophrenia, both in those showing florid signs of psychosis and those showing marked social withdrawal, retardation, and apathy. The combination of slowing and lack of interest with increased physiological arousal might appear paradoxical. It is possible, however, that as a result of persistent 'over-arousal' the schizophrenic seeks to minimize the intensity and frequency of stressful stimuli to which he may be exposed. Left to himself, he quickly becomes socially withdrawn, apathetic, retarded, and often even mute. Such a withdrawal does not significantly affect his levels of arousal but in fact only results in the so-called 'secondary' and 'tertiary' handicaps seen in this condition. Such handicaps, seen in patients exposed to understimulating conditions in long-stay, poorly staffed mental hospitals, inadequately planned and ill-equipped hostels, and even in their own homes, have given rise to the stereotyped picture of the chronic mental patient as a stooped, apathetic, mumbling figure, impervious to all external stimuli, and totally withdrawn into a world of his own.

This theory suggests that schizophrenics require careful

and supervised exposure to emotionally arousing situations and stresses. In a study of discharged male schizophrenics (Brown, Carstairs, and Topping 1958) it was found that close emotional ties with parents or wives indicated a poor prognosis. A further study (Brown *et al.* 1962) found that those patients who returned home to live with relatives who were highly emotionally involved with them (as judged by ratings of the relatives' behaviour) were more likely to suffer a relapse of florid symptoms. Schizophrenics have been shown to react badly to high levels of 'expressed emotion' (Brown, Birley, and Wing 1972) and over-enthusiastic attempts to reactivate unprepared, long-stay patients have been shown to lead to a sudden relapse of symptoms, even when these have not been obvious for years (Wing, Bennett, and Denham 1964).

So it would appear that an environment that is too stressful can result in an exacerbation of so-called 'positive' symptoms (florid hallucinations, delusions, anxiety, excitement, and symptomatology) whereas one that is lacking in colour, interest, and stimulation can lead to the development of 'negative' symptoms (apathy, retardation, poverty of movement, stupor). There are obvious practical implications in this for all those involved in living with and caring for schizophrenic patients, such as parents and other relatives as well as employers, voluntary helpers, and professional therapists.

Associations have been sought between schizophrenic rates and such factors as maternal age, sibling size, birth order, and season of birth. Some slight evidence suggests that there is an association in large families between schizophrenia and low birth order (Zubin *et al.* 1961). There is some evidence too that suggests that a marked excess of winter births is found amongst schizophrenic patients. Dalan (1968) has reported on a study of schizophrenic patients selected from all patients born and treated in Sweden in which he compared their season-of-birth distribution with that of the general population averaged over a ten-year period. He found a very significant difference in the month-of-birth distribution between schizophrenics and the general population, the schizophrenics having an excess of births in January to April and a deficiency in July to October. Hare, Price, and Slater (1974) examined the season-of-birth distribution in 46,000 patients admitted for the first time to a psychiatric bed in England and Wales during 1970 and 1971 and who had been born in England and Wales during 1921–1955. Their quarterly distribution of birth was compared on a year-by-year basis with that of all live births in England and Wales and a highly significant excess of births in the first quarter of the year was noted for schizophrenia (and for manic-depressive psychosis). Possible explanations include abnormal sexual behaviour traits on the parts of the parents of schizophrenics leading to an abnormal seasonal distribution in the births of their children (unlikely on its face value but could perhaps be proved or disproved by taking a look at the season of birth of the patients' siblings), and the suggestion that winter-born children are prone to nutritional deficiencies or infections which in some way damage the constitution and so facilitate the manifestations of a functional psychosis in those genetically at risk.

Opinions about the role of precipitating factors in the genesis of schizophrenia have been complicated by the tendency to make assumptions about *cause*, e.g., to assume that since close family ties can *provoke* a schizophrenic relapse they therefore *cause* it, that because certain biochemical disturbances are *associated* with an acute schizophrenic episode this means that they underlie and *produce* it, that because schizophrenia tends to be seen more in the lower social classes, this proves that social deprivation *causes* schizophrenia to appear.

The psychoanalytical view of schizophrenia

The process of understanding psychic material as it arises from other psychic material has been termed 'psychological understanding'. It is a subjective activity and the natural scientist, concerned in the main with what can be perceived by the senses and concerned also with *causal* explanations, 'expresses an understandable and justified disinclination towards the psychological explanation where it is used to take the place of his own work' (Jaspers 1913). All psychoanalytic thinking, however, is based on the assumption that psychological phenomena are amenable to understanding and that the verbal and non-verbal communications of patients can be comprehended, albeit with the considerable effort that analytical exploration involves. Such a view has made its own contribution to the confusion, discussed in more detail in Chapter 3, between *meaningful* connections and *causal* ones. The analyst, in his evaluation of his patient's psychopathology, draws meaningful connections between the latter's personal, subjective experiences, thoughts, and feelings and the genesis and development of his psychological disturbance. That such connections can become transmuted with ease into statements of cause is illustrated by the elaborate explanatory theories of the various psychoanalytic schools and by the dogmatic certainty with which they tend to be asserted.

It is worth noting that Freud never deliberately attempted to analyse a psychotically ill patient. He believed that psychoanalysis involved working with the patient's transference and, since psychotic patients were deemed to be wholly narcissistic and therefore incapable of sustaining a transference relationship in therapy, analysis had little to offer. However, many analysts disagreed, arguing that nobody is totally psychotic and that even in the severely ill schizophrenic there are areas of personality that are neurotic and capable of forming the basis of analytic treatment. A number of analysts in the United States, including Frieda Fromm Reichman and H. Searles, worked with schizophrenic patients on the assumption that treatment of these healthy areas of the personality would strengthen them and allow them to become dominant in relation to the psychotic parts (a situation believed to occur in remissions of the disorder). Such analysts argue that while schizophrenic patients can form transference relationships, such relationships differ qualitatively from those seen in neurotic patients.

A somewhat different approach was initiated by Melanie Klein and currently commands a number of adherents in this country (Klein 1952). This system holds that schizophrenia is a regression to an infantile stage of personality development. The small child, according to Mrs Klein, is capable of forming intense transferences, both positive and negative. Early in life the ego is organized to experience anxiety, to build defence mechanisms and to form primitive 'object relations' both in real life and in phantasy forms. In defence against the overwhelming anxiety of annihilation, for example, the ego develops the capacity to project and introject, to split off good and bad parts of the self and project them into objects which, through 'projective introjection', become identified with these parts of the self. A prominent Kleinian, Hanna Segal, describes the infant's mechanisms for dealing with anxiety thus:

'When an infant has an intolerable anxiety, he deals with it by projecting it into the mother. The mother's response is to acknowledge this anxiety and do whatever is necessary to relieve the infant's distress. The infant's perception is that he has projected something intolerable into his object, but the object was capable of containing it and dealing with it. He can then reintroject not only his original anxiety but an anxiety modified by having been contained. He also introjects an object capable of containing and dealing with anxiety. The containment of the anxiety by an internal object capable of understanding it is a beginning of mental stability.' (Segal 1975: 96)

However, such a stability may be disrupted in two ways. The mother may be unable to cope with the infant's projected anxiety and the infant may reintroject an experience of even greater anxiety than the one he had projected. Or it may also be disrupted by 'excessive destructive omnipotence of the infant's phantasy'.

Within the analytical model of treatment the analyst acts as a container into which the patient can project his intolerable anxieties and impulses. The analyst, by his tolerance and understanding, enables the patient to reintroject these projected parts plus the functions of the analyst with which he can identify.

Inevitably, since this approach declares itself to be a 'treatment', the question arises – what is its value? Psychoanalysis is time-consuming, expensive, and is not readily available within the NHS. It is a theoretical system and, in the opinion of its critics, it does not possess that criterion of falsifiability which, it is argued, is the mark of a truly *scientific* hypothesis (Eysenck and Wilson 1973; Popper 1963). It is not my purpose, however, to go over old ground in this controversy. Instead, it is worth noting that many analysts at the present time appear to recognize that the applicability of a treatment such as psychoanalysis is severely limited in schizophrenia. Hanna Segal (1975) believes it is useful in 'rare cases' in which 'all the conditions are right', but it is clear from all that has gone before that such patients represent a tiny fraction of psychotically ill people and are not especially representative of schizophrenic patients in general. She goes on to argue the doubtful proposition that psychoanalysis by virtue of its capability to throw light on 'the actual psychopathology of the illness' has a key role to play in 'all other psychotherapeutic endeavours, such as management, group therapy, individual psychotherapy, community care, etc.'.

That psychoanalysis has made a significant contribution towards the understanding and elucidation of schizophrenia is far from self-evident. Placed beside the pharmacological developments, the social advances, the genetic evidence, and the epidemiological knowledge now available, and little of this amounts to very much, the insights provided by analytic speculation are modest indeed.

Summary

So where, it may be asked, does all this research, these hypotheses, and the few findings worthy of the name leave the question of what causes schizophrenia? A strong genetic component does appear to be important, but although genetic factors may be necessary they are not always sufficient for the occurrence of a schizophrenic illness. There are well-known physical precipitants, such as an acute illness or childbirth, which may usher in a serious schizophrenic episode, and certain drug intoxications, for example, with mescaline, amphetamines, and LSD, which produce a mental disturbance that is in a number of important respects similar to schizophrenia. A number of environmental and psychological stresses appear to be important in 'triggering' the illness, and in so far as disturbed family relationships and interactions contribute to the development of the condition it is as 'agent provocateur' that they appear to do so. A number of neurochemical hypotheses currently look promising, but to date no acceptable finding of aetiological significance has emerged.

Not a lot of gold-dust to show for over a century of painstaking observation, sifting, and sieving of the mud of human experience. Amidst all the plasma levels, the elaborate multidimensional schemata of the family theorists, the physiological models of the laboratory scientists, the fanciful speculations of the analysts, it is sometimes easy to lose sight of the seriousness of the condition and of the suffering, the often unbearable anguish of the schizophrenic's experience. Personal accounts by patients of their agony and mental pain provide a necessary balance to the aseptic world of fluid levels and abnormal globulins, the dry, desiccated jargon of birth-order statistics and national prevalence, the bland jargon of repertory grids and psychological tests. Clifford Beers has provided a valuable if horrifying account of the sensory disturbances experienced by him at the height of his illness:

'Soon after I was placed in my room all my senses became perverted. I still heard "false voices" which were doubly false for truth no longer existed. The tricks played upon me by my perverted sense of taste, touch, smell and sight were the source of great mental anguish. None of my food had its usual flavour. This soon led me to that common delusion that some of it contained poison . . . Stifling fumes of sulphur are as the crisp air of wooded glens compared to the odour of burning flesh and other pestilential fumes which seemed to assail me . . . All these horrors I took for the work of detectives who sat up nights racking their brains in order to rack and utterly wreck my own with a cruel and unfair "Third Degree". Imaginary breezes struck my face – they seemed to come from cracks in the walls and ceilings and annoyed me exceedingly. I thought them in some way related to that Chinese method of torture by which water is allowed to strike the victim's forehead, a drop at a time, until death releases him.' (Beers 1908: 28–9)

Few of us, indeed few schizophrenics, can portray the sufferings and the hallucinations of the schizophrenic's experience so powerfully. For all the advances, in understanding and in treatment, the condition remains a baffling and enigmatic one, a harrowing experience for the individual sufferer, and a challenge to the ingenuity and skill of those intent on unlocking its secrets.

References

ALLEN, M.G., COHEN, S., and POLLIN, W. (1972)
Schizophrenia in Veteran Twins: A Diagnostic Review.
American Journal of Psychiatry **128**: 939–90.

BATESON, G., JACKSON, D., HALEY, J., and WEAKLAND,
J. (1956) Towards a Theory of Schizophrenia.
Behavioural Science **1**: 251–64.

BEERS, C.W. (1908) *A Mind that Found Itself: An
Autobiography.* New York: Longmans, Green & Co.

BOOK, J.A. (1953) A Genetic and Neuro-Psychiatric

Investigation of a North-Swedish Population. *Acta Genetica et Statistica Medica* 4: 1–100.

BROWN, G.W. and BIRLEY, J.L.T. (1968) Social Change and the Onset of Schizophrenia. *Journal of Health Behaviour* 9: 203.

BROWN, G.W., BIRLEY, J.L.T., and WING, J.K. (1972) Influence of Family Life on the Course of Schizophrenic Disorders: A Replication. *British Journal of Psychiatry* 121: 241–58.

BROWN, G.W., CARSTAIRS, G.M., and TOPPING, G.G. (1958) The Post-Hospital Adjustment of Chronic Mental Patients. *Lancet* ii: 685.

BROWN, G.W., MONCK, E.M., CARSTAIRS, G.M., and WING, J.K. (1962) The Influence of Family Life on the Course of Schizophrenic Illness. *British Journal of Preventive and Social Medicine* 16: 55.

CARLINI, E.A., SANTOS, M., and SAMPAIO, M.R.P. (1965) Potentiation of Histamine and Inhibition of Diamine-Oxidase by Mescaline. *Experimentia* 21 (72): 1–4.

CLARE, A.W. (1974) Mental Illness in the Irish Emigrant. *Journal of the Irish Medical Association* 67 (1): 20–24.

CLARK, R.E. (1948) The Relationship of Schizophrenia to Occupational Income and Occupational Prestige. *American Sociological Review* 13: 325–30.

COHEN, D.J., DIBBLE, E., CRAWE, J.M., and POLLIN, W. (1973) Separating Identical from Fraternal Twins. *Archives of General Psychiatry* 29: 465–9.

COULTER, J. (1973) *Approaches to Insanity.* London: Martin Robertson.

CROW, T.J. (1980) Molecular pathology of schizophrenia: More than one disease process? *British Medical Journal* 280: 66–8.

CROW, T.J., FERRIER, I.N., and JOHNSTONE, E.C.(1979) Characteristics of patients with schizophrenia or neurological disorder and virus-like agent in cerebrospinal fluid. *Lancet* i: 842–4.

DAHLBERG, G. (1926) *Twin Births and Twins from a Hereditary Point of View*. Uppsala.

DALAN, P. (1968) Month of Birth and Schizophrenia. *Acta Psychiatrica Scandinavica* (Supplement 203): 48–54.

DOHAN, F.C. (1966) Cereals and Schizophrenia. Data and Hypothesis. *Acta Psychiatrica Scandinavica* **42**: 125–52.

DURRELL, J. (1973) Introduction. In J. Mendels (ed), *Biological Psychiatry*. New York: Wiley.

EYSENCK, J. and WILSON, G. (1973) *The Experimental Study of Freudian Theories*. London: Methuen.

FARIS, R.E.L. and DUNHAM, H.W. (1939) *Mental Disorders in Urban Areas*. Chicago: Hafner.

FISCHER, M., HARVALD, B., and HAUGE, M. (1969) A Danish Twin Study of Schizophrenia. *British Journal of Psychiatry* **115**: 981–90.

FRIEDHOFF, A. (1973) Biogenic Amines and Schizophrenia. In J. Mendels (ed.), *Biological Psychiatry*. New York: Wiley.

FRIEDHOFF, A. J. and VAN WINKLE, E. (1962) Isolation and Characterisation of a Compound from the Urine of Schizophrenics. *Nature* **194**: 897–8.

FROHMAN, C.E. (1973) Plasma Proteins and Schizophrenia. In J. Mendels (ed.), *Biological Psychiatry*. New York: Wiley.

GARRONS, G. (1963) Étude statistique et génétique de la schizophrenia à Geneve de 1901 à 1950. *Journal de Génétique Humaine* **11**: 89–219.

GOLDBERG, E.M. and MORRISON, S.L. (1963) Schizophrenia and Social Class. *British Journal of Psychiatry* **109**: 785–802.

GOTTESMAN, I.I. and SHIELDS, J. (1966) Contribution of Twin Studies to Perspectives on Schizophrenia. In B. A. Maher (ed.), *Progress in Experimental Personality Research*. New York: Academic Press.

—— (1972) *Schizophrenia and Genetics – A Twin Study Vantage Point*. New York: Academic Press.

—— (1973) Genetic Theorizing and Schizophrenia. *British Journal of Psychiatry* **122**: 15–30.

HARE, E.H. (1967a) Mental Illness and Social Conditions in Bristol. *Journal of Mental Science* **102**: 349–57.

—— (1967b) The Epidemiology of Schizophrenia. In A. Coppen and A. Walk (eds.), *Developments in Schizophrenia. Royal Medico-Psychological Association Special Publication* No. 1.

HARE, E., PRICE, J.S., and SLATER, E. (1974) Mental Disorder and Season of Birth. *British Journal of Psychiatry* **124**: 81–6.

HAWKINS, D. and PAULING, L. (1973) *Orthomolecular Psychiatry: Treatment of Schizophrenia*. San Francisco: W. H. Freeman.

HENRY, J. (1973) *Pathways to Madness*. New York: Vintage Books.

HESTON, L. (1966) Psychiatric Disorders in Foster Home Reared Children of Schizophrenic Mothers. *British Journal of Psychiatry* **112**: 819–25.

—— (1972) Genes and Psychiatry. In J. Mendels (ed.), *Biological Psychiatry*. New York: Wiley.

HIRSCH, S.R. and LEFF, J.P. (1971) Parental Abnormalities of Verbal Communication in the Transmission of Schizophrenia. *Psychological Medicine* **1**: 118–27.

HIRSCH, S.R. and LEFF, J. P. (1975) *Abnormalities in Parents of Schizophrenics*. Maudsley Monograph No. 22. Oxford University Press.

HORNYKIEWIEZ, D. (1963) Topische Localisation des Verhalten von Noradrenalin und Dopamin (3-hydroxytyramin) in der Substantia nigra des normalen und Parkinsonkranken Menschen. *Wien Klin. Wochenschr.* **75**: 309–12.

HORROBIN, D.F. (1979) Schizophrenia: Reconciliation of the Dopamine, Prostaglandin and Opioid Concepts and the Role of the Pineal. *Lancet* **i**: 529–30.

HUGHES, J. and KOSTERLITZ, H.W. (1977) Opioid Peptides. *British Medical Bulletin* **33**: 157.

INOUYE, E. (1961) Similarity and Dissimilarity of Schizophrenia in Twins. *Proceedings of the Third World Congress on Psychiatry*. Montreal: University of Toronto Press.

IVERSEN, L.L. (1978) Biochemical and Pharmacological Studies: The Dopamine Hypothesis. In: *Schizophrenia: Towards a New Synthesis* (Ed. J. K. Wing). Chapter 4, p. 92. London: Academic Press.

JACKSON, D.D. (1960) *The Aetiology of Schizophrenia*. New York: Basic Books.

JASPERS, K. (1974) Causal and 'Meaningful' Connexions between Life History and Psychosis. In S. R. Hirsch and M. Shepherd (eds.), *Themes and Variations in European Psychiatry*. Bristol: John Wright.

KALLMANN, F. (1938) *The Genetics of Schizophrenia*. New York: Augustin.

—— (1946) The Genetic Theory of Schizophrenia. *American Journal of Psychiatry* **103**: 309–22.

KARLSSON, J.L. (1970) The Rate of Schizophrenia in Foster-Reared Close Relatives of Schizophrenic Index Cases. *Biological Psychiatry* **2**: 285–90.

—— (1974) Inheritance of Schizophrenia. *Acta Psychiatrica Scandinavica* (Supplement 247).

KETY, S.S. (1973) Problems in Biological Research in Psychiatry. In J. Mendels (ed.), *Biological Psychiatry*. New York: Wiley.

KETY, S.S., ROSENTHAL, D., WENDER, P.H., SCHULSINGER, F. and JACOBSEN, B. (1975) In: *Genetic Research in Psychiatry* (Eds R. R. Fieve, D. Rosenthal, and H. Brill) pps. 147–65. Baltimore: Johns Hopkins University Press.

KETY, S.S., ROSENTHAL, D., WENDER, P.H., and SCHULSINGER, F. (1968) The Types and Prevalence of Mental Illness in the Biological and Adoptive Families of Adopted Schizophrenics. In D. Rosenthal and S. S. Kety (eds.), *The Transmission of Schizophrenia*. Oxford: Pergamon Press.

KLEIN, M. (1952) Notes on Some Schizoid Mechanisms. In E. Jones (ed.), *Developments in Psychoanalysis*. London: Hogarth Press.

KOHN, M.L. (1968) Social Class and Schizophrenia. A Critical Review. In D. Rosenthal and S. S. Kety (eds.), *The Transmission of Schizophrenia*. Oxford: Pergamon Press.

KOHN, M.L. and KLAUSEN, J.A. (1956) Parental Authority Behaviour and Schizophrenia. *American Journal of Orthopsychiatry* **26**: 297–313.

KRINGLEN, E. (1967) *Heredity and Environment in the Functional Psychoses*. Oslo: Universitetsforlaget.

LAING, R.D. (1967) *The Politics of Experience*. Harmondsworth: Penguin.

Lancet (1974) Dimethyltryptamine and Psychosis (editorial). *Lancet* **ii**: 140–41.

LIDZ, T. (1968a) Quoted by D. Rosenthal in D. Rosenthal and S. S. Kety (eds.), *The Transmission of Schizophrenia*: 424–5. Oxford: Pergamon Press.

—— (1968b) The Family, Language and the Transmission of Schizophrenia. In D. Rosenthal and S. S. Kety (eds.), *The Transmission of Schizophrenia*. Oxford: Pergamon Press.

LIDZ, T., FLACK, S., and CORNELISON, A. (1965) *Schizophrenia and the Family*. New York: International Press.

LUXENBURGER, H. (1928) Vorlaufiger Bericht über Psychiatrische Seri nuntersuchungen an Zwillingen. *Zeitschrift für die Gesamte Neurologie und Psychiatrie* **116**: 297–326.

MCISAAC, W.M. (1961) A Biochemical Concept of Mental Disease. *Postgraduate Medicine* **30**: 111–18.

MECHANIC, D. (1973) The Contributions of Sociology of Psychiatry (editorial). *Psychological Medicine* **3** (1): 1–4.

MISHLER, E.G. and WAXLER, N.E. (1965) Family Interaction Processes and Schizophrenia. A Review of Current Theories. *Merrill-Palmer Quarterly* **2**: 269.

MURPHY, H.B.M. (1968) Cultural Factors in the Genesis of Schizophrenia. In D. Rosenthal and S. S. Kety (eds.), *The Transmission of Schizophrenia*. Oxford: Pergamon Press.

NEWMAN, H.H. (1923) *The Physiology of Twinning*. Chicago: University of Chicago Press.

ØDEGAARD, O. (1936) Emigration and Mental Health. *Mental Hygiene* **20**: 546–53.

POLLIN, W. (1972) The Pathogenesis of Schizophrenia. *Archives of General Psychiatry* **27**: 29–37.

POLLIN, W., CARDEN, P., and KETY, S.S. (1961) Effect of Aminoacid Feedings in Schizophrenics. *Nature* **194**: 897–8.

POPPER, K. (1963) *Conjectures and Refutations*. London: Routledge & Kegan Paul.

PSYCHIATRIC REHABILITATION ASSOCIATION (1973) Report quoted in D. Ennals, *Out of Mind*. London: Arrow.

RAHE, R.H., MCKEAN, J.D., and ARTHUR, R.J. (1967) A Longitudinal Study of Life Change and Illness-Patterns. *Journal of Psychosomatic Research* **10**: 355.

RODNIGHT, R. (1971) Biochemical Research in Psychiatry (editorial). *Psychological Medicine* **1** (5): 353–5.

RODNIGHT, R., MURRAY, R.M., OON, M.C.H., BROCKINGTON, I.F., NICHOLLS, P. and BIRLEY, J.L.T. (1977) Urinary dimethyltryptamine and psychiatric symptomology and classification. *Psychological Medicine* **6**: 649–57.

ROGLER, L.H. and HOLLINGSHEAD, A.B. (1965) *Trapped: Families and Schizophrenia*. New York: Wiley.

ROSENTHAL, D. (1968) Confusion of Identity and the Frequency of Schizophrenia in Twins. *Archives of General Psychiatry* **3**: 297–304.

—— (1972) Three Adoption Studies of Heredity in the Schizophrenic Disorders. *International Journal of Mental Health* **1**: 63–75.

SEGAL, H. (1975) Psychoanalytical Approach to the Treatment of Schizophrenia. In M. H. Lader (ed.), *Studies of Schizophrenia*. Ashford, Kent: Headley Bros.

SHIELDS, J. (1978) Genetics. In: *Schizophrenia: Towards a New Synthesis* (Edited by J. K. Wing). Chapter 3, pps. 53–87. London: Academic Press. New York: Grune & Stratton.

SIEMENS, H.W. (1924) *Die Zwillingspathologie. Ihre Bedeutung, Ihre Methodifi, Ihre bisherigen Ergebnisse*. Berlin: Springer Verlag.

SINGER, M.T. and WYNNE, L. (1965) Thought Disorder and Family Relations of Schizophrenics. IV. Results and Implications. *Archives of General Psychiatry* **12**: 201–12.

SLATER, E. (1968) A Review of Earlier Evidence on Genetic Factors in Schizophrenia. In D. Rosenthal and S. S. Kety (eds.), *The Transmission of Schizophrenia*. Oxford: Pergamon Press.

SLATER, E. and COWIE, V. (1971) *The Genetics of Mental Disorder*. London: Oxford University Press.

SROLE, L., LANGNER, T.S., MICHAEL, S.T., OPLER, M.K., and RENNIE, T.A.C. (1962) *Mental Health in the Metropolis: The Midtown Manhattan Study*. Vol. 1. New York: McGraw-Hill.

STABENAU, J.R., POLLIN, W., MOSHER, L.R., FROHMAN, C., FRIEDHOFF, A.J., and TURNER, W. (1969) Study of Monozygotic Twins Discordant for Schizophrenia. *Archives of General Psychiatry* **20**: 145–58.

STIERLIN, H. (1974) Psychoanalytic Approach to Schizophrenia in the Light of a Family Model. *International Review of Psycho-Analysis* **1**: 169–78.

SUNDBY, P. and NYHUS, P. (1963) Major and Minor Psychiatric Disorders in Males in Oslo: An Epidemiological Study. *Acta Psychiatrica Scandinavica* **39**: 519–47.

TIENARI, P. (1971) Schizophrenia and Monozygotic Twins. *Psychiatrica Fennica* 97–104.

TURNER, R.J. and WAGONFELD, M.O. (1967)
Occupational Mobility and Schizophrenia. An
Assessment of the Social Causation and Social
Selection Hypothesis. *American Sociological Review*
32: 104–113.

VENABLES, P.H. (1966) The Psychophysiological Aspects of
Schizophrenia. *British Journal of Medical Psychology* **39**: 289.

WALSH, D. and WALSH, B. (1968) Some Influence on the
Intercounty Variation in Irish Hospitalisation Rates.
British Journal of Psychiatry **114**: 15–20.

WENDER, P.H., ROSENTHAL, D., and KETY, S.S. (1968)
A Psychiatric Assessment of the Adoptive Parents of
Schizophrenics. In D. Rosenthal and S. S. Kety (eds.),
The Transmission of Schizophrenia. Oxford: Pergamon
Press.

WING, J.K. (1973a) Schizophrenia: Medical and Social
Models. Lecture delivered at the University of Vienna,
December 1973.

—— (1973b) Social and Familial Factors in the Causation
and Treatment of Schizophrenia. In L. I. Iverson and
S. P. R. Rose (eds.), *Biochemistry and Mental Illness*.
London: The Biochemical Society.

WING, J.K., BENNETT, D.H., and DENHAM, J. (1964)
The Industrial Rehabilitation of Long-Stay
Schizophrenic Patients. *Medical Research Council* Memo.
No. 42. London: HMSO.

WYATT, R.J., SAAVEDRA, J.M., and AXELROD, J.
(1973) A Dimethyltryptamine-Forming Enzyme in
Human Blood. *American Journal of Psychiatry* 130: 754–60.

WYNNE, L.C. and SINGER, M.T. (1963) Thought Disorder
and Family Relations of Schizophrenics. 1. A Research
Strategy. *Archives of General Psychiatry* **9**: 191–8.

ZUBIN, J., SUTTON, S., SALZINGER, S., BURDOCK,
E.I., and PERETZ, D. (1961) A Biometric Approach to
Prognosis in Schizophrenia. In P. Hoch and J. Zubin
(eds.), *Comparative Epidemiology of the Mental Disorders*.
London and New York: Grune & Stratton.

6

Electroconvulsive therapy

Of the many treatments of the severe mentally ill, none is so effective for specific clinical disorders and so misunderstood as induced convulsions or electroshock.   MARTIN M. KATZ 1974: xi

I have met many people who have been treated with ECT. Few regard it with anything short of abhorrence. Most refuse to recall their experiences, which they have well buried. The mindless nature of the process apart, it represents an experience of being treated as a thing.   MICHAEL BARNETT 1973: 45

THERE IS scarcely a more controversial or a more widely used treatment in contemporary British psychiatry than electroconvulsive treatment – ECT. Accounts of the procedure by hostile critics and by some patients who have experienced it suggest a treatment approach whereby minds are blown apart, memories erased, and feelings blunted by a procedure more closely resembling an amateur mechanic kicking his defective car than a scientifically validated medical treatment. First-hand accounts tell of bodies writhing, people whimpering, and limbs thrashing uncontrollably, and there is a firm body of opinion that testifies to the irreversible damage to the brain itself said to occur in patients who have undergone hundreds of shock treatments.

The roots of electrical treatment lie buried deep in the history of psychiatry. That electricity can stun was known to Hippocrates and his colleagues by way of their familiarity with the electric torpedo or cramp-fish found in Mediterranean waters. In an address delivered to the Royal Society in 1774, Sir John Pringle (1774) described how before the days of Galen the torpedo fish was applied to affected parts of the body and was particularly effective in easing persistent headaches. Earlier in 1756, John Wesley procured an apparatus that could deliver electric shocks and found the treatment so effective that he declared 'hundreds, perhaps thousands, have received unspeakable good' (p. 420). A surgeon at St Thomas's Hospital, John Birch, was one of the first dedicated advocates of electricity as a therapeutic agent and in 1792 in a letter to George Adams, an instrument-maker who provided Birch with many of his electricity machines, he explained how he administered the treatment to a porter suffering from a melancholic state for almost a year. Six small shocks were passed through the brain in different directions on each of three successive days, following which the patient regained his spirits, went back to his work, and remained perfectly well for seven years (Birch 1792).

In his *A Treatise on Madness*, published in 1758, William Battie noted that 'one species of spasm, however occasioned, seldom fails to put an end to that other which before subsisted'. At this time the belief that massive excitation or exposure to some form of physical stress might have a beneficial effect on mental distress flourished. An extraordinary array of 'treatments' based on such a belief appeared: burning, cupping, whirling, starving, immersing in freezing or boiling water, bleeding, binding – these were among the formidable activities inflicted on the unfortunate patient in the hope that he might be shaken out of his distracted state. Long before electroshock was first used, methods for inducing epileptic fits were employed in the hope of triggering a therapeutically useful reaction. In 1785, Dr W. Oliver published an account of the results of administering camphor in a case of melancholia. In high doses, camphor, which is extracted from a particular type of laurel tree, can induce epileptic seizures. Dr Oliver gave the camphor by mouth, following which the patient became sick and dizzy and had to be put to bed. Shortly afterwards

'. . . his senses returned to him, and something like a flash of lightening, he said, preceded their return. He now quitted his confinement and trials were made of his behaviour in various companies, at different houses. Parties were formed for him, at his own house; he became natural,

easy, polite, and in every respect like himself, and played
his game at whist with great accuracy.'

(Oliver 1785)

The patient did subsequently relapse, becoming melancholic again, and a further dose of camphor was given, following which he became cheerful and in good heart once more.

Interest in camphor-induced fits waxed and waned
throughout the following two centuries. Early in the 1930s,
the Hungarian psychiatrist Dr Laszlo Meduna hit upon an
ingenious modification. The camphor method of inducing fits
was slow and unreliable and was supplanted when Meduna
discovered that intravenous injections of metrazol, a soluble
component of the synthetic camphor preparation, produced
more reliable convulsions. While he refined this technique,
Ugo Cerletti, a psychiatric research worker in Rome, was
investigating changes in brain tissue produced by convulsions
in animals. To avoid excess damage, Cerletti had so perfected
his technique that a fit could be induced with as little as sixty
to seventy volts passed between two electrodes for less than
one-tenth of a second. When Meduna published his preliminary results with metrazol, Cerletti read them and it
immediately occurred to him, and to those members of his
research team who were daily inducing fits on an experimental basis in dogs, that such electrical methods might be
technically more acceptable and therapeutically more effective in man than chemically induced convulsions.

As David Impastato (1960) points out in his account of the
first ECT, most of Cerletti's colleagues 'were timid and feared
causing death, irreversible brain changes and epileptic states'.
Cerletti, however, was made of sterner stuff. He undertook
further studies, applying electrodes to the heads of pigs, made
available to him in the slaughter-house in Rome. (It was
commonly believed that the pigs were killed by the electric
current in the slaughter-house. In fact, they were rendered
unconscious thereby enabling the butchers to stab and bleed
them without difficulty.) Cerletti endeavoured to find out the

quantity of current and the length of time it had to be applied for death to occur. He discovered that a very large amount of current applied over a prolonged period of time was needed and that there was a significant difference between a *convulsant* and a *lethal* dose of electricity. It was then that he decided to go ahead and use this method in man.

Until this time Cerletti had refrained from applying the electrodes to the skulls of his experimental animals, attaching them instead to different parts of the body, usually the mouth and rectum. His findings in the Rome slaughter-house convinced him that application of the electrodes to the head was both safe and feasible. His colleague Bini, together with an electrical engineer, devised the first electroshock box, which had two circuits: a direct circuit to measure the resistance of the patient's head (in ohms) and an alternating circuit to elicit the convulsion. This circuit included a timer which measured time in tenths of a second up to a minute, a potentiometer which allowed the voltage to vary from 50 to 150 and an ammeter to indicate the milliamperage which flowed between the electrodes.

The rationale for the use of convulsive therapy, like the treatment itself, had become somewhat refined since Battie's somewhat crude statement. Several investigators had suggested that the correlation between epilepsy and schizophrenia was unusually low and that when they did occur together the occurrence of an epileptic seizure appeared to modify the schizophrenic symptoms. Meduna summarized this view as follows:

> Between schizophrenia and epilepsy there exists a sort of biological antagonism which must be expressed in the pathological course of the two diseases. Without being able to characterise these pathological actions, I feel justified in asserting a priority that these courses are either mutually exclusive or they do, at least to a certain degree, weaken each other in their mutual effects.'

(Meduna 1938: 44–5)

Such a hypothesis has not stood the test of time. There is no worthwhile evidence to support the idea of a 'biological antagonism' between the two conditions; indeed there is some firm data showing a strong positive association between a certain form of epilepsy, temporal lobe epilepsy, and schizophrenia. However, Cerletti, in common with most of his contemporaries, accepted Meduna's hypothesis. He had his shock box. All that was needed now was a suitable patient.

He arrived in the shape of an incoherently gibbering 'catatonic schizophrenic' from Northern Italy, found wandering in a Rome railway station by the police. He appeared confused, was quite unable to provide the simplest information about himself, and expressed himself in a severely thought-disordered fashion. No one could identify him. David Impastato takes up the story:

'The patient was brought in, the machine was set at one-tenth of a second and 70 volts and the shock given. Naturally the low dosage resulted in a petit mal reaction. After the electric spasm, which lasted a fraction of a second, the patient burst into song. The Professor (Cerletti) suggested that another treatment with a higher voltage be given. The staff objected. They stated that if another treatment were given the patient would probably die and wanted further treatment postponed until the morrow. The Professor knew what that meant. He decided to go right ahead then and there, but before he could say so the patient suddenly sat up and pontifically proclaimed, no longer in a jargon, but in clear Italian: "Non una seconda." (Not again, it will kill me.) This made the Professor think and swallow, but his courage was not lost. He gave the order to proceed at a higher voltage and a longer time; and the first electroconvulsion in man ensued.'

(Impastato 1960: 1113–14)

This first ECT was administered in 1938. Over the next twenty years electroconvulsive treatment gradually became established as the major physical treatment in psychiatric practice. Attention was paid to what constituted the appropriate number and frequency of induced convulsions, the optimal strength and type of current, the most suitable part of the head to which to apply the electrodes, and the psychiatric conditions for which it seemed most appropriate. The development of a group of drugs capable of briefly paralysing muscles (curare, gallamine, succinylcholine) and of short-acting anaesthetic agents (thiopental, methohexital) meant that ECT could be administered with reasonable safety, few side-effects, and a minimum of discomfort. The muscle relaxant ensured that a fit could be induced without a concomitant and massive spasm of the major muscles (a spasm which, if severe enough, could result in a fracture of the spine) while the anaesthetic relieved the patient's understandable anxiety during the treatment and much of his post-seizure anxiety as well.

How ECT is given

The patient is instructed to abstain from food for at least four hours before treatment, to rule out any danger of vomiting while under the anaesthetic. One milligram of atropine (a routine pre-anaesthetic medication) is given some thirty minutes before the treatment to dry up salivary and bronchial secretions and to reduce the likelihood of anaesthetic or shock-induced heart irregularities. The patient lies on a bed or couch with the pillow removed and the usual precautions (e.g., removal of false teeth, spectacles, etc.) observed. He is then given an intravenous injection of a short-acting anaesthetic (usually thiopental in a dose of 125–250 mg) and, through the same needle, a dose of muscle relaxant (usually 30–50 mg of succinylcholine). Within fifteen to twenty seconds of the injection, slight rippling of the muscles under the skin can be seen (muscle fasciculations) which serve to indicate that muscle paralysis is imminent and the anaesthetist takes over respiration of the patient by way of a face mask and a pressure bag. When the fasciculations have ceased and the patient is well oxygenated (skin colour good, blood pressure and pulse steady), the shock can be safely administered. Two electrodes, dampened with a bicarbonate solution to prevent skin burns at their points of contact, are applied to the anterior temporal areas of the scalp (at each side of the head, above and in front of each ear). A gag is inserted in the patient's mouth to prevent him biting his tongue. An electric current, usually eighty volts with a duration of 0·1–0·3 second, is given which results in a 'modified' convulsion, as evidenced by mild tonic-clonic movements in the facial muscles and in the muscles of the hands and feet. After the convulsion, the gag is removed, the patient is turned on his side, and the anaesthetist maintains an oxygen supply until the muscle relaxant wears off (this occurs within several minutes of it having been given) and the patient starts to breathe on his own. Within five to twenty minutes the patient gradually returns to full consciousness although he may feel sleepy and indeed sleep for up to an hour after treatment. The usual course of treatment consists of between five and twelve treatments, given at a rate of two to three treatments per week.

Does ECT work?

It is more than thirty-five years since Cerletti's first electrical treatment, yet there still rages an acrimonious dispute over whether it actually works or not! At first sight, such a situation might seem remarkable. After all, one review (Riddell 1963) of the literature on research into ECT conducted during the years 1955–60 revealed over 200 studies! However, only forty-two of these studies concerned the therapeutic effects of ECT and of these only ten met the most minimal requirements of a scientifically valid and reliable research effort. Most studies of ECT make no use at all of a *control group*, i.e., a group of patients resembling in every way the *ECT-treatment group* except that the former has not received an electric shock. Admittedly, it is not as easy to design a suitably controlled trial of ECT as it is to set up a trial testing, say, of an anti-depressant drug. In the case of a drug trial, the *treatment group* can be given the drug being tested while the *control group* receives a similar tablet or capsule which, however, is made of an inert, harmless substance such as sugar. Nobody intimately involved in the trial – the patients, nurses, doctors – need know which patients receive the drug and which receive the placebo. Only when the code is broken, is it known. With ECT, however, the situation is not so simple. For a valid trial of ECT to be undertaken, the *control group* of patients would need to receive exactly the same treatment as the *treatment group* except the shock; that is to say, the *control group* would have to receive the anaesthetic, the muscle relaxant, and the oxygen, and all the attention and care given to the *treatment group*.

An alternative approach compares patients given ECT with patients who are given no treatment whatsoever. Such a research design, however, means that there are a number of factors which differentiate the *treatment* from the *control group* over and above the fact that the former receives ECT whereas the latter does not. For example, patients in the control group do not receive any injection (a dramatic treatment in itself – injections of water have a remarkable 'placebo' effect in a number of psychiatric conditions) nor are they the beneficiaries of the concentrated nursing and medical care and attention lavished on ECT treated patients.

Other approaches to answering the question of whether ECT works or not include comparing the various methods of administering the treatment and comparing the efficacy of ECT with that of other treatments. Thus ECT studies can be divided into four main groups:

1. studies in which the control group patients are anaesthetized but do not receive any electric shock;
2. studies in which the control group patients receive no treatment at all;
3. studies in which different methods of administering ECT are compared;

4. studies in which ECT is compared to other methods of treatment.

1 Studies with an anaesthetized control group ('Simulated ECT')

In the years that have passed since Ugo Cerletti's initiative, thousands of people have received electrical treatment for a variety of psychiatric disturbances. Yet there have only been a handful of studies in which an attempt was made to compare a group of patients given an anaesthetic, a muscle relaxant, *and* electrical treatment with a similar group given the anaesthetic and muscle relaxant but no shock. For reasons that will become clear, those few studies that have been undertaken in this way have not established whether ECT is therapeutically effective or not.

One of the first studies (Miller *et al.* 1953) assigned thirty seriously disturbed patients to three treatment groups: (1) orthodox electrical treatment; (2) thiopental sodium anaesthesia; (3) thiopental sodium plus non-convulsive electrical stimulation. None of the three groups showed any change in the state of their psychoses which were categorized by their authors as schizophrenic. A somewhat similar approach (Brill *et al.* 1959) attempted to determine the role played by each of the major components of ECT in its alleged therapeutic effect. Patients were randomly assigned to one of five treatment groups: (1) orthodox ECT; (2) ECT with sufficient muscular relaxation to abolish the contraction; (3) ECT under anaesthesia; (4) anaesthesia alone; (5) nitrous oxide alone. There were ninety-seven patients involved, of whom about two-thirds were diagnosed as schizophrenics and the remainder as suffering from a variety of depressive and neurotic conditions. This study also failed to show that ECT was more effective than anaesthesia alone. A third study (Ulett *et al.* 1956) did suggest that electroconvulsive and photoconvulsive shock achieved very much better results than either subconvulsive shock or sedation with barbiturates.

In 1960, Robin and Harris designed a study in which suitably depressed patients were given either a course of ECT or 'conservative' treatment and were then compared. 'Conservative' treatment consisted of two weeks treatment with the antidepressant phenelzine ('Nardil') followed by two weeks treatment with matched placebo tablets. Cases selected for ECT were given either twice weekly ECT and placebo tablets, twice weekly injections of anaesthetic plus phenelzine tablets, or twice weekly injections of anaesthetic plus placebo tablets. Little antidepressant effect was obtained with phenelzine. In contrast, patients treated with ECT responded well whereas those who received the anaesthetic plus placebo or the anaesthetic plus phenelzine did relatively poorly. Unfortunately, the clinicians rating the patients' responses knew which patients received 'true' and which received 'simulated' ECT and hence this portion of the study cannot be considered to be truly blind.

More recently, two British workers published the results of a more systematic and thorough attempt to compare simulated and real ECT.

'The study involved two groups of 16 patients suffering from depressive psychosis. One group received six unilaterally administered shocks under conventional anaesthesia and muscle relaxation; the second group underwent the same procedure without receiving any shocks. Outcome was assessed by a separate investigator using the Hamilton Rating Scale for Depression under double-blind conditions. The results showed that this form of ECT was only superior to the control treatment for one item in the scale, a finding which could have occurred by chance.'

(Lambourn and Gill 1978)

The authors themselves point out that there may be features of this study which might explain its negative result. Unilateral ECT was used although many clinicians (though not so many research workers) believe that it is less effective than bilateral ECT. Assessment of the efficacy of the course of six treatments was made after only two weeks which may have been too early to allow for the full therapeutic effect to develop. Six treatments may not be enough. However, the referring clinicians were able to add extra ECT or medication afterwards yet there was no difference between the groups one month later. However, this subsequent part of the study was not conducted blind.

However, a somewhat similar study by Freeman and his colleagues at the Royal Edinburgh Hospital, found that ECT *was* 'significantly superior to simulated ECT in the treatment of depressive illness':

'40 patients prescribed ECT for treatment of a depressive illness were randomly allocated to two groups. One group had bilateral ECT twice weekly while the other group had the first two treatments replaced by simulated ECT. The anaesthetic procedure was identical for both groups and the entire procedure was double-blind, i.e. neither patient nor rater knew which treatment had been given. After the first two treatments, patients who received the "real" ECT were significantly less depressed than before treatment and were less depressed when compared with the patients receiving 'simulated' ECT. Both groups continued to improve until their final treatment and when the two groups were now compared all measures showed that the "simulated" treatment patients, having lagged behind throughout treatment, had now caught up.'

(Freeman *et al.* 1978)

Because of the earlier study by Lambourn and Gill, Freeman and his colleagues examined the effects of the two forms of treatment on anxiety. In both groups, nearly all anxiety relief occurred with the first two 'real' ECTs and, unlike with depression, no further relief occurred with additional treatment. However, all the patients in this group were primarily depressed and the results, therefore, do not indicate that ECT has any specific anti-anxiety effect. Freeman (1978) explains the discrepancy between the findings of the Edinburgh study and those of Lambourn and Gill by pointing out that the latter study compared simulated ECT with unilateral and not bilateral ECT as in his own study and that while criteria for inclusion of patients in both trials were similar, many more of the Lambourn and Gill patients were outpatients and as a result may have been less severely depressed to start with. However, the Edinburgh study has been criticised for the fact that many of the patients were on antidepressants, that the actual numbers studied were small, that there was no definition of what constituted a 'course' of ECT and that if allowance is made for patients who discontinued treatment during the trial simulated ECT appears more effective than real. (Crow *et al.* 1978; Cutter 1978). The definitive trial of ECT is still awaited.

2 Studies using a no-treatment control group

One study that involved straightforward comparison of a group of patients given ECT with a group that did not is that of Shapiro and his colleagues at the Maudsley Hospital (Shapiro *et al.* 1958). These workers were interested in the effect of ECT on mental slowing and distraction in depressed patients. The experimental group was given ECT with an anaesthetic and a relaxant, the number of treatments being determined on clinical grounds and ranging from three to ten, while the control group had no treatment. Significant clinical improvement was reported by patients having ECT although there was no evidence that the treatment reduced distraction effects or psychomotor slowing in depression.

Thirty depressed patients were allocated at random in the two groups. Psychomotor slowness and the distraction effect were assessed by means of a number of psychological tests given before and after the treatment in the case of the experimental group and twice with a comparable interval between them in the case of the control group. The patient's symptomatology was assessed twice by means of a five-point rating scale carried out by the doctor and a subjective scale in which the patient assessed his own condition. (Shapiro *et al.* 1958)

Some controlled drug trials make use of a drug group, an ECT group, and a placebo group, and it is possible in these cases to regard the placebo group as a 'no-treatment' group and to compare it with the ECT group. The most significant study along these lines conducted in Britain was the Medical Research Council study of 1965:

The MRC study compared ECT (a course of four to eight treatments), imipramine (a tricyclic antidepressant in doses of 200 mg/day), phenelzine (a monoamine oxidase inhibitor in doses of 60 mg/day), and an inert placebo in the treatment of in-patients suffering from depression. The patients, aged between forty and sixty-nine, had suffered from illnesses of less than eighteen months' duration and had not been in receipt of adequate treatment before the trial. Treatments were randomly allocated and were maintained for a minimum of four weeks. If the rater deemed the response to a particular treatment to be satisfactory, it was continued. Otherwise, patients failing to respond to ECT were switched to tablets and those failing to respond to tablets were switched to ECT. (Medical Research Council 1965: 881)

At four weeks, 71 per cent of the patients receiving ECT had few or no symptoms compared with 52 per cent for imipramine, 30 per cent for phenelzine, and 39 per cent for placebo. ECT was easily the quickest effective treatment in cases of severe depression. More long-term evaluation over a six-month period did not affect these results except to show that most of the patients who had been switched from phenelzine to ECT responded remarkably well.

A variety of other such studies (Greenblatt, Grosser, and Wechsler 1964; Kristiansen 1961; Kiloh, Child, and Latner 1960; Carney, Roth, and Garside 1965) appear to support the claims of ECT in the treatment of depression and particularly its role in the management of severely psychotically depressed patients. Certain anti-depressant drugs, such as imipramine ('Tofranil') and amitriptyline ('Tryptizol'), do appear to produce as powerful a response as ECT, but there is some evidence that ECT may bring about a speedier response.

The major methodological defect inherent in simple studies of comparison between ECT, drugs, and/or placebo is that they are not 'blind'; i.e., the researchers know which patients receive the drug/placebo and which receive ECT. Thus it can be argued that the fact that the clinical assessments in these studies are carried out by raters who are aware of the treatment each patient receives could be responsible for the reported superiority of ECT over other treatments. It is not easy, however, to accept that the significant differences in studies, such as that of Leslie Kiloh and his colleagues in Newcastle (1960), in which a good therapeutic response was seen in 89 per cent of depressed patients treated with ECT compared with 11 per cent of those treated with a placebo, could be completely explained away in this fashion.

3 Studies comparing different types of ECT

Orthodox electroconvulsive treatment has been given in an *unmodified* form (i.e., without an anaesthetic or muscle relaxant), in a *modified* form, with an *anti-convulsant*, using a *subconvulsive* stimulus (administering an electric current too weak to induce a fit), and *unilaterally* (both electrodes are applied to *one* side of the head only). These various methods of administration of the treatment have been compared with each other, as a consequence of which it has been possible to establish which of the many factors involved in ECT appears to exert the therapeutic effect.

In a number of studies C. P. Seager found that modified and unmodified ECT showed similar results and he concluded that those factors modified by the anaesthetic and the muscle relaxant (i.e., the state of the patient's alertness during treatment and the peripheral muscular contractions caused by the fit) were not crucial to its beneficial therapeutic effects (Seager 1958, 1959). Two Scandinavian workers, Cronholm and Ottosson, artificially shortened the duration and the extent of the epileptic discharge induced by ECT by administering an anti-convulsant drug, lidocaine, and found that this did reduce the therapeutic efficacy of the treatment. In a number of detailed studies Ottosson (1960) has shown that the memory disturbances reported with ECT and the treatment's anti-depressant effect arise, at least in part, via different mechanisms; whereas the memory defect is mainly determined by the amount of electrical current, and partly by the seizure, the anti-depressant effect is bound to the cerebral seizure activity induced by the electrical stimulation.

Ottosson compared the relief of depression and the performance on formal memory tests of three groups of patients in a double-blind trial. The first group was given the *minimum* shock necessary to produce a fit. The second group was given a shock *well above* the convulsive threshold. The third group had their fit *modified* by a previous injection of the anaesthetic lidocaine which shortens the epileptic discharge without affecting the convulsive threshold. The liminal and supraliminal shocks (group 1 and 2) produced fits of the same duration (as monitored on an electroencephalogram).

Ottosson found that patients in the first two groups showed a similar therapeutic response to ECT but the group receiving the larger shock (the second group) showed more severe memory impairment following treatment. In the third group the length of the seizure-discharge was much shortened by the lidocaine and following this treatment the patients showed significantly *less* relief of depression. (Ottosson 1960)

As Michael Pare points out, in a comment on Ottosson's findings, 'these results appear to have the clear implication that the optimal technique for administering ECT would deliver to the patient the minimum shock necessary to reliably produce an epileptic fit' (Pare 1968). Giacomo d'Elia (1974) has distinguished three main trends which are involved:

1. modification of the type of electrical current employed in stimulation;
2. replacement of the electrical current by a chemical agent;
3. modification of the position of the stimulating electrodes.

The transformation of electrical stimuli from diphasic sinusoidal waveform pulses to unidirectional fractionated ones made it possible to induce generalized convulsions with a reduced amount of energy and consequently with reduced memory disturbances. The replacement of an electric current by a chemical convulsive agent, flurothyl, has, however, not shown any obvious advantages and has languished. With unilateral electrode placement, however, a considerable reduction of side-effects, without a loss of therapeutic efficiency, has been claimed.

The development of unilateral ECT is based on the well-established fact, sometimes elevated to the status of a law, that man's intellectual functions depend more on one cerebral hemisphere than the other. This hemisphere is called the *dominant hemisphere*. Extensive lesions to the dominant hemisphere can result in serious impairment in the production and the comprehension of speech and in other related intellectual functions, whereas lesions affecting the non-dominant hemisphere do not produce such effects. The explanation of such dominance is a complete mystery. In right-handed individuals, the dominant cerebral hemisphere is the *left* one, such dominance correlating with the greater degree of skill with which such individuals use their right hand, foot, and eye. However, in two-thirds of left-handed people, it is also the left hemisphere which is dominant.

In 1957, Lancaster, Steinert, and Frost (1958) introduced the unilateral technique whereby both electrodes are placed on the 'non-dominant' side of the head (i.e., the right side of the head in right-handed and most left-handed people). They noted that such unilateral application resulted in much less post-treatment disorientation and memory impairment than occurred with bilateral treatment yet there did not appear to be any diminution in therapeutic effect.

Many other investigators have reported similar findings. Two main types of memory impairment are seen with ECT: *anterograde amnesia* (i.e., difficulty in remembering inform- ation acquired *after* treatment) and *retrograde amnesia* (i.e., difficulty in remembering information acquired *before* treat- ment). Both forms of amnesia are reportedly less obvious after unilateral ECT. Not all studies have shown this, however, and to date bilateral ECT remains the commoner form of treatment in Britain. Those who argue in favour of a lowered incidence of side-effects after unilateral ECT suggest that this may be due to a lower quantity of electrical energy reaching the brain tissues or to different or more limited spreading of the current.

In a review of twenty-nine studies of unilateral versus bilateral ECT, Giacomo d'Elia and Heino Raotma (1975) conclude that both types of treatment appear to produce the same anti-depressive effect but that the unilateral form results in less memory disturbance. Such a finding is in line with the claim that the anti-depressive effects of ECT and the memory disturbance seen with the treatment are not causally related; the anti-depressive effect is related to the seizure whereas the mechanism of the memory disturbance appears to be related to the strength of the current

4 Studies comparing ECT with other treatment methods

There have been numerous studies in psychiatry that have compared ECT with other physical treatments. During the 1950s, an important group of drugs, the tricyclic anti-depressants, was developed and researchers immediately began comparing the efficacy of these new drugs with that of ECT in the treatment of severe depressive illnesses. Ashley Robin and John Harris (1962), in a controlled comparison of imipramine ('Tofranil') and ECT in thirty-one depressed patients found the latter to be therapeutically superior:

> The thirty-one patients were treated in random order with bi-weekly ECT, relaxant, anaesthetic and matched placebo tablets *or* with bi-weekly anaesthetic and imipramine tablets. An attempt was made to standardize all additional treatments and the symptom ratings were conducted 'blind', i.e., by a clinician who did not attend the treatment sessions and thus was unaware as to which treatment had been given to each patient he rated. Imipramine did produce an adequate anti-depressant response but this was not as marked as that produced by ECT.
>
> (Robin and Harris 1962)

Other tricyclic anti-depressants have been developed, including amitriptyline ('Tryptizol'), trimipramine ('Surmontil'), and desimipramine ('Nortriptyline'). All of these compounds, and particularly amitriptyline, have proved to be effective anti-depressants but, as Bennett (1967) has pointed out in a comprehensive review of the subject, ECT appears to be marginally more potent, especially in the more severe forms of depression. Many controlled studies have confirmed the superiority of ECT over the other main group of anti-depressants, the monoamine oxidase inhibitors – tranylcypromine ('Parnate'), phenelzine ('Nardil'), iso-carboxazid ('Marplan'), iproniazid ('Marsilid') – in the treatment of moderate and severe depression.

The development, some twenty-five years ago, of the 'anti-psychotic' drugs, the phenothiazines, represented a breakthrough in the physical treatment of the major psychoses, schizophrenia and manic-depressive illness. The majority of British psychiatrists appear to prefer such drugs to ECT in the management of *schizophrenia*; indeed, apart from the usefulness of ECT in modifying the catatonic disturbances (marked excitement or stupor) occasionally seen in this condition, there is no convincing evidence that it has any effect on the more common forms of the illness (see below).

Indications

The majority of psychiatrists in this country appear to agree with the view expressed by Lothar Kalinowsky and Hans Hippius (1969) to the effect that the quick and predictable effect of electroconvulsive therapy in certain *depressive illness* represents one 'of the most spectacular results obtainable in psychiatry'. As we have seen, the proportion of patients showing a good response to ECT is usually reported as 70–80 per cent. However, not all depressed patients are helped by ECT. Certain clinical features are reputed to be associated with a good response; these include a family history of depression, a pyknic body build, a history of weight loss, and a particular pattern of sleep disturbance characterized by early morning waking. Other hopeful signs in terms of a good response to ECT are the patient manifesting a marked retardation of his physical and psychological processes and expressing certain 'delusional' beliefs which appear to rise out of his depressed mood.

One type of delusional belief, sometimes seen in severely depressed people, is the so-called 'nihilistic delusion'. Influenced by the profound emotional malaise which is central to depression, the patient's mood may become completely negativistic. He may declare he has no name, no age, no parents, relatives, wife nor children. He may insist he has no head, no chest, no body, may deny everything, oppose everything, resist everything. Such a patient may become mute, may refuse to eat and may resist every medical and nursing initiative aimed at maintaining his very life. Such a patient usually blames himself for being useless and a burden, for bringing unhappiness and shame on his family. He may even believe that because of his innate wickedness, he is going to be tortured, imprisoned or even executed.

Robert Hobson at the Maudsley Hospital (1953) constructed a check-list based on an analysis of the history and clinical state of 127 depressives treated with ECT and identified six items associated with a good response to ECT and nine items associated with a poor response (see *Table 1*).

Table 1 *Prediction of response to ECT*

favourable features (score 1 for each feature *absent*)	*unfavourable features* (score 1 for each feature *present*)
1 sudden onset	1 hypochondriasis
2 good insight	2 depersonalization
3 obsessional previous personality	3 emotional lability
4 self-reproach	4 neurotic traits in childhood
5 duration of illness less than one year	5 neurotic traits in adult life
6 pronounced retardation	6 hysterical attitude to illness
	7 above average intelligence
	8 fluctuating course since onset
	9 ill-adjusted or hysterical previous personality

(Hobson 1953)

He scored one point for the *absence* of each favourable item and one for the *presence* of each unfavourable one; the higher the total score, the less likely the patient is to respond. M. W. P. Carney, Roger Garside, and Martin Roth (1965) assessed thirty-five individual aspects of depressive illness affecting 108 patients treated with ECT and found that ten items correlated significantly with the mental state six months after completion of the treatment. These items and their weightings are shown in *Table 2*. Such attempts to predict have not been wholly successful, however. For example, of the forty-four patients included in the Carney, Roth, and Garside study, who showed a good response to ECT, nine would have been predicted as responding poorly, while of sixty-four patients showing a poor response, eight would have been predicted as good responders. Nonetheless, the factors

Table 2 *Prediction of response to ECT*

feature	score*
weight loss	+3
pyknic body build	+3
early wakening	+2
somatic delusions**	+2
paranoid delusions	+1
self pity	−1
anxiety	−2
worse in evenings	−3
hysterical features or attitude	−3
hypochondriasis***	−3

*Score only if feature present. Ignore features which are absent.
**Delusions of body change or disease, usually of a bizarre nature.
***Excessive or morbid preoccupation with bodily sensations that have little or no organic basis.

(Carney, Roth, and Garside 1965: 659)

identified by Hobson, Carney and his colleagues, and a number of other workers, as helpful predictors of response to ECT, are currently accepted as such in clinical practice.

Kenneth Granville-Grossman has summarized current British views on the usefulness of ECT in depression as follows:

'The best results are obtained in cases of severe depression with retardation, arising suddenly in patients with good premorbid personalities, where guilt feelings and delusions are prominent, where the symptoms are much worse in the mornings and where there is early wakening. (This clinical picture corresponds to that of classical "endogenous depression".)'   (Granville-Grossman 1971 : 9)

Electroconvulsive therapy is sometimes used in the management of *manic excitement*, but to be effective it may have to be given very frequently, i.e., at a rate of two to three treatments per day. Such a frequency rate often leads to a serious degree of confusion on the part of the patient and it is more common nowadays for mania to be treated with one of the more powerful major tranquillizer drugs, such as the phenothiazine, *chlorpromazine* ('Largactil'), or the butyrophene, haloperidol ('Serenace').

Does ECT help in the treatment of *schizophrenia*? In contrast to the near unanimity of agreement among British psychiatrists concerning its efficacy in severe depression, there is utter confusion over its role in schizophrenic states. One textbook on physical treatments, by Professor Michael Shepherd and his colleagues at the Institute of Psychiatry (Shepherd, Lader, and Rodnight 1968), is of the opinion that ECT has been replaced by the phenothiazines in many centres in Britain, whereas another, by Eliot Slater and William Sargant (1972: 59), declares that 'all recently ill schizophrenic patients should receive combined drug and convulsive therapy as early as possible'! The evidence, such as it is, is far from convincing and it does appear as if clinical faith in ECT's role underpins the use of the treatment in schizophrenia rather than any objective evidence that it actually works. The few comparative studies of ECT and the phenothiazines in schizophrenia provide unimpressive results for ECT despite enthusiastic claims by some clinicians. One British reviewer of the usefulness of physical treatments in this condition has observed that 'the superiority of modified

ECT to pentothal anaesthesia alone has never been satis-factorily demonstrated' (Cawley 1967: 105), a fact under-lined in a number of studies in this country and in the United States.

It is frequently argued that ECT is not helpful in the treatment of the so-called *'reactive' depressions*, i.e., those depressions alleged to occur in response to clearly identifiable physical, social, or psychological stresses. Yet, straight away there is a serious difficulty here. Stresses are only identifiable if they are discovered. Many psychiatrists are accused of being too busy to do more than undertake a cursory examin-ation of their patients' history and mental state and accord-ingly tend to diagnose an excessive number of depressions as arising 'out of the blue'. It is only after a full course of electrical treatment has been given without any noticeable effect that a reappraisal is made of the situation, an 'identi-fiable stress' is located, and the diagnosis is altered to 're-active' depression. Indeed, Sargant and Slater actually advocate using ECT as a diagnostic tool; if you are in doubt as to what sort of depression your patient suffers from, give him a couple of ECTs. If he responds, press ahead, it is 'endogenous'; if he doesn't, it is reactive! Such an approach, employed on a wide scale, accounts for the large number of people who at some time or another have had ECT for no other reason than that their psychiatrist thought it would not do any harm and might even cast light on the situation. Not surprisingly, such patients look upon ECT with little favour and many of them spend some time and effort denigrating ECT as a degrading and useless form of treat-ment. In the final analysis, it would be better not merely for psychiatric patients but for the reputation of ECT and of psychiatry in general, if ECT was used, like any serious treatment, in a limited and prudent fashion in cases which show the *presence* of clear-cut symptoms which have been shown to benefit from such a treatment rather than in cases selected for ECT because they have failed to respond to anything else.

Side-effects

Any serious physical treatment in medicine has side-effects. The life-saving antibiotic, penicillin, can, in certain people who are allergic to it, provoke a life-threatening reaction. Anti-cancer drugs can so suppress a patient's resistance as to result in serious, even fatal infections. The potent pain-relievers, the opiates, can lead to a debilitating dependence. Powerful treatments all have powerful side-effects and the current, widespread reliance on medication increases the likelihood of their being accidentally or quite deliberately abused.

There is a tendency for clinicians to play down the side-effects of treatments. For example, Peter Hays, in a passage describing ECT, writes:

> '[ECT] produces a transient memory difficulty which may upset a patient who is already concerned about himself and may feel that his memory is specially vulnerable; it is not infrequently followed by a severe headache . . . [which] occasionally produces in patients a pronounced fear of the treatment that is unexplained and is out of all proportion to the triviality of the procedure.'

(Hays 1964: 98)

Michael Barnett, in his book *People Not Psychiatry* (1973), regards the above passage as one which 'reeks of dehumaniz-ation' with its dismissive tone and patronizing attitude. Hays's passage does not indeed reflect that curious tendency of certain advocates of physical treatments subtly to imply if not frankly to state that patients who develop side-effects or express fear of a 'trivial' procedure such as ECT are in some way to 'blame' for such a bothersome situation. However, it is worth remembering that ECT is not a trivial procedure – no procedure that involves a general anaesthetic and a muscle relaxant can be so described – and it does no service to the treatment to pretend it is. If it were trivial one would anticipate that it would be none too efficacious.

Most treatments that are perfectly safe are perfectly useless as well.

William Sargant and Eliot Slater (1972) take a more serious view of the procedures; 'it should not be undertaken in a light-hearted spirit and should never be employed as a mere placebo'. This is not to suggest that it is a dangerous procedure. The risk of death with ECT is negligible. In 1953, Maclay reported that he could only find sixty-two deaths associated with ECT in the mental hospitals of England and Wales during the period 1947–52, a period during which thousands of convulsive treatments had been given. William Sargant (1972) reports that in twenty years of clinical practice at St Thomas's Hospital in London, during which time he has given thousands of treatments, he has seen only one death, and that of a man aged eighty-four years. The absolute numbers of deaths due to ECT have declined over the past twenty years so that whereas thirty-four patients died in 1954–6 and eleven in 1957–8, only twenty-five died during the years 1959–66 (Williams 1966). It would be unwise to attribute such a decrease to a fall in the use of ECT. *Tables 3*

Table 3 *Attendances at ECT clinics (Warley Hospital)*

year	in-patients		out-patients	
	new patients	total attendances	new patients	total attendances
1965			141	873
1966			158	931
1967			212	1308
1968			173	940
1969			175	966
1970			207	1133
1971			177	1030
1972*	244	2929	160	951
1973	483	2713	151	918
1974	483	3173	145	748

* No records available of in-patient clinic attendances prior to 1972

Table 4 *Pattern of ECT administration (Bethlem Royal and Maudsley Hospitals)*

	Maudsley					Bethlem		
	1970	1971	1972	1973	1974*	1972	1973	1974*
no. of treatments given	975	871	721	797	335	419	574	255
no. of patients given ECT	113	111	86	85	39	64	90	42
average no. of ECTs per patient	8·6	7·9	8·4	9·4	8·6	6·5	6·3	6·0

* For six months only

and *4* show the use of ECT in several British hospitals, and while the pattern is uneven, it does not support the view that ECT is becoming obsolete as a therapy. However, there is evidence of a dramatic decline in ECT use in the United States (Morrisey *et al.* 1979). A survey of its popularity in all types of psychiatric facilities showed a 49 per cent reduction from 1972 to 1977. The single largest decline was experienced by State psychiatric centres (64 per cent) followed, in turn, by private for-profit mental hospitals (54 per cent), public general hospitals (47 per cent), private nonprofit general hospitals (45 per cent) and private non-profit mental hospitals (39 per cent). Private mental hospitals continue to administer the largest volume of ECT treatments. Such a finding conflicts with the assertion frequently made by the critics of ECT that it is a method of punitive and social control particularly favoured in the intimidation and oppression of radical and minority groups (Scheflin and Opton 1978; Frank 1978). In fact, as Morrisey and his colleagues point out, their study of the use of ECT by the psychiatric facilities of New York show that the 'vast majority of ECT treatments occur in the private sector for white, middle-class outpatients or short-term in-patients'.

The most widely publicized side-effect of ECT is the associated memory disturbance. Moyra Williams (1966) has shown that the nature of the memory disorder in ECT resembles that seen following a mild head injury. There is a short and rapidly dwindling amnesia for the time-period preceding each treatment (retrograde amnesia) and a longer post-shock (anterograde) amnesia. The most obvious defect is in the patient's ability to retain material he has recently learned. This defect outlasts the short (twenty to forty minutes) post-ECT confusional period and has been shown to affect information presented to the patient either just before the shock or during recovery from it. The late Professor Erwin Stengel (1951) demonstrated how the retrograde amnesia slowly and gradually shrinks so that the patient remembers more and more of what occurred before each treatment. Some degree of memory deficit may persist for several weeks after the completion of a course of ECT.

Can a permanent memory defect result from a course of ECT as critics claim? There have been a number of intensive studies carried out in recent years which have focused on the impact of ECT not only on recently acquired memories but on memory for information acquired over a lengthy period prior to ECT (Squire *et al.* 1976; Task Force Report 14, 1978). It does now seem that a conventional course of ECT can affect memories acquired many years prior to treatment. The effect on memory is greater for recent memories and less for more remote ones while very remote memories appear to recover fully following ECT in a manner which suggests that such recovery is spontaneous and does not require relearning. However, memories acquired during the days immediately preceding a course of ECT may be permanently lost. As yet, however, there is no evidence to suggest that ECT produces permanent loss of memory for events occurring during the one or two years preceeding ECT. Nevertheless, a recent Task Force on ECT, established by the American Psychiatric Association, admits that 'a fully satisfactory study of this issue with maximally sensitive tests has not yet been accomplished'.

D. J. Spencer (1968), in a study that analysed the aspects of ECT to which patients appeared to take most exception, found memory impairment to be well down the list. Factors such as 'waiting for treatment', the doctor probing 'for veins' (to administer the anaesthetic and relaxant), 'hearing other patients having treatment', and 'being conscious yet unable to breathe' (an avoidable complication if the muscle relaxant is not given until the patient is well and truly anaesthetized) were much more prominent than complaints about memory loss. Spencer noted that another major cause of anxiety is the idea of having electricity passed through the brain. He found that such anxiety was allayed simply by explaining to the patient that it is not the electricity that matters but the convulsion. 'Most surgical patients have the rudiments of their treatment explained to them,' declares Spencer, 'so why not those who are having ECT?' Why not, indeed? Psychiatrists are forever complaining about how general physicians, surgeons, and obstetricians refrain from taking patients into their confidence and, as a result of an aloof and chilling failure to tell their patients what is going on, cause unnecessary anxiety. Yet it is far from clear when it comes to some of the treatments used in psychiatry whether psychiatrists themselves are any more forthcoming.

Other side-effects from ECT are now rarer with better technique and the use of modifying drugs. Fractures of the spine, limbs, and jaw used to be serious though rare complications of the convulsion prior to the use of muscle relaxants, but now they are even rarer. Similarly, respiratory difficulties, cardiovascular complications, and strokes are uncommon because clinicians are careful to exclude any serious heart, lung, or brain disease before declaring a patient fit for treatment.

How does ECT work?

For over thirty years ECT has been a mainstay of treatment in clinical psychiatric practice, yet how the treatment actually works remains obscure. One of the main problems in psychiatry relates to the fact that when knowledge is absent, mythical explanations thrive. Certain myths concerning ECT and how it works possess a remarkable resilience and, despite the accumulation of evidence that categorically invalidates them, they sturdily persist. One mythological explanation of ECT is as a punishment, another as a method erasing unpleasant experience. Finally, there are a number of biologically based hypotheses currently being explored for clues as to the nature of ECT's therapeutic effect.

1 *Punishment theories*

It is argued, perhaps most effectively by Dies (1969), that ECT punishes undesirable behaviour and as a consequence of such punishment the behaviour ceases.

'In social learning theory terms, ECT can be characterised as having a decidedly negative reinforcement value. The patient learns that ECT has been recommended for him because of his pathological behaviour. Demonstration of symptoms will result in punishment ... The patient is punished for his pathology and the psychological rug is virtually pulled out from under him.'   (Dies 1969:334)

Furlong (1972) quotes an excerpt from that well-known contemporary template of informed public opinion, *Playboy* magazine, which reports a student 'privileged to spend a summer working with mental patients', describing ECT as 'absurdly archaic ... [it is] not only degrading for the patient but reduces psychology from science to superstition'. A nurse is quoted as declaring that 'one attendant holds the patient's legs and another his arms ... cruel' while a self-identified PhD states, 'In the 15th and 16th centuries it was believed that the mentally ill were possessed by devils and that torturing the patient's body would force the demons to seek residence elsewhere. Today's electroshock therapy simply uses 20th century gadgetry to effect this magical cure.'

An article in the *Sunday Times* (King Deacon 1974) conjured up a vision of ECT worthy of a Hammer Films horror production – patients hurling their limbs in the air, drooling from the mouth, 'whimpering as they were led to that room'. Other writers have drawn attention to the way ECT is used as a punishment and have made the not unreasonable assumption that since it is so used then this must be its *raison d'être*.

At least one analyst (Brill *et al.* 1959) has described an elaborate series of dynamic factors to explain the efficacy of ECT in the treatment of severe depression which include the fulfilment of the patient's repressed desire for pain and punishment, an unconscious hope for death and rebirth, and the need to be a passive and helpless victim of the therapist's phantasies. Another analyst, Good (1940), commenting on chemically induced convulsive treatment, sweepingly denied that any beneficial effects of such treatment resulted from the convulsion. The induction of *fear* was the crucial factor. He noted that during the post-convulsive phase, some patients moved their lips, some their bowels, and some touched their genitals. In such movements, he saw clear and unquestionable evidence that the adult level of genital development was absent during the post-convulsive period and thus that convulsive treatment operated by producing a regressed state. He noted the 'utter helplessness' of the patient during treatment, a state which 'seems to be of great significance reminiscent as it is of descriptions of primal anxieties'.

2 *Memory impairment theories*

The idea that the disturbance of memory which accompanies ECT may be the means whereby improvement is brought about resiliently survives the relatively extensive literature that effectively shows it to be false. Some psychiatrists, who clearly know as little about such a literature as do the many lay critics of ECT, have contributed to the confusion. Thus Myerson (1943) believes that the whole purpose of using ECT is to 'knock out the brain and reduce the higher activities . . . to impair memory and thus the newer acquisition of the mind, namely the pathological state, is forgotten'.

Others have written loosely of ECT damaging nerve cells (Freeman and Watts 1948) and of producing 'a psychological jolt to bring the patient face to face with reality' (Morgan 1940). Many apologists for ECT, as well as critics, have argued that the whole purpose of the treatment is to make the patient forget the disturbing thoughts that have made him sick.

Is there any basis for either of these theories? Does ECT act as a punishment? Does it work by blotting out painful memories? If the ritual involved in lying on a couch, having an injection, being rendered unconscious, and receiving a 'treatment' is perceived as a 'punishment' and is thereby therapeutic, then such an effect should be independent of whether a shock has or has not been administered. As we have seen, a properly controlled trial of 'simulated' versus 'real' ECT in depressed patients remains to be performed, but such evidence as there is appears to point to the induced seizure as the therapeutically effective factor. This does not support those who argue in favour of ECT as a punishment. We have seen how subconvulsive shocks, i.e., shocks of insufficient strength to produce a convulsion, have not been found to be as effective in producing a therapeutic response as convulsive shocks. If the punishment theory were valid, then such factors as the strength of the shock should not affect the response. Likewise, the finding that lidocaine-modified seizures are less effective is difficult to reconcile with any of the psychological theories of pain, punishment, atonement, and fear. As far as Jan Ottosson (1974: 20), one of the leading researchers into ECT, is concerned, it is clear that 'a therapeutically active component is contained in the convulsion' and 'it is unnecessary to waste words on theories which do not take this fact into account'.

The view that it is the memory loss that is the important therapeutic factor is one that does not take Ottosson's 'fact' into account at all. Nor does it take account of the fact that long after the memory disturbance associated with ECT has worn off, and when the patient can clearly recall how he felt and suffered during his depression, the therapeutic effect of the treatment remains. By altering electrode placement it is possible to separate anti-depressant activity and memory impairment, and it has been shown that the judicious selection of electrode locations and the rate of seizure inductions can allow many patients to obtain a therapeutic result without any objective or subjective memory impairment. Such a dissociation of memory impairment and therapeutic response emphatically disproves the theory that the therapeutic response is dependent on the production of amnesia.

Finally, such 'explanations', based on fear, punishment, and memory impairment, fail to explain why certain types of psychiatric disturbance appear to respond to ECT whereas other types do not. Dies (1969), somewhat ingeniously, does attempt to explain such a discrepancy: 'It is general knowledge in our culture', he declares, 'that ECT as a treatment procedure is almost specific to depression.' Such an argument is absurd, ignoring as it does the fact that public confusion concerning ECT, about what it is, how it is given, and how it might work, is widespread and profound.

In a recent review of the current status of research into how ECT might work, Jan Ottosson declares:

'Clinical experience indicates that there is a specific effect of ECT in the following senses:
(a) ECT is better than any other treatment in endogenous depression
(b) The antidepressive effect of ECT is better than any other effect of ECT (antipsychotic, antimanic etc.)
(c) The antidepressive effect is not bound to and not dependent upon the "organic" effect (memory disturbance, deterioration).'   (Ottosson 1974: 20)

3 Biochemical theories

For Ottosson, the key to the understanding of ECT lies in obtaining a greater knowledge of the fundamental biological processes involved in 'endogenous' depression. Particular interest has recently been focused on the role of specific biochemical substances that act as *neurotransmitters* in the brain (Schildkraut *et al.* 1967) (i.e., conveying electrical impulses from brain cell to brain cell). One such neurotransmitter, *noradrenaline*, is found in particularly high concentrations in regions of the brain, such as the limbic system and the brainstem, which are involved in the regulation and modification of emotional experiences (see Chapter 7). Interest in the role of noradrenaline in depression was stimulated by the finding that the drug *reserpine*, which is used to lower blood pressure in hypertensive subjects, can precipitate in certain patients a mental state identical to that designated 'endogenous' depression and that the drug also *reduces* the brain concentration of noradrenaline. In contrast, a number of drugs which can *elevate* the mood and which are therefore useful as anti-depressant agents appear to *potentiate* the neurotransmitter effects of noradrenaline in the brain either by *inhibiting* its breakdown, *increasing* its production, or rendering its site of action more *sensitive* to its effects. If a decrease in the neurotransmitter activity of noradrenaline were a crucial factor in depression and if the beneficial effects of anti-depressant drugs were attributable to their ability to counteract such a decrease, then one might expect that ECT would induce similar changes in the availability of the substance in the brain.

Studies in rats have shown an increase in the production of noradrenaline following electrical shock administration. Likewise, there is some suggestion that changes in noradrenaline may occur in the brains of patients in association with the clinical improvement noted after ECT. For example, Schildkraut and Draskoczy (1974) have recently reported that the urinary excretion of a breakdown product of noradrenaline (methoxy-hydroxy-phenylglycol), which orginates mainly in the brain, was increased during the course of ECT in a patient. (This increase in breakdown product, they speculate, may reflect an increase in the general metabolic activity of noradrenaline.) There was a significant rise during the course of the patient's clinical improvement, an even greater rise after the course of ECT was terminated, and a greater rise again when the patient became a little elated. It may be that, by increasing the availability of noradrenaline (and other neurotransmitters) to brain receptors, ECT produces similar anti-depressant effects to those of various stimulants, euphoriants, and anti-depressive drugs. However, the levels in the peripheral blood and in the urine of neurotransmitters such as noradrenaline, various associated substances such as *serotonin,* and breakdown products such as *methoxy-hydroxy-phenylglycol* (MHPG), may not accurately reflect what is going on in the brain. For this reason, research workers have begun to concentrate on developing ways of measuring levels in the cerebrospinal fluid (the fluid system that surrounds the brain and that is in constant, intimate contact with its cellular activity). Some workers have already reported rises in certain neurotransmitter levels in the cerebrospinal fluid following ECT and associated with clinical improvement, but other workers have contested such findings and have failed to replicate them.

In view of the fact that the improvement that follows ECT persists long after the treatment has been discontinued, some workers have suggested that a long-term change, such as an adaptive alteration in an enzyme system governing the synthesis or breakdown of neurotransmitter substances, may occur. Because changes in protein synthesis rates could theoretically account for the way ECT works, such rates have been fairly extensively studied. However, there is some evidence that, whereas variation in protein synthesis following ECT may well occur, such a change appears to be related not to ECT's anti-depressant effects but to its effects on memory. Protein synthesis appears to be closely related to the consolidation of memory traces and several workers have reported a significant interference in brain protein synthesis after ECT which persists for a relatively brief period. However, such studies have been conducted on animals and it may not be valid to extrapolate their findings to man.

A variety of other ECT effects (increased permeability of the blood vessels in the brain, lack of oxygen, alteration in steroid levels) have been monitored without any resultant clarification of how the treatment might work. Another more hopeful area concerns alterations in body concentrations of water and electrolytes. In depression, and more especially in manic illnesses, increases in the amount of sodium and water in the body cells and a decrease in potassium have been reported. Following recovery from depression, these concentrations return to normal. Unfortunately the picture with regard to ECT's possible role in water and electrolyte metabolism is still a confused one and it may well be that such changes are secondary to the recovery process and are not part of ECT's direct effects.

Certain functions markedly disturbed in depressive illness include body weight, appetite, sleep, circulation, temperature, libido, and menstruation. These activities are regulated by nerve cells buried deep in the middle of the brain, in the hypothalamic centres of the *diencephalon*. These diencephalic centres control the rhythmic cycles that govern these functions (e.g., the sleep–waking cycle, the menstrual cycle, daily temperature changes, etc.). Lesions in the diencephalon, in addition to causing disturbances in such cyclical activities, can produce manic as well as depressive symptoms. Brain-wave tracings, taken after the administration of ECT, have reportedly shown a pattern of waves thought to be diencephalic in origin and which appear to be related to the stability of an ECT-induced remission from a depressive illness (Roth *et al.* 1957). On the basis of such observations one might be tempted to speculate that ECT exerts its therapeutic effects by way of the diencephalon and it may be that further research aimed at clarifying the role of certain neurochemical events, perhaps those involving transmitters such as noradrenaline, in this part of the brain may ultimately explain not merely the way in which ECT works but the underlying biochemical processes involved in depression itself.

Summary

The most widely expressed criticism of electrical treatment is that nobody knows how it works. Not surprisingly, such ignorance worries many people. The modern era of 'scientific' medicine has already produced much unnecessary, hazardous, and even tragic therapeutic procedures such as hysterectomy for non-specific backache and total teeth extraction for rheumatoid arthritis. It has produced skin cancer as a consequence of irradiation treatments for acne and drug addiction as a result of indiscriminate treatment of insomnia. It is not surprising, therefore, to find scepticism mixed with anxiety concerning the application of electric shocks to an organ as delicate, sensitive ,and mysterious as the brain in the absence of any but the most crudely based theory of how such shocks might actually work. The object, however, of the experimental method is to discover the relations that connect any phenomenon with its immediate cause. In medicine the history of therapeutic endeavour is replete with examples of how efficacious treatments became available long before it was in any way clear how such treatments worked. Digitalis was known to improve the failing heart long before anything was known of the mechanism of such an effect. In many ubiquitous conditions, such as the common cold, the experimental method is mainly devoted to finding some treatment that might work, but in many others it is to find out *why* a treatment, already discovered, does work. Lind discovered that oranges and lemons helped to eliminate scurvy years before anyone suspected the existence of any vitamin, let alone vitamin C, while Jenner's vaccination against smallpox pre-dated by over a century the microscopic identification by Paschen and Nauck of the first virus. At the present time, many breast and blood cancers show a remarkable response to certain treatment approaches even though the underlying cause of cancer still eludes us.

Like all effective treatments, such as antibiotics, anticonvulsants, anti-cancer agents, and surgical interventions,

ECT has its prime indications, its secondary indications, and its contraindications. When the procedure is baldly described as in the *Sunday Times* article mentioned above (King Deacon 1974), it sounds crude, grim, and primitive, but it is necessary to realize that a similar unvarnished account of a common surgical procedure such as an appendicectomy ('patient drooling on operating table . . . crude gash made on fragile abdominal wall . . . surgeon's hand clumsily inserted in open wound . . . abdominal organs extracted like string of sausages at butcher's shop . . . patient moaning and delirious for hours afterwards . . .') would hardly encourage anyone to undergo the experience. In the last resort, such emotionally loaded objections are irrelevant. The only worthwhile question concerning ECT is whether it relieves the pain and suffering of severe depression. I have attempted to present some of the evidence relating to this question and the reader is left to make up his own mind. In view of the alarmist reports of ECT regularly published, it is worth reading the account of ECT in the *British Journal of Psychiatry* written, anonymously (1965), by a psychiatrist who had received a course of treatment for a depressive illness. It is a clear, calm, and dispassionate account of how the treatments were given, the memory disturbance experienced, and the response of his depression to the shocks. He ends his account with the hope that it will help to

' . . . dispel the erroneous belief that E.C.T is a terrifying form of treatment, crippling in its effects on the memory and in other ways. The technique is today so refined that the patient suffers a minimum of discomfort, and the therapeutic benefits are so great in those cases where it is indicated that it is a great pity to withhold it from mistaken ideas of kindness to the patient.'

(Anonymous 1965: 367)

'In those cases where it is indicated' – nothing has done the cause of ECT more harm than its indiscriminate use by overenthusiastic and uncritical clinicians. Fitting the patient to the treatment rather than the other way around is a particular hazard of psychiatric practice, and 'stretching' a diagnosis so that a patient can fall under its rubric and so 'qualify' for a treatment such as ECT is not unknown! Yet, it must also be remembered that severe depressive illnesses can be fatal – a recent analysis of 100 suicides by Brian Barraclough and his colleagues in Chichester (1974) showed that 70 per cent suffered from well-established depressive illness – as Robert Burton observed many years ago, 'black bile is a shoeing horn to suicide'. The practice of psychiatry, like that of medicine, demands knowledge, judgement, and skill; it demands that the physician knows when to intervene and when to refrain from interfering. Such judgement is as important in deciding whether to recommend a patient to have ECT as it is in deciding to operate to remove a possibly inflamed appendix. Yet such judgement is, I believe, often overwhelmed by extraneous considerations. It is easier to give a course of ECT than to explore a patient's social and personal circumstances. It is easier to recommend ECT than to patiently tease out complex factors such as occupational stress, marital difficulties, personal doubts, sudden bereavement, and financial anxieties. It is easier for a psychiatrist, overwhelmed by sheer numbers of patients, to reach for the ECT machine than to resort to more time-consuming and difficult approaches. And, because it is easier, ECT is a much abused and over-used method of treatment. Psychiatrists who persist inso abusing it have only themselves to blame if the public, impressed by the many who have received ECT without benefit, concludes that the treatment is a fraud and an anachronism and demands its abolition.

The polarization of the discussion concerning the efficacy of ECT has been more pronounced in the United States. In an effort to clear away some of the ambiguity and un-certainty surrounding the treatment, the Council on Research and Development of the American Psychiatric Association set up a task force on ECT which was to study the current use of the treatment, review the evidence of its usefulness, make recommendations about its future use and consider the civil liberties of patients and informed consent in the management of treatment programmes. The Task Force reported in 1978. It concluded that the weight of clinical and published evidence supported the status of ECT as an effective treatment in cases of severe depression where the risk of suicide is high and where the use of drug or other therapy entails high risks and/or will take an unacceptably long period to manifest a therapeutic response, in a case of severe catatonia which has not responded to drugs and where the patient's life is in danger, and severe manic illnesses where the use of drug therapy entails unacceptable risks and/or where co-existing medical problems (e.g. recent heart attack) either require prompt resolution of the mania and/or make drug therapy unacceptable. It expressed doubts about the efficacy of ECT in schizophrenia and recommended that ECT should not be used to control symptoms or violent behaviour in the absence of clear-cut evidence of the existence of one of the illnesses for which ECT is a recognised treatment. It found no established usefulness in the administration of ECT to children, to people exhibiting long-standing character disorders, or in so-called reactive depressions (Task Force, Report 14; 1978).

In Britain, in 1976, allegations of maltreatment of patients at St Augustine's Hospital in Kent and of the use of ECT against patients' wishes and as a form of punishment led to the formation of a Committee of Enquiry. This Committee's Report revealed sufficient evidence for its authors to recommend strongly that the Royal College of Psychiatrists 'should give urgent consideration to these problems and issue clear guidance' (Report of Committee of Enquiry, 1976). In response, the Royal College set up a Special Committee which, in 1977, issued a comprehensive Memorandum on the use of ECT (Royal College of Psychiatrists 1977). Like its American counterpart, it too reviewed the evidence concerning the effectiveness of the treatment and came to very similar conclusions.

Both these reports also attempted to lay down guidelines concerning certain ethical questions relating to the use of ECT, questions which Salzman (1977) has identified as (1) the right to receive ECT, (2) the right to refuse ECT, and (3) the nature of informed consent about ECT and its potential hazards. The right to receive ECT, like the right to receive any treatment, hinges on the view that ECT is an effective, reasonably safe and rapid treatment. In Alabama, the courts ruled that a patient cannot be confined involuntarily if he/she is not offered treatment. (Wyatt v. Stickney 1971). In a related case, the Judge dealt in some detail with the use of ECT, describing it as an extraordinary and potentially hazardous mode of treatment. (Wyatt v. Hardin 1975). He ruled that before it can be administered to patients in the state hospitals of Alabama its use must be recommended by a qualified mental health professional trained and experienced in the use of ECT; that the recommendation must be accompanied by supportive documents recording the clinical justifications and rejected alternatives; that the recommendation must be agreed to by another qualified mental health professional trained and experienced in the use of ECT and that the treatment must be approved by the director of the hospital. In addition to the patient's clearly informed consent, if he or she is deemed competent to give it, additional approval of an 'Extraordinary Treatment Committee' is to be obtained. This Committee, appointed by the Human Rights Committee of the hospital, is to consist of five members to include at least one psychiatrist, one neurologist, and one attorney. In summary, before ECT can be given to a consenting patient in the state hospital of Alabama, its indications are to be considered by at least four psychiatrists and one neurologist with at least two attorneys monitoring the proceedings!

It is worth remembering that Judge Johnson's criteria arose in the context of the right to *adequate* treatment. While the APA Task Force on ECT rejected the Judge's description of ECT as an extraordinary and potentially hazardous treatment, they acknowledged the judge's concern with the provision of adequate treatment in Alabama's state hospitals where he had been struck by 'the unacceptable standards of treatment that existed, the inadequate medical care and the fact that only unmodified ECT was available'.

It cannot be assumed that the Judge would have imposed the same restraints in a different and more professionally acceptable situation although American lawyers have ignored such considerations and quote the Alabama ruling across the USA. In Britain, the Royal College of Psychiatrists views such a massive array of legal controls as unnecessary. ECT is seen as a treatment like any other offered to mentally ill patients. Problems only arise with compulsorily committed patients and the College Memorandum recommends that in the case of such patients and any others who are unable to understand the nature and the purpose of the treatment proposed and therefore 'unable to give consent', the procedures adopted in the case of administering any treatment to compulsorily detained patients should apply.

A field study of fourteen treatment centres found broad agreement between clinical practice in Britain and the Royal College of Psychiatrists' Memorandum on the Use of ECT (Lambourn and Murrills 1978). No instance of treatment being given without anaesthesia and muscle relaxants (i.e. 'unmodified'), as in the case of the Alabama State Hospital, was revealed. Yet there is still unease on both sides of the Atlantic (Clare 1978) concerning the danger that poorly staffed and excessively strained hospitals may use ECT to excess and that the boundary line between therapy and punishment may be crossed despite the confidence of psychiatric authorities that when this does occur it is an occasional lapse to be corrected by a general improvement in professional standards and the provision of adequate treatment facilities rather than by the implementation of further legal controls.

The report has been much quoted and is apparently regarded by many mental health professionals in the United

States as a balanced and realistic appraisal of the present situation. However, it is clear from events occurring on the other side of the continent that Dr Greenblatt's task force has not had the last word. As a result of pressure from a group of former mental hospital patients calling themselves 'Network Against Psychiatric Assault', a bill was passed by the California State Assembly on October 30, 1974, placing rigid restrictions upon physicians using ECT. The bill lays down the conditions under which ECT may be performed and provides for a civil penalty of up to $10,000 for each violation or revocation of licence or both. ECT may only be performed after 'all other appropriate treatment modalities have been exhausted' and after the application has been reviewed by a committee of three physicians, one appointed by the department involved and two by the local mental director.

The implementation of the bill was halted by a temporary restraining order following representations to the effect that, amongst other defects, it violated patients' rights to confidentiality. (According to the Northern California Psychiatric Society, the bill as originally drafted would allow members of the state legislature or members of county boards of supervisors to peruse a patient's treatment record without the patient's consent.) However, the fact that it was drafted and passed through the Assembly in a single legislative session reflects the intensity of feelings against ECT and the vigour of the political activity directed against it.

Throughout the discussion concerning electroconvulsive treatment, we see once again the remarkable and apparently irresistible tendency for practitioners, patients, and members of the public to adopt a posture of absolute faith or incorrigible antagonism and to adhere to such a position with a fervour comparable to that accompanying a religious conviction. In the absence of conclusive evidence, one way or the other, it would seem prudent to maintain a cautious attitude towards a treatment that is empirical. It would in addition be a significant contribution towards the general level of the discussion if participants would remember that many of the most effective treatments in modern medicine are empirical and that the use of a physical treatment, such as ECT, in no way militates against the simultaneous use of other treatment modalities, such as psychotherapy or behaviour therapy, in the management of psychiatric disorders.

References

AMERICAN PSYCHIATRIC ASSOCIATION (1978) Task Force Report 14. *Electroconvulsive Therapy*. American Psychiatric Association: Washington, D.C.

ANONYMOUS (1965) The Experience of Electroconvulsive Therapy by a Practising Psychiatrist. *British Journal of Psychiatry* **111**: 365-7.

ASNIS, G.M., FINK, M., and SAFERSTEIN, S. (1978) ECT in Metropolitan New York Hospitals. A Survey of Practice, 1975-76. *American Journal of Psychiatry* **153**: 4: 479-82.

BARNETT, M. (1973) *People Not Psychiatry*. London: George Allen & Unwin.

BARRACLOUGH, B., BUNCH, J., NELSON D., and SAINSBURY, P. (1974) A Hundred Cases of Suicide: Clinical Aspects. *British Journal of Psychiatry* **125**: 355-73.

BATTIE, W. (1758) *A Treatise on Madness*. London: Whiston & White.

BENNETT, I.F. (1967) Is There a Superior Antidepressant? In S. Faratini and M.N.G. Dukes (eds.), *Antidepressant Drugs*. Excerpta Medica Foundation.

BIRCH, J. (1792) In G. Adams (ed.), *An Essay on Electricity, Explaining the Principles of that Useful Science and Describing the Instruments* (4th edition). London.

BRILL, N.Q., CRUMPTION, E., EDISUN, S., GRAYSON, H.M., HILLMAN, L.I., and RICHARD, R.A. (1959) Relative Effectiveness of Various Components of

Electroconvulsive Therapy. *Archives of Neurological Psychiatry* **81**: 627–35.

CARNEY, M.W.P., ROTH, M., and GARSIDE, R.F. (1965) The Diagnosis of Depressive Syndromes and the Prediction of ECT Response. *British Journal of Psychiatry* **111**: 659.

CAWLEY, R. (1967) The Present Status of Physical Treatments in Schizophrenia. In A. Coppen and A. Walk (eds.), *Recent Developments in Schizophrenia. British Journal of Psychiatry*, Special Publication No. 1. Ashford, Kent: Headley Bros.

CLARE, A.W. (1978) Therapeutic and Ethical Aspects of Electro-Convulsive Therapy: A British Perspective. *International Journal of Law and Psychiatry* **1, 3**: 237–53.

COTARD, M. (1882) Nihilistic Delusions. In S. R. Hirsch and M. Shepherd (eds.), *Themes and Variations in European Psychiatry*. Bristol: Wright.

CROW, T.J., JOHNSTONE, E.C. and FRITH, C.D. (1978) How Does ECT Work? *Lancet* **ii**: 432–3.

D'ELIA, G. (1974) Unilateral Electroconvulsive Therapy. In M. Fink, S. Kety, G. McGaugh, and T. A. Williams (eds.), *Psychobiology of Convulsive Therapy*. New York: Wiley & Sons.

D'ELIA, G. and RAOTMA, H. (1975) Is Unilateral ECT less Effective than Bilateral ECT? *British Journal of Psychiatry* **126**: 83–9.

DIES, R.R. (1969) Electroconvulsive Therapy: A Social Learning Therapy Interpretation. *Journal of Nervous and Mental Disease* **146**: 334.

FRANK, R.F. (1978) *The History of Shock Treatment*. San Francisco. London: Wildwood House.

FREEMAN, C. P. (1978) How Does ECT Work? *Lancet* **ii**: 893.

FREEMAN, C.P.L., BASSON, J.V. and CRIGHTON, A. (1978) Double-Blind Controlled Trial of Electroconvulsive Therapy (E.C.T.) and Simulated E.C.T. in Depressive Illness. *Lancet* **i**: 738–40.

FREEMAN, W. and WATTS, J.W. (1949) (eds.)
Psychosurgery in the Treatment of Mental Disorders
and Intractable Pain. In *Psychosurgery*. Springfield:
Thomas.

FURLONG, F.W. (1972) The Mythology of
Electroconvulsive Therapy. *Comprehensive Psychiatry*
13 (3): 235–9.

GOOD, R. (1940) Some Observations on the Psychological
Aspects of Cardiazol Therapy. *Journal of Mental Science*
86: 491.

GRANVILLE-GROSSMAN, K. (1971) (ed.) Convulsive
Therapy. In *Recent Advances in Clinical Psychiatry*. London:
J. & A. Churchill.

GREENBLATT, M., GROSSER, G.H., and WECHSLER, H.
(1964) Differential Response of Depressed Patients to
Somatic Therapy. *American Journal of Psychiatry* **120**:
935.

HARRIS, J.A. and ROBIN, A.A. (1960) A Controlled Trial
of Phenelsine in Depressive Reactions. *Journal of Mental
Science* **106**: 1432–7.

HAYS, P. (1964) *New Horizons in Psychiatry*.
Harmondsworth: Penguin.

HOBSON, R.F. (1953) Prognostic Factors in Electric
Convulsive Therapy. *Journal of Neurology, Neurosurgery
and Psychiatry* **16**: 275–81.

IMPASTATO, D. (1960) The Story of the First
Electroshock Treatment. *American Journal of Psychiatry*
116: 1113–14.

KALINOWSKY, L. and HIPPIUS, H. (1969)
*Pharmacological, Convulsive and Other Somatic Treatments in
Psychiatry*. New York: Grune & Stratton.

KATZ, M.M. (1974) Introduction. In M. Fink, S. Kety,
J. McGaugh, and T. A. Williams (eds.), *Psychobiology of
Convulsive Therapy*. Washington, DC: Winston & Sons.

KILOH, L.G., CHILD, J.P., and LATNER, G. (1960) A
Controlled Trial of Iproniazil in the Treatment of

Endogenous Depression. *Journal of Mental Science* **106**: 1425–8.

KING DEACON, A. (1974) *Sunday Times*, July 14, 1974.

KRISTIANSEN, E.S. (1961) A Comparison of Treatment of Endogenous Depression with Electro-Convulsive Therapy and Imipramine. *Acta Psychiatrica Scandinavica* (Supplement 162): 179.

LANCASTER, N., STEINERT, R., and FROST, I. (1958) Unilateral Electroconvulsive Therapy. *Journal of Mental Science* **104**: 221–7.

LAMBOURN, J. and GILL, D. (1978) A Controlled Comparison of Simulated and Real ECT. *British Journal of Psychiatry* **133**: 514–19.

LAMBOURN, J. and MURRILLS, A.J. (1978) Actual Practice of ECT in a Health Region of Britain. *British Journal of Psychiatry* **133**: 520–23.

MACLAY, W.S. (1953) Death Due to Treatment. *Proceedings of the Royal Society of Medicine* **46**: 13.

MEDICAL RESEARCH COUNCIL (1965) Report by Clinical Psychiatry Committee. *British Medical Journal* **1**: 881.

MEDUNA, L. VON (1938) General Discussion of the Cardiazol Therapy. *American Journal of Psychiatry* (Supplement) **94**: 40–50.

MILLER, D.H., CLANCY, J., and CUMMING, E. (1953) A Comparison between Unidirectional Current Nonconvulsive Electrical Stimulation Given with Reiter's Machine, Standard Alternating Current Electroshock (Cerletti Method) and Pentothal in Chronic Schizophrenia. *American Journal of Psychiatry* **112**: 759–802.

MORGAN, J.J.B. (1940) Shock as a Preparation for Readjustment. *Journal of Psychology* **10**: 313.

MORRISSEY, J.P., BURTON, N.M. and STEADMAN, H.J. (1979) Developing an Empirical Base for Psycho-legal Policy Analyses of ECT: A New York State Survey. *International Journal of Law and Psychiatry*, **2**: 1, 99–111.

MYERSON, A. (1943) Borderline cases treated by Electric Shock. *American Journal of Psychiatry* **100**: 355.

OLIVER, W. (1685) Account of the Effect of Camphor in a Case of Insanity. *London Medical Journal* **6**: 120–30.

OTTOSSON, J.D. (1960) Experimental Studies in the Mode of Action of Electroconvulsive Therapy. *Acta Psychiatrica Scandinavica* **35** (Supplement 145): 5–235, 468.

—— (1974) Comments on Induced Seizures and Human Behaviour by M. Fink. In M. Fink, S. Kety, J. McGaugh, and T. Williams (eds.), *Psychobiology of Convulsive Therapy*. London: John Wiley.

PARE, C.M.B. (1968) Recent Advances in the Treatment of Depression. In A. Coppen and A. Walk (eds.), *Recent Developments in Affective Disorders. British Journal of Psychiatry*. Special Publication No. 2. Ashford, Kent: Headley Bros.

PRINGLE, J. (1774) Discourse on the Torpedo. Lecture delivered at the Royal Society. In R. Hunter and I. Macalpine (eds.), *Three Hundred Years of Psychiatry*. London: Oxford University Press.

REGISTRAR-GENERAL (1970) *Statistical Review of England and Wales for the Year 1966. Part III Commentary*. London: HMSO.

REPORT OF COMMITTEE OF ENQUIRY, St. Augustine's Hospital, Chartham, Kent (1976). South East Thames Regional Health Authority, London.

RIDDELL, S.A. (1963) The Therapeutic Efficacy of ECT. *Archives of General Psychiatry* **8**: 42–52.

ROBIN, A.A. and HARRIS, J.A. (1962) A Controlled Comparison of Imipramine and Electroplexy. *Journal of Mental Science* **126**: 217–19.

ROTH, M., KAY, D.W., SHAW, J., and GREEN, J. (1957) Prognosis and Pentothal Induced Electroencephalographic Changes in Electroconvulsive Treatment. An Approach to the Problem of Regulation or Convulsive Therapy. *Electroencaphalography and Clinical Neurophysiology* **9**: 225–37.

ROYAL COLLEGE OF PSYCHIATRISTS (1977)
Memorandum on the Use of Electroconvulsive Therapy.
British Journal of Psychiatry **131**: 261–72.

SALZMAN, C. (1977) ECT and Ethical Psychiatry.
American Journal of Psychiatry **134**: 1006–9.

SARGANT, W. and SLATER, E. (1972) *An Introduction to
Physical Methods of Treatment in Psychiatry* (5th edition).
London: Churchill Livingstone.

SCHEFLIN, A.W. and OPTON, E.M. JR. (1978)
The Mind Manipulators. London: Paddington Press.

SCHILDKRAUT, J.J. and DRASKOCZY, P.R. (1974)
Electroconvulsive Shock and Norepinephrine
(Noradrenaline) Turnover. In M. Fink, S. Kety,
J. McGaugh, and T. A. Williams (eds.), *Psychobiology
of Convulsive Therapy*. London: John Wiley.

SCHILDKRAUT, J.J., SCHANBURG, S.M., BREESE, G.R.
and KOPIN, I.J. (1967) Norepinaphrine (Noradrenaline)
Metabolism and Drugs Used in the Effective Disorders.
A Possible Mechanism of Action. *American Journal of
Psychiatry* **124**: 600–608.

SEAGER, C.P. (1958) A Comparison between the Result
of Unmodified and Modified Electroplexy (ECT).
Journal of Mental Science **14**: 206–20.

—— (1959) Controlled Trial of Straight and Modified
Electroplexy. *Journal of Mental Science* **105**: 1022–8.

SHAPIRO, M.B., CAMPBELL, D., HARRIS, A., and
DEWSBERRY, J.P. (1958) Effects of ECT upon
Psychomotor Speed and 'Distraction Effect' in
Depressed Psychotic Patients. *Journal of Mental Science*
104: 681–95.

SHEPHERD,M.,LADER,M.,andRODNIGHT,R.(1968)*Clinical
Psychopharmacology*. London: English Universities Press.

SPENCER, D.J. (1968) Some Observations on E.C.T.
Medical World **105**: 26–9.

SQUIRE, L.R., CHACE, P.M., and SLATER, P.C.
(1976) Retrograde amnesia: Temporal judgements about

remote events following electroconvulsive therapy.
Nature **260**: 775–7.

STENGEL, E. (1951) Intensive ECT. *Journal of Mental Science* **97**: 139–42.

ULETT, G.A., SMITH, K., and CLESER, G.C. (1956) Evaluation of Convulsive and Subconvulsive Shock Therapies Utilizing A Control Group. *American Journal of Psychiatry* **112**: 759–802.

WESLEY, J. (1756) In R. Hunter and I. Macalpine (eds.), *Three Hundred Years of Psychiatry*. London: Oxford University Press.

WILLIAMS, M. (1966) Memory Disorders Associated with Electroconvulsive therapy. In C. M. Whitby and O. L. Zangwill (eds.), *Amnesia*. London: Butterworth.

Wyatt v. Hardin No. 3195-N (M.D. Ala. Feb. 28. 1975, modified July 1, 1975).

Wyatt v. Stickney 325 F. Supp. 781 (M.D. Ala. 1971); 334 F. Supp. 1341 (M.D. Ala. 1971).

7

Psychosurgery

If there is no meaning in it, that saves a lot of trouble, you know, as we needn't try to find any. The King of Hearts in *Alice in Wonderland*

IN THEIR attempts to cope with the ill-defined nature of contemporary psychiatric theory and its lack of a firm, comprehensive foundation, psychiatrists have constructed 'models', 'systems', all-embracing frameworks within which the mechanisms and processes of thought and behaviour, rational and irrational, are explained and understood. Inevitably, in a field that lacks the solid, tested, theoretical base of a natural science, such as physics, and that has yet to achieve the impressive pragmatic achievements of a clinical science, such as medicine, individual psychiatrists fall prey to the temptation to adhere to this or that explanatory system with a dogmatism redolent of religious fanaticism. There is, in addition, a slow, gradual, and pervasive influence exerted by such stout believers so that students in psychiatry are often led to feel that it is only because of resistance or prejudice on their part that they cannot see the truth of what their teachers affirm with such conviction.

This tendency to elevate unproved assumptions to the realm of established truth is seen not only in the area of clinical practice in psychiatry but in the area of research as well. Once elevated, such a 'truth' is liable to be enthusiastically and passionately endorsed by one group of supporters while vehemently and sharply rejected by another. Developments in the field of psychosurgery illustrate this tendency with a special clarity. Some psychiatrists boast of never having referred a single patient for a psychosurgical operation and make plain their utter contempt for what they see to be a crude mutilation of the most delicate of organs. Other psychiatrists appear equally convinced that the new operative techniques represent an exciting breakthrough in the diagnosis and management of what have hitherto been among the most intractable and crippling conditions in psychiatry.

In so far as there is an *official* medical view of the value of psychosurgery in Britain, it is probably close to that put forward in a *Lancet* editorial written in 1972:

'This is no field for the euphoric novice; but the caustic advice to beginners can be passed on to the whole profession – "don't give it up, take it up". If a neurosurgeon, interested in psychosurgery, will build up a liaison of confidence and understanding with a few psychiatric colleagues there is no lack of material. It is essential that such a group should have a common language for description of clinical manifestations. Already individual results are so strikingly good that this time there can be no turning back.'

The 'turning-back', referred to in the editorial, recalls an earlier phase in the history of psychosurgery when, disillusioned with the results, many clinicians quietly abandoned interest. If the *Lancet* is to be believed, brain surgery in psychiatry has something to offer and merits cautious and scrupulous examination. The response fired by critics has been a double-barrelled one to the effect that psychosurgical procedures do not produce any specific therapeutic effect but merely blast the patient's mental faculties, leaving him a shattered, blunted wreck, and that even if such procedures were to be proven effective they would not be acceptable on ethical grounds. As one of psychosurgery's most uncompromising and hostile critics, Dr Peter Breggin, makes plain:

'To the extent that psychosurgery "blunts" the individual, I personally feel that it partially kills the individual. If we accept this concept, then we can allow the person the right to suicide or partial suicide but we cannot allow a second party to aid him in the suicide. Just as it is against the law to take a person's life, even with his consent, so it should be against the law to take *part* of a person's life even with his consent.'

(Breggin 1972: 5576)

The dispute is hardly helped by the fact that there is even some confusion over the precise definition of psychosurgery itself. A World Health Organization publication (1976) defined psychosurgery as 'the selective removal or destruction ... of nerve pathways ... with a view to influencing behaviour.' This definition provoked a critical response from Bridges and Bartlett (1977) who point out that much modern psychosurgery is concerned with the treatment of intractable affective illnesses without any intended effect on behaviour at all and they suggest as an alternative definition 'the surgical treatment of certain psychiatric illnesses by means of localized lesions placed in specific cerebral sites.' However, this too seems an inadequate definition for it fails to account for those operations which are intended to modify behaviour and for those where there does not appear be any specific cerebral target. The recent report of the US National Commission for the Protection of Human Subjects of Biomedical and Behavioral Research (1977) acknowledged these difficulties and eventually adopted the following definition for use in its exhaustive survey of the available literature and its final assessment of the efficacy of operative procedures:

'Psychosurgery means brain surgery on (1) normal brain tissue of an individual who does not suffer from any physical disease, for the purpose of changing or controlling the behavior or emotions of such individual, or (2) diseased brain tissue of an individual, if the primary object of the performance of such surgery is to control, change or affect any behavioral or emotional disturbance of such individual.'

Within the terms of this definition, surgery with a dual purpose, for example the relief of epileptic seizures as well as relief of emotional disorder, would be classifiable as psychosurgery if the predominant reason for performing the operation was to affect the behavioural or emotional disturbance.

Historical development

In 1875 the British neurologist Sir David Ferrier described how the removal of a large portion of the frontal lobes of the brain in monkeys appeared to have little or no effect on sensory or motor abilities but produced a remarkable change 'in the animals' character and disposition', the monkeys becoming more tame and docile (Ferrier 1875). The first published account of a psychosurgical intervention in man was that of Dr Gottlieb Burckhardt, who in 1890 attempted to interrupt the connecting nerve fibres between the frontal lobes and the remainder of the brain in severely disturbed and actively hallucinating patients (1891). His results were poor – some of the patients while reportedly more easy to manage on their hospital wards remained acutely psychotic and Burckhardt encountered fierce opposition from medical colleagues. Twenty years later the Russian neurosurgeon Ludwig Puusepp severed the fibres connecting the frontal lobe on one side of the brain with the remainder of the organ in three patients adjudged to be suffering from manic-depressive disorder. In his report he admits to producing a miserable result and declared that as a consequence he would not perform any more operations.

Such crude procedures and unpromising results did noᵥ bode well for such an approach and it is not surprising to find that little interest was shown in psychosurgery for several decades. However, experimentation continued into brain function in animals, with Karl Lashley's ingenious studies of the relationship between the cerebral cortex of rats and learning and memory, Heinrich Kluver's experiments on the temporal lobe, and Carlyle Jacobsen's exploration of the function of the frontal lobes in monkeys. At their Yale laboratory Jacobsen and Professor John Fulton (1935), in a series of experiments, showed how the frustrational responses of normal chimpanzees to being denied rewards in test situations disappeared completely after destruction of their frontal lobes. 'Temper tantrums and anxiety behaviour' vanished and the animals appeared to forget why they might have been angry or distressed. Later Fulton reported that 'the most ferocious specimens have been reduced to a state of friendly docility' (Fulton 1949).

The Portuguese neurologist Egaz Moniz was excited by these findings and speculated on the possible application of frontal lobe destruction in patients suffering from psychiatric disturbances characterized by irrational fears, severe anxiety, and crippling obsessional behaviour. In 1936, he began his first series of neurosurgical interventions, initially using alcohol injections and later a steel cutter ('leucotome') to cut the fibres connecting key, emotion-regulating centres deep in the subcortical areas of the brain and the frontal lobes. An enthusiastic account of this approach in twenty cases was published (1936) and Moniz's work was quickly taken up by two American surgeons, Walter Freeman and James Watts at Georgetown University in Washington. (Moniz's career as a psychosurgeon was cut short when a leucotomized patient shot him in the spine, rendering him hemiplegic. He retired in 1944 and five years later received, with Walter Hess, the Nobel Prize in Physiology and Medicine for his work in establishing the therapeutic value of leucotomy in certain psychoses.) The two Americans modified Moniz's surgical procedure and devised the so-called 'standard leucotomy' (*Figure 1*) which was to be widely used until early in the 1950s. By 1950, Freeman and Watts had operated on over 1,000 patients and the estimated world figure for such procedures has been given as over 20,000.

The 'standard leucotomy' consists of making a burr hole in the side of the head, above and in front of the ear, inserting a cutting instrument, sweeping it in an arc in the

Figure 1 *Technique of leucotomy as performed by Freeman and Watts*

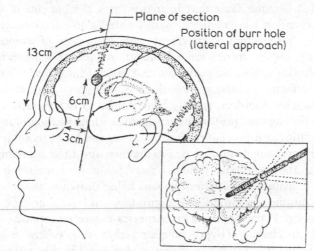

A leucotomy is guided by bone rather than by cerebral landmarks.
(Elliott, Albert, and Bremmer 1948)

coronal plane and thereby dividing as much white matter
as possible. The same procedure was then repeated on the
opposite side of the head. This operation was extremely
crude in that at post-mortem there was found to be
extreme variation in the positioning of the cuts.

As with every new and dramatic treatment procedure,
first reports positively glowed with success. Of Moniz's first
twenty patients, seven were considered to have completely
recovered from their disabling psychiatric difficulties and a
further seven had improved. He claimed best results with
agitated depressive patients, relatively poor ones with
schizophrenics. The British neurosurgeon Peter Schurr, in a
review of the subject (1973), has stated that in Britain
'enormous numbers of patients were operated upon by the
"standard" technique and between a third and a half of the
patients so treated were discharged with a relapse rate of
only about 3 per cent'. However, as he goes on to point out,

post-operative evaluation in such cases was often superficial and it became clear that in many cases the benefits of the intervention were clouded by unwanted side-effects ranging from 'intellectual impairment and disorders of emotion (flattening or troublesome lability) to lack of self-control, euphoria, aggressive outbursts and lack of initiative'. Other side-effects, including incontinence, epilepsy, and certain metabolic disorders, greatly contributed to the growth of a reaction against psychosurgery and the identification of it by its critics as a procedure that made vegetables of its subjects and deprived them of their intelligence and their humanity.

At about the same time as Egaz Moniz was embarking on the leucotomy trail, attention was being drawn to the role of the limbic system in the regulation and modification of emotional responses. The American neuroanatomist C. Judson Herrick (1933) suggested that this system might influence the 'internal apparatus of general bodily attitude, disposition and affective tone' and in 1937, in a classic paper, Dr James Papez (1937) proposed that the limbic system, composed of the hypothalamus, the anterior thalamic nuclei, the cingulate gyrus, the hippocampus and their interconnecting fibres might constitute 'a harmonious mechanism which may elaborate the functions of central emotion as well as participate in emotional expression' (*Figure 2*). According to this theory, hypothalamic stimuli are projected to the cingulate gyrus by way of the anterior nucleus of the thalamus. Associated fibres from the cingulate gyrus relay this activity to other parts of the cortex and produce the emotional colouring that accompanies psychic processes generated there. The reverse side of this process supplies a possible explanation of how emotional display and experience are produced by psychic activity. Impulses generated in the cerebral lobes are funnelled through the cingulate gyrus to the parahippocampal gyrus and thence to the hippocampus. By way of the fornix, and possibly the mamillary bodies, these impulses are then conveyed to the hypothalamus, which activates the peripheral autonomic

Figure 2 *Main connections between the hypothalamus and the cerebral cortex*

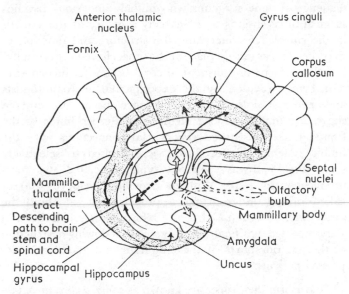

The limbic lobe is shaded. Solid arrows show the hypothetical circulation of impulses during the experiencing of emotion. The thick dotted arrow indicates the descending path to the brain-stem and spinal cord for expressing emotion. Olfactory afferent fibers are lightly dotted.
(Gatz 1970: Figure 36)

system and plays a crucial role in such factors as the pulse, blood pressure, appetite, sleep cycle, sexual functions, and general arousal. If, as some theorists suggest, this entire circuit is a reverberatory one then it may be possible for impulses to circulate repetitively and result in an emotional experience which is both intense and persistent. Peter Schurr comments:

'Unfortunately this ray of light was unheeded by the psychiatrists who referred their patients for leucotomy and by those who carried out the operations – these included any surgeon of whatever experience who was willing to undertake them.   (Schurr 1973:53)

The sting in this quote underlines the 'knife happy' tendency of some surgeons who blithely undertook psychosurgical interventions with scarcely a glance at the growth in the knowledge concerning the structure and function of the crucial areas taking place at the time. However, gradually, if belatedly, psychosurgical theory began to incorporate data being provided by the experimental neuroanatomists and neurophysiologists. As evidence began to emerge suggesting that the more medial and deeper fibres of the frontal lobes constituted the crucial connections with the limbic system, so procedures were devised to selectively sever these pathways while leaving associated structures untouched. In 1948, William Scoville developed the so-called 'orbital undercutting' approach while, at about the same time, Sir Hugh Cairns at Oxford and Dr J. LeBeau in Paris reported significant improvements following destruction of the anterior parts of the cingulum in agitated and depressed patients.

> To perform the procedure known as *orbital undercutting*, two burr holes are drilled in the temple, one over each orbit. A retractor is inserted and the frontal lobes are lifted enabling the surgeon to directly visualize the undersurface of the lobes and cut the medial fibres connecting them to the thalamus.

In a review of the two procedures, the British neurosurgeon Walpole Lewin declared that 'the results from the various centres together with the experimental evidence on which these operations are based, make cogent arguments for directing surgery to the orbital (area of the frontal lobes) for symptoms of anxiety and depression and to the cingulate gyrus for aggression and obsessional disorder' (Lewin 1961).

As the concept of discrete and key centres began to replace more diffuse and vague ideas of brain function, so the variety of surgical techniques employed in the treatment of severe, intractable mental disturbance developed. Stereotactic techniques, introduced by Ernest Speigel and Henry Wycis of Temple University, Philadelphia, for the purpose of destroying specific areas in the brain to relieve intractable physical pain, began to be applied in the late 1940s to the treatment of mental illness. In 1949, these same workers used such an approach to destroy the dorsomedial thalamic nucleus in psychotic patients.

The stereotactic approach consists of the introduction of a probe into the brain under x-ray guidance and control When the tip of the probe is adjacent to the chosen target the destructive lesion is made. This may be achieved by electricity, cold (cryosurgery), heat (diathermy or radio-frequency), or by way of a cutting wire introduced via the probe. Alternatively, radio-active seeds, such as Yttrium-90, may be placed in position and the centre destroyed over a period of time.

Ernest Spiegel (1969) surveyed the members of the International Society for Research in Stereoencephalotomy and reported that approximately 26,000 stereotactic operations had been performed up to 1965 and that an estimated 12,000 had been undertaken during 1965–8. Such operations were, in the main, designed to produce relief from certain behavioural and emotional disturbances (aggression, over-activity, and psychosis) by selectively destroying areas of the limbic-hypothalamic circuit such as the anterior or dorsomedial thalamic nuclei, the amygdala, the posterior hypothalamus, the cingulum, and the pathways to the frontal lobes (*Figure 3*).

What is the theoretical foundation for surgical mutilation of these delicate areas of the brain, areas which in Walle Nauta's (1973) words 'encompass neural mechanisms that allow man to be human'? Other than empirically and clinically based observations of behaviour before and after surgery, is there an appropriately sophisticated neuro-anatomical and neurophysiological model of emotional function in the brain? It is worth briefly reviewing available

Figure 3 *Diagram of pathways linking three main subdivisions of the limbic system*

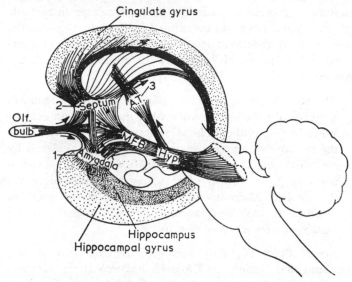

The ring of limbic cortex is shown in light and dark stipple. See text for further anatomical details and functional significance. Abbreviations: A.T. – anterior thalamic nuclei; Hyp. – hypothalamus; MFB – medial forebrain bundle; Olf. – olfactory.
(Maclean 1958: 62)

data on the functions of the major areas of the brain which neurosurgeons have singled out for attention as sites of possible relief in chronic mental impairment.

The frontal lobes

Apart from David Ferrier's observations on behavioural changes in monkeys following destruction of their frontal lobes, subsequently confirmed by numerous experimenters, and the studies of Fulton and Jacobsen, there was little in the way of objective data on the role of the frontal lobes in the modification and expression of emotion at the time of Moniz's historic surgical interventions. It is now known that there are intimate connections running between the frontal lobes and the deeper centres of the limbic system. Fibres of nerve cells situated in the anterior and dorsomedial nuclei of the thalamus, in the hypothalamus, in the amygdala, and in portions of the fornix run to restricted and localized areas in the anterior portions of the frontal lobes. Likewise, fibres of cells in different parts of the anterior frontal areas are known to run to subcortical structures which include the thalamic nuclei and the hypothalamus. Walter Scoville argued that the beneficial effects of frontal lobe surgery were due to interrupting these connections. Milton Greenblatt and Harry Solomon in Boston suggested that as a result of the destruction of parts of the frontal lobes:

'Reduction of cells and circuits theoretically may have the following consequences: (1) The individual loses drive, force, energy. (2) He is less affected by past experience and more bound to immediate stimuli. (3) He is less able to elaborate experiences or sustain experience.'
(Greenblatt and Solomon 1953: 19–34)

These workers admit that at first glance psychosurgical interventions, resulting in the irreversible destruction of apparently normal brain tissue, and the consequent interference with the patient's powers of adaptation appear indefensible. Their answer reflects the beliefs held by psychosurgeons concerning the nature of their operations on the frontal lobes:

'If the patient is less affected by past experiences and more bound to immediate stimuli, he may be freed from past emotional entanglements and given an opportunity for a new line of development . . . abnormal emotional states might gradually evaporate, the distorted fantasy life becomes uncharged; tension, agitation, hostility, brooding and preoccupation would be less disorganising and although the individual might be more superficial and shallow, adaptation at a simpler level would be possible.
(Greenblatt and Solomon 1953: 19–34)

In some fashion, cutting the linking pathways between lobes and the limbic system defuses the emotions experienced by the patient so that one is left with a person who can be described as shallow, blunted, and superficial but *emotionally* relieved. In fact, so destructive were the early frontal lobe operations that these blunting effects put many surgeons off such procedures altogether. Such personality changes as a consequence of frontal lobe damage have been known for over a century. In 1848, Phineas Gage, a young construction worker on a railroad in Vermont, had an iron rod, some 3½ feet long and 1¼ inches in diameter, driven through his left cheek and out through the front side of his skull as a result of an explosion. Gage recovered, to the astonishment of his workmates and medical attendants, and was left with a 3½-inch tubular channel running through the frontal area of his brain and out through the opening in his cheek. Before the accident, Gage had been reliable, trustworthy, hardworking, and likeable. Afterwards, the change was remarkable. His physician, Dr John Harlow, described how

'. . . the equilibrium or balance, so to speak, between his intellectual faculties and animal propensities, seems to have been destroyed. He is fitful, irreverent, indulging at times in the grossest profanity (which was not previously his custom), manifesting but little deference for his fellows, impatient of restraint or advice when it conflicts with his desires, at times pertinaciously obstinate, yet capricious and vacillating, devising many plans of future operation, which no sooner arranged than they are abandoned in turn for others appearing more feasible. A child in his intellectual capacity and manifestations, he has the animal passions of a strong man.'   (Harlow 1866)

Similar, if less dramatic, effects were reported after the early and unmodified frontal lobe cuts. Denny-Brown (1951), in a study of the functional deficits caused by psychosurgery, concluded that it is the inability to 'visualise consequences which is the unique effect of leucotomy' and he pointed out that damage to the frontal lobes resulted in an alteration in personality producing a 'euphoria with peculiar indifference to the seriousness or indeed painful consequences of any station'. However, while some patients who had undergone such surgery showed signs of intellectual deficits, by no means all did. The McGill University psychologist Donald Hebb (1945), on the basis of a review of the leucotomy literature available up to 1945 and ot a careful six-year assessment of a man who had had over one-third of his frontal lobes removed for treatment of severe epilepsy, concluded that the frontal lobes were not necessary for ordinary adjustment nor for adequate performance on intelligence tests.

The frontal lobes nonetheless do appear to be crucially important for those conscious intellectual processes that are essential to well-planned and organized initiative, and which enable the individual to anticipate the future consequences of his actions. True, the more anterior and superficial areas of the lobes do not seem to have any significant role to play in terms of motor or sensory function or in the recording of memories, and such areas can be removed without causing a serious impairment in intellectual performance. In practice, leucotomies restricted to these areas are no longer popular in that they have little to offer clinically and have been superseded by more sophisticated operative procedures. More extensive surgery of one or both frontal lobes can, however, produce serious defects in a patient's ability to plan ahead and to organize the execution of such plans.

With the fall from grace of frontal lobe surgery, on account of its serious sequelae, interest shifted to the role of the limbic system. Support for Papez's theory of limbic function came from experimental work in which it had been noted that when those areas in the frontal lobe which appeared to mediate beneficial changes in the behaviour and emotional state of psychotic patients were stimulated, nervous impulses were produced which appeared to travel via intermediate circuits in the limbic system to outflow pathways in the hypothalamus and in the arousal system in the brain-stem, resulting in alterations in certain physiological functions of emotion such as the blood pressure, the pulse, and the respiratory rate. Kenneth Livingston, in a review of the history of frontal lobe surgery, concluded:

'On the basis of this evidence it could be postulated that the "key" to understanding the effects of frontal lobotomy lay in the elucidation of functional fronto-limbic relationships – the mechanisms by which frontal lesions may alter limbic system function.'   (Livingston 1969: 92)

The limbic system

In a recent review of the possible role of the limbic system in the production and modification of certain emotional states, the American physiologist Paul MacLean (1969) suggested that man has inherited the structure and the organization of three basic cerebral types, which he has labelled *'reptilian'*, *'old mammalian'*, and *'new mammalian'* (*Figure 4*). The 'reptilian' portion comprises the brain-stem and includes much of the reticular system, the mid-brain, and the basal ganglia. MacLean argues that, according to ethological observations, this 'reptilian' brain 'programmes stereotyped behaviours according to instructions based on ancestral learning and ancestral memories'. It is the most instinctive and automated of the three brain areas and is primarily concerned with such responses as homing, mating, breeding, imprinting, etc. A standard example of the reptilian brain in action is that of the turtle returning year by year to the same place to lay its eggs or a salmon returning up-stream to spawn.

It seems obvious that the 'reptilian' brain is ill-equipped to deal with novel and unpredictable situations. The 'new mammalian' cortex, on the other hand, is a highly differentiated, specialized, and complex organ, capable of the highest intellectual functions. This new brain, evolutionarily speaking, consists in the main of the two large cerebral hemispheres and includes the frontal lobes. The 'old mammalian' brain comprises the limbic cortex and its major connections.

Figure 4 *Schema of 'holonarchic' organization of three basic brain types*

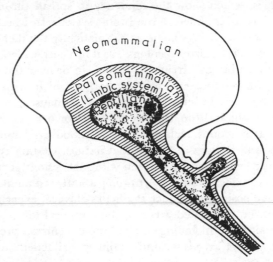

Schema of 'holonarchic' organization of the three basic brain types which, in the evolution of the mamammalian brain, became part of man's inheritance. Man's counterpart of the old mammalian brain comprises the so-called limbic system which has been found to play an important role in emotional behaviour.
(Maclean 1967: 374–82)

Because of its close relationship with the olfactory apparatus (the sense of smell is a primitive perceptual modality), the limbic system had been dismissed as of little consequence *vis-à-vis* the higher cognitive and emotional functions of the brain until Papez's classic paper. It was he who pointed out that whereas this 'old mammalian' brain or limbic system is structurally somewhat primitive, it has strong connections with a number of key areas, among them the *hypothalamus*, a centre that plays a crucial role in the integration of emotional experience and certain viscero-somatic behaviours such as appetite, sleep, sexual drive, body temperature, and hormonal function.

MacLean has demonstrated how the limbic system is functionally as well as anatomically an integrated system by mapping the propagation of, for example, hippocampal seizure discharges, which show the tendency to spread throughout and be largely confined to the limbic system. In MacLean's words, 'nothing brings home so dramatically the dichotomy of function, or "schizophysiology" as it has been called, of the old and new brains'. Irritative lesions, in or near the limbic cortex, can produce epileptic discharges which are accompanied by basic feelings of hunger, thirst, nausea, choking, cold, warmth, and the need to defaecate or urinate, and by emotional reactions such as terror, foreboding, familiarity, sadness, and feelings of a paranoid nature. Certain types of automatic behaviour can be seen with such lesions, including eating, drinking, vomiting, running about, screaming, and aggressive posturing. Wilder Penfield's classical experiments, in which he stimulated areas of the temporal lobes of conscious patients, including their limbic centres, produced feelings of *deja vu*, visual and auditory hallucinations, and illusions.

A 16-year-old girl had seizures, before the onset of which she would hear music; the music, which was always the same, was a lullaby her mother had sung, 'Hushabye my baby . . .' During an exploratory operation, Penfield electrically stimulated various parts of the temporal lobe during which the girl reported hearing pieces of music and experiencing a dream-like state in which she could hear numerous voices talking indistinctly.

A 43-year-old French Canadian housewife experienced seizures in which she would hear voices which seemed to be coming from the right. Often she would hear music and would go to see if her children had left the radio on. She sometimes heard people sing and at all times the voices and the singing were completely realistic and convincing. At operation, a tumour was found which was pressing on the temporal lobe and the deeper limbic centres.

(Penfield and Jasper 1954)

Penfield and Jaspers have provided excellent descriptions of other psychical phenomena accompanying seizures originating within the temporal and limbic systems, including the phenomenon whereby the patient feels thoughts of a stereotyped and basic nature flooding into his mind.

One 12-year-old boy experienced seizures for over a year although no obvious cause was ever discovered. The first thing he noticed, prior to a fit developing, was that many thoughts crowded into his mind. For example, there was a piece of bread on the table and he thought that it was necessary to turn or move the bread. He seemed to see less of the surroundings but the bread remained clear. He complained of experiencing a succession of thoughts and strange ideas which he found very difficult to explain.'

(Penfield and Jasper 1954)

It should be recalled that the original circuit described by James Papez was formed by a pathway passing from the hippocampus via the fornix to the mammillary body, anterior thalamic nucleus, cingulate gyrus, and then back to the hippocampus (*Figure 2*). Electrical experimentation in monkeys revealed that stimulation of the anterior cingulate gyrus resulted in autonomic responses associated with emotion such as vocalization, increase in the size of the pupils, changes in respiration, and cardiovascular responses. When lesions were made in this area, more tame and less fearful animals were produced Ward (1948). Upon such an experimental basis did Sir Hugh Cairns perform his first anterior cingulectomy in man. Cairns believed that the benefit such an operation conferred on obsessional patients suggested that the operation interrupted a 'reverberating circuit' of impulses in Papez's limbic circuit.

The concept of a 'reverberating circuit' is one that crops up again and again in discussion of limbic function and mental disorders. Penfield's experiments and the work of psycho-physiologists such as MacLean support the idea that the emotions represent an amalgamated and integrated form of internally and externally derived experience. Penfield's electrical stimulations and the reports of patients with so-called psychomotor epilepsy, such as the three patients described above, demonstrate that the experience of certain emotions does not depend on simultaneous activation of sensory systems. For example, the epileptic experience of fear arises centrally in association with an epileptic discharge and not from the perception by the peripheral sensory organs (the eyes, ears, smell, etc.) of any external threat. MacLean (1969) describes how he once treated a young man who, at the beginning of each seizure, had a feeling of fear that someone was standing behind him. If he turned to see who it might be, his feeling of fear intensified. During intervals between seizures, such patients often become preoccupied by persistent persecutory feelings. Such observations have led to speculation that the similarity between the phenomena seen in patients with temporal lobe epilepsy and patients with schizophrenia may reflect a common or similar underlying basis. Likewise, the persistence of severe anxiety, depression, or repetitive forms of behaviour (obsessive-compulsive actions) or thought (ruminations) may be a consequence of limbic system pathology whereby impulses generated within the system reverberate throughout it and are transmitted to the frontal lobes to be experienced in the form of fully fledged and unpleasant cognitive and physical experiences.

An additional circuit to that of Papez's within the limbic system, the 'defence reaction circuit', is said to run from the amygdala to the hypothalamus via the stria terminalis and back to the amygdala by a return pathway (*Figure 5*). For instance, it has been shown that electrical stimulation of these centres produces a defence reaction in the cat (Hilton and Zbrozyna 1960). As the intensity of the electrical stimulation is increased, so the conscious cat progresses from rest to looking alert, becoming agitated, and finally attacking in response to auditory and visual stimuli. Such a behavioural pattern is accompanied by alterations in respiration, heart rate, and muscle blood flow which appear to prepare the animal for 'fight or flight'. Electrical stimulation of the posteromedial nucleus of the hypothalamus in patients has caused them to complain of severe anxiety, flushing, a sensation of fullness, and palpitations (Abrahams, Hilton, and Zbrozyna 1960). Anxiety produced by certain external

Figure 5 *The Papez circuit and the defence reaction circuit*

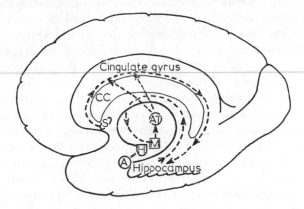

The Papez circuit (broken line) passes via the cingulum bundle, in the cingulate gyrus, from septem (S) to hippocampus, and via fornix to mamillary body (M), via anterior thalamic radiations to cingulum bundle. *The defence reaction circuit* (solid line) passes from hypothalamus (H) via stria terminalis to amygdala, and via amygdalo-fugal pathway to hypothalamus.
(Laitinen and Livingston 1973: 165)

stresses, such as a mental test or a sudden fright, is usually accompanied by similar experiences and similar alterations in pulse, respiration, and muscle blood-flow. Some psycho-surgeons have since claimed that destruction of the postero-medial hypothalamic nucleus produces a reduction of anxiety in severely disturbed patients (Sano 1966).

Stimulating the amygdala produces a similar defence reaction to that obtained by stimulating the hypothalamus

(Magnus and Lammers 1956). According to Paul MacLean and his colleagues, the amygdaloid reaction is characterized by a gradual build-up of the defensive response during stimulation and the persistence of the response after the stimulation has been discontinued. Again, it is on the basis of such experimental observations that the operation of amygdalotomy (the destruction of the amygdala) has been tried in the treatment of some seriously aggressive and hyperactive patients.

It is difficult reading the clinical and experimental literature on psychosurgery to avoid getting submerged in a measure of surgical cuts, localized circuits, specialized centres, and reverberating pathways. I have only picked out for brief discussion a number of what appear to be the key theories currently being discussed. Stripped of their technical clothing, they tend to appear primitive and vague. It is said that stimulation of such-and-such a centre produces such-and-such a response, yet as Janice Stevens and her colleagues in Boston (1969) have pointed out (and she is by no means alone) there appears to be marked variability in the responses elicited by the same implanted electrode. This may well be because it is difficult to place an electrode with precision and in any event each individual's 'limbic circuitry' may differ from another's, just as his face does. Or again, it may be that an individual responds to electrical stimulation in ways that significantly depend on his previous experiences, his personality, and the circumstances in which such experimentation occurs. However, what has been clarified over the years is the way in which various parts of the central nervous system (the frontal lobes, the limbic system, the reticular arousal system in the brain-stem, the peripheral sensory system, the motor, and the hormonal systems) interrelate in the elaboration and modification of the emotional response accompanying behaviour (*Figure 5*).

Kenneth Livingston and Alfonso Escobar (1973) have recently attempted to summarize available data on limbic system function and have proposed tentative models of how this system might contribute to certain psychiatric disturbances. They first consider the 'Papez' or *medial limbic* circuit and note the extensive evidence indicating that destructive lesions of such a circuit produce states of psychic and motor *hypoactivity*. Clinical syndromes of mutism and apathy have been reported with traumatic, vascular, and neoplastic lesions of the medial limbic pathways (Nielson 1953). Conversely, they suggest that irritative lesions might produce the opposite effect, i.e., that irritative medial limbic lesions might produce psychic and motor *hyperactivity*. Psychiatric disorders which are characterized by anxiety, restlessness, irritability, and obsessive-compulsive disturbances would fall into this category. They point out that selective destructive surgical lesions of the cingulate pathways and medial limbic-frontal connections are claimed to be effective in the treatment of such disorders (Le Beau 1952; Foltz 1968) and declare 'There is thus a good correlation between the anatomical, experimental and clinical evidence relating to functions of the medial limbic system' (Livingston and Escobar 1973: 348).

Regarding the *basolateral* limbic circuit (which is essentially the 'defence reaction circuit' described above), they suggest that it is concerned in the main with the activities of the sensory-receptive and the interpretative functions of the cerebral cortex (in contrast to the medial limbic system which is concerned in the main with arousal and activity and is closely linked with the reticular core or arousal system in the lower brain-stem). They believe that there is 'considerable indirect evidence' that the limbic components of this interpretative cortex are involved in those psychiatric disorders in which altered sensory perception and interpretation may be considered to be the underlying functional disturbance provoking complex hallucinatory and delusional experiences. Such surgical interventions in this basolateral circuit include lesions to relieve intractable depression and destruction of the amygdala and its hypothalamic connections in the management of intractable aggressive behaviour.

Extent of psychosurgery

Such theories may appear simplistic and vague, yet this has not prevented a veritable plethora of operations from being performed. In Britain, Geoffrey Knight and his colleagues at the Brook Hospital in London use a stereotactic approach which involves placing radioactive yrttrium seeds on each side of the posterior orbital aspect of the frontal lobes – the so-called 'subcaudate tractotomy'. Good results are claimed in severely and chronically depressed and obsessional patients (Knight 1969; Bridges *et al.* 1973). Alan Richardson at the Atkinson Morley Hospital in Wimbledon performs stereotactic operations with a cryogenic probe which produces a small permanent lesion by freezing up to 1 cubic centimetre of white matter. He and his colleagues report particularly beneficial results in patients with anxiety, depression, and obsessional neurosis with lesions placed in the anterior part of the cingulum and the medial quadrant of the frontal lobe (Kelly *et al.* 1973a, b). Eric Turner at the Queen Elizabeth Hospital in Birmingham performs partial removal of both temporal lobes or removal of the posterior portion of the cingulate gyrus* in cases of serious persisting aggression (Turner 1970) while Edward Hitchcock and his co-workers at Edinburgh's Royal Infirmary use stereotactic bilateral amygdalotomy for similar conditions (Hitchcock *et al.* 1972).

Outside Britain, a comparable array of surgical approaches is being employed. Ballantine and his team at the Massachusetts General Hospital (1967) stereotactically place lesions in the anterior cingulum, Lauri Laitinen in Finland does likewise (Laitinen and Vikki 1972), and Hunter Brown and his Californian colleagues surgically attack multiple limbic targets including the cingulum, the amygdala, and the medial portions of the frontal lobe in patients variously described as suffering from 'hard-core schizophrenia',

*Cingulectomy refers to removal of part or all of the cingulum; cingulotomy refers to cutting a portion of this area; likewise the distinction between amygdalectomy and amygdalotomy, lobectomy and lobotomy, etc.

'sociopathic aggression', anxiety, and chronic depression (Hunter Brown and Nighthill 1968). Keijo Sano (1966) in Tokyo has called his approach by the perhaps deceptively reassuring title of 'sedative therapy'; he surgically destroys the posterior medial hypothalamus in hyperactive and aggressive states. At the University of Göttingen in Germany, a surgical team has been treating paedophilic homosexuals (men who seek out sexual opportunities with prepubertal or teenage boys) by means of a stereotactically placed lesion of the ventromedial nucleus of the hypothalamus and have reported on the outcome in approximately twenty patients (Roeder, Orthner, and Muller 1972). Some surgeons do not seem to pay too much attention to the theoretical speculations of the physiologists and appear to try all sorts of interventions in all sorts of cases. Not surprisingly, the results appear somewhat confusing. Yet psychosurgeons are by no means dismayed.

It is generally agreed that the popularity of psychosurgery has waxed and waned rather dramatically during its brief modern history. In a survey of leucotomy in Britain published in 1961 more specific information about the extent and nature of its use was provided (Tooth and Newton 1961). Between the years 1942 and 1954, 10,365 people underwent leucotomies for serious mental illness. Only 14 per cent of these patients had been ill for less than two years prior to surgery whereas over 40 per cent had been ill for at least six years. Two-thirds of the patients were chronic schizophrenics. Eighty-four per cent had a 'standard' leucotomy, a further 7 per cent had a modification of the standard approach, leaving only 9 per cent operated upon by the more recent techniques developed since 1948. The least satisfactory results were amongst the schizophrenics; only 17 per cent of the men and 20 per cent of the women were adjudged to be totally or socially recovered. By 1959 the numbers of patients undergoing surgery had fallen dramatically. Whereas there had been an average of 1,100 operations a year during 1948–54, the number had declined to about 400 in 1959. For example, in the triennium 1952–4, a total of ninety-one leucotomies were performed at the Bethlem Royal and Maudsley Hospitals, whereas by the triennium 1961–3 this figure had fallen to thirty. During 1967–9, only seven leucotomies were performed on patients in these hospitals. The significant factor contributing to the fall, in the opinion of these authors, was the incidence of undesirable side-effects. Not surprisingly, those psychiatrists who had to look after the failures of neurosurgery in mental hospitals became prejudiced against such procedures (Livingstone 1969). The development of powerful drugs, such as the phenothiazines and the anti-depressants, and the increasing attention paid to behavioural and social techniques of treatment further reduced interest in surgical procedures. Thus did the first wave of psychosurgery subside and by 1961 only eleven hospitals in Britain reported performing more than ten leucotomies apiece that year, their collective sum being 189 leucotomies or 45 per cent of the national total. Sixty-five hospitals, providing 42 per cent of all the mental hospital beds in the country, did no leucotomies whatsoever in the same year.

Since only a relatively small number of those neuro-surgeons who practise psychosurgery actually publish their results, and such published articles as do appear tend to be reviews of operations performed over a number of years, it is difficult to estimate with any accuracy the current popularity of the procedure. However, while the Swedish surgeon Gosta Rylander (1973) speaks of a 'renaissance of psychosurgery' after its decline some twenty years ago, a questionnaire survey undertaken on behalf of the Task Force on Psycho-surgery of the American Psychiatric Association found a decline in the number of psychosurgeons in the US and Canada performing psychosurgery over the three years studied, 1971–3, a decline attributed to the deterrent effect of the public controversy over the subject in addition to the effect of several well-publicized law suits against neuro-surgeons. On the basis of this survey's results and those of

Gildenberg (1975), Valenstein (1977) suggests that the average number of psychosurgical procedures performed is very likely to have been between 400 and 500 per year during the years 1971–3. The average number of such operations performed each year seems to have decreased each year since 1973 but there is a paucity of reliable data. Robin and Macdonald (1975) have estimated that approximately 200 procedures were performed in Britain in 1974 but a recent retrospective review (Barraclough and Mitchell-Heggs 1978) suggests the lower figure of 158 for the number of operations done that year and lower figures still, 154 and 119, for 1975 and 1976 respectively. The authors of this report suggest that adverse publicity may well be causing the fall in the amount of surgery. Replies to a questionnaire sent on behalf of the US National Commission for the Protection of Human Subjects of Biomedical and Behavioral Research indicated that some twenty neurosurgeons in fifteen surgical units in Britain perform stereotactic psychosurgery with some degree of regularity. Staff at the Geoffrey Knight Psychosurgical Unit in London reported that they had performed fifty-four, thirty-nine, and forty-six operations in 1973, 1974, and 1975 respectively. Neurosurgeons at St George's Hospital average about twenty operations annually while those at the Maudsley-Guys King's College neurosurgical unit reported that they had performed only one, six, and four operations in these same three years.

An Australian survey (Smith 1977) estimated that just over eighty operations were done there in 1973 and this rate is thought to have remained constant since then. In India, surgery is almost entirely confined to the Madras Institute of Neurology. Estimates of the number performed between 1973 and 1975 vary from eighty-six to 132. The procedures performed include amygdalectomies, hypothalamotomies, cingulotomy, and prefrontal leucotomies. There is also a group of sixty-five patients on whom cingulotomies were performed for dependence on narcotics. In Japan, approximately twenty-five operations were performed in 1972, but the following year an active protest movement developed and gradually the number of operations performed has fallen. As far as can be ascertained (Valenstein 1977) no operations were performed in 1975. The figures for Czechslovakia range from 110 to 141 operations performed between 1973 and 1975. Some degree of psychosurgical activity occurs in Spain, Argentine, Poland, France, Germany, Holland, Denmark, Sweden, and Finland but estimates of frequency are difficult to make with any degree of accuracy. Psychosurgery was banned in the Soviet Union in the early 1950s and as far as one can tell no operations have been performed since that time. However recent reports indicate that 'therapeutic electrical stimulation' through implanted electrodes have been used to treat intractable pain, and temporal lobe epilepsy associated with aggression or psychiatric disorders (Bechtereva *et al.* 1973; 1975; 1976).

The results of psychosurgery

'The object of surgery', declare William Sargant and Eliot Slater, in what is the most popular textbook on physical treatments in psychiatry in use in Britain (Sargant and Slater 1972: 103), 'is to remove or modify severely in-capacitating symptoms when all other methods have failed; and limbic leucotomy often enables further treatment to be much more useful.' These authors appear to be in no doubt that psychosurgery has much to offer. Side-effects are acknowledged as a hazard, but, it must be said, these acknowledgements are made with some reluctance and the side-effects tend to be attributed to the earlier 'standard leucotomy', much less popular nowadays, or are accepted as a reasonable price to pay for the remarkable pay-off, i.e., 'the relief of symptoms [that] can be of the order that makes a sane man of a lunatic' (p. 127). They accept that after surgery a patient, particularly an elderly one, may exhibit some signs of intellectual impairment and they admit that patients with certain tendencies held under control by means of associated feelings of anxiety and guilt may show exacerbation of these tendencies, e.g., drinking, sexual proclivities, gambling, without any accompanying feelings of guilt, regret, or remorse. 'It is probable that nearly every individual after operation is happier than before', they surmise with a degree of confidence not shared by psychosurgery's critics, although they do add that such contentment can be bought at somebody else's or society's expense (pp. 124–5). Post-operative irritability, severe and undesirable personality changes, epilepsy, emotional blunting, and haemorrhage are all mentioned as undesirable sequelae, but in such a way as to suggest that when they do occur it is the technique, the misplacement of the cut, or the patient's personality that is to blame. Some idea of the crudity of their assessment of psychosurgery (and Sargant and Slater are by no means atypical in this regard) is illustrated by their reference to Walter Freeman's observation that in the professions 'where fine qualities of personal appreciation of the feelings of others are so necessary more caution in recommending operation should be exercised than when the patient comes from the world of business or commerce'. Why? Because one might end up blunting the emotional life of a doctor instead of a banker? No – rather because 'a little ruthlessness' is often seen post-operatively and while 'a little ruthlessness' may not be helpful to someone seeking a University Chair in Psychiatry (some psychiatrists would demur), it is a positive asset to the ambitious, thrusting, competitive businessman and speculator fighting for survival and success.

The two authors sum up their view of psychosurgery by dismissing the suggestion that it represents an assault on the patient's personality with the following words:

'Those who are familiar with the effects of the modern modified operation carried out by highly skilled hands know that this idea is out of place. The damage done, even to a mature and differentiated personality, as a rule, is so slight as to be beyond detection by clinical methods.'   (Sargant and Slater 1972: 127)

They indicate an impressive list of conditions likely to benefit from surgery – long-standing depression, anxiety states, obsessional neurosis, anorexia nervosa, certain organic conditions, impulsivity, and aggressivity. With regard to schizophrenia, they regret the reduction of surgical treatment of this condition in the United States, attributing this to 'ideological issues', whereas the similar decline in the United Kingdom they blame on the more prosaic and pragmatic grounds of a shortage of sufficiently skilled neurosurgeons. They quote John Pippard's view that by 1962 half of Britain's mental hospitals had stopped psychosurgery and sourly comment that, as a result, hundreds of patients 'are being cheated' of the 'excellent chances' of 'great improvement' which can be provided to chronic sufferers by the combination of surgery and post-operative treatments with phenothiazines (p. 117).

Leaving aside their enthusiasm for psychosurgery in other conditions, their unabashed advocacy for it in schizophrenia seems curious. They are quite unable to quote a single study since 1955 to support their claims and they fall back on several studies, undertaken in the early part of that decade, to justify their enthusiasm. The measure of improvement after surgery of which they appear particularly proud is 'discharge from hospital' and they mention several studies which appear to show especially striking figures. It can, of course, be objected that social methods, involving planned programmes of work rehabilitation, the development of social skills and behavioural shaping aimed at minimizing the effects of withdrawal and apathy and at preventing chronicity, have enabled many otherwise long-stay patients to leave hospital, return home or to a hostel, take up a job, and maintain themselves, and that all this can be achieved without recourse to a dangerous and crude operation on the patient's brain. Sargant and Slater reply by asserting that those schizophrenic patients eventually treated by surgery had, of course, been previously exposed to social rehabilitative methods without success, an unlikely occurrence, however, since social methods of treatment only began to be undertaken seriously and applied intelligently about ten years after the widespread application of surgery in schizophrenia. A similar argument can be made for the role of the antipsychotic drugs; once they began to be used in significant amounts towards the end of the 1950s, the psychosurgical treatment of schizophrenics began to wane. .

This is not to suggest that as a result of such pharmacological and social developments all schizophrenic patients can now be effectively treated. But to argue a place for psychosurgical intervention in this condition one would have to refer to studies somewhat more recent than those of some twenty-five years ago. Sargant and Slater fail to refer to more recent work, a surprising omission in view of the fact that such studies as have been done do not support their claims for surgery in schizophrenia. An interesting example of their selectivity is a study by Desmond Kelly and his colleagues (1972) to which they refer *vis-à-vis* the favourable results it reports for psychosurgery in *severe depression*. This same study, however, is not referred to when these two authors come to consider *schizophrenia*, which is a pity, for the conclusion of Kelly and his colleagues is that 'in schizophrenia, leucotomy may help depression or anxiety, but the effect of modified operations on delusions and hallucinations is often disappointing and only relatively few patients with this diagnosis were selected for operation'.

The absence of any properly controlled studies in this whole area is quite remarkable. When one recalls the elaborate, often intricate studies performed to assess the effects of certain drugs, one can only marvel at the ability of surgeons to convince others of the success of their results, using only their enthusiasm and persuasiveness. Ashley Robin (1958) at Runwell Hospital did attempt to properly assess the clinical outcome in 198 patients treated with

leucotomy with the same number of patients not so treated –
the two groups matched for chronicity, age on admission to
hospital, and sex. He found that leucotomy did not appear to
improve the chances of discharge from hospital, accelerate
discharge, reduce the possibility of readmission, delay
readmission, reduce the number of admissions, nor improve
hospital behaviour as judged at ward level. What does the
textbook by Sargant and Slater, a text described by the
Practitioner as providing 'an authoritative clear and concise
review of the present situation', have to say about Robin's
findings? Nothing at all, for nowhere is the study mentioned.
Robin's work has been criticized elsewhere on the grounds
that his patients had been treated with the standard leucotomy
and of course this crude approach has since been superseded
by more sophisticated, refined, and effective procedures.
However, the studies that Sargant and Slater *do* quote
likewise used the standard approach, an approach it
should be remembered that was employed in at least
20,000 patients.

Geoffrey Knight is reasonably candid about the efficacy of
surgery in schizophrenia. 'Of the large number of operations
which were performed in the early years, two-thirds were
upon schizophrenics, a group which yield the least satisfactory results, fewer than one-fifth making a good recovery
and only one-third being ultimately discharged from hospital'
(Knight 1965). John Fulton had pleaded in 1949 for a slow-
down in 'the already massive clinical assault on the frontal
lobes', not because of 'ideological issues', so caustically
referred to by Sargant and Slater, but because more needed
to be known of the underlying physiology of the brain. Yet
surgeons carried on with almost religious zeal. Walter
Freeman, the doyen of American psychosurgery, recently
reported (1971) on a follow-up of 415 private patients
suffering from 'schizophrenia' who had been treated during
the early years of frontal lobe surgery. His paper was
published in the *British Journal of Psychiatry*, a journal famed
internationally for its normally stringent academic standards.

(For example, relatively few papers of psychoanalytic importance have been published in the journal because of its editorial board's insistence on the need for properly controlled testing of therapeutic claims and hypotheses.) At the time Freeman's paper was published, the editor of the journal was none other than Eliot Slater (co-author with William Sargant of the textbook praising the effectiveness of leucotomy in schizophrenia), a psychiatrist well known in Britain for his harsh criticism of psychoanalysis and its claim to be scientific. It is of some interest, therefore, to note the appearance in his journal of a paper reporting on the long-term follow-up of the efficacy of psychosurgery in schizophrenia in which the diagnostic criteria are never described, in which next to nothing is recorded about the condition of the patients prior to surgery, in which no mention is made of the spontaneous recovery rate in acute and chronic variants of the condition, and in which no reference is made to the possibility that at least some of the patients might have improved as a consequence of alterations in treatment occurring about the same time as the surgery. Instead we are provided with a series of anecdotal accounts of Freeman's 'achievement' of which the following two extracts are typical examples:

'A physician who had been discharged from two internships because of aggressive paranoid behaviour completed an internship, served as a liaison officer among several military hospitals in Germany for three years, married and fathered two children. He established a ten man medical clinic and flies his own plane.'

'A psychiatrist with a drive towards homicide or suicide returned to his post in a state mental hospital four months after operation, was promoted to chief of service, gave lectures on mental hygiene in the community, established an after-care clinic and after a few years went into private practice.'   (Freeman 1971: 621–4)

Freeman's paper is somewhat more interesting with regard to the insight (unwittingly provided?) which he gives his readers into his conception of illness and health than for what it has to say about a formidable, irreversible method of treatment. The only indices of improvement which he makes use of to illustrate his claim that surgery is effective relate to whether the patient lives outside hospital and is employed or not. His category of 'Employed' includes part-time occupations, of which the vast majority of quite seriously handicapped schizophrenic patients are quite capable without their having to undergo brain surgery. Despite the use of such a loose measure of response, however, less than half his patients appeared to have achieved it, scarcely a dramatic advertisement for such an approach. Freeman, however, is not at all abashed. He notes that those 'schizophrenics' operated upon early in their hospitalizations did better than those who did not undergo surgery until after they had been many years in hospital and he concludes that 'in a dangerous disease such as schizophrenia it may prove safer to operate than to wait'!

It is scarcely believable that a reputable journal such as the *British Journal of Psychiatry* would publish such a deplorable paper. It is not easy to believe that the same journal would publish a paper enthusiastically endorsing the efficacy of psychotherapy (or indeed of certain drugs) in the management of schizophrenia without demanding that it contain a definition of the terms employed, some reputable and independent measures of clinical improvement, and some attempt at evaluating a matched, control group of patients. Yet here we have a paper which on the basis of four pages of casual anecdote, potted history, and amateur statistics argues for more frequent use of a most serious, indeed arguably the most serious method of treatment that can be employed in schizophrenia and indeed insists, in the absence of any objective evidence, that it can be *more dangerous not to operate than to do so* – and the *British Journal of Psychiatry* publishes it. Is it surprising, therefore, that critics of psychosurgery, appalled by the apparent double standards employed by its supporters, tend to write it off as grotesque mutilation and knife-happy sorcery?

There is more general agreement that patients suffering from severe disturbances of mood and emotion are more likely to benefit from psychosurgical treatment than schizophrenics. The more intense and persistent the emotional responses, the more appropriate, it is argued, is the referral for psychosurgery (Bridges and Bartlett 1977). Crippling phobias, ritualistic and compulsive behaviours, and profound, intractable and suicidal depression figure most prominently in the mental state reports of patients referred for psychosurgical treatment. Such disturbances are usually described as being of long duration and resistant to alternative treatments such as psychotherapy, electrical treatment, and drugs. However, the criteria whereby psychiatrists refer patients for treatment (in those countries, such as the UK and the United States, where most if not all psychosurgical candidates are psychiatrically referred) and the criteria whereby neurosurgeons accept them are only rarely made explicit. The declaration commonly made to the effect that 'all therapeutic alternatives have been exhausted' lacks precision. One Canadian psychiatrist (Lehmann 1973) has attempted to be more specific about the criteria and has suggested that, for example, a patient referred for psychosurgical treatment of anxiety and depression should have had at least one but preferably two courses of ECT, disabling symptoms for at least two years, adequate doses of both minor and major tranquillisers, and psychotherapy by a trained therapist for a minimum period of six months. Kelly (1976), in his less specific description of selection criteria, tends to agree broadly with such recommendations.

Several studies have also been undertaken with a view to clarifying the role of psychosurgery in the treatment of severe *obsessive-compulsive disorders*. Tan, Marks, and Marset (1971) compared twenty-four patients who had had a modified leucotomy for anxiety with severe obsessions with a group of thirteen matched controls over a period of five years after treatment and found that the leucotomized patients did significantly better than the controls. Obsessions were reduced from a severe to a moderate degree of handicap, work adjustment improved, and such personality changes as occurred after operation were mild and unrelated to outcome. Bridges and his colleagues at the Brook Hospital Neurosurgical Unit in London (1973) compared twenty-four obsessional patients with twenty-four severely depressed patients who had also had psychosurgery. After three years, definite symptomatic improvement had been noted in 16 per cent of the obsessional and 17 per cent of the depressed patients.

Yet, despite such impressive figures, and the marked relief of symptoms in even such a low proportion of chronically and severely disabled patients is impressive, there still remain some nagging doubts. First, there is the apparent confusion over the best site for the operation, despite all those elaborate theories painstakingly described by the physiologists and referred to earlier in the chapter. For example, according to limbic system theory, operations on the cingulate gyrus should benefit those suffering from obsessive-compulsive illnesses. Some workers are quite adamant that they do, whereas others, including Geoffrey Knight, appear equally adamant that they do not. Again, when the surgeons leave describing the statistical results and provide illustrative case histories, doubts begin to grow. Here is an example provided by Geoffrey Knight to illustrate the effects of a subcaudate tractotomy (an operation directed at an area in the medial portion of the frontal lobe):

'A woman of 38 suffered from tension and anxiety since childhood. Following *marriage to a sadist* [my italics] she developed multiple jerks and sweating, so severe that she had to change her clothes several times a day, and obsessional tidiness and depression. The effort to tidy her wardrobe was exhausting. She was unable to face meeting

people. Strong suicidal impulses developed. Following operation 9 years ago she was immediately dramatically improved. Within two months the jerking, sweating and suicidal ideas were gone; she was able to put things away in the wardrobe and forget all about abnormal tidiness. "Formerly it had taken me ages to get away from it – I seemed glued to it". She has maintained this complete cure.'
(Knight 1973: 101)

Such an anecdote raises as many questions as it attempts to answer. One might be forgiven for concluding that the correct management of a wife made anxious and obsessed by a sadistic husband would be a brain operation on the husband. Knight, in this extract, however, appears to believe that it is the wife's brain that required treatment, not the husband's sadism. The marriage, it would appear from this totally insufficient account, provoked a deterioration in the poor woman's state, yet we are told nothing of any attempts to clarify the marital state, provide some form of therapy, or suggest separation, and one must conclude that such attempts were not made. If the marriage is not relevant, why did Knight include it in his account? If it is relevant, why and what was done about it?

There may be those who feel that such an example is unfair and that Knight left out the information I seek because he was only using a brief anecdote to illustrate the potentially beneficial effect of a specific surgical approach, in this case subcaudate tractotomy. Yet, I have to say that, regrettably, such an example is only too typical of what the psychosurgeons and their supporters provide. Take this account given by Sargant and Slater in their textbook:

'Another type of depressive illness that may be helped by leucotomy is the reactive depression in which environmental factors of an irremediable kind are involved. A depressed woman, for instance, may owe her illness to a psychopathic husband who cannot change and will not accept treatment. Separation might be the answer but is ruled out by other ties such as children, by the patient's financial or emotional dependence or by her religious views. Patients of this type are often helped by antidepressant drugs. But in the occasional case where they do not work, we have seen patients enabled by a leucotomy to return to the difficult environment and cope with it in a way which had hitherto been impossible.'

(Sargant and Slater 1972: 105–6)

It is difficult to believe that what is being advocated here is a brain operation on a woman to enable her to live with a seriously disturbed man, yet that is precisely what it amounts to. Is it any wonder that the critics of brain surgery become ever more vocal, ever more bitter, ever more extreme?

Evaluating the effects of surgery is greatly dependent on the reliability, validity, and comprehensiveness of the data as they are presented in the literature. One recent literature review (Valenstein 1977), covering 153 articles published between 1971 and 1976, offers little room for complacency. The majority of reports lacked any objective measurement and relied on clinical acumen and subjective impression. A rating scale of scientific merit, ranging from 1 to 6, whereby psychosurgery reports can be judged has been proposed (May and Van Putten 1974). A rating of one is applied only to those studies that have matched controls, use objective tests, evaluate patients for an adequate pre- and postoperative period, employ independent raters, analyse data statistically and do not confound any variables (e.g. drug treatment, psychotherapy etc.) A rating of six, on the other hand is applied to reports that provide only descriptive information on the patients and have no comparison group. When Valenstein (1977) applied these criteria to the 153 papers included in his review, most of them received a rating of five or six. Almost 90 per cent of the articles from the US received rating between four and six. Valenstein points out that 'it is important to note that a rating of four would be given only to articles of low scientific value'. 'It is unlikely', he adds, 'that an animal study with such a low rating would be accepted for publication by the editors of a respected experimental journal.'

One of the harshest and most unrelenting critics of psychosurgical procedures is the Washington psychiatrist Peter Breggin. Breggin opposes all forms of brain surgery in psychiatric patients and in 1972, with the assistance of Congressman Cornelius Gallagher of New Jersey, had a massive indictment of such procedures, entitled *The Return of Lobotomy and Psychosurgery*, entered in the *Congressional Record* (1972). Breggin's criticisms can be briefly summarized. He sees no scientific justification in operating, on the basis of naive and unproven neurophysiological theories, upon ostensibly normal brains. He believes that the methods of measuring success after such operations are crude and biased, and in so far as there is any post-operative 'success' it is due to the emotional blunting, apathy, and disinterest that he believes follows every operation. Finally, he is fearful of the potential future use of psychosurgery as a tool of political control within society.

'We are in danger of creating a society in which everyone who deviates from the norm will be in danger of surgical mutilation. The increasing application of these methods to "neurotics" and to people who are already well enough to work and to live with their families raises the spectre of wide scale applications, particularly to women, who continue to be the majority of victims.'

(Breggin 1972: 5576)

Unfortunately, Dr Breggin's analysis of psychosurgery is blatantly one-sided and tendentious. Unwisely, he dismisses the role of psychosurgery in relieving intractable physical pain and seems throughout his *Congressional Record* report to be uncertain whether psychosurgery should be banned because it *does not work* or banned because it *does work* and may be abused in a sinister and fearful fashion. He ruins his case by his tendency to wild exaggeration and, on occasion, a somewhat cavalier approach to the use of facts. As perhaps befits a contemporary assailant of psychiatric orthodoxy, Breggin mounts his attack with a series of sweeping assertions, selected quotations, and random examples which together constitute an indictment of such staggering proportions that it leaves the casual reader stunned and in disbelief that any-one professing himself to be a physician would indulge in such shameful practices. An example of his approach is the use he makes of a study by Marks, Birley, and Gelder (1966) at the Maudsley Hospital of the effects of leucotomy in twenty-two cases of agoraphobia. 'Marks and his colleagues', declares Breggin,

> 'somehow come up with 22 cases of "agoraphobia" – fear of open spaces – and lobotomised them (again) with the bimedial frontal lobotomy. They present no case material so we can't judge what they mean by "agoraphobia" or why they would destroy a person's brain to cure such a symptom. In fact, agoraphobia as an isolated symptom is so rare that one must distrust their clinical judgment in its entirety. People crippled by such a symptom almost in-variably demonstrate a complex of psychiatric symptoms, as do almost all individuals who are psychologically crippled.' (Breggin 1972: 5570)

In point of fact, Marks and his colleagues never loboto-mized anyone and are never likely to since not one of them is a qualified surgeon. What they did, and this they describe in some detail, was to assess retrospectively the progress of agoraphobic patients who had had a modified leucotomy some time in the past with a matched series of similar patients who had not undergone surgery. This, however, is a small quibble. More serious is Breggin's assertion that 'we can't judge what they mean by "agoraphobia"' – if he truly means this it suggests that he never read the paper in the first place, for had he done so he would find on its very first page the statement:

'The term agoraphobia is used here to describe fears of
going out in streets, shops, crowds, lifts, cars, trains,
tunnels, bridges or remaining alone at home, in varying
combinations. Several patients in each group (the surgically treated and the control groups) had depression or
obsessions at some stage of their illness.'

(Marks, Birley, and Gelder 1966: 757)

One might contest such a definition, but can one say, as
Breggin does with such brazen confidence, that no definition
has been provided? And again, despite his insistence, we
need not disregard these authors' clinical judgement. Nowhere do they claim, as he implies they do, that agoraphobia
is an 'isolated symptom', but they make it plain both in this
paper and in a number of other studies referred to in it
(Gelder and Marks 1966; Gelder, Marks, and Wolff 1967)
that the term is commonly applied to those patients in whom
agoraphobia is the *predominant* rather than the only symptom.
Finally, to accuse Marks, Birley, and Gelder of leaving their
readers in the dark as to the reasons 'why they would destroy
a person's brain to cure such a symptom' is to indulge in the
sharpest of debating tactics. Note the subtle shift whereby
cutting the fronto-thalamic fibres becomes transformed into
destroying a person's brain, a shift that leaves the accused
little alternative than to acknowledge his role as brain-
basher and plead forgiveness. In actual fact, these three
authors do give reasons, not for destroying brains, which
they would deny doing, but for trying to assess the results of
psychosurgical intervention. First, and Breggin would have
known this had he read some of the other papers written
by these authors (not to mention Isaac Marks's excellent
account of phobic anxiety states, *Fears and Phobias* (1969)),
the symptom complex 'agoraphobia' is extremely distressful
and handicapping. As far back as 1872, when Westphal in a
celebrated monograph first coined the term 'agoraphobia',
some of the classic features of the syndrome were described –
the agony experienced on walking through deserted streets,

the relief obtained from company or alcohol, the terror of being left alone, an affliction of the mighty ('Augustus Caesar durst not sit alone in the dark') as much as the ordinary man. 'They that live in fear', wrote Westphal, 'are never free, resolute, secure, merry, but in continual pain . . . no greater misery, no rack, no torture like unto it.' Numerous treatments, including behaviour therapy, psychotherapy, and drugs, have been employed with varying effects, but a residual number of cases remain resistant to all attempts at modification. Second, not one of the three authors had an axe to grind for psychosurgery; two of them, Marks and Gelder, might well be accused of having a preference for behavioural approaches while Birley is a socially inclined psychiatrist not overly enthusiastic about physical treatments in psychiatry. Third, while concluding that their study suggests that leucotomy produces a dramatic fall in anxiety, following which phobic symptoms gradually improve, they take great pains to emphasize that their analysis is retrospective, that there is a serious need for careful selection of the relatively small number of patients likely to benefit from such an approach, and that 'there is a danger that a favourable report about any treatment may lead others to use it too widely.'

The manner in which Breggin abuses this paper illustrates the way in which many controversies in psychiatry evolve and for this reason I have dwelt on it at some length. Walter Freeman makes enthusiastic and unsupported claims for the efficacy of psychosurgery and he is published in the *British Journal of Psychiatry*. Peter Breggin makes a wild and ill-judged onslaught on the same subject and he ends up enshrined in the *Congressional Record* of the United States Congress. Somewhere in the middle of this furore, there are those, such as Marks and his co-workers, who are trying to make sense of the available data while at the same time laying down criteria whereby more studies might be undertaken to clarify the situation further. Typical, too, of controversies in psychiatry, is the tendency for the valid doubts expressed by Breggin to become submerged and lost to sight within the sea of rhetorical vituperation in which he gratuitously indulges. For he does have a valid argument. His indiscriminate attacks only play into the hands of those who wish to portray all criticism of brain surgery in psychiatry as misplaced idealism and cranky ideological crusading. Yet, is it merely 'ideological issues' that lead one to feel unease reading about the Madras neurosurgeon, Balasubramaniam, and his psychosurgical interventions in patients with 'hyperactivity' (1970)? In one account he describes the results of operation in 115 patients, of whom three were *under five* and another thirty-six were *under eleven*. Using diathermy or the injection of substances such as olive oil to destroy centres in these children's brains, he declares:

'The improvement that occurs has been remarkable. In one case, a patient had been assaulting his colleagues and the ward doctors; after the operation he became a helpful addition to the ward staff and looked after other patients. In one case, the patient became quiet, bashful and was a model of good behaviour.'

(Balasubramaniam *et al.* 1970: 21)

Assessments made post-operatively inevitably emphasize the fact that patients become more manageable and are less troublesome. Yet the simple classification system used by Balasubramaniam is crude and provides remarkably little information about the patients' subsequent state. It is a system especially liked by some psychosurgeons and is made up of six grades which range from 'no need for any drug; patient mixes well' to 'died'. Interestingly enough, there is no category for 'made worse'. Balasubramaniam performs stereotactic operations directed against the amygdala and appears to do so without trying drugs beforehand; this is a surprising approach, for in aggressive and epileptic states in childhood a number of drugs, including certain anti-convulsants, have been found to be particularly effective.

Two Japanese surgeons, Narabayashi and Uno in Tokyo, have reported on a follow-up of twenty-seven children, ages ranging from *five* to *thirteen*, who had had amygdalotomies (1966). These workers operate on children characterized by 'unsteadiness', hyperactive behaviour disorders and poor concentration rather than violent behaviour'. Good results include 'a degree of satisfactory obedience and of constant, steady mood which enabled the children to stay in their social environment, such as kindergarten or school for the feebleminded'. In the United States, O. J. Andy and his colleagues at the University of Mississippi School of Medicine in Jackson frankly admit that the goal of surgery in children is to reduce 'hyperactivity' to levels which can be managed by their parents (1966). They insist that there is something organically wrong with the children upon whom they operate, but in the great majority of cases they provide little in the way of evidence as to what such pathology might be. A triad of symptoms exists, consisting of hyperactivity, aggression, and emotional instability, which allegedly responds to surgical intervention. Andy provides a description of such a case. In 1966 he provided an account of a boy of nine who 'had seizures and behavioural disorders (hyperactive, combative, explosive, destructive, sadistic)' (Andy 1970). He began surgery with a bilateral destruction of the thalamus. Nine months later, clinical conditions necessitated a further attack on the thalamus on one side. After a further year, the patient showed some additional signs of excessive irritability, aggressiveness, and 'combativeness', and had a further operation. At this stage, Andy reported the patient as 'adjusted to his environment' and showing 'a marked improvement in behaviour and memory'. Four years later, Andy included this case in a follow-up report and revealed that whereas the boy was reportedly easy to manage he was showing signs of steady intellectual deterioration. And by this time the boy was thirteen years and four brain operations old.

Rylander's 'renaissance of psychosurgery' has led some practitioners into somewhat grandiose positions, perhaps the most flamboyant being that adopted over the role of brain operations in the control of violent, antisocial behaviour. In 1967 a letter was published in the *Journal of the American Medical Association* on the 'Role of Brain Disease in Riots and Urban Violence' (Mark, Sweet, and Ervin 1967). It was written by three American surgeons: William Sweet, chief of neurosurgery at the famed Massachusetts General Hospital in Boston, Vernon Mark, neurosurgery chief at Boston City Hospital, and Frank Ervin, a psychiatrist and neurologist currently on the faculty of the University of California in Los Angeles and associated with the Center for the Prevention of Violence. The letter, written at the height of the racial and urban disturbances which had racked American cities for a number of years, pointed out that whereas 'poverty, unemployment, slum housing and inadequate housing' obviously played an important part in provoking civil unrest, more subtle factors, such as 'brain dysfunction' in those rioters engaged in arson, sniping, and physical assault, should also be taken into account and yet tended to be ignored. These experts drew attention to the fact that only a small number of slum dwellers took part in riots and that an even smaller number participated in violent behaviour. 'Yet if slum conditions alone determined and initiated riots', they observed, 'why are the vast majority of slum dwellers able to resist the temptation of unrestrained violence?' Fear? Apathy? Lack of opportunity? No – the answer to this hardy perennial as to what it is that differentiates the 'silent majority', those long-suffering souls who take everything that is thrown at them passively and with little outward sign of protest, from the far from silent minority who rise up, rebel, and run rampant appears obvious to these experts. Look to the brain:

'The real lesson of the urban rioting is that beside the need to study the social fabric that creates the riot atmosphere we need intensive research and clinical studies of the individuals committing the violence. The goal of such studies would be to pinpoint, diagnose and treat those people with low violence thresholds before they contribute to further tragedies.'

(Mark, Sweet, and Ervin 1967: 895)

At least one cynical commentator (Holden 1973) has dismissed this argument as a shrewd attempt to exploit public anxieties and obtain research funds. However, to others, the simple equation linking social unrest and subtle brain pathology is a harbinger of a brave new scientific world wherein dissent and confrontation will be deemed pathological and the remedy for social injustice will be the surgeon's knife. In 1970 these three experts persuaded the United States Congress to direct the National Institute of Mental Health to award them a grant of half a million dollars to continue their research. Indeed, so impressed was the Senate Labor, Health, Education and Welfare appropriations subcommittee with Sweet's testimony that a further million dollars was earmarked for research into possible biological causes of violence and the 'NeuroResearch Foundation', set up by these three workers, received enthusiastic backing from the law enforcement community in the United States.

In support of their contention that a significant proportion of urban violence is a consequence of brain disease, Mark and Ervin, in a book entitled *Violence and the Brain* (1970), cite a number of highly publicized crimes. For example, much is made of the fact that Charles Whitman, who shot forty-four people and killed fourteen of them from a tower on the campus of the University of Texas in Austin, was found at post-mortem to have a malignant tumour in his brain. The tumour was situated in the region of the amygdala. It is of course possible that there is a causal connection between the tumour and the violence (which is clearly implied by Mark and Ervin), but other evidence, particularly the contents of a diary that Whitman kept methodically for over four years, runs counter to the view that his murderous exploit resulted from a sudden, impulsive, tumour-generated outburst. Whitman's diary provides considerable detail about how he planned his crime, his defence of the tower, and his escape afterwards. The night before the shoot-out on the campus he attacked his mother and his wife. His explanations for these actions, in his diary, do not support the implicit contention in Mark and Ervin's book that Whitman was acting out sudden pathological impulses generated in his diseased brain, but rather that he acted in a carefully planned and methodical way for a lengthy period of time. It is to go beyond the available evidence to argue that at the root of many, if not the majority of, violent crimes there is specific brain disease. This dubious claim is bolstered by highly selected cases, such as Whitman's, and a perverse use of statistics – one favourite trick is to stack the number of rapes, muggings, homicides, and child assaults on one side and the incidence of epilepsy, cerebral palsy, head injuries, and other manifestations of brain damage on the other to create an impression that both sets of phenomena are intrinsically linked in a causal manner. The purpose of all this rhetoric is to emphasize the need

> '. . . to develop an *early warning test* of limbic brain function to detect those humans who have a low threshold for impulsive violence, and we need better and more effective methods of treating them once we have found who they are.'
> (Mark and Ervin 1970: 160)

In the face of such enthusiasm, one has to forcefully remind oneself that at the present time little in the way of objective and reliable information is known about how the limbic system functions. Little is known of the relationship between the various centres and for the moment psychiatrists and psychosurgeons have to be content with a number of theoretical suppositions such as those of Papez and MacLean upon which to proceed gingerly in highly selected cases. Ever since Sir Denis Hill and his colleagues drew attention to abnormalities in the electroencephalographic tracings of a group of personality-disordered, emotionally unstable, impulsive patients (Hill and Watterson 1942), there has been intense interest in the possibility of identifying potentially violent people before violence occurs. Yet, and Mark and Ervin would do well to contemplate the experience gained in this area, it is still unclear, a quarter of a century later, how specific such findings are, i.e., how common such abnormalities are in EEG tracings of normal, non-institutionalized populations.

We are asked to believe that psychosurgeons have a significant role to play in the reduction of contemporary violence, but when it comes to defining what is meant by violence a certain unease and evasiveness can be detected. Vernon Mark and Robert Neville, in an article in the same issue of the *Journal of the American Medical Association* (1973) which carried the letter from Erwin, Mark, and Sweet, calling for studies 'to pinpoint, diagnose and treat those people with low violence thresholds before they contribute to further tragedies', concede that there is some disagreement in contemporary society as to what constitutes violence. Many political activists, they admit, are called violent. Many more, they neglect to say, are viewed as *potentially* violent. The police are constantly accused of using violent tactics; dissidents regularly complain of being *provoked* into violence. Mark and Neville attempt to reassure an increasingly nervous public (and a somewhat wary medical profession) with a defiintion of violence as:

'. . . personal violent behaviour, unwarranted and usually unprovoked acts that directly attempt to, or actually do, injure or destroy another person or thing. This does not include violence organised for a political motive. Of course we would not approve neurosurgery unless *the personal violence could be traced to organic brain disease and could not be treated by non-surgical methods.*'

(Mark and Neville 1973: 768)

It seems a somewhat extreme claim to assert that many of the rioters, looters, and arsonists out on the streets of American cities in the mid-1960s suffered from 'organic brain disease' not amenable to non-surgical methods of treatment. What are we to make of the decline in urban rioting, looting, and arson in the same cities since those long hot summers ended? Are we to conclude that all those diseased brains spontaneously recovered, all those malfunctioning limbic circuits regained their stability?

That some psychosurgeons make expansive claims which cannot be justified appears undeniable. Whenever a serious attempt is made to carry out a properly controlled pre- and post-operative assessment in patients undergoing psychosurgical procedures, the results of such interventions almost invariably tend to be less impressive than those reported by researchers who do not take such care. When Edward Hitchcock and his Edinburgh colleagues (1973) implemented an elaborate system of assessment of their patients' psychiatric, behavioural, and social status prior to and following amygdalotomy, they found the short-term response in fourteen cases of severe, intractable impulsive violence to be much less impressive than that reported in a number of highly publicized studies performed in other centres (Narabayashi *et al.* 1963; Heimburger, Whitlock, and Kalsbeck 1966). Such, invariably, is the life history of treatments in psychiatry. When, for example, a new drug appears on the market, loud and insistent are the claims made on its behalf. However, when the enthusiasm for its remarkable efficacy in a number of conditions has died away, there commences a period of some disillusion which may reach a point where people feel that the drug has nothing to offer at all. Finally, after a series of properly controlled and standardized trials of the drug have been undertaken and published, it becomes clear that the drug has a useful role in the management of a small number of patients suffering from a particular condition. So, one suspects that the proper study of psychosurgery will reveal that as a treatment it has a role in psychiatry, but a limited role. In a number of highly selected cases of chronic, distressing, and intractable psychological suffering, leucotomy may be found to be useful and, as we have seen, the indications are that this is so.

If psychosurgery does not work, if the theories are all fraudulent and the results all cooked, then clearly the future of psychosurgery is doomed, for in medicine, as elsewhere, truth eventually will out. But, and the anxiety one senses in its critics appears increasingly related to this possibility, what if it is effective, if in a number of highly selected, chronically distressed, and intractable cases it is found to provide considerable improvement and relief? 'To the extent that psychosurgery "blunts" the individual I personally feel that it partially kills the individual', declares Breggin in a passage quoted at the beginning of this chapter. But to the extent that it does not 'blunt' and that it does relieve intense psychological agony what do Breggin and like-minded critics feel? Let us take as an example the crippling obsessive compulsive disorders. Obsessions (see Chapter 3) are persistent distressing impulses or thoughts which are experienced by the subject as unwanted and irresistible. Compulsions are acts that result from obsessional thoughts. Freud, in 1917, provided the following description of the clinical picture in such conditions:

> 'The obsessional neurosis takes this form: the patient's mind is occupied with thoughts that do not really interest him, he feels impulses which are alien to him, and he is impelled to perform actions which not only afford him no pleasure but from which he is powerless to desist. The thoughts (obsessions) may be meaningless in themselves or only of no interest to the patient; they are often only absolutely silly . . .' (Freud 1955: 153)

The actions which the patient feels compelled to perform are usually in the form of repetitive, stereotyped acts of counting, touching, arranging objects, moving in certain ways, washing, and dressing. Such ritualistic behaviour acts as a defence against disaster – e.g., ritualistic hand-washing serves to protect against the anxiety-provoking idea of contamination. Yet the performance of the anxiety-relieving ritual itself becomes the focus for obsessional ruminations and doubt. As Karl Jaspers points out:

'Performance [of the ritual] becomes scrupulously exact, distraction must be excluded and there is an engagement of the whole mind. Every possibility of error arouses doubt as to the effectiveness of the ritual and increases the demand for further acts to make certain, and, if there is further doubt, there must be a full repetition from the start . . . When the compulsive urges are surrendered to there is . . . a vivid feeling of relief. If, however, they are resisted, severe anxiety arises . . . To get rid of the anxiety, patients must once more carry out the meaningless ritual of harmless acts.'   (Jaspers 1963: 136)

The fear of suffering such anxiety is enough to provoke it and, within such a vicious and tormenting cycle, the patient wrestles with the increasingly painful and preoccupying phenomena. Those patients who suffer from severe forms of this condition experience terrible psychic agony. Their waking hours are dominated by the obsessional ruminations and impulses, their mental life overwhelmed by the requirements of repetitively carrying out elaborate, meaningless rituals. To date, treatment for the severer varieties of such states is far from impressive. Drugs have a limited value while psychotherapy has not proved particularly effective. In a number of patients, and especially in those who exhibit symptoms of depression alongside their obsessional and compulsive symptoms, psychosurgery, allegedly, has provided some relief.

It is this criterion, namely the relief of severe and disabling symptoms, that serves as a justification of psychosurgery for many British psychiatrists. In those cases where a new, non-surgical treatment appears which is effective, brain surgery is discarded, but in those patients, and they should be relatively few in number, who do not respond to any of the more orthodox forms of treatment surgery can be the last hope of some escape from crippling and incessant suffering. (It is worth noting in this regard that Marks, Hodgson, and Rachman (1975) have reported impressive success using behavioural modification of obsessive-compulsive rituals in twenty patients; it is a matter of some irony that Dr Marks, castigated by Peter Breggin for acknowledging the possible benefits of surgery in certain psychiatric states, should contribute to a situation wherein surgery may become obsolete as a treatment modality.)

So we are left with the two central questions concerning psychosurgery: does it work and should it be used? Taking the second question first, the Report of the US National Commission for the Protection of Human Subjects of Biomedical and Behavioral Research (1977) is highly relevant. The Commission, a multiprofessional group of lawyers, physicians, psychologists, and specialists in ethics, undertook a thorough review of published work on the subject and assessed several studies specially performed for it. To the chagrin of psychosurgery's critics, the Commission endorsed the use of psychosurgery under properly supervised conditions. Its recommendations included the setting up of Institutional Review Boards to supervise and monitor psychosurgical procedures performed at approved institutions on patients properly informed of their rights and adequately assessed pre- and post-operatively. The Report did not rule out psychosurgery on prisoners, involuntarily committed patients, or patients under the supervision of legal guardians but recommended that the IRBs should withold approval pending authorization by a court and consent by a legal guardian. The Commission acknowledged that the ability of prisoners and mental patients to make free choices may be diminished by institutionalization or by suggestions to the effect that alterations in probation, parole, sentence, release, or otherwise may be dependant on acceptance of surgery. However, it felt that it would be unfair 'to exclude prisoners or involuntarily confined patients from the opportunity to seek benefit from new therapies on the basis of an unrebuttable presumption of diminished capacity or by prohibiting third-party consent'. One of the Commission members, however, dissented from the report, arguing that all persons in institutions such as psychiatric hospitals, whether voluntary or involuntary patients, should be evaluated by a court before the performance of psychosurgical procedures.

These American recommendations are similar to those made by the New South Wales Committee of Inquiry (Kiloh 1977). The Committee recommended the setting-up of a Psychosurgery Review Board which would have the power to assess all proposed psychosurgical procedures. In cases of doubt about the capacity of the patient to provide informed consent, a Judge of the Supreme Court would consider the question. The Australian Committee, however, ruled against psychosurgical procedures being employed in the case of patients presumed to be incapable of giving informed consent, namely persons under sixteen, under sentence, awaiting trial, on probation, or involuntarily committed.

At the time of writing, the use of psychosurgery in Britain is regulated by the usual restrictions on any medical treatment including the Mental Health Act (1959). Bridges and Bartlett (1977) have made clear the policy at one British unit, the Geoffrey Knight Unit at the Brook Hospital in South London, concerning informed consent. The Unit does not accept patients for psychosurgery who are the subject of a committal order under the 1959 Mental Health Act. Current British practice seems to be to use psychosurgery treatments but only as a last resort. For example, in a detailed study of the effects of stereotactic limbic leucotomy in sixty-six patients (Mitchell-Heggs et al. 1976), all but seven had previously received at least one course of ECT, thirty-five had undergone formal psychotherapy or psychoanalysis, while the majority had received 'supportive, non-interpretative psychotherapy' throughout the greater part of their illnesses.

The US Commission's emphasis on the need to restrict psychosurgery to a number of approved centres reflects the view that only experienced surgeons working closely with psychiatrists should undertake the work. Several leading experts insist that it may not be possible to maintain an adequate level of surgical expertise if the procedure is performed infrequently and thus argue for a concentration of the surgery in a small number of special centres. However, it is clear from the results of a recent survey (Barraclough and Mitchell-Heggs 1978) that such a situation has not been reached in Britain. While it is true that four major neurosurgical units accounted for two-thirds of the operations, a further twenty-seven units were performing five or less operations each year. A similar situation exists in the US where Valenstein (1977) has estimated that about 25 per cent of the operations are done by surgeons who perform three or less operations per year and that approximately 70–80 per cent of neurosurgeons perform less than three operations annually.

Does it work? The US Commission believed it did in certain cases but it was unable to base its findings on any adequately controlled and prospective trial for the very good reason that none has taken place. Yet ever since the initial period of enthusiasm for psychosurgery, there have been calls for a proper trial. 'Carefully controlled studies are needed if we are to assess lobotomy', declared an editorial in the *American Journal of Psychiatry* in 1949 (Finesinger 1949). Fifteen years later, a British psychiatrist is insisting that 'Further evaluations of the operation can best be done, perhaps can only be done, by controlled clinical trials' (Birley 1964). Later again, another British psychiatrist, showing an irritation that may reflect the failure of psychosurgeons down through the years to take much notice of such strictures, asks: 'It is too much to ask that the same stringent criteria (as used for new drugs) should be adopted in dealing with potentially more dangerous, and certainly more expensive, surgical procedures?' (Levy 1972).

A research committee of the Royal College of Psychiatrists did propose such a trial which was to be carried out in a number of centres in Britain. Patients referred for consideration for psychosurgery were to be assessed and randomly allocated to surgical and non-surgical treatments (Research Committee, R. C. Psychiatrists 1977). For reasons which a *Lancet* editorial described as 'shadowy but which have been related to active political lobbying by the critics of psychosurgery' (there were eleven separate questions on the subject in the House of Commons during 1976 alone), the trial never received the necessary financial backing and was dropped, yet one more example, it should be noted, of opposition from the critics of psychosurgery to attempts to establish the usefulness or otherwise of the procedure condemned by them because it has yet to be shown to be useful!

The formidable difficulties involved in such a study can hardly be exaggerated. The selection of patients for operation, the selection of a properly matched control group, the particular operative procedure to be studied, the nature and extent of the pre- and post-operative assessments, are only some of the features of such a trial that will pose methodological problems. Difficult as such problems may be, there seems to be no alternative to such a study if the fundamental and controversial questions of efficacy and ethics are ever to be answered.

References

ABRAHAMS, V.C., HILTON, S.M., and ZBROZYNA, A. (1960) Active Muscle Vasodilation Produced by Stimulation of the Brain Stem; Its Significance in the Defence Reaction. *Journal of Physiology* **154**: 491–513 (London).

ANDY, D.J. (1966) Neurosurgical Treatment of Abnormal Behaviour. *American Journal of the Medical Sciences* **252**: 232–8.

—— (1970) Thalactomy in Hyperactive and Aggressive Behaviour .*Confinia Neurologica* **27**: 168–71.

BALASUBRAMANIAM, V., KANAKA, T.S., RAMANUGAM, P.V., and RAMANURTHI, B. (1970) Surgical Treatment of Hyperkinetic and Behaviour Disorders. *International Surgery Bulletin* **54**: 18–23.

BALLANTINE, H.T., CASSIDY, W.L., FLANAGAN, N.B., and MARINO, R. (1967) Stereotaxic Anterior Cingulotomy for Neurospsychiatric Illness and Intractable Pain. *Journal of Neurosurgery* **26**: 488–95.

BARRACLOUGH, B.M. and MITCHELL-HEGGS, N.A. (1978) Use of neurosurgery for psychological disorder in the British Isles during 1974–6. *British Medical Journal* **2**: 1591–3.

BECHTEREVA, N.P. and BUNDZEN, P.V. (1973) Neurophysiological organization of mental activity in man. In: *Biological diagnosis of Brain Disorders* pp. 3–23. New York: Spectrum Publications.

BECHTEREVA, N.P., BONDARTCHUK, A.N., SMIRNOV, V.M., MELIUTCHEVA, L.A. and SHANDURINA, A.N. (1975) Method of electrostimulation of the deep brain structures in treatment of some chronic diseases. *Confinia Neurologica* **37**: 136–40.

BECHTEREVA, N.P., KAMBAROVA, D.K., SMIRNOV, V.M. and SHANDURINA, A.N. (1976) The principles and tactics of using the brain's latent abilities for therapy. Chronic intracerebral electrical stimulation for phantom limb pain, hyperkineses and epilepsy. In: *Neurosurgical Treatment in Psychiatry* (Ed. W. H. Sweet). Baltimore: University Park Press.

BIRLEY, J.L.T. (1964) Modified Frontal Leucotomy: A Review of 106 Cases. *British Journal of Psychiatry* **110**: 211.

BREGGIN, P. (1972) The Return of Lobotomy and Psychosurgery. *Congressional Record* **118**: E1603–E1612 (February 24).

BRIDGES, P.K. and BARTLETT, J.R. (1977) Review article: Psychosurgery: yesterday and today. *British Journal of Psychiatry* **131**: 249–60.

BRIDGES, P.K., GOKTEPE, E.D., MARATOS, J., BROWNE, A., and YOUNG, L. (1973) A Comparative Review of Patients with Obsessional Neurosis and with Depression Treated by Psychosurgery. *British Journal of Psychiatry* **123**: 663–74.

BURCKHARDT, G. (1891) Rindenexcisionen, als Bertrag zur operativen Therapie der Psychosen. *Allgemeine Zeitschrift für Psychiatrie* **47**: 463–548.

DENNY-BROWN, D. (1951) The Frontal Lobes and Their Functions. In A. Feiling (ed.), *Modern Trends in Neurology*. London: Butterworth.

ELLIOTT, H., ALBERT, S., and BREMMER, W.A. (1948) A Program for Prefrontal Lobotomy with Report of the Effect on Intractable Pain. *Treatment Services Bulletin* **3**: 26–55.

FERRIER, D. (1875) The Croonian Lecture. Experiments on the Brain of Monkeys (second series). *Philosophical Transactions of the Royal Society of London* **165**: 433–88.

FINESINGER, J.E. (1949) Comment: Prefrontal Lobotomy as a Therapeutic Procedure. *American Journal of Psychiatry* **110**: 211.

FOLTZ, E.L. (1968) Cingular Lesions: Current Status and Use of Rostral Cingulotomy. *Southern Medical Journal* **61**: 899.

FREEMAN, W. (1971) Frontal Lobotomy in Early Schizophrenia: Long Follow-Up in 415 Cases. *British Journal of Psychiatry* **114**: 1223–46.

FREUD, S. (1955) Notes Upon a Case of Obsessional Neurosis. In *Standard Edition of the Complete Psychological Works of Sigmund Freud* Vol. 10. London: Hogarth Press.

FULTON, J.F. (1949) *Physiology of the Nervous System*. New York: Oxford University Press.

FULTON, J.F. and JACOBSEN, C.G. (1935) The

Functions of the Frontal Lobes, a Comparative Study in Monkeys, Chimpanzees and Man. *Advances in Modern Biology* **4**: 113–23 (Moscow).

GATZ, A.J. (1970) (ed.) *Manters Essentials of Clinical Neuroanatomy and Neurophysiology* (4th edition). Philadelphia: F. A. Davis.

GELDER, M.G. and MARKS, I.M. (1966) Severe Agoraphobia: A Controlled Prospective Trial of Behaviour Therapy. *British Journal of Psychiatry* **112**: 309–19.

GELDER, M.G., MARKS, I.M., and WOLFF, H.H. (1967) Desensitization and Psychotherapy in the Treatment of Phobic States: A Controlled Inquiry. *British Journal of Psychiatry* **113**: 53–73.

GILDENBERG, P.L. (1975) Survey of stereotactic and functional neurosurgery in the United States and Canada. *Applied Neurophysiology* **38**: 31–7.

GREENBLATT, M. and SOLOMON, H.C. (1953) *Frontal Lobes and Schizophrenia*. New York: Springer.

HARLOW, J.M. (1866) Recovery from the Passage of an Iron Bar through the Head. *Massachusetts Medical and Social Publication* **2**: 329–47.

HEBB, D.D. (1945) Man's Frontal Lobes: A Critical Review. *Archives of Neurology and Psychiatry* **54**: 10–24.

HEIMBURGER, R., WHITLOCK, C.C., and KALSBECK, J.E. (1966) Stereotaxic Amygdalotomy for Epilepsy with Aggressive Behaviour. *Journal of American Medical Association* **198**: 741.

HERRICK, C.J. (1933) The Functions of the Olfactory Parts of the Cortex. *Proceedings of the National Academy of Science* **19**: 7 (Washington).

HILL, D. and WATTERSON, D. (1942) Electroencephalographic Studies of Psychopathic Personalities. *Journal of Neurological Psychiatry* **5**: 47–65.

HILTON, S.M. and ZBROZYNA, A.W. (1963) Amygdaloid Region for Defence Reactions and its Efferent Pathway to the Brain Stem. *Journal of Physiology* **154**: 491–513 (London).

HITCHCOCK, E.R., ASHCROFT, G.W., CAIRNS, V.M., and MURRAY, L.G. (1972) Pre-Operative and Post-Operative Assessment and Management of Psychosurgical Patients. In E. R. Hitchcock, L. V. Laitinen, and K. Vaernet (eds.), *Psychosurgery*. Springfield, Illinois: Charles C. Thomas.

—— (1973) Observations on the Development of an Assessment Scheme for Amygdalotomy. In L. V. Laitinen and K. E. Livingston (eds.), *Surgical Approaches in Psychiatry*. Lancaster, England: Medical and Technical Publishing Co.

HOLDEN, C. (1973) Psychosurgery: Legitimate Therapy or Laundered Lobotomy? *Science* **179**: 1109–11.

HUNTER BROWN, M. and LIGHTHILL, J.A. (1968) Selective Anterior Cingulotomy: A Psychosurgical Evaluation. *Journal of Neurosurgery* **29**: 513–19.

JASPERS, K. (1963) *General Psychopathology*. Manchester: Manchester University Press.

KELLY, D. (1976) Psychosurgery in the 1970s. *British Journal of Hospital Medicine*: 165–74.

KELLY, D., RICHARDSON, A., and MITCHELL-HEGGS, N. (1973a) Stereotactic Limbic Leucotomy: Neurophysiological Aspects and Operative Technique. *British Journal of Psychiatry* **123**: 133–40.

KELLY, D., RICHARDSON, A., MITCHELL-HEGGS, N., GREENUP, J., CHEN, C., and HAFNER, R.J. (1973b) Stereotactic Limbic Leucotomy: A Preliminary Report on 40 Patients. *British Journal of Psychiatry* **122**: 141–8.

KELLY, D., WALTER, C.J.S., MITCHELL-HEGGS, N., and SARGANT, W. (1972) Modified Leucotomy Assessed Clinically, Physiologically and Psychologically. *British Journal of Psychiatry* **120**: 19–29.

KILOH, L.G. (1977) Commentary on the Report of the Committee of Inquiry into Psychosurgery. *Medical Journal of Australia* **ii**: 296–301.

KNIGHT, G.C. (1965) Stereotactic Tractotomy in the Surgical Treatment of Mental Illness. *Journal of Neurology, Neurosurgery and Psychiatry* **28**: 304–10.

—— (1969) Stereotactic Surgery for the Relief of Suicidal and Severe Depression and Intractable Psychoneurosis. *Postgraduate Medical Journal* **45**: 1–13.

—— (1973) Additional Stereotactic Lesions in the Cingulum Following Failed Tractotomy in the Subcaudate Region. In L. V. Laitinen and K. E. Livingston (eds.), *Surgical Approaches in Psychiatry*. Lancaster, England: Medical and Technical Publishing Co.

LAITINEN, L.V. and VIKKI, J. (1972) Stereotaxic Ventral Anterior Cingulotomy in Some Psychological Disorders. In E. R. Hitchcock, L. V. Laitinen, and K. Vaernet (eds.), *Psychosurgery*. Springfield, Illinois: Charles C. Thomas.

Lancet (1972) Psychosurgery (editorial). *Lancet*, July 8.

—— (1975) Psychosurgery on Trial (editorial). *Lancet* **i**: 1175.

LE BEAU, J. (1952) The Cingular and Precingular Areas in Psychosurgery-Agitated Behaviour, Obsessive-Compulsive States, Epilepsy. *Acta Psychiatrica Neurologica Scandinavica* **27**: 304.

LEHMANN, H.E. and OSTROW, D.E. (1973) Quizzing the expert: Clinical criteria for psychosurgery. *Hospital Physician* **9**: 24–31.

LEVY, R. (1972) Psychosurgery. *Lancet* **ii**: 185.

LEWIN, W. (1961) Observations on Selective Leucotomy. *Journal of Neurology, Neurosurgery and Psychiatry* **24**: 37.

LIVINGSTON, K.E. (1969) The Frontal Lobes Revisited. The Case for a Second Look. *Archives of Neurology* **20**: 90–95.

LIVINGSTON, K.E. and ESCOBAR, A. (1973) Tentative Limbic System Models for Certain Patterns of Psychiatric Disorders. In L. V. Laitinen and K. E. Livingston (eds.), *Surgical Approaches in Psychiatry*.

Lancaster, England: Medical and Technical Publishing Co.

MACLEAN, P. (1958) *The American Journal of Medicine* **25**: 61.

—— (1967) The Brain in Relation to Empathy and Medial Education. *Journal of Nervous and Mental Disease* **144**: 374–82.

—— (1969) The Paranoid Streak in man. In A. Koestler and J. Smythies (eds.), *Beyond Reductionism*. London: Hutchinson.

MAGNUS, D. and LAMMERS, H.J. (1956) The Amygdaloid-Nuclear Complex. *Folia Psychiatrica, Neurologica et Neurochirurgica Neerlandica* **59**: 555–82.

MARK, V.H. and ERVIN, F.R. (1970) *Violence and the Brain*. New York: Harper & Row.

MARK, V.H. and NEVILLE, R. (1973) Brain Surgery in Aggressive Epileptics. *Journal of American Medical Association* **226** (7): 765–72.

MARK, V.H., SWEET, W.H., and ERVIN, F.R. (1967) Role of Brain Disease in Riots and Urban Violence (letter to the journal). *Journal of American Medical Association* **201**: 895.

MARKS, I.M. (1969) *Fears and Phobias*. London: Heinemann.

MARKS, I.M., BIRLEY, J.L.T., and GELDER, M.G. (1966) Modified Leucotomy in Severe Agoraphobia: A Controlled Series Inquiry. *British Journal of Psychiatry* **113**: 53–73.

MARKS, I.M., HODGSON, R., and RACHMAN, S. (1975) Treatment of Chronic Obsessive-Compulsive Neurosis by *in Vivo* Exposure. A Two-year Follow up and Issues in Treatment. *British Journal of Psychiatry* **127**: 349–64.

MAY, P.R.A. and VAN PUTTEN, T. (1974) Treatment of schizophrenia 11. A proposed rating scale of design and outcome for use in literature surveys. *Comprehensive Psychiatry* **15**: 267–75.

MITCHELL-HEGGS, N., KELLY, D. and RICHARDSON, A. (1976) Stereotactic limbic leucotomy – a follow-up at 16 months. *British Journal of Psychiatry* **128**: 226–40.

NARABAYASHI, H., NAGAO, R., SAITO, Y., YOSHIDA, M., and NAGAHATA, M. (1963) Amygdalotomy for Behaviour Disorders. *Archives of Neurology* **9**: 11 (Chicago).

NARABAYASHI, H. and UNO, M. (1966) Long Range Results of Stereotaxic Amygdalotomy for Behaviour Disorders. *Confinia Neurologica* **27**: 168–71.

NAUTA, W.H.J. (1973) Connections of the Frontal Lobe with the Limbic System. In L. V. Laitinen and K. E. Livingston (eds.), *Surgical Approaches in Psychiatry*. Lancaster, England: Medical and Technical Publishing Co.

NIELSON, J.M. (1953) Correlation of Sites of Lesion with Symptoms. *Journal of Mental and Nervous Disease* **118**: 429.

PAPEZ, J.W. (1937) A Proposed Mechanism of Emotion. *Archives of Neurological Psychiatry.* **38**: 725–43 (Chicago).

PENFIELD, W. and JASPER, H. (1954) *Epilepsy and the Functional Anatomy of the Human Brain.* London: J. and A. Churchill.

RESEARCH COMMITTEE, ROYAL COLLEGE OF PSYCHIATRISTS (1977) In: *Neurosurgical Treatment in Psychiatry, Pain and Epilepsy.* (Eds W. H. Sweet, S. Obrador and J. G. Martin-Rodriguez) p. 175. Baltimore.

ROBIN, A.A. (1958) A Retrospective Controlled Study of Leucotomy in Schizophrenia and Affective Disorders. *Journal of Mental Science* **104**: 1025–37.

ROEDER, F., ORTHNER, H., and MULLER, D. (1972) The Stereotaxic Treatment of Pedophilic Homosexuality and Other Sexual Deviations. In E. R. Hitchcock, L. V. Laitinen, and K. Vaernet (eds.), *Psychosurgery*. Springfield, Illinois: Charles C. Thomas.

RYLANDER, G. (1973) The Renaissance of Psychosurgery. In L. V. Laitinen and K. E. Livingston (eds.), *Surgical Approaches to Psychiatry*. Lancaster, England. Medical and Technical Publishing Co.

SANO, K. (1966) Sedative Stereoencephalotomy-Fornicotomy Upper Mesencephasic Reticulotomy and Postero-Medial Hypothalamotomy. In T. Takizane and J. P. Schade (eds.), *Progress in Brain Research*. Amsterdam: Elsevier Publishing Co.

SARGANT, W. and SLATER, E. (1972) *Introduction to Physical Treatment in Psychiatry* (5th edition). Edinburgh: Livingstone.

SCHURR, P.H. (1973) Psychosurgery. *British Journal of Hospital Medicine* 10 (1): 53–60.

SMITH, J.S. Quoted in E. S. Valenstein (1977).

SPIEGEL, E.A. (1969) Indications for Stereoencephalotomies. A Critical Assessment. *Confinia Neurologica* 31: 5–10.

STEVENS, J.R., MARK, V.H., ERVIN, F., PACHACO, P., and SUEMATSU, K. (1969) Deep Temporal Stimulation in Man. Long Latency, Long Lasting Psychological Changes. *Archives of Neurology*: 157–69 (Chicago).

TAN, E., MARKS, I.M., and MARSET, P. (1971) Bimedial Leucotomy in Obsessive-Compulsive Neurosis: A Controlled Serial Enquiry. *British Journal of Psychiatry* 118: 155–64.

TOOTH, G.C. and NEWTON, M.P. (1961) *Leucotomy in England and Wales, 1942–1954*. London: HMSO.

TURNER, E.A. (1970) Operations for Aggression. Bilateral Temporal Lobotomy and Posterior Cingulectomy. *Proceedings Second International Conference on Psychosurgery*. Copenhagen.

US NATIONAL COMMISSION FOR THE PROTECTION OF HUMAN SUBJECTS OF BIOMEDICAL AND BEHAVIORAL RESEARCH (1977) *Report and Recommendations: Psychosurgery*. US DHEW Publ. No. (OS) 77–0001.

VALENSTEIN, E.S. (1977) The practice of psychosurgery: a survey of the literature (1971–1976). In *Psychosurgery* Appendix 1–1–1–143. US National Commission for the Protection of Human Subjects of Biomedical and Behavioral Research. US DHEW Publ. No. (OS) 77–0002.

WARD, A.A. (1948) The Anterior Cingular Gyrus and Personality. *Research Publication of the Association for Research in Nervous and Mental Diseases.* **27**: 438–45.

WESTPHAL, G. (1871–2) Die Agoraphobia: eine neuropathische Erscheinung. *Archive für Psychiatrie und Nervenkrankheiten* **3**: 138–71; 219–21.

WORLD HEALTH ORGANIZATION (1976) *Health Aspects of Human Rights.* Geneva: WHO.

8

Responsibility and compulsory hospitalization

Involuntary mental hospitalisation is like slavery. Refining the standards for commitment is like prettifying the slave plantations. The problem is not how to improve commitment but how to abolish it.

SZASZ 1974a: 79

Compulsory psychiatric care is not a threat but a right. Every citizen should have the right to be admitted against his will to the care of a first-class psychiatric service.

BIRLEY 1973

I T IS somewhat fashionable to stress the similarities between physical and mental disorder. Yet one obvious and crucial difference is that a mentally ill person may be legally deprived of his rights and his liberty and be detained, against his wishes, for observation and treatment in hospital, whereas someone suffering from a physical illness, even a lethal one, is free to disregard medical advice, refuse treatment, and risk his own life in the process. In Britain, compulsory hospitalization is governed by the *Mental Health Act* (1959), a piece of legislation that resulted from the lengthy and searching deliberations of the Royal Commission on the Law Relating to Mental Illness and Mental Deficiency which sat between 1954 and 1957. The Commission recognized that 'advances in medical knowledge, new methods of treatment and the development of new organs of government and new social services' demanded changes in the medical and administrative methods whereby such objects were pursued. The *Mental Health Act* laid down the obligations and the functions of the hospitals and the local authorities in the treatment of the mentally ill. The statutory limitation of treatment of 'persons of unsound mind' in specially designated hospitals was removed and hospital authorities were enabled to arrange for any kind of hospital to receive any type of mental patient whether on an informal (i.e., voluntary) basis or under a compulsory order.

One of the central features of the 1959 Act is that as much treatment as possible should be carried out on a voluntary basis. At the present time the great majority of admissions to psychiatric hospitals and units in this country are informal (*Table 1*). Patients so admitted are free to take their own discharge at any time and many frequently do. Less than one in

Table 1 *Admissions to mental illness and mental handicap hospitals 1962 and 1970 (England and Wales)*

	1962	1970	
Section 25 Section 29	27,692	11,143 17,260	28,403
Section 26	1,858	1,140	
Sections 135/6	740	1,493	
other	1,584	1,725	
	31,874 (20%) 124,884 (80%)	32,761 (17%) 161,958 (83%)	
total	156,758	194,719	
resident patients 31 December	197,081	171,051	

Ministry of Health (1962)
Department of Health and Social Security (1970)

every five hospital admissions involves a compulsory certification and the great bulk of these are made up of twenty-eight-day and three-day orders. This is in sharp contrast with the situation in the United States where approximately 80 per cent of all mental hospitalizations are on a compulsory basis.

It is important to note at the outset that the *Mental Health Act* does not in fact define what it means by 'mental illness'. The looser concept of 'mental disorder' is employed and is defined as follows:

'In this Act mental disorder means mental illness, arrested or incomplete development of mind, psychopathic disorder, and any other disorder or disability of mind.'

(Part 1, Section 4 (i))

Arrested or incomplete development of the mind is split into *severe subnormality* and *subnormality*, By *severe subnormality* is meant a state of arrested or incomplete development of the mind, which includes subnormality of intelligence, and which is of such a nature or degree that the patient is incapable of living an independent life or of guarding himself against serious exploitation or will be so incapable when of an age to do so. By *subnormality* is meant a lesser state of arrested or incomplete development whereby the individual requires or is susceptible to medical treatment or other special care or training and is capable to some extent of living an independent or semi-independent life. *Psychopathic disorder* is defined as 'a persistent disorder or disability of mind which results in abnormally aggressive or seriously irresponsible conduct on the part of the patient and which requires or is susceptible to medical treatment'. The Act refrains, however, from defining the term 'mental illness'.

As a result of the reluctance of the framers of the 1959 Act to provide a legal definition of mental illness it is not at all clear what the term actually means in law. A legal decision in the Court of Appeal in 1973 provoked the following interesting comment from Lord Justice Lawton:

'Like the Master of the Rolls, Lord Denning, and the Lord Justice Orr, I agree that this appeal has called attention to the difficulties which arise under the Mental Health Act 1959 from the definition of mental disorder which is set out in Section 4 of the Act. For the purpose of seeing what was the intention of the Act, this Court has looked at the Report of the Royal Commission on the Law relating to Mental Illness and Mental Deficiency 1958. The Royal Commission seems to have overlooked that their recommendations would not result in a definition of

mental disorder which would meet the requirements of
doctors . . . The facts of this case show how difficult the
fitting of particular instances into the statutory classification
can be. Lord Denning and Lord Justice Orr have pointed
out that there is no definition of mental illness. The words
are ordinary words of the English language. They have no
particular medical significance. They have no particular
legal significance. How should the Court construe them?
The answer in my judgement is to be found in the advice
which Lord Reid gave in Cozens v. Brutus (*Appeal Court
Cases, 1973, pp. 834, 861*) namely that ordinary words of
the English language should be construed in the way that
ordinary sensible people would construe them.'

(*Weekly Law Reports*, 1973: 857–83)

So, Lord Justice Lawton asked himself what would an
ordinary person have to say about the mental state of the
person involved in the case before the Court of Appeal and
he concluded that he would declare him to be obviously
mentally ill. Such a legal verdict would appear to vindicate
the views of those who insist that mental illness is what
ordinary people think it is; it is, as one observer has put it, 'a
social judgement of our present age' (Tucker 1973). This
being so, the compulsory hospitalization of persons deemed
to be suffering from 'mental illness' would seem to be a
somewhat sophisticated process whereby society declares
what it will and will not tolerate in the shape of unusual,
deviant, and antisocial behaviour on the part of its individual
members.

One is always reluctant to argue with a member of the
judiciary, and particularly one as erudite and eminent as
Lord Justice Lawton. Yet it is not easy to see how it can be
confidently asserted that the words 'mental illness' have 'no
particular medical significance'. Agreed there is difficulty
and disagreement as to what does and does not constitute
mental illness (Chapter 1), yet such disagreement tends to
relate more to problems over specific diagnostic categories

and the exact boundary between illness and health than to the question of the existence of mental illness itself. That is to say, psychiatrists may and do differ over whether this or that symptom is schizophrenic or manic but there is, in general, less disagreement over whether the symptom is a mark of illness or health.

The various sections of the *Mental Health Act* (1959) governing compulsory certification are detailed in the Appendix at the end of this chapter. In brief: *Section 25* allows a patient to be detained for observation (with or without treatment) provided that he is suffering from mental disorder of a specified kind and degree and that his detention is necessary for the sake of his own safety or health or for other people's protection. Two medical opinions, in addition to an application from the patient's nearest relative or an approved social worker, are required and the order is valid for twenty-eight days. *Section 26* allows a patient to be detained for treatment for up to one year in the first instance, given the same provisions. Two medical opinions are required and the order can be renewed for one further year after the first year and then for two years at a time. *Section 29* allows for emergency detention for up to three days on the same grounds on one medical recommendation, while *Section 30* allows for a patient already in hospital to be held there for up to seventy-two hours. *Sections 135* and *136* permit the police to remove those who appear to be suffering from mental disorder and to be in need of care and control to a psychiatric hospital or other 'place of safety' where they may be detained for up to three days. *Sections 60* and *65* govern the referral of patients to hospitals by the Courts, while *Sections 72* and *74* govern the transfer of mentally abnormal offenders from prison to mental hospitals.

The decision to hospitalize a patient against his will rests on two separate judgements. First, the patient concerned is judged to be suffering from a mental disorder. Second, he is considered to be a danger to his own health or safety or to the safety of others. There are obvious limitations involved in each of these judgements. The formulation of a psychiatric diagnosis (Chapter 3) is a formidable undertaking and is subject to varying degrees of error. Deciding whether a given individual constitutes a danger to himself and/or to others is not an easy task either. Psychiatrists have not shown themselves to be particularly skilled at predicting dangerousness. Nor have they been too astute in distinguishing the potential suicide from the pretender. The belief that psychiatrists have a particular skill whereby they can readily identify the potential homicidal or suicidal individual may well reflect the layman's idea that the majority of psychiatric patients are potentially or actually violent. This is quite erroneous. The vast majority of mentally ill people are not especially violent or self-destructive. It is only in a minority of individuals that the possibility of violence has to be considered by the psychiatrist. It is this minority which poses particular diagnostic and management problems. These problems can be looked at in more detail by taking a closer look at the question of suicide, remembering all the time that many of the issues and principles raised therein concern the potentially homicidal patient as well.

Suicide

Suicide, as A. Alvarez points out in his courageous and imaginative study, has 'come big' (1971). Clinical investigations, statistical analyses, epidemiological surveys multiply. A new science – suicidology – has been born. Once concealed and ignored, the fearful, unforgivable sin of despair, suicide is now the subject of international conferences, television discussion shows, mawkish exposés in the Sunday colour supplements. In Britain, about 1 per cent of all deaths are the result of suicide. Although numerically more elderly than young people die this way, suicide is the fourth most common death in the 15–34 age-group. In England and Wales, twelve men and eight women in every 100,000 of the population kill themselves each year.

Is a person who kills himself, by definition, mentally ill? George Cheyne, the British physician, in a treatise on the subject of suicide, entitled *The English Malady*, written in 1733, appeared to believe so:

'. . . the late frequency and daily encrease of wanton and uncommon self-murderers, produced mostly by this distemper . . . [persuaded him] to try what a little more just and solid philosophy, join'd to a method of cure, and proper medicines could do, to put a stop to so universal a lunacy and madness.'   (Cheyne 1733: 1–3)

The distemper referred to by Cheyne, and which earned the reproach 'universally thrown on this island by foreigners', was related to the moisture of the air, the variability in the weather, the richness of the food, the inactivity of 'the better sort (among whom this evil mostly rages)', and the effects of living in towns. So, in his view, the 'lunacy and madness' of suicide had environmental causes. William Battie, on the other hand, was reluctant to dub all suicidal activity as evidence of mental disturbance. In *A Treatise on Madness*, published in 1758, he noted the relationship between 'the perpetual tempests of love, hatred and other turbulent passions provoked by nothing or at most by very trifles' and suicidal acts and declared that frequently

'. . . cases of suicide, though generally ascribed to lunacy by the verdict of a good-natured jury, except where the deceased left no assets, are no more entitled to the benefit of passing for pardonable acts of madness than he who deliberately has killed the man he hated deserves to be acquitted as not knowing what he did.'

(Battie 1758: 36–7)

The debate between these two views has flourished to this day. In practice, most psychiatrists incline to Battie's view and accept that there are cases of self-destruction that are not a consequence of mental illness. There are, of course, those who, like Cheyne, believe that such a deed can only be explained by postulating mental unbalance, but much more attention is given at the present time to one who takes the completely contrary view and declares suicide to be at *all* times an exercise and expression of human freedom. Professor Thomas Szasz, characteristically unambivalent about this as about so much else, insists that attempts to prevent suicide represent attempts to curtail human freedom. He compares the would-be suicide with the would-be emigrant:

'. . . both want to leave where they are and move elsewhere. The suicide wants to leave his homeland and settle in another country. A crucial distinction between open and closed societies is that people are free to leave the former but not the latter. The medical profession's stance toward suicide is like the Communists' toward emigration: the doctors insist that the would-be suicide survive, just as the Russians insist that the would-be emigrant stay home.'

(Szasz 1973: 206–7)

What do we know of those who commit suicide? Are they emotionally ill or are they, as Szasz somewhat picturesquely paints them, would-be emigrants seeking passage to another shore? Some recent studies, which have relied on extensive interviews with the relatives, friends, and doctors of consecutive cases of suicide, and comparisons with matched, random controls drawn from the population, have helped clarify certain factors in the individual's history and in his clinical state which appear to predispose him to take his life. Brian Barraclough and his colleagues in Chichester adopted such an approach in their study of 100 cases of suicide (1974). Using reasonably strict criteria, they concluded that ninety-three of the suicides had been obviously mentally disturbed at the time of their action. Eighty-five were suffering from morbid depression or alcoholism. Eighty had seen a doctor around the time of their suicide and a similar number were receiving drugs for psychiatric troubles. Well over 50 per cent had given reasonably clear warnings of suicidal thinking.

Follow-up studies of samples of mentally ill patients and of the general population illustrate the increased risk of suicide seen in psychiatric disorders. Some 3 per cent of schizophrenics will eventually kill themselves as will about 7 per cent of organic brain syndromes associated with epilepsy. According to Peter Sainsbury (1973), early dementia in the elderly, in whom insight is preserved (i.e., those elderly people who realize that their brain functioning is becoming seriously impaired), carries a high risk of suicide, especially if there is an associated depression. Manic-depressive illness carries the highest risk: approximately one in every six commits suicide. A follow-up of over 200 alcoholics discharged from hospital found that approximately 8 per cent had committed suicide (Kessel and Grossman 1961).

Apart from the Communists and their success in curbing emigration, the medical profession, despite Szasz's strictures, appears to be relatively ineffective in curbing suicide. A more fundamental criticism would appear to be that the medical profession pays less attention than it should to appeals from patients. Indeed, Neil Kessel, now Professor of Psychiatry at the University of Manchester, has drawn attention to the way the profession has contributed to the current situation in which, in his opinion, it is easier to kill oneself then ever before:

'The growth of self-poisoning has come about in the train of a rapid rise in the number of highly dangerous preparations employed therapeutically, together with a great contemporaneous increase in prescribing. The effect of this medical revolution has been to make poisons both readily available and relatively safe. The way has thus been opened for self-poisoning to flourish . . . Facilities for self-poisoning have been placed within the reach of everyone.'   (Kessel 1967: 35)

As suicide by means of drugs has increased, so other methods of killing oneself, hanging, shooting, jumping, cutting, have decreased. As Alvarez remarks (1971) with some irony, 'there has been a technological breakthrough which has made a cheap and relatively painless death democratically available to everyone'.

People who suffer from depressive illnesses constitute a particular risk. The depressive most prone is usually a man whose first depressive illness occurs after the age of forty. He may well be living alone, have suffered a recent loss, such as the death of his spouse, and is likely to have had previous psychiatric treatment. The risk of suicide is very much higher if he has made a previous attempt. A family history of alcoholism or depressive illness is also often found. The onset of depression is likely to have occurred shortly before the suicide attempt and just prior to the attempt he may have been discharged from active psychiatric treatment. Peter Sainsbury (1973) has drawn attention to the social isolation that is a feature of many suicides. Suicides more often live alone in disorganized urban areas and there is a higher prevalence amongst divorced and separated people. Moving house and losing a job in the recent past are two stresses seen more frequently among successful suicides than in matched, controlled, non-suicidal population samples.

Barraclough and his colleagues (1974) found that many of the suicides in their study had visited their general practitioner in the week before they died. Over 70 per cent had done so in the previous three months. The GP apparently recognized in most cases that the patient was 'emotionally disturbed' because he prescribed tranquillizers or psychotropic drugs to approximately 80 per cent of them, mostly in the form of barbiturates. However, the patient's depression was not usually recognized, for relatively few were given anti-depressant drugs and then usually in deficient doses. Worse, 45 per cent died from barbiturate poisoning and fifteen of the seventeen suicides categorized as 'impulsive' killed themselves with barbiturates recently prescribed by their general practitioners! Peter Sainsbury concludes:

'It would therefore appear that a substantial proportion of suicides could be prevented if their family doctors or hospital physicians were as well trained in the recognition and management of depression, and of other psychiatric conditions known to have high rates of suicide, as they are, say, in the diagnosis and treatment of pneumonia.'

(Sainsbury 1973: 579)

It is in the light of these findings and those of other studies (Robins *et al.* 1959; Copes, Freeman-Browne, and Robin 1971; Bunch *et al.* 1971) that Szasz's portrayal of suicide as an uncomplicated, clear-cut, and 'free' decision is simplistic and even irresponsible. His performance at the BBC 'Controversy' programme on mental illness in 1973, where he declared that the fact that doctors have a higher suicide rate than that of the general population reflected their ability to preserve their own civil right to suicide while abrogating that of others, represented a triumph for debating skill and verbal opportunism. But it cynically clouded and twisted the issue. The greater availability of drugs, and especially the barbiturates, to members of the medical, nursing, and pharmaceutical profession is an explanation which, at the very least, merits consideration by any serious analyst.

There is little evidence to support Szasz's claim that medicine has been mobilized to prevent legitimate 'emigration' from life. There is plenty to suggest that doctors, far from restricting freedom of movement at the port of exit, actually, if unwittingly, provide the means of travel! We know, not alone from the retrospective examination of the last weeks and months in the lives of successful suicides, but from the accounts and experiences of those who have made attempts and for one reason or another have failed, that the motivation of people at the time they take their overdose or kick the chair away is bewilderingly complex. No one can ever say with certainty whether the failed suicide really wanted to die or live, the successful one to live or die. Arbitrary, even banal, factors can turn an attempt into a success. Alvarez recounts how the poetess Sylvia Plath made two attempts on her life. The first, a serious one, failed. She had disguised the theft of the sleeping tablets, left a 'misleading note' to put people off the trail, and swallowed fifty sleeping pills in a disused cellar. She was found late and almost dead – by sheer accident. The second, in Alvarez's view, was not a serious attempt. 'I am convinced by what I know of the facts', he writes, 'that this time she did not intend to die' (Alvarez 1971: 28). Very depressed, she saw her doctor, a sensitive but overworked man who prescribed sedatives. An appointment was made with a psychotherapist, but the letter went astray – the postman delivered it to the wrong address. The therapist's reply, with the details of the appointment, arrived a day or two after she died.

If the problem of suicide, complex to others, is simple to Szasz, the situation with regard to the pros and cons of compulsory hospitalization is much the same. In the preface to the British edition of his book, *Law, Liberty and Psychiatry*, he declares:

'If "mental illness" is a bona fide illness – as official medical, psychiatric and mental health organizations, such as the World Health Organization, the American and British Medical Associations, and the American Psychiatric Association, maintain – then it follows, logically and linguistically, that it must be treated like any other illness. Hence, mental hygiene laws must be repealed. There are no special laws for patients with peptic ulcer or pneumonia; why then should there be special laws for patients with depression or schizophrenia?'   (Szasz 1974b: xi–xii)

Why indeed? A patient suffering from a bleeding stomach ulcer can refuse a blood transfusion, pull out his intravenous drip, reject his medication, dress, and discharge himself without incurring any legal sanctions whatsoever. Clearly he is ill, indeed seriously so, yet he is free to do what he chooses, even if he should thereby place his own life in jeopardy. A patient suffering from severe depression, however, who believes that his life is without hope, that there is little point in carrying on, that he is a nuisance to others and a burden on himself, can be taken and placed in a hospital against his will, despite his protestations that he is not ill, and that anyway, ill or not, he wants to dispose of himself in his own way. The one is adjudged ill yet responsible for his actions and decisions; the other is adjudged ill but, in addition, his responsibility is questioned.

Questions of responsibility do not arise in every case of mental illness. It is only in those mentally disturbed people who act out (or threaten to act out) their depressive, persecutory, or aggressive preoccupations that the degree and extent of their responsibility for their actions is queried.

A young schizophrenic believed that a neighbour was controlling his mind, inserting horrible ideas and thoughts into his consciousness, and causing hallucinatory voices to laugh and jeer at his actions, call him a homosexual, and mock his virility. On a number of occasions, when such experiences threatened to overwhelm him, he remonstrated with the neighbour and, at length, driven to distraction by his hallucinations, he attacked him, causing him serious injury. Remanded in prison, he continued to complain of the voices and made a determined but unsuccessful suicide attempt.

To what extent was this young man responsible for his actions? Was his judgement at the time of his attack clouded or clear? Was his ability to control himself impaired? Was his responsibility *diminished* by virtue of his obvious mental disturbance?

For the layman, the concept of a diminution in personal responsibility presents little difficulty. Alcoholics appear unable to control their drinking, kleptomaniacs their stealing, obsessionals their ritualistic behaviour, impulsive individuals their anti-social activities. Deciding in each individual case as to the extent of such an impairment in responsibility, however, presents many more problems. This is another issue of contemporary psychiatric practice which has been argued about furiously down through the centuries. In the third century AD, a Roman jurist argued that the insane were not responsible for any criminal acts. Marcus Aurelius had earlier stated that 'Furiosus satis ipso furore punitur' (the madman is sufficiently punished by his madness). de Bracton, jurist and Archdeacon of Barnstable, insisted in 1265 that a madman lacked reason and did not know what he was doing. In what has been termed 'the first systematic treatise in English law' (Loucas and Udwin 1974), he wrote,

'. . . an insane person is one who does not know what he is doing, is lacking in mind and reason and is not far removed from the brutes.'

It took a number of somewhat bizarre cases involving eminent personages for the law to develop to a level of sophistication somewhat more appropriate to the delicacy and subtlety of the issue involved. In May 1800, Hadfield shot at King George III in Drury Lane Theatre in an attempt to bring about his own execution. A veteran of the French wars in which he had sustained a sword wound of his brain, Hadfield was convinced that he had a divine mission to save the world by forfeiting his own life. He was acquitted, held in Newgate Prison, and dealt with, retrospectively, under the Act of 1800 'for the safe custody of insane persons charged with offences'. He was subsequently committed to the care of the staff of Bethlem Hospital. In January 1843, Daniel M'Naghten, believing himself persecuted by the Church of Rome and the police, shot and killed the Prime Minister's private secretary, having mistaken him for Sir Robert Peel himself. As in the case of Hadfield, a special verdict – 'Not guilty, on the ground of insanity' – was returned and M'Naghten was committed to Bethlem Hospital. Following this verdict, there was a tremendous outcry, the decision being seen as an acquittal and a weakness in the enforcement of the law. The whole question of the unsoundness of mind as a restriction on the degree of personal responsibility was debated in the House of Lords and the judges of England were asked to put forward their views on the criteria for such an acquittal. Their conclusions were that –

> 'The jury ought to be told in all cases that . . . to establish a defence on the ground of insanity, it must be clearly proved that, at the time of committing the act, the party accused was labouring under such a defect of reason, from disease of the mind, as not to know the nature and quality of the act he was doing, or if he did know it, that he did not know he was doing what was wrong.'
>
> (Weihofen 1933: 28)

The interpretation of the outcome of the Hadfield trial was that an individual, knowing that what he was doing was wrong, might nonetheless be compelled to act in that manner by his delusional ideas. The so-called M'Naghten Rules allowed for a defence justified only by unawareness of the nature of the act, ignorance of the wrongness, or in response to a delusion which, if true, would justify the act. Further confusion was introduced following the attempted assassination of Queen Victoria by MacLean, when the concept 'Guilty but insane' was inserted into the *Criminal Lunatics Act* of 1883. The Home Secretary of the time, believing that the Queen might be interested in the disposal of her would-be assassin, told her that the verdict had been 'Not Guilty by Reason of Insanity'. The Queen, on this occasion as on another, was far from amused and replied with acerbity 'Insane he might or might not be; not guilty he is certainly not' (McGrath 1973: 135). A finding of 'Not Guilty by Reason of Insanity' was reintroduced into the criminal code in the *Criminal Procedures (Insanity) Act*, 1964.

Attempting to discover whether a deluded offender knew the nature of what he was doing and its wrongfulness resulted in varying interpretations of the responsibility of the mentally ill for acts committed by them. One uncompromising view of the M'Naghten Rules was that given by the Lord Chief

Justice to the Royal Commission on Capital Punishment in 1950. Referring to the trial of Thomas John Ley, Lord Goddard maintained that a man might be insane and yet so wicked in his madness as to be quite properly sentenced to death and executed (Royal Commission 1957). A delusion might excuse a criminal act but only if the act were legally excusable had the delusion been true. The significance of the delusion as evidence of a mentally abnormal mind was not felt to be important.

The introduction of the concept of *diminished responsibility* has allowed such formidable and uncompromising interpretations of the M'Naghten Rules to lapse. The relevant clauses in the *Homicide Act* of 1957 are as follows:

1. 'Where a person kills or is a party to the killing of another, he shall not be convicted of murder if he was suffering from such abnormality of mind (whether arising from a condition of arrested or retarded development of mind or any inherent causes or induced by disease or injury) as substantially impaired his mental responsibility for his acts and omissions in doing or being a party to the killing. (Part I, Section II (i))

2. On a charge of murder, it shall be for the defence to prove that the person charged is by virtue of this section not liable to be convicted of murder.

(Part I, Section II (ii))

3. A person who but for this section would be liable, whether as principal or as accessory, to be convicted of murder shall be liable instead to be convicted of manslaughter. (Part I, Section II (iii))

4. The fact that one party to a killing is by virtue of this section not liable to be convicted of murder shall not affect the question whether the killing amounted to murder in the case of any other party to it.'

(Part I, Section II (iv))

The concept of an excusing condition in law was formulated at around this time by Professor H. L. A. Hart, who noted that a characteristic of advanced legal systems is that an individual's liability to punishment, particularly for serious crimes carrying severe penalties, is made by law to depend on, among other things, certain mental conditions. He drew attention to what he termed 'excusing conditions' –

'. . . the individual is not liable to punishment if at at the time of his doing what would otherwise be a punishable act he is, say unconscious, mistaken about the physical consequences of his bodily movements or the nature or qualities of the thing or persons affected by them, or, in some cases, if he is subjected to threats or other gross forms of coercion or is the victim of certain types of mental disease . . . If an individual breaks the law when none of the excusing conditions are present, he is ordinarily said to have acted of 'his own free will", "of his own accord", "voluntarily"; or it might be said, "He could have helped doing what he did".'   (Hart 1958)

Thomas Szasz, who quotes Hart, believes that he and other eminent legal authorities, are mistaken in their assumption that there is a category called mental illness. This view of Szasz is well known and even popular among radical critics of psychiatry and has been strongly supported by those who believe it represents enlightened and progressive thinking in contrast to the authoritarian and coercive philosophy allegedly permeating orthodox psychiatry. But let us take Szasz's view further. Not content with arguing that mental illness is a myth, and that therefore attempts to diminish the responsibility of some offenders by pleading the existence of mental impairment is fallacious, Szasz then indulges in a typical piece of debating guile:

'To the extent that a person acts involuntarily, he cannot be regarded, in the social sense of the term, as a human being. This then leads to the dilemma typical of contemporary forensic psychiatry. Either we regard offenders as sane and punish them; or we regard them as insane, and, though excusing them of crimes officially, punish them by treating them as beings who are less than human. It seems to me that there is a more promising alternative. Let us not consider mental illness an excusing condition. By treating offenders as responsible human beings, we offer them the only chance, as I see it, to remain human.'

(Szasz 1974: 137)

Here Szasz sets up his basic premise – a person acting involuntarily cannot be regarded 'in the social sense of the term' as a human being – from which all else flows. But what does such a premise mean? A driver, intoxicated at the wheel of his car, is doubtless 'under the influence of alcohol' and to that extent his mental abilities are impaired, but is he in any sense, leave aside the 'social' one, any less a human being? Can a patient, confused and delirious in a toxic confusional state, be regarded as 'a human being' and if not what is he? Szasz cleverly and cunningly pairs two concepts – impairment of mental abilities and loss of essential humanity – in such a way that those psychiatrists and lawyers who mount a defence of diminished responsibility in a given case can be accused of denigrating their client's humanity and reducing his dignity. This he then proceeds to do. The choice, as Szasz ingeniously constructs it, lies between finding the offender guilty and punishing him and finding him mentally impaired and punishing him! Underpinning Szasz's entire approach to the problem of responsibility in mental disorder is his belief that all compulsory psychiatric treatment is punishment masquerading under a more acceptable name. It should be said that Szasz has provided a sizeable body of evidence testifying to disgraceful abuse of involuntary hospitalization procedures in the United States and that his lack of enthusiasm for such a procedure is, for this reason, readily comprehensible. But this is to confuse abuse of a procedure with the procedure itself. Some compulsory hospitalizations appear to differ little from incarcera-in prison. Szasz's account (1974c) of the Ezra Pound case is a particularly pertinent example. He is right to draw attention to the gross abuses of liberty which can and do result from therapeutic enthusiasm, ignorance, omnipotence, and incompetence. But he is not alone in his criticisms. They have been as skilfully, if more constructively and less intemperately, argued by a number of commentators (Kittrie 1971; Scheff 1966) who have, perhaps, received less attention because they have made less noise. In Britain, as in the United States, people are confined in mental hospitals for indefinite periods to receive 'treatment' which is often either unavailable or ineffective with few of the safeguards against wrongful confinement available to ordinary offenders. But abuse of a procedure is not a conclusive argument in favour of the procedure's abolition. It is, however, a reason for ensuring that the legal protections surrounding such a procedure are sufficiently developed and effective. For Szasz, such legal protections are irrelevant. The problem is not how to improve commitment but how to abolish it:

'. . . in the final analysis, what makes a medical intervention morally permissible is not that it is therapeutic, but that it is something the patient wants. Similarily what makes the quasi-medical intervention of involuntary psychiatric hospitalization morally impermissible is not that it is harmful but that it is something the so-called patient does not want.' (Szasz 1974: 78–9)

In short, it is not the abuse of compulsory hospitalization but its existence that Szasz condemns. He is in no doubt that there is *never* any difference, ethical, philosophical, or psychological, between the patient with the ulcer coolly (or indeed, heatedly) rejecting medical advice, returning home, and possibly haemorrhaging to death, and the patient sunk in a melancholic gloom choosing to kill himself. In each case, the judgement of the patient is unimpaired; in each case, the patient is fully responsible. The findings of Barraclough, Sainsbury, Robins and those other research workers who have taken the trouble to investigate in some detail the antecedents of suicidal behaviour are ignored. Szasz, fearlessly and courageously allowing his patient freely to kill himself, places himself modestly in the tradition of Pascal and La Rochefoucauld, Voltaire and Nietzsche, Bierce and Mencken, in the forefront of the battle against 'the parentification of authority and the infantilization of nearly everyone else'. The psychiatrist, who interprets his responsibility to his patient somewhat differently, finds himself placed in the company of Inquisitors, witch-hunters, slavers, and political interrogators for his pains. Obviously, any psychiatrist of sensitivity and integrity would be clear as to which tradition he should follow.

Szasz avoids case-histories in his writings. Doubtless he would argue that they are superfluous for his purpose, which is to examine and critically assess the general principles underlying the day-to-day clinical practice of psychiatry. Occasionally, however, he does provide a glimpse of how he himself operates in practice. It provides a valuable picture of the doughty liberal champion in action. Answering his own question as to why psychiatrists pay more attention to the symptoms of schizophrenic patients than their rights, he observes:

'Perhaps because many schizophrenics conduct themselves as if others had no rights: they violate their privacy, not to mention their sense of reality. Hence the schizophrenic may be treated as: 1. a dangerous madman; 2. a person having highly dramatic and unusual experiences; or, 3. a person disrespectful of the rights of others. The first view is that of traditional psychiatry; the second that of the glamorizers of schizophrenia; the third is my own.'

(Szasz 1974: 104)

Concerning paranoid delusions, he believes that many are, in effect, 'the expression of a lack of courage':

'For example, the elderly woman who complains that her husband is poisoning her. She accuses. She complains. But she does not act. Why doesn't she kill him. Or leave him? Why doesn't she put her money where her mouth is? Because she lacks courage. She wants someone else to act on her belief, and to be responsible for the consequences.'

(Szasz 1974:105)

In short, psychotic disturbances are games and mental illness is 'self-enhancing deception, self-promotive strategy' (p. 88). Not a shred of worthwhile evidence does he provide in support of such a view. His 'explanation' of the nature of the elderly woman's delusions ignores the fact that many patients do not restrict themselves to making verbal complaints and accusations but frequently *act* on their beliefs. Such patients are notoriously litigious and often pursue with tenacity the innocent objects of their accusations through the courts. They are well known to the police and to lawyers and, when they fail to persuade these representatives of the law of the truth of their assertions, they not infrequently take the law into their own hands, sometimes with tragic consequences. To at least one practising psychiatrist, the conceptualization of a paranoid patient as someone lacking in courage is a singularly unhelpful, uninformative, and inappropriate declaration.

This view of schizophrenia as 'self-enhancing deception, self-promotive strategy' and schizophrenics as nuisances is re-emphasized in the latest book to appear from the prolific Szasz entitled, appropriately, *Schizophrenia*. The book also contains the savage assault on Laing which first appeared in the literary journal *New Review* on this side of the Atlantic (Szasz 1977). Poor Laing gets a bloody nose for not charging his schizophrenic patients at Kingsley Hall and ends up accused of displaying the same contempt for his patients as 'the keepers of madmen at the Burgholzli, Maudsley or Salpetriere have always displayed'.

As we discussed in Chapter 1, Szasz's arguments all rest on the fundamental premise that diseases are grounded on recognised and recognisable histological and biochemical changes. It is an unshakeable premise for the very good reason that Szasz steadfastly ignores attacks made upon it. I once myself debated with Szasz over the existence or otherwise of mental illness. (Clare 1978; Szasz 1978). Disdaining to acknowledge the smear with which he associated Nazism and psychiatry, ignoring his semantic gymnastics concerning tuberculosis, and deflecting his merry quips about state medicine, I enquired as to the conceptual status of diseases *before* their biological features are known. What was epilepsy before the EEG? What was tuberculosis before the discovery of the bacillus? What was amphetamine psychosis before the association between the mental symptoms and the drug were noted? What is migraine now? What was the correct classification of the psychological symptoms of pellagra before the underlying vitamin deficiency was identified? Have all diseases been discovered? Szasz, the normally loquacious, verbally dazzling Enoch Powell of contemporary psychiatry, maintained a steadfast silence.

Szasz, while for the most part contemptuous of psychiatry, appears to regard law as an internally consistent entity which has only trouble when it comes into contact with psychiatry. Not all lawyers share his view. Hans Mohr, Professor of Law and Sociology at York University in Ontario, Canada, points out that there is a tendency to forget that criminal law is 'a highly controversial area of law' and that criminal lawyers are often viewed with 'ambivalence' by their colleagues (Mohr 1978). 'There are many claims to legality in the criminal law', he remarks, 'which on close examination turn out to be no more than arguments by analogy'. Shades of Szasz's views on psychiatry!

Let the law deal with power and coercion, says Szasz, and let the physician get on with healing. He considers only compulsion but Mohr draws attention to the question of compassion and points out that as curious as a form it may sometimes take it cannot be defined away:

'The criminal law, as we know it, and have it, must make the presumption of rational men who intend the consequences of their acts. But what is a policeman to do if he finds somebody on the streets obviously out of his mind (and in many cases he does not need a subtle diagnostician to determine that)? It is easy to say that it all depends on whether or not the person committed a crime. But shouting, threatening, creating other disorders, breaking windows and so on are all crimes and justify the invocation of the criminal process. What do we expect the Justice of the Peace to do if, in a bail hearing, the person before him is confused and cannot give a rational answer? What should the Prosecutor do if he finds that a person charged with a minor offence is deeply depressed and suicidal? What about the Judge who finds that the accused before him does not understand what he is charged with and what is happening? Or how would he sentence a mother who has killed her child whom she loved so much that she could not bear seeing him grow up in a rotten world?

(Mohr 1978)

However, it is not just the issue of compulsion that gives rise to the controversy between law and psychiatry. There is the fact that in the name of public protection psychiatrists, judges, and parole authorities are detaining people against their will for longer periods than they can justify on other grounds. There is also the fact that people are detained because of the danger of something they *might* do in the future rather than because of something they have already done. Walker (1978) discussed the issues raised by the concept of *dangerousness* in some detail. He concludes a masterly review with the judgement that it is defensible from the moral point of view to detain, or otherwise control certain people for the protection of others and that from the legal point of view it is not impossible to draft provisions for this purpose with satisfactory safeguards. But he does enter two notable caveats. The first is that so far as the problem is concerned no system of rules 'can avoid the need for decisions by human beings, with all their biases and irrational fears'.

The other is that custodial institutions, however liberally managed, are places of last resort, whether for the mentally ill or for offenders.

Birley's declaration concerning a patient's 'right to be admitted against his will' speaks of a 'first-class psychiatric service'. After all, if the legislation enacted is to enable those who are ill to receive treatment, then the facilities should be such as to facilitate delivery of *effective* treatment. The problem is, as Walker points out, that some of the patients compulsorily detained because of the fear that their mental state will result in crimes of violence, e.g. markedly paranoid individuals threatening to kill, do not actually benefit from any available psychiatric intervention. What is to be done when the psychiatrists have done their therapeutic best and the only justification for further detention is that he might still do what he talks of doing? The public and the media are not exactly enthralled by the arguments of progressive penologists in favour of close supervision of potentially dangerous individuals in the community. Yet neither is the public happy with the idea of committing people to periods of indefinite detention in psychiatric hospitals.

And, there is no denying that the compulsory admission provisions of the 1959 Mental Health Act are abused. The wide regional variation in the number of patients compulsorily hospitalized is difficult to explain. Figures for 1970 for psychiatric hospitals and units revealed that the number of admissions under *Section 26*, for example, ranged from three per 1,000 to fifteen per 1,000, while the rates for all compulsory admissions ranged from 215 per 1,000 to 143 per 1,000 (*Patients' Rights* 1974). Such statistically significant differences may of course be due to certain regions having better after-care facilities than others with the result that their voluntary admission rates fall and their proportion of compulsory admissions rises. However, other factors, such as the relative simplicity of some compulsory admissions, the comparative inexperience of some social workers, and even the distance from the patient's home to the hospital (giving the voluntary patient more time to change his mind!) have been suggested as possible, non-psychiatric reasons for the variation in rate. The MIND Report on Patients' Rights (1974) noted that there are hospitals that are reluctant to admit patients in the absence of consultants (at night and on weekends) unless the patient is on a compulsory order. The Report notes sarcastically that 'it is advisable in such areas not to become ill at weekends'. Another way in which compulsory admission rates can be affected by non-medical considerations came to light during the nurses' dispute in 1973. At that time, a ranking list of emergencies was drawn up and it was made clear that only such emergencies would be handled by those hospitals particularly affected by the industrial action. The only psychiatric emergency that qualified for inclusion on the list was compulsory admission, which meant that psychiatrists were under immense pressure to certify severely ill patients to get them into hospital even though many of these patients were quite willing to enter hospital voluntarily.

Once certified, can a patient appeal? Under the terms of the 1959 *Mental Health Act*, a patient can appeal to an independent enquiry body called the Mental Health Review Tribunal. These tribunals are set up in each of the fifteen administrative areas of the National Health Service and they have the power to discharge patients detained in hospital, except in those cases where there is an order restricting discharge (Sections 65 and 74). The membership of a Mental Health Review Tribunal consists of a lawyer, a medically qualified member (usually a psychiatrist), and a lay person, chosen from a pool of people who have special experience in administration or the social services or who have some other special qualifications. The chairman is the lawyer and all the members are appointed by the Lord Chancellor's Office.

The procedure is relatively straightforward. The patient, or his nearest relative, can apply to have a compulsory order removed. The applicant fills in a form and sends it to the tribunal. He does not have to specify why he wishes to be released. The hearing usually takes place within the hospital. In advance, the hospital prepares a medical report on the patient stating the details of his case, the reasons for his detention, and what facilities in the community are available in the community for the care of the patient should his discharge be ordered. After hearing from both the patient and the psychiatrist looking after him, the tribunal members confer and their decision is announced in writing shortly after the tribunal has finished its hearing.

In 1973 a total of 676 applications to Mental Health Review Tribunals were made and 563 of these were actually heard. Of these, ninety-four patients were discharged. However, these figures do not tell the whole story by any means. The MIND Report, quoted above, has claimed that the working of these tribunals appeared in fact, though not in intention, to be weighted against the patient. The Report mentions 'substantial intellectual and psychological difficulties' facing patients making an appeal. Such patients are often unfamiliar with the procedure and even when they persevere with their appeal they may act ineffectually. A project of the National Council for Civil Liberties in the years up to 1967 provided lay assistance to patients in presenting their case before the Mental Health Review Tribunals. The project produced the remarkable result that of seventy-eight patients who were so assisted, thirty-two (or 41 per cent) were successful in obtaining their release against a general average in unassisted cases of about $12\frac{1}{2}$ per cent. Understandably, MIND has concluded that there is a case for the provision of a service of lay representation for all patients at Review Tribunals.

The MIND Report also claims that many patients who have had their status altered from 'detained' to 'informal' at Hospital Management Committee reviews are not always aware that they can now discharge themselves from hospital if they so wish. 'The change', observes the Report, 'is often not fully explained by the consultant. Few hospitals are so well staffed by social workers that they have time to discuss with patients the implications of their new "informal" status.' But the Report comes to the conclusion that whereas there are many people in hospital who do not need to be there, this is due not so much to their being detained against their will as to the fact that there are not enough half-way houses, hostels, and other community facilities outside hospital to which such patients could be discharged.

This is not to suggest that abuses of the power to compulsorily detain patients in mental hospitals in Britain do not occur. They can and do occur. It is a treacherous area, however, and establishing the 'dangerousness' of a patient is hazardous, as reference to one well-publicized case shows. In February 1973 the medical correspondent of the *New Statesman* drew attention to the case of a seventeen-year-old Welsh girl, Gillian Gwyther, who following a two and a half year spell as an in-patient at Morgannwg Hospital was transferred to Broadmoor Hospital (Gould 1973a). Her original admission followed several episodes of unpredictable and aggressive behaviour and the application for a Section 26 was signed by the girl's mother. During her stay in Morgannwg, Gillian was lethargic and apathetic, which was attributed by her doctors to her condition (she was diagnosed as suffering from schizophrenia) but which Dr Gould and the girl's mother blamed on the drugs she was being given and the impoverished environment of the ward. Throughout her daughter's period in hospital, Mrs Gwyther claimed that no one had ever given her 'the smallest explanation' of her legal rights. Nonetheless, a appeal was eventually made to the area Mental Health Review Tribunal and a date was fixed for the hearing. Before the hearing could be held, however, Gillian was transferred to Broadmoor. Two acts of violence, according to Dr Gould, precipitated this turn of events. The first involved an attack on the ward sister. The doctor implied that this was a serious assault. Dr Gould's article frankly doubts this and notes that on the day after the attack the said sister was back on duty and was going about her work 'in a reasonably brisk and energetic fashion'. The second attack, also on a nursing sister, resulted in the staff member losing some of her hair, but Dr Gould points out that the nurse later admitted that her hair did tend to come out easily! Doubtful that she required a transfer to Broadmoor (a hospital for dangerously aggressive and refractory patients) Dr Gould bitterly criticized Morgannwg Hospital and the fact that while there this 'charming young woman had 30 months of her youth needlessly destroyed'.

A follow-up article appeared in March of the same year (Gould 1973b). This recounted how Gillian had had her case heard by a Mental Health Review Tribunal but her appeal to be released had been rejected. (The original article had implied that one of the reasons she had been so abruptly transferred to Broadmoor was to avoid a Tribunal hearing, but this was not so. The rules governing such appeals operate in the Special Hospitals of Broadmoor, Moss Side, and Rampton as well as in ordinary mental hospitals and units.) Dr Gould, in the course of this article, described the workings of the Review Tribunals, but he declared that appeals have 'a small chance of success' and quoted a chairman of one of Broadmoor's tribunals as saying 'Everything hangs on the medical reports'. But, and more important, he focused on the fact that the *Mental Health Act*'s Section 26 allows a person to be detained 'in the interests of his own *health* or safety'. By what right, he demanded, does society incarcerate somebody for their own *health*? Their own safety, perhaps; for other people's safety, certainly; but for their own personal *health*?

> 'We should all be appalled by the suggestion that somebody suffering from, say, high blood pressure should be forced by law to stay in hospital until pronounced cured. Why should we assume the right to lock up people with a sickness of the mind, unless that sickness (like smallpox) does indeed threaten the rest of us.' (Gould 1973b)

An 'atrocious piece of legislation', Dr Gould declares of the 1959 *Mental Health Act*, denying 'thousands of citizens their most fundamental human rights'. In the case of Miss Gwyther, her detention in Broadmoor brought about an improvement in her behaviour although she was still actively hallucinating and severely incapacitated. The doctors there felt she could probably return to her area hospital, but Morgannwg Hospital indicated that it would be preferable if Gillian could have a year free of aggressive behaviour before such a transfer back occurred. Her mother insisted that Gillian could be managed at home, but Broadmoor's doctors and the Mental Health Review Tribunal disagreed.

Was Gillian a danger to others? The doctors say she was and point to episodes in her family prior to admission and the two assaults at Morgannwg. Dr Gould declares that the physical violence in the home is 'a myth' and suggests, somewhat blithely perhaps, that the attacks on the nurses did not amount to very much. Was she ill? Both the doctors and Dr Gould agree that Gillian was – but Dr Gould, by felicitous choice of phrasing and emphases, strongly implies that her hospital experiences made her very much worse and that it would have been better if she had never been admitted in the first place. Was her Mental Health Review Tribunal hearing a fair and independent one? Dr Gould is doubtful, although it turned out later that Gillian was independently represented by counsel and, as the NCCL project showed, had a very much higher chance of being discharged than might otherwise have been expected. Finally, if no longer aggressive (and the Broadmoor doctors concluded within a few months of her arrival there that she was not), could she not have been returned to Morgannwg or even discharged? Herein lies an awkward dilemma facing doctors. A patient, at one time aggressive and acutely disturbed, improves and becomes more amenable and less unpredictable. Yet he/she remains seriously psychotic. In such a situation, and Gillian Gwyther's state appeared to resemble it fairly closely, the relationship between the state of the patient's 'health' and his/her own and/or other's 'safety' becomes a matter of crucial importance. Dr Gould, and other champions of the rights of the individual, insist that detaining persons because of the state of their mental health is always wrong. If no longer actually aggressive, the patient should be free to decide whether he stays or goes. But such champions are not always so consistent. Those Broadmoor doctors who today find themselves castigated for their excessive caution in releasing a disturbed person from their care are likely tomorrow to be as fiercely attacked for the premature discharge of an apparently improved patient who promptly commits an assault.

Recently, there has been considerable discussion about the 1959 Mental Health Act and proposals for changes have come from the Royal College of Psychiatrists (1974), the National Association for Mental Health (Gostin 1975; 1977), the British Association of Social Workers (BASW 1977) and the Butler Committee (Report of the Committee on Mentally Abnormal Offenders 1975). A one-day conference followed the appearance of a consultative document and more recently there appeared the long-awaited White Paper (HMSO 1978).

At the heart of the movement for reform of the 1959 Act (an Act long regarded as highly progressive and liberal) are four main aims. The first is that people suffering from mental disorder should be treated as far as is possible in the same way as those with physical illnesses. Secondly, treatment should whenever possible be voluntary, involuntary measures being reserved for emergencies and the last resort. Thirdly, special legal 'labelling' of the mentally retarded should be abolished and these people should have the same access as other citizens to appropriate education and rehabilitation. Fourthly, mental health should be integrated into the general health and social services, particularly at their point of delivery in the hospitals and the community.

The development of acute psychiatric units within general hospitals, the emphasis on effective treatment within the primary health care sector and the growing awareness of psychological and social factors in the genesis of psychiatric ill-health are all regarded as indicators of a gradual integration of the medical and psychiatric services. Much pride, too, is taken in the fact that over 90 per cent of all admissions to British psychiatric hospitals are voluntary. The White Paper endorsed the principle that the mentally ill should be treated similarly to their physically ill counterparts.

Yet there are surprising anomalies and contradictions contained in the White Paper. The document advocates that informally admitted psychiatric patients should always be given a statement of their legal rights on admission to hospital despite the fact that physically ill patients do not receive such information. Indeed, the *Lancet* was moved to enquire whether the DHSS intended that in future all patients, physically as well as mentally ill, should receive such a declaration of rights and if not, why not? (*Lancet* 1979). 'After all', the editorial observed, 'a patient with chronic renal disease often has a good reason to know his civil rights as a patient with phobic anxiety.'

However, the most controversial proposals concern the detention and treatment of involuntary psychiatric patients. The existing Mental Health Act is ambiguous concerning the administration of treatment to compulsorily detained patients. This is especially true in the case of Section 25 which provides for the detention of a patient for 'observation with or without medical treatment' but does not explicitly allow treatment to be imposed without consent. The Royal College of Psychiatrists points out that the whole point behind detention is in order that treatment be given. Detaining a patient in hospital without providing treatment is tantamount to turning hospitals into penitentiaries and psychiatrists into jailers. MIND argues for the separation of the process of detention from the process of treatment. In addition to pressing for a tightening of the legislation concerning psychiatric powers to detain, MIND argues for greater controls to be introduced governing the administration of treatment to detained patients. MIND proposed a quasi-judicial, multi-disciplinary review of all treatment decisions which had any of the following components: (i) the patient objects to the treatment or otherwise does not give a legally effective consent; (ii) treatments involving noxious or aversive stimuli or involving restraint or seclusion; (iii) other treatments which irreversibly or unpredictably affect the patient or are not fully established. If the review board considers the patient's refusal to be informed and reasonable under the circumstances the treatment should not be given (Gostin 1975).

The Royal College of Psychiatrists, worried by what its members saw as a threat to medical control over clinical decisions, suggested an amendment to the existing law clarifying the ultimate authority of the responsible medical officer (RMO) to impose treatment upon a detained patient. The RMO would be guided by a non-legislative code of practice which would involve, where possible, consulting with the next-of-kin and obtaining an independent consultant psychiatric opinion in writing. The final decision, however, would rest with the RMO who would record his reasons for carrying out the treatment particularly where the independent consultant held a contrary view.

The Butler Committee proposed that if the patient is unable to appreciate what is involved in the treatment procedure the RMO should be authorized to impose it upon him save where the treatment is irreversible or hazardous. In cases where the patient is competent but refuses to give consent, the RMO may only impose treatment in the following circumstances: (i) where (not being of a hazardous or irreversible nature) it represents the minimum interference with the patient to prevent him from acting dangerously to himself or others; or (ii) where it is necessary to save the patient's life; or (iii) where (not being irreversible) it is necessary to prevent him from deteriorating (Butler Committee 1975).

The White Paper, in a section which reflected the influence which MIND exerted on those who drafted it, attempted to clarify what it meant by 'hazardous, irreversible or not fully established' without specifying which if any psychiatric treatments it had in mind:

Hazardous treatments are those where the risk of adverse reaction or the severity of such reaction would be disproportionate to the degree of benefit the treatment is likely to confer or the prospect of success.

Irreversible treatments are those which necessitate the removal or destruction of brain tissue or are designed to effect irreversible changes in cerebral or bodily functions.

Treatments which are *not fully established* are those not in general use or whose safety and efficacy have not yet been confirmed by clinical research.

It is not at all clear which treatments are covered by such definitions. The *Lancet* commented a trifle sarcastically that it was difficult to see 'how any doctor could employ such treatments without running a serious risk of legal action' (*Lancet* 1979). MIND seems to have had treatments such as ECT in mind but many doctors would disagree and would argue that it is less hazardous than many other treatments in medicine, no more nor less irreversible than the administration of a potent drug and no less established as an effective treatment than antidepressants or psychotherapy. One of the reasons that psychiatrists have reacted so heatedly to MIND's proposals in this regard is that they feel that definitions such as those put forward above could quite legitimately be ascribed to almost every treatment in psychiatry, not to mention medicine itself. If anytime a doctor wished to administer any treatment of reasonable potency to a patient compulsorily admitted to his care for treatment he had to go before a multidisciplinary panel to justify that decision what would be the point of the years of training to enable him to make such a decision and the reasonable level of remuneration paid to him as reward for carrying such a responsibility. The Royal College of

Psychiatrists' review of the White Paper expressed the view of British psychiatrists with uncharacteristic bluntness:

'. . . the responsibility for invoking compulsory powers (in relation to admission and treatment) is a clinical matter and the College considers that the professional background and higher professional training of psychiatrists prepare them to make fundamental decisions in the field of clinical psychiatric practice and to take the primary responsibility for these decisions.'

(Report of Special Committee,
Royal College of Psychiatrists 1979)

Dr Gerald Vaughan, the present Minister of Health, who will be crucially involved in the new Conservative Government's decision *vis-à-vis* a reformed Mental Health Act, shared this opinion when, in opposition, he attacked the then Secretary of State, David Ennals, for appearing to endorse MIND's demands:

'What seems strange is that the Secretary of State appears to be suggesting that if an experienced psychiatrist has decided that a particular kind of treatment is necessary he should turn, not to another experienced psychiatrist but to a panel of people, some of whom will have no experience in that field. It makes absolute nonsense of a lot of medical training. Why spend up to ten years training to become a psychiatric consultant and then have one's view of what is best for a patient reversed by someone working in a different specialty who may have spent only two or three years in training.'
(Vaughan 1979)

This is an area which provokes passionate debate. I, myself, once believed that although I did not regard ECT as a particularly hazardous or irreversible treatment many people did and the argument for a multidisciplinary review committee reviewing its use in cases of compulsorily detained patients was a persuasive one (Clare 1979). I have since changed my mind, mainly on account of the fact that it has become increasingly clear that such multidisciplinary reviews would not stop and could not stop at ECT. Intramuscular injections, potent drugs, certain forms of behaviour therapy – all these and more would fall under the scrutiny of such bodies. The function of the clinical psychiatrist *vis-à-vis* the detained and seriously disturbed psychiatric patient would become that of a jailer while he awaited the deliberations of a multidisciplinary panel concerning the appropriateness or otherwise of various suggested treatments.

Yet some form of review would appear indicated. In this respect, it is worth noting that the World Psychiatric Association's Declaration of Hawaii, a statement of psychiatric ethics largely provoked by the controversy over Soviet abuse of psychiatry, states: 'Whenever there is compulsory treatment or detention there must be an independent and neutral body of appeal for regular enquiry into these cases' (WPA 1977). How independent and how neutral is not, however, defined. The White Paper is also in a quandary when it comes to the problem of balancing the need to protect staff against violent patients against the need to protect patients against violent staff. Section 141 provides that civil or criminal proceedings against a person acting or purporting to act in pursuance of the Mental Health Act can be brought only with the leave of the High Court. The White Paper proposes that criminal actions should be removed from the scope of Section 141 and that patients should be permitted to proceed if there are 'reasonable' rather than the at present 'substantial' grounds for the contention that the defendant acted in bad faith or without reasonable care. MIND points out that psychiatric patients seldom resort to legal action but the Confederation of Health Service Employees (COHSE) disagrees (COHSE 1977). Already staff organizations are refusing to cope with patients likely to cause serious nursing and other management problems (see below) and this increasing tendency is having serious implications for the courts, the prisons, and the community.

The MIND Report is critical of psychiatrists for being 'over-cautious' in their predictions of violent behaviour and of being reluctant to discharge patients who almost certainly represent little danger to themselves or to others. It is very doubtful, however, if psychiatrists, as a group, are over-cautious. It is a matter of some irony that shortly before the appearance of this Report, massive newspaper, television and radio coverage was devoted to the release of a young woman who had been detained in the Maudsley Hospital for seven months after she had killed two of her four children. Despite the fact that the psychiatrist involved, Dr Peter Scott, is one of this country's foremost forensic experts, the bulk of the comment was critical. The newspaper headlines flaunted the words 'Killer' and 'Madness' and the overwhelming impression given was that of a gullible and soft psychiatrist who had unthinkingly released into the community a psychopathic murderess. It is in itself a reflection of the Press's capacity for self-examination that when the time came to publicize the MIND Report and its strictures on the conservatism of psychiatrists, no mention was made of Dr Scott's willingness to endure a remarkable amount of public criticism in giving a disturbed woman the opportunity of informal treatment outside hospital. A further incident around this time casts even greater doubt on the MIND Report's claim. A man who had murdered his wife, while morbidly jealous and psychotic, was refused admission to Glenside Hospital in Bristol despite the fact that the psychiatrist involved did not consider him to be a danger to others and felt he could be quite effectively treated in an ordinary mental hospital setting. The opposition to the patient's admission came from the Confederation of Health Service Employees (COHSE), the union of which most of the hospital's non-medical staff were members. COHSE did not oppose the patient's admission because they believed him to be safe and hence in no need of in-patient treatment, however. They did so because they believed him to be *very dangerous* and certainly more dangerous than the psychiatrist appeared to believe! The judge involved, Mr Justice Mais, was moved to observe:

> 'I find it very difficult to understand how it is that medical opinion has been overturned by those who are not nursing and who have not had the experience and skill of the doctors, and I find it hard to understand how it is that an order of this court is apparently incapable of being carried out.'   (*The Times*, November 1, 1975)

The judge had issued a *Section 60*, sending the man to Glenside Hospital after he had pleaded guilty to manslaughter on the grounds of diminished responsibility. The order had to be rescinded, however, after COHSE members at the hospital threatened to strike if the patient was admitted.

It is clear that not all psychiatrists are 'over-cautious'. An editorial in *The Times*, commenting upon the affair and upon the simultaneous and coincidental appearance of the MIND Report, remarked that it was perhaps an unfortunate time for the publication of views which felt that too many people were in mental hospitals against their will. Noting that MIND proposed that compulsory hospital admission should only follow a prediction of dangerous behaviour 'based on recent overt acts', the editorial declared the suggestion to be too restrictive and proffered the following opinion:

> 'The [MIND] report is deeply mistrustful of the efficiency of psychiatrists on the ground that they tend to err on the side of prudence in judging whether a patient is dangerous or not. No doubt they do: it is an error in the right direction.'   (*The Times*, November 3, 1975)

So there it stands. MIND believes that psychiatrists play it too safe. I am not so sure that they do. *The Times*, however, is in no doubt but thinks it is just as well! On this issue, I feel *The Times* most closely approximates to the feelings of the general public on this matter.

Summary

The *Mental Health Act* legislates for the compulsory hospitalization not merely of those who, by virtue of mental disorder, represent a danger to the *safety* of themselves or others but also of those whose mental state constitutes a threat to their own *health* or the health of others. The Act recognizes that an individual's mental abilities and judgements can be so impaired by virtue of a mental disorder that he cannot be regarded as fully *responsible* for his actions. At the heart of the controversy over the question of compulsory hospitalization is the problem of responsibility. There are those critics, and Thomas Szasz is one of them, who appear content to accept that an individual's mental faculties can be and often are impaired in those 'mental illnesses' in which an associated physical, usually brain, abnormality can be detected, but who reject the possibility of such an impairment in those mental illnesses, the so-called 'functional' mental illnesses, in which no organic pathology can be discovered. However, as the British philosopher Antony Flew points out (1973), such a position appears somewhat imprudent when we entertain the permanent possibility of discoveries requiring the transfer of some condition previously rated as only functional into the other, the organic, category'. The crucial question for Flew is whether an individual indulging in some form or other of unwanted behaviour is able to inhibit such inclinations if he so wishes. The law of most countries, as Hart reminds us, requires that the person liable to be punished

'. . . should, at the time of his crime, have had the capacity to understand what he is required by law to do or not to do, to deliberate and to decide what to do, and to control his conduct in the light of such decisions.'

(Hart 1968: 218)

The phrase 'when the balance of his mind was disturbed', often used apropos of a successful suicide attempt or a bizarre criminal act, reflects the view that there are mental disturbances of such a nature as to affect the psychological integrity of the individual and impair his judgement. The legislation governing compulsory hospitalization of the mentally ill embodies an attempt to provide the individual with protection in the event that his mind or that of another should be so impaired and his health or that of another should be so threatened.

Psychiatrists, sensible ones anyway, know full well that they cannot prevent people from killing themselves. Nor can they prevent them from killing each other. It is a rare day that does not claim at least one suicide victim, that does not see at least one newspaper story of the muffled appeal that a GP did not hear, of the ambivalent gesture of despair that a psychiatrist did not understand. Less frequently, but more dramatically, appears a tale of frenzied killings, cold-blooded assaults, and the tortured, deluded, crazy inner world of some unfortunate psychotic man is laid bare before the public's uncomprehending and bewildered eye. In some public courtroom, a psychiatrist testifies to the complexity of the relationship between the violent phantasy and the violent act, to the fact that only a small fraction of the mentally ill is dangerous, to the reality that in a society which proudly and justifiably cherishes the individual's freedom there will always be risks. The media cry out for more security and every psychiatrist subsequently faced with a potentially aggressive patient resolves to take no chances.

Yet, as I have said earlier, the public's stance is not a consistent one. It recoils with disgust and amazement when some unfortunate soul, locked away years before for a trifling peccadillo, stumbles awkwardly and uneasily out of a mental hospital and into the outside world like some forgotten soldier emerging from a foreign jungle to find the war long since ended. The psychiatrist once more stands indicted, this time for his zeal as a jailer and his indifference to his patient's rights.

It takes courage for the psychiatrist and the social worker to decide to compulsorily admit a patient to a hospital. It takes courage on occasions to decide not to. Whatever the decision, it is essential for the protection and the integrity of all concerned – patient, relatives, psychiatrist, social worker, GP – that there should be an effective and independent court of appeal to which it can be taken by any of them for an honest, fair, and thorough assessment.

Appendix: Sections of the Mental Health Act (1959) governing compulsory admission to hospital

Section 25: a patient may be compulsorily admitted to hospital under this section provided that

  (a) he suffers from mental disorder of a nature or degree which warrants his detention in a hospital for observation (with or without treatment) for at least a limited period;

and (b) he ought to be so detained 'in the interests of his own health or safety or with a view to the protection of other persons'.

A person may be detained on a Section 25 for up to twenty-eight days, beginning with the day he is admitted to hospital and, unless he is dealt with under another section of the Act, he is free to leave hospital at the end of this period. An application for admission of a patient on a Section 25 rests on the written recommendations of *two* medical practitioners. One of these doctors should have known the patient prior to certification and one must be recognized by a local authority as having special competence in the area of mental disorder. In addition to the medical recommendations, an application to the hospital involved, made out by the patient's nearest relative or, if such a relative is unobtainable or prefers not to sign, by a social worker approved by a local authority as having the necessary competence to undertake such a task. A patient so detained may be discharged by his doctor at any time or by three or more members of the Area Health Authority, authorized for the purpose. The nearest relative has *not* the power to discharge a patient detained on a Section 25.

Section 26: A patient may be detained for treatment under this section provided:−

(a) he is suffering from mental disorder being
   (i) in the case of a patient of any age, mental illness, or severe subnormality;
   (ii) in the case of a patient *under the age of 21*, psychopathic personality or subnormality.

and (b) his disorder is 'of a nature or degree which warrants the detention of the patient in a hospital for medical treatment' *and* is necessary 'in the interests of the patient's health or safety or for the protection of other persons that the patient should be so detained'.

Again, two medical recommendations are required. Both doctors have to state the psychiatric condition affecting the patient and both have to specify whether other methods of dealing with the patient are available and if so why they are not appropriate. As with a Section 25, an application may be made by the patient's nearest relative or by a suitably approved social worker. A patient admitted on a Section 26 may be detained for treatment for up to one year in the first instance. The order can, however, be renewed for one further year after the first year and then for two years at a time. It is of course possible (and common) for the responsible medical officer to discharge a patient before the order has elapsed. Again, three or more members of the Area Health Authority involved may exercise the right to discharge. The nearest relative *has the power to discharge* a patient provided he gives notice in writing to the hospital authorities of his proposed action. If the consultant responsible for the patient believes that if the patient were to be discharged he would be likely to act in a manner dangerous to other persons or to himself, he can bar the relative's application to discharge. The patient or his nearest relative can apply to a Mental Health Review Tribunal for a review of the patient's case.

Section 29: In a case of urgent necessity, a patient may be admitted compulsorily for observation for up to seventy-two hours. Any such application must be made to the hospital involved and must include a statement, signed by the nearest relative or by an approved social worker (who must have seen the patient sometime during the preceding three days), stating that it is a matter of great urgency. Such an application must be accompanied by one medical recommendation. For this section to be converted to a Section 25, a second medical recommendation must be received by the hospital authorities within seventy-two hours.

Section 30: Under this section, a patient already in hospital on a voluntary basis may be detained compulsorily on the recommendation of one doctor and the nearest relative or an approved social worker. Such a holding operation can last only seventy-two hours unless during that time a second medical recommendation has been received converting the order into a Section 25.

Section 136: When a police constable finds in a public place any person who *appears* to be suffering from a mental disorder or in immediate need of care or control he may take the person to a place of safety where he can be detained for a period not exceeding seventy-two hours. Places of safety include any residential accommodation provided by local authorities, a police station, a mental nursing home, a residential home for mentally disordered persons and a hospital. In the ordinary course of events, the patient is so grossly disturbed and the offence committed so trivial (commonest include loitering and disturbing the peace) that the police use such discretionary powers to take such a person to hospital.

Section 60: A person, convicted before a Court of Assize or Quarter Sessions of an offence (other than an offence, the sentence for which is fixed by law) or by a Magistrate's Court of an offence punishable on summary conviction with imprisonment, may be detained under this Section in a hospital specified in the order. The Court must be satisfied, on the written or oral evidence of two medical doctors, that:–

'the offender is suffering from mental illness, psychopathic disorder, subnormality or severe subnormality and that the disorder is of a nature or degree which warrants the detention of the patient in a hospital for medical treatment.'

The Court must also be satisfied that having regard to the details of the offence, the character, and antecedents of the offender, and to other methods of dealing with him, that the most appropriate disposal would be by the Hospital Order. There must also be evidence that the specified hospital is willing to accept the patient within twenty-eight days. This is by far the most important and the most frequently used penal procedure and accounted for 1,130 cases of 11,933 remanded for medical report in 1972.

Section 65: When a person is to be detained under a Hospital Order, the Court of Assize or Quarter Sessions (a Magistrate's Court does not possess this power) may also make an *order restricting discharge.* The Court may apply such a restriction after considering the patient's behavioural background and the gravity of his offence. In effect, this means that if a Court considers the circumstances to be so serious that for the protection of the public there should be no easy discharge it restricts this discharge so that the patient cannot be discharged, transferred, granted leave of absence without the consent of the Home Secretary. Neither the patient nor his nearest relative have direct access to a Mental Health Review Tribunal.

Section 72: Where a person is undergoing a term of imprisonment and the Home Secretary is satisfied on medical evidence of two practitioners that the person is suffering from any form of mental disorder which is of a nature or degree which warrants the detention of the patient in a hospital for medical treatment he may order the transfer of the patient to a specified hospital. Should a prisoner so transferred no longer require treatment for mental disorder he may be returned to prison or to another establishment to complete his sentence. The Home Secretary, in the interest of public safety, may place restrictions on the transfer (Section 74) and discharge of the patient. Such restrictions are similar to those embodied in Section 65.

In addition to these sections of the *Mental Health Act* (1959), Section 4 of the *Criminal Justice Act* (1948) can be used in the management of the mentally abnormal offender. Under Section 4, a probation order can be made on the evidence presented to a court by a medical practitioner, suitably approved as having competence in the area of mental disorder, and who is usually a consultant on the staff of the hospital to which the offender may be admitted. The offences for which these orders can be made cover a very wide range indeed from, for example, attempted murder to petty larceny.

References

ALVAREZ, A. (1971) *The Savage God*. London: Weidenfeld & Nicolson.

ANONYMOUS (1973) Review of *The Myth of Mental Illness*. *Times Literary Supplement*, June 15.

BARRACLOUGH, B., BUNCH, J., NELSON, B., and SAINSBURY, P. (1974) A Hundred Cases of Suicide: Clinical Aspects. *British Journal of Psychiatry* **125**: 355–73.

BATTIE, W. (1758) *A Treatise on Madness*. London: Whiston & White.

BIRLEY, J.L.T. (1973) Coercion and Care. Lecture delivered to London Medical Group.

BRITISH ASSOCIATION OF SOCIAL WORKERS (1977) *Mental Health Crisis Services – A New Philosophy*. Birmingham: BASW.

BUNCH, J., BARRACLOUGH, B., NELSON, B., and
SAINSBURY, P. (1971) Suicide Following Bereavement
of Parents. *Social Psychiatry* **6**: 193–9.

CHEYNE, G. (1733) *The English Malady or A Treatise on
Nervous Diseases of all Kinds, as Spleen, Vapours, Lowness of
Spirits, Hypochondriacal and Hysterical Distempers*. London:
Strahan & Leoke.

CLARE, A.W. (1978) Therapeutic and Ethical Aspects of
Electro-Convulsive Therapy: A British Perspective.
International Journal of Law and Psychiatry **1**: 237–53.

CLARE, A.W. (1978) In Defence of Compulsory
Psychiatric Intervention. *Lancet* **i**: 1197–8.

CONFEDERATION OF HEALTH SERVICE EMPLOYEES
(1977) *The Management of Violent or Potentially Violent
Patients*. London: COHSE.

COPES, J.B., FREEMAN-BROWNE, D.L., and ROBIN,
A.A. (1971) Danger Periods for Suicide in Patients under
Treatment. *Psychological Medicine* **1**: 400–404.

DECLARATION OF HAWAII ON PSYCHIATRIC ETHICS
(1977). London: World Psychiatric Association.

DEPARTMENT OF HEALTH AND SOCIAL SECURITY
(1970) *Psychiatric Hospitals and Units in England and Wales*.
London: HMSO.

FLEW, A. (1973) *Crime or Disease?* London: Macmillan.

GOSTIN, L.O. (1975) *The Mental Health Act from 1959 to
1975. Observations, Analysis, and Proposals for Reform*,
Vol. 1. A MIND Special Report. London: MIND
(National Association for Mental Health).

GOSTIN, L.O. (1977) A Human Condition. *The law
relating to mentally abnormal offenders: Observations, analysis
and proposals for reform*. Vol. 2. A MIND Special Report.
London: MIND (National Association for Mental
Health).

GOULD, D. (1973a) Trapped. *New Statesman*, February 9.
—— (1973b) The Broadmoor Girl. *New Statesman*, March 23.

HART, H.L.A. (1958) Legal Responsibility and Excuses.
In S. Hook (ed.), *Determinism and Freedom in the Age*

of Modern Science. New York: New York University Press.

—— (1968) *Punishment and Responsibility: Essays in the Philosophy of Law.* Oxford: Clarendon Press.

H.M. GOVERNMENT (1957) *Royal Commission on the Law Relating to Mental Illness and Mental Defficiency Report.* London HMSO.

—— (1959) *Mental Health Act.* London: HMSO.

KESSEL, N. (1967) Self Poisoning. In E. S. Shneidman (ed.), *Essays in Self Destruction.* New York: Basic Books.

KESSEL, N. and GROSSMAN, G. (1961) Suicide in alcoholics. *British Medical Journal* **ii**: 1671.

KITTRIE, N. (1971) *The Right to be Different.* Baltimore: Johns Hopkins.

Lancet (1979) Editorial: *Law and Mental Disorder* **i**: 759–61.

LOUGAS, K. and UDWIN, E.L. (1974) The Management of the Mentally Abnormal Offender. *British Journal of Hospital Medicine,* September.

MCGRATH, P.G. (1973) *Medico-Legal Journal* **41**: 135.

MILL, J.S. (1859) *On Liberty.* London: Henry Regnery.

MINISTRY OF HEALTH (1962) *Annual Report.* London: HMSO.

MOHR, H.W. (1978) Law and Mental Disorder: A Critique of the Law Reform Commission of Canada. *International Journal of Law and Psychiatry* **1, 1**: 51–62.

MONAHAN, J. (1977) John Stuart Mill on the Liberty of the Mentally Ill: A Historical Note. *American Journal of Psychiatry* **134**: 12: 1428–9.

NATIONAL ASSOCIATION FOR MENTAL HEALTH (1974) *Patients' Rights: The Mentally Disordered in Hospital.* Mind Report No. 10. London.

REPORT OF THE COMMITTEE ON MENTALLY ABNORMAL OFFENDERS (1975). Cmnd. 6244. London: HMSO.

ROBINS, E., MURPHY, G.E., WILKINSON, R.H., GASSNER, S., and KAYES, J. (1959) Some Clinical Considerations in the Prevention of Suicide Based on a

Study of 134 Successful Suicides. *American Journal of Public Health* **49**: 888.

ROYAL COLLEGE OF PSYCHIATRISTS (1979). Report of the Special Committee of Council on the White Paper on the Mental Health Act.

ROYAL COLLEGE OF PSYCHIATRISTS' WORKING PARTY. *News and Notes Supplement* October 1974.

SAINSBURY, P. (1973) Suicide: Opinions and Facts. *Proceedings of the Royal Society of Medicine* **66**: 579.

SCHEFF, T. (1966) *Being Mentally Ill*. Chicago: Aldine.

SZASZ, T.S. (1973) In *The Listener:* 206–7, August 16.

—— (1974a) *The Second Sin*. London: Routledge & Kegan Paul.

—— (1974b) *Law, Liberty and Psychiatry*. London: Routledge & Kegan Paul.

—— (1974c) Politics and Psychiatry: The Case of Mr. Ezra Pound. In *Law, Liberty and Psychiatry*.

The Times (1975) Search for Hospital for Wife Strangler. November 1, p. 2.

—— The Total Banishment of Bedlam. November 3, p. 13.

The Weekly Law Reports (1973) (3): 857–83.

SZASZ, T.S. (1976) Anti-Psychiatry: The Paradigm of the Plundered Mind. *New Review* **3, 29**: 3–14.

SZASZ, T. (1978) The Case Against Compulsory Psychiatric Interventions. *Lancet* **i**: 1035–6.

SZASZ, T.S. (1979) *Schizophrenia*. London: Oxford University Press.

TIDMARSH, D. (1973) Psychiatric Illness, Destitution and Crime. Paper read to meeting of the Association of Psychiatrists in Training at Institute of Psychiatry, London. November 15.

TUCKER, G. (1973) The Law and Mental Illness. Letter to *New Psychiatry*, October 3.

VAUGHAN, G. (1979) *Hansard*, 22 February at 670.

WALKER, N. (1978) Dangerous People. *International Journal of Law and Psychiatry* **1, 1**: 37–49.

WEIHOFEN, H. (1933) *Insanity as a Defense in Criminal Law*. New York: The Commonwealth Fund.

WHITEHEAD, A. and WINN, D. (1974) The Case for Reforming the 1959 *Mental Health Act*. *New Psychiatry* 1 (5): 9–10.

9

The contemporary state of psychiatry

Patient's name: Psychiatry.
Age: In middle years.
History: European born; after sickly youth in the US, travelled to Vienna and returned as Dr. Freud's Wunderkind. Amazing social success for one so young. Strong influence on such older associates as Education, Government, Child Rearing and the Arts, and a few raffish friends like Advertising and Criminology.
Complaint: Speaks of overwork, loss of confidence and inability to get provable results. Hears conflicting inner voices and insists that former friends are laughing behind his back. Patient agrees with Norman Mailer: It's hard to get to the top in America but it's even harder to stay there.
Diagnosis: Standard conflictual anxiety and maturational variations, complicated by acute depression. Identity crisis accompanied by compensatory delusions of grandeur and a declining ability to cope. Patient averse to the therapeutic alliance and shows incipient overreliance on drugs.
Recommended treatment: Requires further study.
Prognosis: Problematic.

(*Time* 1979)

THUS DID that faithful monthly recorder of the American pulse, *Time* magazine, sum up the state of contemporary psychiatry in that part of the world. In Britain, the subject appears to be in no better shape. A submission made by the Royal College of Psychiatrists in 1974 to the Central Manpower Committee of the Department of Health and Social Security declared that 'the average standard of psychiatric practice in Britain is abysmally low' and admitted that while psychiatrists are understandably reluctant to publicize this fact 'the evidence is overwhelming' (Royal College of Psychiatrists 1974). Over the past decade, the mental hospital headlines have documented a horrifying story of neglect, squalor, and ill-treatment – Ely, Farleigh, Whittingham, Napsbury, St Augustine's, Normansfield and, perhaps the most appalling of all, Rampton.

Sadly, there is little evidence that the highly publicized scandals and the public inquiries they provoke actually contribute to the development of an informed public opinion concerning the fundamental realities of psychiatric care in Britain. The more sensational aspects of these cases inevitably and perhaps understandably are highlighted by the media while the public are invariably shocked and angered by the disclosures of serious professional incompetence and misconduct. However, those conditions which greatly foster such abuses receive much less in the way of serious investigation. Indeed, Inskip, who chaired the South Ockenden and St Augustine's Inquiries, has reluctantly concluded that such inquiries 'burn up money that is desperately needed to improve the Health Service, disrupt the work of the hospital, and often have a devastating effect on individual and group morale, leaving in their wake a legacy of corrosive bitterness. They should be avoided wherever possible' (Inskip and Edwards 1979).

In a letter to the *Lancet* in 1972, a consultant psychiatrist, exasperated by the recurrent crises, the obligatory expression of concern by the political planners, the ephemeral interest of the general public, pointed an accusing finger at the flimsy financial fabric of the service:

'I do not know whether the country can afford adequate staffing of psychiatric hospitals and rebuilding the majority of them. Without that I fear that inspection, inquiries and Ombudsmen will no more improve the psychiatric service than court martials improve the morale of the army'

(Last 1972: 630).

The public, while dimly aware of the shortage of funds and skilled manpower, is more preoccupied with the effects of such deficiencies on the quality of the services it receives.

An undue emphasis on physical treatments and a remarkable lack of time are among the more popular criticisms made by psychiatric patients, their relatives, and observers of the contemporary psychiatric arena. Thus the mother of a schizophrenic boy wrote to me complaining of the treatment her son had received – 'It's drugs, drugs, drugs all the time . . . cannot medical students be taught that part of their job is to listen?' Again, in a report on the need for more psychotherapeutically based treatment within the Health Service, the National Association for Mental Health (MIND) expressed the view that many patients complain of being treated as objects, given drugs instead of the opportunity to talk about their feelings and their problems. 'Even when pills are the right answer', declared the Report, 'there is a need for discussion and, perhaps most important of all, for a willing ear to listen to their problems, anxieties and fantasies' (1974a: 3).

A willing ear and time – such modest requirements, it might be thought, given the gargantuan size of the NHS and its available manpower. Yet, as is made abundantly clear by the College of Psychiatrists' memorandum, the manpower situation is in a dreadful state at precisely the time when the apparent demand for skilled psychiatric assistance and more time-consuming treatments than drugs has risen to a raucous clamour. An excessive emphasis will continue to be placed on physical treatments, patients will find it difficult to have enough time with their therapists, and scandals will erupt from time to time for as long as the demand for psychiatric advice and care outstrips the resources that the country devotes to the psychiatric services.

If the nationalized psychiatric services struggle through insufficient funding, the American psychiatric services, a mixture of public and private endeavours, appear no better off. Non-white, lower class patients are treated by the public system with its over-crowded state hospitals, its lower-status mental health professionals, and its emphasis on drug-based treatments while the better-off patient obtains psychoanalysis or analytically-based psychotherapy from psychiatrists trained at some of America's finest medical schools. In a recent review of the American scene from a British vantage-point, Murray (1979) picked metropolitan Washington to illustrate the inequitable distribution of resources which bedevils not merely American psychiatry but medicine in general. In Washington, there are thirty-five psychiatrists per 100,000, a concentration which must make America's capital the most analyzed city in the world. However, these psychiatrists, Murray points out, 'huddle together in the affluent districts, profiting from the generous health-insurance benefits of the federal employees' while the public psychiatric services are probably the worst in America and standards at the once renowned St Elizabeth's Hospital have deteriorated so badly that the Joint Commission on American Hospitals has removed its accreditation (Murray 1979).

The demand

The degree to which psychiatric ill-health is recognized depends very much on the zeal with which it is sought and the measure by which it is identified. It also needs to be remembered that the *prevalence* of a disorder is not the same thing as the *demand* for it to be treated. As we shall see, minor neurotic ill-health is not an uncommon problem. If every person so afflicted was to seek treatment, the psychiatric services (and the general medical services too) would be quickly overwhelmed. Fortunately, many of these conditions are self-limiting and have high rates of spontaneous recovery.

At a first step, however, in assessing demand, it is necessary to arrive at some estimate of the prevalence of psychiatric disorders in the community. Reporting on the wide variation in the findings of various surveys, Taylor and Chave comment:

'The size of the catch depends on the size of the mesh of the net that is used; mental institutions find the least, community studies find more, and direct interviews find the most. Indeed, the over-enthusiastic psychiatric diagnostician can find evidence of psychiatric ill-health in most human beings; such findings perhaps tell us more about the observer than the observed.'

(Taylor and Chave 1964: 189)

Bearing in mind such strictures, we can turn to the major sources of data on psychiatric morbidity, namely the statistics of in-patient hospitalizations, out-patient and day-patient attendances, general practice surveys, and randomly sampled surveys of the general population.

If we look at the number of people in mental hospitals, we are confronted with a dramatic decrease occurring over the past decade. Immediately prior to the First World War, the number of patients in mental hospitals in England and Wales was about 100,000. This figure rose steadily to a peak of 154,000 in 1954. Since that time, there has been a steady fall so that by 1976 there were approximately 105,000 resident patients in mental hospitals in England, Scotland and Wales. The percentage fall over the period 1970–76 was a dramatic 19·8 (Royal Commission on the NHS 1979).

However, if we turn from the number of patients resident in mental hospitals to the number of individual admissions to such hospitals each year the picture changes. Prior to the First World War, there were about 20,000 admissions each year to mental hospitals. By 1950, the figure had risen to 57,000 and in 1964 there were 159,000. *Table 1* shows the steady increase in the number of admissions in England and Wales between 1964 and 1972. It is worth noting that, whereas first admissions increased between 1964 and 1972 by about one-sixth, re-admissions went up by almost one-half, an increase that probably reflects a more active treatment policy. From the admission data for 1964–9, it has been estimated that the life-time chance of being admitted to a mental hospital is about one in nine for men and one in six for women.

Concurrent with this contraction in the number of resident patients in mental hospitals has been a dramatic expansion

Table 1 *Admissions to mental illness hospitals (England and Wales)*

year	total admissions	first admissions	non-first admissions
1964	158,861	76,194	82,667
1965	159,452	80,566	78,986
1966	163,980	82,305	81,675
1967	168,438	85,780	82,658
1968	172,485	89,021	83,464
1969	174,709	89,931	84,778
1970	176,163	65,552	110,611
1971	176,028	65,563	110,465
1972	185,131	63,838	121,293

in out-patient and day-patient services. Between 1970 and 1976 the number of patients receiving out-patient care in Britain rose from 149,000 to 244,000, a rise of 63·8 per cent, while the number of patients attending day hospitals rose from 580,000 to over one million, an increase of just over 100 per cent. Figures obtained from the four psychiatric case registers operating in Britain at the present time (Aberdeen, Camberwell, Nottingham, and Salford) and which monitor all the contracts made with the specialized psychiatric services by patients in these areas suggest that in any one year twenty people per 1,000 of the population make contact for the first time with the services. On any one day of the year, about 8·5 people in every 1,000 are in such contact. All four registers report a higher contact rate for the single compared with the married, the divorced compared with the still married or widowed. About 50 per cent of the patients in contact with the services are seriously mentally ill. The annual 'use of service' prevalence rates for women greatly exceed those for men and for both sexes there is a sharp increase with age.

It has to be remembered, however, that hospital-based statistics do not reflect accurately the total amount of psychiatric morbidity within the community. Those patients who filter through to the specialized psychiatric services tend to be a highly selected group. A wholly different perspective on the size and nature of the demand for psychiatric help is provided from the vantage-point of primary medical care. A family doctor in the NHS will, on average, see 70 per cent of the patients on his list in one year and 90 per cent in two years. He is thus uniquely positioned to provide a reasonably informed opinion as to the extent of psychiatric disturbance within his practice. Surprisingly, there has only been one large-scale and comprehensive specialized psychiatric survey in Britain (Shepherd *et al.* 1966) and this revealed an overall prevalence rate for psychiatric disturbance of about 140 per 100,000 of the general population. Patients suffering from so-called neurotic conditions represented about 63 per cent of the total whereas schizophrenic and personality disordered patients each accounted for only 4 per cent. The remainder was made up of a variety of other conditions. Such a diagnostic distribution contrasts sharply with that seen in hospital-based surveys. The study revealed that there was considerable variation between the doctors in the amount of psychiatric morbidity they reported and much of this variation was accounted for by the doctors' attitudes to psychiatry. This same survey found that, whereas about half of the psychiatrically disturbed patients had been ill for at least a year, only about one in twenty had been referred for specialized help or, even though social factors had been recognized, to the social services. For almost one-quarter of the patients, no treatment whatsoever was recorded, and for one in every eight, prescriptions for sedatives or tranquillizers were the sole treatment given.

Other smaller general-practice surveys have confirmed the finding that a significant proportion of mental distress goes unidentified and/or untreated. Of a random group of patients aged forty to sixty-four on the lists of five general practitioners, 19 per cent of men and 27·5 per cent of women with clear-cut and well-established psychiatric symptoms had *not* been identified as in need of treatment by their family doctors. Goldberg and Blackwell (1970) found that among 553 consecutive attendances at a GP's surgery, 'hidden psychiatric morbidity' accounted for one-third of the disturbed patients.

The elderly

When we turn to consider the needs of special groups and the prevalence of particular psychiatric disorders, the demand for psychiatric help appears insatiable. In 1931, people over sixty-five years of age accounted for just over 5 per cent of the total population of Britain. This figure had risen to 9·5 per cent by 1966 and it is now estimated that by 1980 about 15 per cent of the population or seven and a half to eight million people will be over sixty-five.

In 1971, there were 50,025 mentally ill patients over sixty-five, representing 46 per cent of all mentally ill patients in hospital and 47 per cent of all long-stay patients. As the proportion of elderly people in the general population increases, so can we expect that the absolute numbers of elderly patients in mental hospitals, and the proportion they constitute of the total patient numbers, to significantly increase. Indeed, surveys by David Kay and his colleagues in Newcastle (Kay, Beamish, and Roth 1964) and by Parsons in Swansea (1965) have illustrated the high level of psychiatric morbidity experienced by people in this age-group. The Newcastle study revealed that just over one in every four people over sixty-five suffered some degree of significant mental disturbance; the elderly at home with such disabilities outnumbering those in institutions by about fifteen to one. The Swansea study was limited to the elderly living at home and it claimed that about 10 per cent had serious psychiatric disturbance. For every person living in the local mental hospital there were ten living at home with similar troubles. Both studies, therefore, suggest that only a fraction of the elderly with psychiatric disturbance are receiving much in the way of treatment.

Children

The situation at the other end of the life-cycle is comparable. Estimates of the proportion of children suffering from psychiatric disturbances range from 5 per cent to 17·9 per cent.

A reasonable overall estimate appears to be that about one in every ten children exhibits overt psychiatric problems. However, here again, one should not simply equate prevalence with demand – the attitudes of the parents towards psychiatric intervention, the severity of the child's disturbance, and the opinion of referral agencies such as the school and the GP all influence the decision whether or not to seek psychiatric help in each individual case. The present position has been neatly summarized (Royal College of Psychiatrists 1973a) as follows: psychiatric disorder exists in approximately 100 children in every 1,000. These 100 children merit different kinds of psychiatric help varying from diagnosis and advice to highly specialized treatment. While help is only acceptable to the families of about fifty of these children, it is currently only available to about twenty of them. The proportion of those families to whom help is acceptable can be expected to rise with the provision of better services.

Forensic psychiatry

Another area in which the demand for psychiatric help is rapidly expanding is forensic psychiatry. Several prison population surveys conducted over the past few years suggest that between 30 and 40 per cent of the sentenced male prison population exhibit significant evidence of serious psychiatric disturbance.

Dr John Gunn, at the Institute of Psychiatry in London, has applied these figures across the country, using the 1972 prison population figures as a baseline, and he has calculated that about 9,000 men in prison require psychiatric assistance (Gunn 1975). The Interim Butler Report (HM Government 1974) has indicated that some 500 men in prison would be more appropriately placed in hospitals outside the penal system, including 127 who should be in the Special Hospitals of Broadmoor, Rampton, and Moss Side. Surveys of women in prisons such as Holloway and Woodside provide very similar figures for psychiatric morbidity to those of the men.

Psychotherapy

The demand for psychotherapeutic skills, while arguably no more urgent than those described above, has been pressed with more public vigour over the past few years. The MIND Report (1974), which referred to psychotherapy somewhat pungently as the 'talking treatment', did not concern itself with the scientific evidence relating to the indications for or efficacy of psychotherapy (there is not a great deal of such evidence available) but preferred to base its claim for a considerable improvement in the psychotherapeutic services on a number of assertions made by patients: 'We are people not cases'; 'I want to be different'; 'I asked for help and was given pills'.

The apparent failure of physical methods of treatment, as evidenced by the high rates of admission and re-admission to hospitals, was also employed as an argument to illustrate the demand for psychotherapy. One study that has attempted to quantify the demand for such treatment is that of John and Lorna Wing. They estimate that to provide 'specialized psychotherapy' throughout England and Wales on the scale that it is practised in Camberwell would require well over 100 psychotherapists working whole-time within the NHS.

Camberwell, by virtue of the Maudsley Hospital situated within its boundaries, is comparatively well served by psychotherapists. Wing and Wing, in their study, classified a patient as in receipt of 'specialised psychotherapy' if he was being seen at least weekly for a minimum of six months by a psychiatrist who was either a trained analyst or analytically orientated or who devoted himself mainly to psychotherapy. Despite being well endowed by the standards of the rest of the country, Camberwell nonetheless had large deficiencies in relation to psychotherapeutic services. If everyone of the type already referred to psychotherapy in this area were referred to psychotherapy – only a very small proportion is actually referred – it would absolutely swamp the whole of the psychotherapy services in this area alone. If one wanted to multiply this on a national scale again, one would produce an enormous requirement.　　　　　　　　　(Wing and Wing 1970)

In addition to the demands of the aged, children, the prison service, and for skilled psychotherapeutic help, there is the growing demand for psychiatric participation in the management of adolescent problems, student ill-health, marital and family crises, alcoholism and drug abuse, the mentally handicapped, and psychological problems in industry. Those patients currently in receipt of psychiatric treatment represent the tip of the iceberg, the bulk of which is submerged within the community, unidentified and untreated.

In the United States, a similar picture emerges. Despite a deliberate programme begun in 1957 to 'deinstitutionalize' the psychiatric population, run down the mental hospital system, and treat the mentally ill mainly at Community Mental Health Centers (CMHCs), 40 per cent of all hospital beds are still filled by psychiatric patients. Rates of mental disorder in the community in general vary according to who is making the estimate and the measures used. One of the better studies, which relied upon psychiatrists' diagnoses, reported mental disorder rates varying between 11·5 and 14·5 per cent, prevalence figures not dissimilar to those in Britain (Roth et al. 1959). Up to 20 per cent of college students are estimated to use mental health services (Gold 1973), while in a study of industrial dispensaries 4·8 per cent of all attenders were diagnosed as emotionally disturbed (Rosen et al. 1970). In out-patient departments, psychiatric illness rates reportedly range from 53 to 88 per cent for women and 21 to 79 per cent for men, using attenders and non-psychiatric physician diagnoses (Hankin and Oktay 1979).

The resources

In 1976, 43 per cent of all the patients in hospital in England were psychiatric. One-third of these were mentally handicapped and the remainder were mentally ill. In general, these patients were (and are still) hospitalized in old, decrepit institutions in a poor state of repair. Sixty-five per cent of the country's mental hospitals were built before 1891; 40 per cent are over a century old. Whereas psychiatry, by virtue of the number of in-patients, out-patients, and day-patients, is one of the largest specialties in medicine, it receives a relatively small slice of the available medical resources. We have seen how psychiatry accounts for 45 per cent of the hospital beds, yet only 11 per cent of all consultants are psychiatrists and only 20 per cent of nurses work in psychiatric hospitals and units. In non-psychiatric hospitals, the average consultant looks after about thirty in-patients. His psychiatric colleague cares for 154 while the average consultant in mental handicap has over 400 patients under his supervision. Whereas in hospitals for the mentally ill there are thirty-six nurses for every 100 patients (thirty-two nurses/100 mentally handicapped patients), in non-psychiatric hospitals there are 121 nurses for every 100 patients.

The disparity in resources between psychiatric and non-psychiatric hospitals does not only concern manpower. The average weekly cost of maintaining a patient in an acute ward of a general hospital is just under ninety pounds. In contrast, it takes £30·34 to maintain a mentally ill patient and twenty-eight pounds a mentally handicapped one. Lest it be thought that such discrepancies could be explained by the relatively high cost of the technical aids and elaborate equipment of modern medical care, it is worth noting that while in 1973 it cost £8·18 to feed a patient in a large acute general hospital ward for one week, it only cost £3·58 to feed a mentally handicapped patient.

And so the grim realities of the psychiatric services – the dilapidated buildings, the miserable food, the overcrowded wards, the inadequate facilities, the sheer impersonal nature of the hospitals – become comprehensible. These are realities which affect the lives not only of the thousands of patients who are in contact each year with the psychiatric services but of the skilled, semi-skilled, and unskilled personnel who have to make such resources suffice.

Not that the psychiatric services are exactly well staffed. One of the commonest criticisms levelled by patients at psychiatric practice is that it is difficult, if not impossible, to see the same doctor twice and even more difficult to see a doctor who is British-born. It is curious that few members of the general public ever ask why it is that this country is unable to produce enough doctors of its own to staff its much-vaunted health service. The public knows it does not, it dislikes the fact, but it does little about it other than grumble in a non-productive fashion. The problem is that Britain is seriously short of doctors and will remain so at least until the end of the decade. To a very great extent such a deficiency arose from a recommendation of the Willink Committee in 1957 (HM Government 1957) to the effect that the country was producing too many doctors and should reduce its output. (This must rank as the most sagacious prediction since Beveridge forecast that with the development of a national health service there would be a fall in the demand for health care.) So from about 2,100 doctors per year in 1957, output fell to only 1,500 doctors in 1964. By the early 1960s the planners had realized their error and immediately instituted an expansion of existing medical schools and the development of a number of new ones. Not until the end of this decade will the beneficial effects of such an expansion be noted. Until then, the country has to make do with what it produces plus the contribution made by overseas-trained medical personnel.

In Britain, there are approximately 1,200 consultants in psychiatry and another 150 in mental handicap. In addition, there are about 1,000 doctors in training positions in psychiatry. Between 1971 and 1977, the percentage increase in the number of psychiatric consultants has been 22·3, a fact which has eased somewhat the pressure on the specialty. The numbers of junior staff have also expanded dramatically. Nevertheless, there are still certain disquieting features about the manpower situation. First, the proportion of overseas doctors in psychiatry rose from just over one-third in 1965 to over a half in 1972. In 1978, almost one-quarter of the consultants specializing in mental illness had been born overseas while 34 per cent of the senior registrars, 66·8 per cent of the registrars, and 53·7 per cent of the senior house officers were from overseas. Between 1965 and 1972, meanwhile, there was a 12 per cent *drop* in the total number of home-trained doctors in the specialty (i.e. doctors trained in Britain or the Irish Republic). It does appear from a number of studies that medical graduates in Britain are not attracted to psychiatry as a career and are turning to other areas of medicine and particularly to general practice. Less than 5 per cent of final year medical graduates indicate psychiatry as their career of first choice whereas 32 per cent nominate general practice as their first-choice (Parkhouse and Palmer 1979).

Does it matter very much that overseas-trained doctors are replacing home-trained graduates in psychiatric posts and that the psychiatric services, in the words of Henry Miller (1973), operate 'by courtesy of the medical schools of Madras and Bombay'? I personally believe that the increasing dependence on overseas doctors poses very serious problems for the practice of psychiatry. First, it is clear that many doctors from overseas come here without any intention to take up the subject. They come here to obtain a higher qualification in medicine, surgery, or obstetrics, but because they have little money and are at a disadvantage when competing with home-trained graduates for the better training posts they have to be content with taking positions in less well-endowed hospitals, posts that British medical graduates would not touch under any circumstances. Peripheral posts in psychiatry are among the easiest in medicine to obtain and it is not difficult to see why an overseas doctor, frustrated in his ambition to continue his postgraduate training in medicine, surgery, or obstetrics, might find himself forced to choose between taking a psychiatric position and staying in Britain or returning home empty-handed. Perinpanayagam has put the problem with almost painful honesty:

'Having chosen a field he is least interested to work in, befuddled by the terminology of dynamically orientated psychiatry, perplexed by the anxiety-provoking interview of an acute psychiatric admission ward, lacking fluency in the English language, let alone familiarity with the English culture and idiom, the postgraduate tries hard to put on a bold front, masking his chronic anxiety created by apprehension as to when he will succeed in obtaining a job of his choice and securing the goal he originally had.'

(Perinpanayagam 1973: 11)

Peter Brook, in his detailed study of psychiatrists in training (1973), found that one-quarter of the trainee psychiatrists who had graduated overseas did not regard themselves as committed to psychiatry and over one-third of these had come to Britain with no intention of entering psychiatry.

Having taken a post in a peripheral hospital, the overseas trainee finds himself at an even greater disadvantage, *vis-à-vis* the home-trained graduate, when it comes to tackling the membership examination of the Royal College of Psychiatrists, the trainee's 'ticket' to a consultancy. *Tables 2* and *3* outline the fortunes of trainees in the first few 'MRCPsych' examinations held. It is clear that one does not need a computer to deduce that if a trainee is white, home-trained, and a senior registrar at the Maudsley Hospital or one of the country's better teaching hospitals or university departments his chances of passing the membership examination are almost twice those of a coloured, overseas-trained medical assistant in a peripheral mental hospital. Only about 20 per cent of all psychiatric trainees work in teaching hospitals, but of these 90 per cent are British-born medical

Table 2 *MRCPsych pass rate by country of origin (per cent)*

origin	Exam I (no. 323)	Exam II (no. 371)	Exam III (no. 337)	Exam IV (no. 137)	Exam V (no. 115)	Exam VI (no. 117)	Exam VII (no. 105)
UK/Republic of Ireland, Australasia, South Africa	80	84	79	78	84	72	77
UAR, Indian sub-continent	47	44	48	73	18	48	18
other	*	*	*	*	*	*	*

* Indicates numbers too small for analysis

Table 3 *MRCPsych pass rate in relation to most senior posts held by country of origin (per cent) (first three examinations held)*

post held	United Kingdom, etc.	Indian/ Arab	other	all candidates
Consultant	81	65·5*	**	77
Senior Registrar/ Lecturer	84	58	64*	79
Registrar/ SHO/Clinical Assistant	83	40	78*	67
SHMO/ Medical Assistant	66	37*	**	55

* Indicates percentages based on small numbers of candidates
** Indicates numbers too small for analysis

graduates and only 10 per cent are from overseas (Russell 1972). Thus there is plenty of evidence to support the Royal Commission on Medical Education in its view that 'the defects and deficiencies of the present system bear more hardly on the overseas doctors who have great difficulty in securing appointments to posts which would provide a good training' (HM Government 1966).

Other commentators (Freeman 1974; Mahapatra 1975) have drawn attention to what one psychiatrist has termed the 'stage army' of junior doctors from overseas who will never qualify for eventual appointment as consultants. The College of Psychiatrists may believe that in failing these trainees in the membership examination it is protecting the public from the possible consequences of their professional inadequacies. The DHSS, too, probably consoles itself that the goats are weeded out from the sheep before any harm is done. Yet, as anyone familiar with the way psychiatry is practised in reality knows, it is the junior doctor who has day-to-day contact with the psychiatrically ill patient and in very many instances the responsibility he carries is in practice greater than consultants and the DHSS are ever prepared to admit. It is somewhat typical of the bureaucrat (be he in the College or down at the Elephant and Castle) that he should believe that depriving somebody of a certificate prevents him from doing too much harm. Doubtless, critics will look back in a decade's time with disbelief at a system that seduced doctors from abroad with promises of excellent postgraduate training, diverted them into the worst-staffed and equipped areas of the psychiatric service, allowed them to diagnose and treat patients during their three or four years 'training', and then, after charging them £70 plus for the dubious honour of sitting the membership examination, decreed that they were not competent to practise psychiatry after all.

Those countries that supply Britain with most of its psychiatric junior staff are relatively impoverished themselves and have for the most part rudimentary services (*Table 4*). How long this country can go on exploiting the medical graduates of India, Pakistan, and the African Continent under the guise of providing postgraduate psychiatric training remains to be seen. If the Royal College of Psychiatrists means business with its hospital approval policy (the College is currently visiting psychiatric hospitals and units and refusing to approve posts as suitable for its membership examination in those with inadequate facilities) and its membership examination, then the outlook for the bulk of overseas trainees is grim. It is also likely to be grim, in the short-term at least, for those hospitals and areas that currently rely almost entirely on overseas staff to maintain their services.

The Committee of Inquiry into the Regulation of the Medical Profession, under the chairmanship of the Vice-Chancellor of Bristol University, Dr A. W. Merrison, took note of 'the widespread belief that present conditions of registration of foreign doctors are unsatisfactory' (HM Government 1975). As a result of its deliberations, the Temporary Registration Assessment Board tests (Trab tests) were

Table 4 *Number of psychiatrists per population of 200,000 in various countries*

country	psychiatrists per 200,000 pop.	no. of psychiatrists	population (millions)
USSR	22·4	20,000 (not clearly defined)	178·4
Denmark	20	409	4·0
Norway	20	350	3·8
USA	19	19,000	201·5
Finland	13	300	4·6
United Kingdom	8·5	2,400 (includes trainees)	55·2
Japan	7	3,548	101·6
Yugoslavia	3·2	315	20·2
West Indies	1·8	40	4·5
India	0·8	200	511·3
Tanzania	0·03	2 (fully trained)	12·5
Kenya	0·02	1	10·2

Compiled from *A Directory of World Psychiatry* (World Psychiatric Association)

introduced in 1975 to test overseas doctors' professional knowledge and knowledge of English. The rate of failure in this test has been in excess of 65 per cent since their introduction. The difficulties experienced by nurses working with and patients treated by some doctors from overseas are neatly illustrated in an excerpt from evidence given to the Committee by the Royal College of Nursing:

'Reference was made by several members to the danger of medical instructions, given either in writing or verbally, being misinterpreted by nurses when the use of English is poor. The use of the telephone to relay messages also presents a problem when there is a language difficulty and evidence of the wrong diagnosis being given, as well as misunderstanding about both the admission and discharge of patients, has been referred to . . . Misunderstandings readily occur between the patient and the doctor when the doctor does not speak English competently; explaining the nature of an operation, discussing the patient's condition and interviewing relatives, present particular problems. Doctors who do not speak English well present a particular difficulty in psychiatric hospitals where the face to face interview between the doctor and the patient is an essential part of diagnostic and treatment procedure. An example was given of the doctor from abroad who interpreted the use of colloquialisms by the patient as a sign of confusion and disorientation . . . The ethical principles and cultural background peculiar to the United Kingdom give rise to a great deal of difficulty for doctors from certain countries where values and principles are different . . . It is the view of the RCN that overseas doctors are given very little introduction into hospital life, its management, policies and procedures.'

(HM Government 1975: 60, paragraph 184)

For the overseas doctor in a hospital post affording little opportunity for training, the possibility of his improving his English and developing his skill and knowledge to the required level is a slim one indeed. However, those home-trained doctors (and the relatively few overseas-trained) who do obtain reasonable training posts in psychiatry do not necessarily acquire a suitably broad-based psychiatric training either. Brook's study (1973) found that less than two-fifths of his trainees were satisfied with their training in psychotherapy while only one-third felt that they had had sufficient exposure to behaviour therapy techniques to enable them to make effective use of such methods in practice. Half of the trainees reported receiving no training whatsoever in the diagnosis and management of alcohol and drug abuse, and the situation with regard to forensic psychiatry, psycho-geriatrics, and mental subnormality was even worse. Brook's finding that almost two-thirds of his samples of registrars and senior registrars were extremely dissatisfied with their training experience in community psychiatry bodes ill for the Departmental plans to turn the average psychiatrist into a catchment-area-based, community-orientated practitioner.

Why do British-trained doctors shun psychiatry as a career? Such lack of interest appears, at first glance, to be somewhat surprising. It is taking place at a time when psychiatry has become well established as a major subject in the average undergraduate medical curriculum and when postgraduate training in the subject is expanding. Over the past decade and a half, most of the country's medical schools have established academic departments of psychiatry, although the London teaching hospitals, in this as in so much else, have chosen to demonstrate their innate wisdom and superiority by lagging behind the rest of the country, so that even now a number of them have relatively small teaching staffs (Guy's, King's College, and Charing Cross have only just appointed Professors, but St Thomas's, doubtless awaiting guidance from above, proudly stands aloof from this Gadarene rush). The past twenty years have witnessed remarkable advances in drug treatments, in group and individual psychotherapy, in social methods of treatment, and in the application of behavioural methods to the management of psychiatric disturbance. More patients than ever are being treated in units attached to general hospitals and in conditions far more attractive than those in the older and isolated mental hospitals. In short, while psychiatry is still a specialty with many problems and few resources it is a specialty on the move, and one would expect that such a momentum would be reflected in a flurry of interest among newly trained doctors rather than the reverse.

Gerald Russell, Professor of Psychiatry at the Royal Free Hospital Medical School, has been particularly concerned at the drop in British recruitment into psychiatry and has suggested two 'part-explanations':

'The first lies in the excessive clinical burden imposed on psychiatrists whose prime professional satisfaction is derived from unhurried personal contact with their patients. The second stems from the discouragement given to potential recruits by the Department of Health and Social Security whose message has been that career prospects in psychiatry are bleak.' (Russell 1973a: 8)

Russell has expanded on these two factors in a number of trenchant articles. His argument is that the development and expansion of psychiatric services have not been matched by a comparable expansion in manpower. Indeed, in the face of such an expansion of work-load, the DHSS *froze* expansion of staff. Official discouragement was conveyed to potential recruits by means of the so-called 'league tables' which the DHSS published at first in the *Lancet* and the *British Medical Journal* and later in its own publication *Health Trends*. (Such tables indicate those specialties, such as radiology and anaesthetics, in which a demand exists for doctors, i.e., in which promotion to consultancy would be rapid, and those, such as internal medicine, in which promotion would be slow.) As recently as August 1972, *Health Trends* was stating that there exists a 'large surplus' in the supply of psychiatric trainees, a view that formed the basis of the Department's refusal to expand the number of junior posts in the specialty. Since that time, the policy has been relaxed. The Department had previously claimed that there were enough junior doctors in post to 'feed' consultant vacancies as they appeared or were created as part of the consultant expansion programme. However, it is clear that their formula did not take into account 'wastage' caused by junior doctors moving into other specialties, going into general practice after a short period in psychiatry, or leaving psychiatry (and medicine) altogether (the last group includes many women leaving for domestic reasons, doctors going into non-NHS posts such as private practice, insurance, and drug companies, and doctors emigrating).

Not all commentators agree that it is the combination of career prospects and overwork that has deterred potential recruits. The psychotherapist Thomas Freeman (1974) has argued that 'a fad for natural science methodology, an uncritical advocacy of biochemical theories of mental illness and a magical relief in the curative powers of chemotherapy' have put off intending psychiatrists when they are told that these constitute the fundamentals of psychiatry. He believes that potential recruits are disenchanted by an extreme emphasis on the biological and a disregard for the patient as a person. He goes further:

'The disillusionment with psychiatry which is so widespread in medical circles is the final expression of the lack of balance which has characterised British psychiatry over the last 50 years. Psychoanalysis was rejected and then allowed to split off from the main stream. This has led to the most serious consequences for the development of psychiatry.'   (Freeman 1974: 11)

Amongst these consequences, Freeman names the devaluation of the importance of the doctor–patient relationship, the value of which has been increasingly questioned by sociologists, social workers, and psychologists, and the sterility that he believes is a feature of clinical data 'deprived of psychoanalytical concepts and explanation'.

Is there any evidence to support Freeman's contention? The studies of Walton (1963, 1966), Kreitman (1962), Pallis and Stoffelmayer (1973) (referred to in more detail in Chapter 1) do suggest that psychiatry does attract those doctors who are more interested in and open to abstract ideas and concepts, who are less interested in somatic and biological factors, and who have more radical and questioning social attitudes. It could be argued that, with the growth of academic undergraduate teaching and the exposure of medical students to a psychiatry whose exponents lay emphasis more on those aspects of the subject that bind it to medicine (its biological and somatic aspects) than on those that distinguish it as a specialty in its own right, potential recruits might well be deterred.

Peter Brook was sufficiently intrigued to learn more about what it is that determines a doctor to take up a psychiatric career that he asked the 146 trainees in his study to rank those items that affected their choice. Far and away the most important career determinants were the prospective psychiatrist's curiosity about and interest in other people's emotions and actions and his view of psychiatry as an important and interesting branch of medicine. Few doctors were attracted into psychiatry because they thought that it might be antipathetic to other branches of medicine or to the scientific and biological bases of medicine in general – a finding which casts doubt on Freeman's viewpoint. Also against Freeman's case is the fact that one hospital which has over the years provided more than its fair share of recruits is St Thomas's Hospital. No one who has heard William Sargant teach could harbour the illusion that there the tenets of psychoanalysis flourished. His impassioned advocacy of biochemical theories of mental illness and his faith in the efficacy of physical treatments do not appear to have had the effect, predicted by Freeman, of deterring recruits to the specialty. Indeed Sargant's success suggests that what attracts doctors into psychiatry is a stimulating presentation of its possibilities, in one or other of its areas of concern, rather than any particular ideological orientation on the part of the teachers.

According to *Time* magazine, the Americans face a similar problem. US psychiatry relies heavily on overseas psychiatrists to staff its large, over-crowded and antiquated mental hospitals. Even with the foreign-trained, it is estimated that the country will be short 9,000 psychiatrists by 1980 while at the present time there are 3,200 unfilled psychiatric posts at the state hospitals (*Time* 1979). While the United States boasts 27,000 psychiatrists, a remarkable expansion given that it managed to survive on 5,800 in 1950, the signs are that psychiatry as a career there has lost some of its attraction. Today, between 4 and 5 per cent of medical school graduates go into psychiatry which, while higher than the equivalent

British figure, is sharply down on the level of 12 per cent recorded in 1970.

One explanation put forward for the lack of appeal possessed by psychiatry is that it offers neither money nor status. In the flourishing days of American psychoanalysis just after the war, a career as a private analyst brought both. However, psychoanalysis in that part of the world is losing its appeal (a 1976 survey by the American Psychoanalytical Association showed that the average analyst had only 4·7 patients under treatment compared with the 6·2 of a decade earlier) and psychiatrists now rank relatively low on the medical pay scale with an average annual income of $47,565, far behind that of surgeons, $73,245 and only slightly above GPs, $47,438.

In Britain, the past decade has seen a dramatic improvement in the GP's financial position at a time when the hospital doctor, trainee and consultant, has benefited hardly at all. Developments in general practice training have meant that today's trainee GP can acquire considerable knowledge and some skill relating to the management of much of the overall pool of psycho-social morbidity in the community. It is therefore understandable that a newly qualified doctor who has an interest in psychiatry, who would like to be reasonably well paid, have an organized working life without on-call duties, have a modest degree of status and the ability to retain some personal contact with and responsibility for his patients (in a way that is becoming increasingly difficult for many psychiatric consultants to do), should enter upon a career in general practice.

Plans for the future

It was Enoch Powell, with a characteristic piece of inspirational rhetoric, who provided the thrust behind the swing away from hospital-based to community-based psychiatric services. His address to the annual conference of MIND (the National Association of Mental Health) in 1961 resulted in the formulation of a ten-year plan which has since become somewhat elongated in terms of time and altered in terms of content but which nonetheless still dominates political and professional thinking on the organization and the delivery of psychiatric care at the present time. His evocative description of the large, decrepit, and physically decaying mental hospitals gave the speech the 'water-tower' epithet by which it has since come to be known:

'There they stand, isolated, majestic, imperious, brooded over by the gigantic water-tower and chimney combined, rising unmistakable and daunting out of the countryside ... It is out of duty to err on the side of ruthlessness. For the great majority of these establishments there is no appropriate use.' (Powell 1961)

Despite Powell's 'ruthlessness', the great majority of these establishments are with us to this day and it is a matter of some controversy within and outside psychiatry as to the appropriateness not so much of their use but of their abolition. Powell's speech, nonetheless, heralded the publication, the following year, of *A Hospital Plan for England and Wales* which envisaged a reduction in the number of hospital beds for the mentally ill from the level of 2·91 beds per 1,000 of the population to 1·8 per 1,000 by 1975 (HM Government 1962). In 1971 the Department of Health Memorandum, *Hospital Services for the Mentally Ill*, foresaw a further reduction to 0·5 bed per 1,000, the gradual phasing-out of the large mental hospitals, and their replacement by psychiatric units attached to district general hospitals. A total of 230 psychiatric units is currently envisaged, from which therapeutic teams, one for every 60,000 of the population, will operate. Of central importance to the plan is the development of non-hospital, community-based facilities:

'Another main element is the provision of adequate community services by local authorities, for example, social work services, homes for the elderly, hostels, group homes and supervised lodging schemes. Without this an effective community service cannot be provided.'

(Department of Health and Social Security 1971)

Support for the new DHSS policy derived from a number of sources. The majority of psychiatrists desired to be recognized as clinicians within the mainstream of medicine and saw the promised transfer of their centre of work from the isolated mental hospitals to new units situated alongside their medical and surgical colleagues as tangible evidence of such recognition. The public demand for treatment nearer their home, the predicted decline in bed usage, and the progressively developing pattern of multiple, short admissions all contributed to the positive response given to the new plan. Economic considerations also counted – it made more sense to treat psychiatric patients on the sites of existing general hospitals than to duplicate hospitals and their ancillary staff. It was also the hope that a vigorous community approach to treatment might further reduce the need for hospital treatment and thereby reduce hospital costs.

It was intended that the mental hospitals be replaced by psychiatric units placed in District General Hospitals supported by small, local in-patient units and by an enhanced provision of services in the community. In the words of the Royal Commission on the National Health Service, 'the feasibility of this has not yet been demonstrated'. The relatively small size of the DGH units, the lack of money to create more of them and the nature and extent of the patient populations making demands on the psychiatric services have frustrated the plans. Since the unfolding of the plan in 1962, only one large mental hospital in England and Wales has closed while only one district has developed a 'hospital hostel' for the long-term mentally ill individual in need of permanent support.

Departmental planning has also depended on an increased provision of facilities in the community by local authorities. Such provision, as we shall see later, has fallen short of expectations. A very similar picture exists on the other side of the Atlantic. America's Enoch Powell was John F. Kennedy who in the early 1960s sent mental health marching into the community to make a 'full-scale attack' on the twin foes of mental illness and mental retardation (Kennedy 1963). Community Mental Health Centers were established to serve the psychiatric needs of all citizens within a large (75,000–200,000 person) population-defined geographic area. The CMHCs were charged not only with treating the identified patient population but also with serving the mentally ill who do not come for treatment, preventing mental illness in the potentially ill in the community and improving the mental health of the rest of the community. While this innovation did lead to some energy and innovation being injected into mental health care, by the late 1960s, according to one observer, some CMH professionals 'began to lose perspective' (Borus 1978) and, instead of providing needed services, made direct attempts under the banner of prevention to change society by organizing protests against social ills, instructing community leaders on what to do and involving themselves in other activities 'clearly beyond their professional expertise'. Robert Okin, the Commissioner for Mental Health for the State of Massachusetts, has drawn attention to the fact that despite the findings that prompted CMHC legislation in the first place, the community mental health statute has not until recently focused adequately on the needs of the chronically ill population:

'For example, residential services and vocational rehabilitation, both essential for the disabled patient, had not been considered until last year "essential services" within the legislation. Influenced by this . . . CMHCs have often allocated only a small percentage of their resources to the chronic psychiatric patient. Although the most recent version of the CMHC statute has been modified to include a requirement that CMHCs provide services to the chronic patient, no new monies were appropriated for this purpose.'
(Okin 1978)

By June 1978, there were 675 funded CMHCs in the US. According to Steven Sharfstein, Director of the Mental Health Service Programs at the National Institute of Mental Health, there is clear evidence that the programme is actually changing from delivering treatment and care for serious mental illness to providing services for the socially 'maladjusted'. (Sharfstein 1978). Complementing such a shift, there was a marked fall in the numbers of medically-trained personnel working in the CMHCs. In 1970, there were on average 6·8 full-time equivalent psychiatrists per CMHC but by 1975 this had fallen to 4·3. The number of registered nurses decreased from 9·7 full-time equivalents per CMHC in 1970 to 8·9 in 1975. During the same time, however, the numbers of psychologists increased from 4·9 full-time equivalents per CHMC to 8·5 and social workers from 9·1 to 12·2 (Sharfstein 1978).

Although the CMHC programme in the US has received considerable publicity, it actually provides care for a relatively small proportion of the total pool of psychiatric morbidity. In the US, it has been estimated that 4·9 million people (2·3 per cent of the population) used the specialized mental health services in 1973. Of this 4·9 million,

'4·1% ... are treated by private practice psychiatrists; 43·4% are treated in general medical care settings; 8·4% in Community Mental Health Centers; 10·4% in general hospitals; 15·6% in free-standing out-patient, campus, multiservice and military clinics; 6·8% in State and County mental hospitals; 2·5% in other public mental hospitals; 1·3% in private mental hospitals; 3·8% in nursing homes; 1·3% in rehabilitation facilities and half-way houses; 1·2% in children's programs; and 1·2% by private practice psychologists.'   (Regier and Goldberg 1976: 19)

But this is merely the tip of the iceberg, that small proportion of people who receive treatment from the specialized services. The vast majority of emotionally stressed people do not see psychiatrists. This fact has led some observers, such as Aldrich (1967) to argue for greater access to psychiatrists for all and others, such as Shepherd, to encourage 'the strengthening of the family doctor in his therapeutic role' so that no more patients and perhaps even less might require the skills of expensively trained psychiatrists (Shepherd *et al.* 1966).

How much of a psychiatrist's work could be done by other personnel? What is it that the psychiatrist, as distinct from social workers, clinical psychologists, psychiatric nurses and general practitioners, do and should do? In response to the shortage of psychiatrists, there has been a growing number of observers of the psychiatric scene who share Shepherd's view and suggest that the primary care physician, i.e. the GP in the British system, and the family physician as he is known in the US, can be a pivotal person in the mental health care system.

The general practitioner

In the developed countries, general practitioners (or primary care physicians as they are often termed, reflecting the fact that they are the doctors of first contact) represent about one-half of all medical practitioners involved in clinical patient care. In the British National Health Service there are approximately 26,000 general practitioners compared to 11,000 hospital consultants or specialists and 20,000 junior hospital doctors. In the United States, although the proportion of family physicians, as general practitioners tend to be called, has fallen to represent less than 30 per cent of all clinicians, when internists, paediatricians, and other medical specialists who provide primary, direct-access, first-contact care are included, then the proportion of true primary physicians is over 50 per cent (Fry and Gambrill 1978). The average consultation rates per person in Britain are between three and four visits per year compared with between four and five in the US. In any year, the family physician can expect to see 60–70 per cent of all the patients in his practice at least once a year. Given that the average British general practice has a patient list of around 2,500, the time per visit which the GP can give to each patient is not long, averaging between five and ten minutes. There is, however remarkable variation.

Figures suggest that in a year, the average GP will deal with 200 minor emotional illnesses; that twelve patients will present with severe depressions; that he will refer eleven patients for psychiatric advice and four to child guidance clinics; and ten of his patients will be admitted to psychiatric wards or hospitals. Fifty-five of his patients with recurrent or chronic mental illnesses will be living in the community and he would be likely to have five patients with severe mental handicap on his list.

The attitudes of family doctors to psychiatric patients and problems vary from intense personal interest to active dislike. The situation, today, is almost certainly a more positive one than when Shepherd and his colleagues conducted their survey of general practice in London, in the course of which they assessed the attitude to psychiatric patients held by the participating GPs:

'One was altogether averse to psychiatry, and blamed psychiatrists for encouraging neurotic patients to avoid their responsibilities; the second stated that the neurotic patients on his lists were so few and so easily identifiable as to render any systematic study unnecessary; the third commented simply that all neurotic patients were ungrateful and that there was nothing to be done for them.'

(Shepherd et al. 1966)

It should not be thought that GPs have a monopoly of such ill-informed views. Many psychiatrists, particularly those who interpret narrowly their professional brief as one of diagnosing and treating psychotically ill patients, often show a marked antipathy to neurotic patients. How far antipathetic views in general practice reflect an ignorance of psychiatry, a shortage of time, or a lack of interest and enthusiasm is unclear. Nor is it clear whether a general practitioner, adequately trained in psychiatry, refers more or less patients for specialized psychiatric consultations than his less well-trained colleague. On the one hand, one might expect the better-informed GP to treat more patients himself; on the other hand, such a psychiatrically oriented practitioner might well uncover more psychiatric morbidity within his practice and, while taking more personal clinical responsibility might actually *increase* his referral rate as well. What seems clear is that a family doctor, given the weight of psychiatric morbidity that does present in the average practice, is under an obligation to possess more than the rudiments of psychiatric knowledge and skills.

There is a consensus growing on both sides of the Atlantic, different methods of organizing health care notwithstanding, 'that the inclusion of mental health services as an integral component of primary health care offers the only feasible means of substantially improving the distribution of mental health services for the population as a whole' (Coleman and Patrick 1976: 655). Indeed, the possible advent of a National Health insurance scheme in the United States makes it likely that mental health benefits will be made available to persons who previously could not afford specialized mental health services (Hankin and Oktay 1979). These new benefits may increase the demand on primary care physicians to provide mental health care. Indeed, this point is made by two health care planners at the US National Institute of Mental Health when they declare:

'among the possible effects of national health insurance it appears almost inevitable that primary care physicians will assume a greater or more visible role in the delivery of mental health services. This trend may also be accelerated by the relative increase in the percent of medical school graduates entering family practice and the corresponding decrease in the percent entering psychiatry.'

(Regier and Goldberg 1976: 15)

However, given that many patients already go to family doctors in Britain and America with psychiatric problems and that more can be expected to do so in future, what can the family doctor, given various constraints on his time and knowledge, do for them? Three principal modes of treatment are available to the GP: the psycho-pharmacological, i.e. drugs; the psychological, i.e. talking and listening to the patient, expressing sympathy, explaining and interpreting his symptoms, and reassuring him; and social treatments which involve attempts to modify directly the patient's social environment. While each of these approaches has a prominent position in the provision of primary mental health care, it is worth noting a World Health Organisation report and its comments on this topic:

'Transcending in importance these three broad methods of treatment, there are certain general needs, such as a tolerant attitude, dependability, continuity, an interest that allows the doctor to take even minor disorders seriously, and attention to the needs of close relatives of the patient.'

(WHO 1973: 11)

The great problem with pharmacological treatments in general practice is that which bedevils their use in psychiatry itself. Because it takes little time to write out a prescription (it is also a very effective method of terminating an interview), the use of drugs in general practice threatens to get out of hand. There is no doubt that the development of a number of effective drugs in psychiatry has greatly strengthened the general practitioner's ability to deal with many minor and even some major psychiatric disorders. However, the proliferation of such drugs and the ready ease with which they can be prescribed, have given rise to a new set of problems. Many general practitioners are insufficiently versed in the indications for individual drugs, their correct dosages, and their possible side-effects.

Current trends in the use of psychotropic drugs reflect the

growing anxiety about excess prescribing (Parish 1971). In England, during 1975, over 45 million prescriptions were written for such drugs (15·3 per cent of all prescriptions) at a cost of over £25 millions. Not all these drugs are prescribed for psychiatric reasons (Williams 1978) but it seems reasonable to suppose that the majority of them are. Yet there is surprisingly little in the way of unequivocal research results to indicate that these drugs are effective in the treatment of the sorts of psychiatric disturbances seen by general practitioners. In Britain, the General Practice Research Group has carried out some useful attempts to evaluate scientifically such drugs (Wheatley 1972). The main aim of the GPRG was 'to try and determine the most suitable drugs for the treatment of the type of case seen by the general practitioner'. The main therapeutic conclusions arising out of several years of work make sobering reading however. The first emphasises the importance of therapeutic faith in the role of drugs on the part of the general practitioner, a conclusion which may well be of importance to any doctor anxious to evaluate his own role in treating psychiatric ill-health. The second emphasises the fact that 'none of the new drugs that we have investigated has proved to be significantly better than the two standard drugs, namely chlordiazepoxide (Librium) in anxiety and amitryptiline (Tryptizol) in depression'.

It is worth emphasising that minor emotional illnesses are notoriously subject to suggestion or reassurance and are responsive to change. They are thus sensitive to placebo and display a high rate of spontaneous remission. Patients in general practice with minor emotional states display a placebo response rate of around 50 per cent in various drug studies compared with active drug response rates of about 75 per cent. Blackwell, in the United States, points out that it is more than likely that the busy general practitioner who makes a habit of ending each interview with a prescription will be gratified and rewarded by the response that many patients report. 'Too often neither the patient nor the doctor pauses to examine the role played by inquiry, discussion and re-assurance' (Blackwell 1973).

In reaction to what appears to be a prevailing tendency towards drug-orientated therapy, some general practitioners have adapted certain relatively formal methods of psycho-therapy to the general-practice situation. In Britain, the strongest single influence in this direction has been that of 'Balint groups', based on the seminars for general practitioners held for many years at the Tavistock Clinic in London (Balint 1957). A related line of development has been the application in general practice of Eric Berne's 'transactional analysis' (1964). Commenting on such trends, the WHO Report (on Psychiatry and Primary Health Care) observes:

'The drift of a small number of general practitioners into psychotherapy, as into other specialties, is unavoidable, and relatively unimportant. The crucial point is that the great majority of general practitioners, with no special interest in psychotherapy, should be competent to under-stand and to tolerate their patients' behaviour, even when markedly deviant; and that they should be prepared to give sympathy, advice and reassurance in all cases. The extent to which individual practitioners fulfil these requirements varies enormously, and must be considered a product of personality, training and conditions of service. The most important need appears to be increased attention to be-havioural studies in both undergraduate and postgraduate medical education.'   (WHO 1973: 13)

It seems clear, therefore, that the general practitioner, or the primary care physician as he is coming to be known, can and must play a crucial role in the recognition and treat-ment of psychiatric ill-health. The Royal College of General Practitioners has shown a keen awareness of this fact and has already inaugurated a number of programmes designed to improve the proficiency of the latest generation of family doctors in the management of such patients.

The social worker

The psychiatric social worker, as Jansen (1972: 647) recently recounted it, was born in the 1930s, 'the "natural" child of Psychiatrist and Social Worker, having a mutual need to share some of their skills in treating the mentally ill and their relatives'. Over the next three decades this hybrid prospered, so that by 1967, according to an estimate made by the Seebohm Committee, approximately 180,000 patients were receiving psychiatric social work assistance and there was approximately one Mental Health Social Worker per 33,000 population in England and Wales. (At that time, there was one social worker of all types – children's officers, welfare officers, mental health workers, etc. – per 20,000 population.) Until quite recently the majority of psychiatric social workers were based on hospitals and clinics. With the Seebohm Report and the *Social Services Act* of 1970, psychiatric social workers, children's officers, social workers with specialist knowledge of the aged, the physically handicapped, and the subnormal, were merged and a new 'generic' social worker to replace the specialist was born. With the reorganization of the National Health Service, the hospital-based social worker came under the aegis of the new Area Health Authorities, so that now social workers work a generic philosophy and are, for the most part, based in the community.

Such a transfer has not been without its headaches. There have been complaints, particularly from psychiatrists, that as a consequence of the abolition of the specialist social worker and the promotion of experienced social workers into the many top-level administrative posts created during the reorganization, the level of psychiatric expertise possessed by social workers in the field is lamentably low. The ratio of qualified to unqualified social workers has definitely fallen. Less than 15 per cent of local authorities surveyed by MIND could boast a ratio approaching the minimum standard laid down by that organization. The DHSS, in its response to such criticism, points out that these are difficult, transitional times, but by the 1980s there will be sufficient trained social workers to cope with the demand. In the meantime, a handful, relatively speaking, of trained social workers, many of whom perhaps expert in the management of child care problems or of the physically handicapped, have to cope with an awesome load of problems, ranging from the committal of patients to mental hospitals and placing children in care, to assessing the complicity of parents in possible cases of baby battering and providing after-care support for psychiatric patients precipitately discharged from hospital.

A strong positive association exists between psychiatric ill-health and various forms of social difficulty (Cooper 1972; Sylph, Kedward, and Eastwood 1969). A large proportion of clients who present to social workers in local authority social services departments suffer from emotional stress (Corney and Briscoe 1977). Studies of social work attachments to general practice have shown that while a large section of the general population consult their GP for guidance and support on a wide range of social and psychological problems most GPs have little contact with any social agency (Harwin *et al.* 1970) and are unsure of the social worker's role (Ratoff *et al.* 1973). There have now been several experiments which have shown how attaching a social worker to a general practice overcomes these obstacles and can be of value whether the social worker focuses especially on psychiatric illness (Cooper *et al.* 1974) or a mixed caseload (Collins 1965; Cooper 1971).

Clearly, there is considerable research support for closer liaison between medical and social services in the community. Whereas Ratoff and his colleagues (1973) found that the majority of schemes involving co-operation between social workers and doctors were in the hospital services, the situation appears to be changing and a recent survey (Gilchrist *et al.* 1978) showed that over half the local authorities in Britain now have attachment schemes involving social workers working alongside general practitioners. It is sad, therefore, to find a review of the opinions of social workers concerning their subject which, in so far as it considers social work – general practitioner liaison at all, does so in almost entirely negative terms (DHSS 1978). However, the next decade may well see a dramatic increase in the shift of social work treatment from local authority settings and to the setting of the primary health care team.

The psychologist

Until recently, the majority of the 690 clinical psychologists working within the National Health Service did so in the hospital system. Success in the management of severe anxiety states, phobic reactions, and obsessive-compulsive disorders has encouraged some of them to move out into the community to see if their particular approaches, and especially behavioral treatments such as desensitisation, relaxation and operant conditioning, would be of value in the management of the less severe and the less specific neurotic disorders presenting there. Davidson (1977) has found considerable interest among GPs of one London borough in the notion of direct access to psychological services and in working with psychologists on the exchange of ideas. Broadhurst (1977), in a postal survey of clinical psychologists, found generally favourable reactions to the idea of working closely with GPs. However, further research is required before any reasonable estimate of the nature and extent of the psychologist's contribution can be made. There are some grounds for caution. One study, by Johnston (1978), reporting on the attachment of a clinical psychologist to practices covering 30,000 patients, found that there were 119 referrals over eighteen months, of which nineteen were agoraphobics, twenty-four were other behavioural problems, and the remainder were composed of undifferentiated anxiety states, sexual and marital difficulties, problems coping with bereavement, difficulties in relationships, and physical ill-health. Such a figure represents a very small proportion of the total amount of such morbidity which could be expected to exist in such a practice population.

The move towards the development of the primary health care team has been facilitated in recent years by changes in the organization of general practice itself. In the British NHS, the past decade has seen the growth of group practice, health centres and teamwork. In 1976, only 20 per cent of general practitioners were still working in a single-handed fashion. All others were working in groups, 40 per cent in groups of two or three physicians, 30 per cent in groups of four or five and 10 per cent in groups of six or more. One in five GPs were working from purpose-built health centres and the numbers are rising each year. 'Co-operation between physicians, nurses, social workers and secretaries', observe Fry and Gambrill (1978), 'has created primary care health teams which now are the pattern in the NHS'.

In contrast, the primary care system of medical care in the United States has been described as a 'non-system' (Hankin and Oktay 1979). Contrary to the British NHS and other European systems with one entry point for care (the general practitioner), Americans have several entry points. They may seek care from a multitude of sites including private office-based physicians or neighbourhood health centers or specialty care directly without first receiving a referral from the primary care physician. Nonetheless, there are distinct signs that the United States was one of the countries it had in mind when the WHO Group on Psychiatry in General Practice concluded: 'It seems probable that the general practitioner, or somebody like him, will emerge as the leading figure in primary medical care in most countries and that he will play a major role in mental health care' (WHO 1973: 27).

One probable impetus behind the new emphasis on primary medical care in the United States is the rising cost of specialist care. The lower overheads and charges of primary care compare favourably with the more expensive hospital and specialist settings. Compared with other countries, there is no overall physician shortage in the US (there are 114 doctors per 100,000 people compared with 100 per 100,000 in Britain) but there are serious inequalities in the distribution of doctors through the nation. However, according to Robert Smith, Director of the Department of Family Medicine at the University of Cincinnati, the new graduates of residency training in family medicine in the US are increasingly choosing practice sites in smaller communities and a recent study shows that 54 per cent of new family physician graduates have set up practice in towns of 30,000 and 89 per cent in towns of under 100,000 (Smith 1978). By 1977, 100 of the 120 American medical schools had established educational programmes in family medicine and over 4,500 residents were in training in 340 separate residency programmes. Whether the family physician approach represents a more co-ordinated, a more rational and a more practical approach to the problem of delivering care to that proportion of the population presenting with psychosocial problems than the more ambitious Community Mental Health Center approach remains to be seen. One advantage of developing a mental health care system which encourages the bulk of patients with psychiatric problems to seek and receive help from a primary health care individual and/or team is that it avoids not just the expense of specialized psychiatric treatment but the major stigma associated with psychiatric treatment which still persists.

Community resources

When Enoch Powell, back at the beginning of what has been since termed the 'decade of rhetoric' (*New Psychiatry*, October 3, 1974), announced the beginning of what he termed 'a colossal undertaking' he made it plain that there would have to be radical changes in the organization and funding of the mental health services and he focussed on one issue which, all these years later, has a contemporary ring:

> 'A hospital plan makes no sense unless the medical profession outside the hospital service . . . can be supported . . . by a whole new development of the local authority services for the mentally ill and mentally subnormal.'
>
> (Powell 1961)

Despite Mr Powell's insistence on the absolute necessity of community services, the years which have passed since his stirring appeal have seen the most pessimistic forecasts of the critics of his plan grimly confirmed. Having grandly outlined a new revolution in mental health care, Mr Powell's Government, and those that have succeeded it, have consistently refused, on economic grounds, requests from local authorities for the finances necessary for the development of adequate community-based resources. Indeed, in the face of its own weighty indifference, the DHSS continued to issue a stream of exhortatory documents to stir the workers in the field. Take the 1971 Memorandum, *Hospital Services for the Mentally Ill*, and this observation:

> 'Another main element is the provision of adequate community services by local authorities, for example, social work services, homes for the elderly, hostels, group homes, and supervised lodgings schemes. Without this an effective comprehensive service cannot be provided.'

Shortly after this statement, guidelines were issued to local authorities which estimated a need for 12,000 residential places and 30,000 day-care places for the mentally ill. At the time there were available in the community about 2,100 residential places (plus 1,300 places provided by voluntary organizations) and 3,700 day-care places. This estimate took no account of the further 10,000 mentally ill and 26,000 mentally handicapped patients who could leave hospital at once if some form of accommodation could be found for them in the community. Many local authorities have been anxious to implement these guidelines but have been handicapped by the refusal of the Department of Health and Social Services to grant the necessary loan sanction. Forty-five authorities informed the National Association for Mental Health (through its MIND 1973 survey of community care provisions) that projects for the year 1973–4 had been refused approval and it has been estimated that some seventy capital projects were deferred, amounting to more than £7½ million.

Such cuts in the community programme affect most seriously those least able to find alternative help, namely those chronic patients whose social breakdown is due to intractable psychosis or severe neurotic or personality disorders. Between 1960 and 1969 the psychiatric hospitals closed 24,000 beds: a triumph for modern treatment methods, said its supporters; a disastrous failure to provide asylum, declared its critics. In 1965, approximately 27,000 men and 2,000 women were living in common lodging-houses, hostels, and shelters, and another 1,000 at least were sleeping rough (Tidmarsh 1974). Between 1950 and 1970 the prison population doubled while the number of men remanded for medical reports increased from 5,000 in 1960 to 12,500 in 1970. These numbers continue to rise.

The running-down of the large mental hospitals has not been accompanied by a significant development of community based resources. Instead, there has been overcrowding in the hospitals, a rise in the number of homeless and poorly housed people, and a shift of people from the mental health and into the prison services. The result of such inept planning has been the debasement of the concept of 'community care'. One consultant working in a South Wales hospital which, because of overcrowding, fire risks, and threats to withdraw nurse training recognition in view of the conditions, had to discharge into the community some of its long-stay patients, wrote to MIND:

'There are a dozen or more men attending the day hospital here, most suffering from chronic schizophrenia, who live in bad lodgings, go to bed at 8 pm. and wander the streets at the weekend. I have no doubt that for them discharge from hospital has meant greater hardship, There are probably many others with similar problems we do not know about. Whatever the short-comings of our large old hospitals, it is clear that at the moment they are sometimes providing a better service than the community.'

(*New Psychiatry*, October 3, 1974)

Such a phenomenon is not limited to South Wales. A one-night census of the Camberwell Reception Centre (Edwards *et al.* 1968), one of the largest of such centres in the country, which provides shelter each night for up to 1,000 men, produces further evidence of the effects of a policy that attempts to reduce the number of patients in mental hospitals without at the same time providing a suitable facility for them anywhere else:

> 'Under one roof are being performed the functions of an Old People's Home, lodging house for the itinerant labourer, alcoholism rehabilitation centre, mental after-care hostel, half-way home for the discharged prisoner and perhaps a dozen other functions besides.'

(Edwards *et al.* 1968: 1037)

Approximately 25 per cent of the men seen were physiologically addicted to alcohol and almost half had been arrested at some time for drunkenness. About 25 per cent of the men had been in mental hospitals – 7 per cent within the previous six months – a reflection on the after-care arrangements made for such patients. Almost 60 per cent had served prison sentences, mainly for trivial offences. David Tidmarsh (1974), a consultant psychiatrist at Broadmoor Special Hospital, has drawn attention to the way in which, as the hospital services ease their own burden by discharging into the community, the prison services begin to feel a rise in pressure. This is not a particularly surprising finding – wandering, mentally disturbed, isolated men inevitably run foul of the law as a result of offences ranging from loitering, petty theft, and alcoholism to breaking and entering and assault. When such ex-patients appear in court, magistrates and judges are anxious to see that they receive treatment rather than imprisonment but they find it increasingly difficult and sometimes impossible to obtain beds in the mental hospitals for such mentally disordered offenders. More and more psychiatric hospitals are claiming that they are unable to accept any sort of responsibility for patients whose offences and potentiality for antisocial behaviour give rise to anxiety. This may well be the direct result of what has been termed the 'open door' policy, which has been in the words of one commentator 'the most important single change in the milieu of the psychiatric hospital' (H. Freeman 1965) in the post-war years. Opening the locked wards was partly a consequence of the development of effective treatment methods and partly the belief that locked doors were an affront to the dignity of the patient and reflected badly on the image of a psychiatric hospital as a place of care, support, and relief. Hugh Freeman succinctly describes the development and reflects the enthusiasm that generated the momentum behind it:

'. . . the Open Door movement has steadily grown, so that . . . most doors in nearly all psychiatric hospitals are unlocked. In this respect, Great Britain is probably ahead of any other country. It has now been shown that psychotic patients in general do not need any measures of physical security . . . out of the whole range of psychiatric patients, only a handful require security precautions, and these are mostly problems of personality disorder rather than psychosis. The opening of doors in this country has been greatly helped by the existence of the Special Hospitals (including Broadmoor) where such patients with criminal propensities can be concentrated.'

(Freeman 1956: 24–5)

The wholesale unlocking of wards was seen as a tremendous step forward and as the single most effective factor in altering the image of psychiatric care over the past quarter of a century. But like so many such movements, it had consequences few of its enthusiastic supporters had foreseen. A crucial mistake, and it is made in the account above, is to divide psychiatric patients into the dangerous (i.e., those with criminal propensities and therefore properly treated in the Special Hospitals) and the safe. There are of course both these categories, but there is in addition a third. This group contains people who *at times*, by virtue of their illness or a disturbance in personality, may be potentially dangerous or may indulge in crime of an often petty but repetitive nature; when such people come into contact with the law, the latter, recognizing that they are ill and/or are more suitably treated in hospital than in prison, looks to the psychiatric services for assistance. To be told, as judges and magistrates are being told, that the majority of psychiatric hospitals cannot provide a minimally secure setting, even on a short-term basis, leaves magistrates and judges with the stark choice of imposing a long sentence in an orthodox prison, as an alternative to a hospital order to a non-secure hospital. As a result of many years of the 'open door' policy, mental hospital staff are far less competent at managing patients who are not exceptionally dangerous and who might have been quite competently managed in such institutions before the current 'advances' in psychiatric philosophy became established. Applications from all sources for beds in the Special Hospitals (Broadmoor, Rampton, and Moss Side) have risen steadily from 311 in 1961 to 582 in 1973, and Tidmarsh (1974) has described how 'recently applications have been received from hospitals lacking closed wards which have stated that unless Broadmoor accept certain disturbed psychotic patients the only alternative was discharge to the community'!

The plight of the elderly mentally disordered is equally precarious. There are currently over 50,000 patients over sixty-five in mental hospitals in Britain, the number of elderly people in the population continues to rise, and there is a frightening lack of facilities for the elderly in the community. The entire national plan for the psychiatrically ill depends on the willingness and ability of Government to provide the necessary funds for the required development and expansion of facilities in the community but whatever the ability, the willingness to do so seems to have disappeared.

Shortly after its election, the Conservative Government in Britain sent a circular to the local authorities asking them to cut spending by 3 per cent for the remainder of the financial year 1979–80. At the time of writing, it seems likely that £335 millions will be cut from the Rate Support Grant, central Government's grant to the local authorities. As part of the Government's plan to cut £4,000 million off public spending in 1980–81 local authorities have been asked to plan cuts of 5 per cent. Despite the Government's insistence that it regards mental illness and mental handicap as priority areas which should be spared the impact of cuts, there is no evidence of any clear policy guidelines being given to local authorities. Meanwhile, local authorities are unveiling their plans, for example, East Sussex plans to close six old people's homes and some children's homes. Hostel development is at a standstill apart from the vigorous efforts of a number of vigorous housing associations formed by voluntary groups working for the care of de-institutionalized patients. The mood overall is gloomy with widespread expectations that, in the trenchant words of the Director of the National Association for Mental Health, 'mental health services will be first for the chop when the decision-makers at local level weigh up the pressures from more powerful quarters like education and the medical lobby' (Smythe 1979).

The situation in the United States seems no better. While Murray (1979) greets with enthusiasm the new emphasis on social and community psychiatry and the arrival of 'a new breed of academic psychiatrists to high-level posts in the powerful federal agencies' it is noticeable that his hopes appear higher for the effects of such a development on research than on services. President Carter's Commission on Mental Health (1978) pointed the finger at many of the more flagrant deficiencies in the psychiatric services but since there were already well known this scarcely represents advanced thinking. There is growing doubt that the US Treasury will continue to bear the costs of the CMHC programme over the next two decades leading one of Murray's 'new breed' to speculate gloomily on the prospects of a return to the 'economies of scale' of isolated large state hospitals and institutions for the many and private mental hospital and office-based practitioner for the few (Sharfstein 1978).

The relatives

In discussing the psychiatric and social services available to the mentally ill and handicapped, I have thus far neglected to consider the role of the relatives. My neglect reflects the stream of Departmental documents and memos that consider the role of the GP, the consultant, the nurse, the social worker, the health visitor, the occupational therapist, but nowhere that individual who more than anyone constitutes the caring community for the average patient in this country. (History is certainly in danger of repeating itself; in medieval England 'custody of the mentally ill generally rested with their relatives and friends . . . Harmless lunatics were permitted to roam through streets and roads'.)

Jacqueline Grad and Peter Sainsbury (1963) compared the family situation of patients treated by a 'community service' (which admitted 28 per cent of referrals) and a 'hospital service' (which admitted 52 per cent of referrals), Chichester and Salisbury respectively, and found that the families of patients in the 'community service' had to carry a heavier burden and sustained more stress.

'Reassessments were made one month after the decision to admit the patient or treat him at home had been taken and on a two-year follow-up. Initially 60% of the patients' relatives reported some effect on their mental health, 35% impairment of social and leisure activities, 29% upsets in domestic routine, 23% interference with the work with others than the patient. 34% reported disturbances in children. The patient's tendency to complain continuously about bodily symptoms caused most upset and this was followed by suicidal behaviour and by importunate and demanding attitudes. Neurotic patients gave fewer problems, the severely personality disordered and the organically ill gave most. Complete relief was provided for the group as a whole by the hospital service to a greater extent than the community service. During the two years of follow-up, 52% of the "community service" patients and 28% of the "hospital service" patients provided serious problems for their relatives. Families in Chichester were left with more residual financial problems and the effect on their mental health was greater.'

(Grad and Sainsbury 1968: 265)

Criticisms have been expressed about the comparability of the groups in this study (Gardner 1970) and Grad has accepted that it would be necessary to see how patients with identical illnesses fared in both services. The specific diagnostic groups, however, were not large enough to allow for the required statistical analysis.

Distinctions have been drawn between 'objective' and 'subjective' burdens. The former include particular effects on the daily life of the household and abnormal behaviour assumed to disturb the household, whereas the latter described how members of the family feel as a consequence of being exposed to the patient's illness. Hoenig (1968) used such a categorization in his comparison of the Macclesfield services (based on a large mental hospital) and the Burnley services (based on a psychiatric unit in a general hospital setting). He claimed to have found no difference in the 'objective' burden produced by the two services. 'Subjective' burden was more frequently found in the mental hospital families even when there were no 'objective' burdens, provoking one group of critics to wonder whether the type of service creates differences in the attitudes of patients and their families. In a more recent study of a mental hospital based service (Runwell Hospital, Essex) and a district general hospital psychiatric unit (at Rochford General Hospital), John Copes and his colleagues (1974) found the strain on the mental health of relatives to be similar in both services. At six months, however, 47 per cent of the Runwell patients' relatives, compared with 20 per cent of the Rochford patients' relatives, required general supportive care. It is still unclear from these studies whether the swing to community care has significantly eased or worsened the burdens on patients' families.

A study of the stresses experienced by relatives of schizophrenic patients does, however, illustrate the lack of recognition given to the fact that so often relatives are the real 'primary care' agents for the patient. The authors of the study, Professor John Wing and Clare Creer, found serious deficiencies in the community services available to the families:

'Problems were experienced [by relatives] at every stage; in getting early diagnosis and prompt treatment; in obtaining advice about medication; and, above all, about home management of disturbed behaviour; in keeping a close liaison with someone who could ensure rapid treatment at the time of a relapse (or even before the relapse occurred, since it could sometimes be predicted). Even if all the general practitioners, psychiatrists and social workers had been as skilled, sympathetic and readily available as the best of them were there was still the major problem of the availability of day centres, sheltered workshops, hostels, group homes and even hospital beds.'

(Creer and Wing 1974: 65-6)

At a time when criticism and blame are being applied to the relatives of the psychiatrically ill, it behoves those who level such attacks to remember that for the majority of patients it is their families and only their families who will cope with and support them. In the majority of cases, patients can be encouraged to return to their families without fear of relapse, However, as a number of workers have demonstrated, relapse can be precipitated when patients are discharged to homes in which there is a high emotional involvement and a negative attitude on the part of the relatives. In the absence of alternative and suitable aftercare accommodation, patients are returned willy-nilly to their families and both family and relatives are expected to cope as best they can with support from community services which are all too often overstretched and understaffed.

Summary

There are little grounds for satisfaction or, indeed, optimism when one examines the current state of psychiatry. In the United States, a professor of psychiatry at Cornell University calls the care and treatment of the severely and chronically mentally ill 'a national disgrace' (Talbott 1979).

Analysis of the situation on the far side of the Atlantic strikes an ominously familiar chord:

> ' . . . while deinstitutionalization has proceeded, states still have not found a way to enable monies to follow patients from state hospitals to community settings and because with the recent fiscal crunch, all levels of government have placed a lower priority on mental health than on education, highways, police, fire and sanitation . . . despite the lesson learned over the past 20 years that chronic patients need a vast array of supportive services including housing, income, education, and vocational and social rehabilitation, in addition to a full range of medical and psychiatric services, there are only isolated examples in the United States of programs providing such comprehensive care.'
>
> (Talbott 1979: 688)

For all the much-emphasised differences between their health care systems, Britain and the United States face remarkably similar problems when it comes to providing a sophisticated, comprehensive, and efficient psychiatric service. On both sides of the Atlantic, mental hospitals are large, old, and isolated from the populations they serve. Staffing is poor, both numerically and qualitatively, and the State mental hospitals of America, like their counterparts in Britain, rely to a disturbing extent on large numbers of inadequately-trained staff from overseas just to keep functioning.

To date, Britain has been spared the effects that private practice has had upon psychiatry. While there are signs that the love affair which many American psychiatrists have had over the years with psychoanalysis is losing some of its ardour, it may be premature to initiate proceedings for a divorce. The newer psychiatrists may, as observers such as Murray (1979) suggest, turn their attention to implementing knowledge gained over two decades of research into the biological and social aspects of psychiatric ill-health. However, the burgeoning of various forms of dilute or otherwise amended forms of psychotherapy, which include the so-called 'fringe' treatments of experiential groups, primal therapy, gestalt, massage, and charismatic movements such as est, suggests that the affluent neurotic members of America's middle class will, in Gore Vidal's classic phrase, continue to 'groove along emotional lines' and consume more than their fair share of psychiatric time and resources.

Nor can there be much ground for optimism when recruitment into psychiatry stagnates and the subject's practitioners are viewed by their medical colleagues as 'purveyors of mumbo-jumbo at the worst and brilliant dialectics at the best' (Peart 1979). Professor Peart's cold and at times contemptuous dissection of the inadequacies of contemporary psychiatry is remarkable only for being so publicly stated. The majority of his medical colleagues almost certainly hold similar views, preferring to whisper them to each other in common rooms and on committees than write them openly in the foremost psychiatric journal in the land.

Not everyone shares such a gloomy perspective, however. In Jerome Frank's view, and he is one of America's most respected psychiatrists, 'while psychiatry may emerge from its current travails somewhat altered in appearance, its future is bright'. One's confidence in Dr. Frank's prognosis is in inverse proportion to the admiration his skilful diagnosis of psychiatry's ills provokes. He sees the subject publicly discredited, harassed by the legal profession, suffering progressive shrinkage of Government monies and medical recruits, and facing increasing competition from both nonmedical therapists and non-psychiatric physicians. But he is still hopeful.

It is best that the public should know of this state of affairs if only because unless they do they will never be able to begin to comprehend the underlying causes of the endless sequence of hospital scandals, legal wrangles and psychiatric abuses which cross and will continue to cross the television screens and the newspaper columns. Whether such understanding will become translated into action remains to be seen. But the notion that understanding leads to change is one buried in the heart of psychiatry itself. So, like Dr Frank, we can but hope.

References

ALDRICH, G.K. (1965) Review of Psychiatric Illness in General Practice. *American Journal of Psychiatry* **123**: 1321.

BALINT, M. (1957) *The Doctor, his Patient and the Illness*. London: Pitman.

BERNE, E. (1964) *Games People Play*. New York: Grove Press.

BLACKWELL, B. (1973) Psychotropic drugs in use today: the role of diazepam in medical practice. *Journal of the American Medical Association* **225**, 13: 1637.

BORUS, J.F. (1978) Issues Critical to the Survival of Community Mental Health. *American Journal of Psychiatry* **135**, 9: 1029–35.

BROADHURST, A. (1977) What part does general practice play in community clinical psychology? *Bulletin of the British Psychological Society* **30**: 305–9.

BROOK, P. (1973) *Psychiatrists in Training. British Journal of Psychiatry* Special Publication No. 7. Ashford, Kent: Headley Bros.

CLARE, A.W. (1979) Brief Psychotherapy: New Approaches. In: *Symposium on Brief Psychotherapy* (Eds

R. B. Sloane and F. R. Staples) Psychiatric Clinics of North America. Vol. 2, No. 1 pp. 93–109.

COLEMAN, J.V. and PATRICK, D.L. (1978) Integrating mental health services into primary medical care. *Medical Care* **14**: 654–61.

COLLINS, J. (1965) *Social Casework in a General Medical Practice*. London: Pitman.

COOPER, B. (1971) Social Work in General Practice: The Derby Scheme. *Lancet* **i**: 539–42.

—— (1972) Social Correlates of Psychiatric Illness in the Community. G. McLachlan (ed.), *Approaches to Action*. Oxford: Nuffield Provincial Hospitals and Oxford University Press.

COOPER, B., DEPLA, C., HARWIN, B.G., and SHEPHERD, M. (1974) An experiment in community mental health care. *Lancet* **ii**: 1356–8.

COPES, J.B., FRYER, M., and ROBIN, A. (1974) *Treatment Settings in Psychiatry. A Comparative Study*. Cambridge: Henry Kimpton.

CORNEY, R.H. and BRISCOE, M.E. (1977) Social workers and their clients: a comparison between primary health care and local authority settings. *Journal of the Royal College of General Practitioners* **27**: 295–301.

CREER, C. and WING, J.K. (1974) *Schizophrenia at Home*. London: Institute of Psychiatry.

DEPARTMENT OF HEALTH AND SOCIAL SECURITY (1971) *Hospital Services for the Mentally Ill*. London: HMSO.

—— (1978) *Social Service Teams: The Practitioner's View* (Eds O. Stevenson and P. Parsloe) pp. 264–7. London: HMSO.

EDWARDS, G., WILLIAMSON, V., HAWKER, A., HENSMAN, C., and POSTOYAN, S. (1968) Census of a Reception Centre. *British Journal of Psychiatry* **114**: 1031–9.

FRANK, J.D. (1977) Psychiatry, the Healthy Invalid. *American Journal of Psychiatry* **134**, 12: 1349–55.

FREEMAN, H.L. (1965) Psychosis. In *Progress in Mental Health*. London: Office of Health Economics.

FREEMAN, T. (1974) Letter to News and Notes Supplement. *British Journal of Psychiatry*, September 1974.

FRY, J. and GAMBRILL, E. (1978) Introduction to *Scientific Foundations of Family Medicine* (Eds J. Fry, E. Gambrill and R. Smith) pp. 1–7. London: Heinemann.

GARDNER, E.A. (1970) Evaluation of Mental Health Services. In E. H. Hare and J. K. Wing (eds.), *Psychiatric Epidemiology*. London: Oxford University Press

GILCHRIST, I.C., GOUGH, J.B., HORSEFALL-TURNER, Y.R., INESON, E.M., KEELE, G., MARKS, B. and SCOTT, H.J. (1978) Social work in general practice. *Journal of the Royal College of General Practitioners* **28**: 675–9.

GOLDBERG, D. and BLACKWELL, B. (1970) Psychiatric Illness in a Suburban General Practice. A detailed study using a new method of case identification. *British Medical Journal* **2**: 439.

GRAD, J. and SAINSBURY, P. (1963) Mental Illness and the Family. *Lancet* **i**: 544.

—— (1968) The Effects that Patients Have on Their Families in a Community Care and a Control Psychiatric Service – a Two-Year Follow-up. *British Journal of Psychiatry* **114**: 265.

GUNN, J. (1975) Personal communication.

HANKIN, J. and OKTAY, J.S. (1979) Mental Disorder and Primary Medical Care: An Analytical Review of the Literature. US Department of Health, Education and Welfare. National Institute of Mental Health: Rockville, Maryland 20857.

HARWIN, B.G., COOPER, B., EASTWOOD, M.R., and GOLDBERG, D.P. (1970) Prospects for Social Work in General Practice. *Lancet* **ii**: 559–61.

HM GOVERNMENT (1957) *Report of the Committee to Consider the Future Numbers of Medical Practitioners and the*

Appropriate Intake of Medical Students (Willink Report). London: HMSO.

—— (1962) *A Hospital Plan for England and Wales.* Cmnd 1604. London: HMSO.

—— (1966) *Report of the Royal Commission on Medical Education* (The Todd Report). London: HMSO.

HM GOVERNMENT (1974) *Interim Report of Committee on Mentally Abnormal Offenders.* Cmnd 5698. London: HMSO.

—— (1975) *Report of the Committee of Inquiry into the Regulation of the Medical Profession.* London: HMSO.

HOENIG, J. (1968) The De-Segregation of the Psychiatric Patient. *Proceedings of the Royal Society of Medicine* **61**: 115.

INSKIP, J.H. and EDWARDS, J.G. (1979) Mental Hospital Inquiries. *Lancet* **i**: 660.

JANSEN, J. (1972) The Death of a Profession. *British Journal of Psychiatry* **120**: 647–9.

JOHNSTON, M. (1978) The work of a clinical psychologist in primary care. *Journal of the Royal College of General Practitioners* **28**, 196: 661–7.

KAY, D.W., BEAMISH, R., and ROTH, M. (1964) Old Age Mental Disorders in Newcastle upon Tyne. Part I. A Study of Prevalence. *British Journal of Psychiatry* **110**: 146.

KENNEDY, J.F. Message from the President of the United States Relative to Mental Illness and Mental Retardation. Document 58, 86th Congress. Feb. 5th 1963, p. 12.

KREITMAN, N. (1962) Psychiatric Orientation: A Study of Attitudes among Psychiatrists. *Journal of Mental Science* **108**: 317–28.

LAST, S.L. (1972) *Lancet* **i**: 630.

MAHAPATRA, S.B. (1975) Problems of Language in Examination for Foreign Psychiatrists. News and Notes Supplement. *British Journal of Psychiatry*, November 1974.

MILLER, H. (1973) *Medicine and Society.* London: Oxford University Press.

MURRAY, R.M. (1979) A Reappraisal of American Psychiatry. *Lancet* i: 255–8.

NATIONAL ASSOCIATION FOR MENTAL HEALTH (1974a) *Psychotherapy: Do We Need More 'Talking Treatment'?* MIND Report No. 12. London.

New Psychiatry (1974) Surveying a Decade of Rhetoric. October 3.

OKIN, R.L. (1978) The Future of State Mental Health Programs for the Chronic Psychiatric Patient in the Community. *American Journal of Psychiatry* 135, 11: 1355–8.

PALLIS, D.J. and STOFFELMAYR, B.J. (1973) Social Attitudes and Treatment Orientation among Psychiatrists. *British Journal of Medical Psychiatry* 46 (i): 75–81.

PARISH, P.A. (1971) The Prescribing of Psychotropic Drugs in General Practice. *Journal of the Royal College of General Practitioners* 21: Supplement 4.

PARKHOUSE, J. and PALMER, M.K. (1979) Career preferences of doctors qualifying in the United Kingdom in 1977. *Health Trends* 11, 2: 35–41.

PARSONS, P.L. (1965) Mental Health of Swansea's Old Folk. *British Journal of Preventive and Social Medicine* 19: 43.

PEART, W.S. (1979) Research in psychiatry: a view from general medicine. Editorial. *Psychological Medicine* 9, 2: 205–6.

PERINPANAYAGAM, M.S. (1973) Overseas Postgraduate Psychiatric Doctors. News and Notes Supplement. *British Journal of Psychiatry*, March 1973.

POWELL, J.E. (1961) Address to National Association for Mental Health, Annual Conference.

PRESIDENT'S COMMISSION ON MENTAL HEALTH (1978). Report for the President. Washington.

RATOFF, L., COOPER, B., and ROCKETT, D. (1973) Seebohm and the NHS: A Survey of Medico-Social Liaison. *British Medical Journal* 2: 51–3.

REGIER, D.A. and GOLDBERG, I.D. (1976) quoted in Hankin and Oktay (see above) p. 49.

ROSEN, B.M., LOCKE, B.Z., GOLDBERG, I.D. and BABIGAN, H.M. (1970) Identifying emotional disturbance in persons seen in industrial dispensaries. *Mental Hygiene* **54**: 271–9.

ROTH, V.E., RURY, J.L. and DOWNING, J.J. (1959) Psychiatric patients in a general practice. *General Practitioner* **20**: 106–10.

ROYAL COLLEGE OF PSYCHIATRISTS (1973) *Norms for Medical Staffing in a Child Psychiatric Service*. Report to Central Manpower Committee. London.

—— (1974) Memorandum on Psychiatric Manpower as it Affects the Psychiatric Services. London.

ROYAL COMMISSION ON THE NATIONAL HEALTH SERVICE (1979) Cmnd 7615. London: HMSO.

RUSSELL, G.F.M. (1972) The Recruitment of Psychiatrists (*British Journal of Psychiatry* **120**: 333–9.

—— (1973a) Problems of Recruitment into General Psychiatry. News and Notes Supplement. *British Journal of Psychiatry*, August.

SHARFSTEIN, S.S. (1978) Will Community Mental Health Survive in the 1980s? *American Journal of Psychiatry* **135**, 11: 1363–5.

SHEPHERD, M., COOPER, B., BROWN, A.C., and KALTON, G. (1966) *Psychiatric Illness in General Practice*. London: Oxford University Press.

SMITH, R. (1978) The Evolution of Academic Family Medicine in the United States. In: *Scientific Foundations of Family Medicine* (Eds J. Fry, E. Gambrill, and R. Smith) Chapter 3, pp. 12–15. London:Heinemann.

SMYTHE, T. (1979) Mental health services face a major crisis. *Mind Out*, July/August. No. 35, p. 2. London: National Association for Mental Health.

SYLPH, J., KEDWARD, H.B., and EASTWOOD, M.R. (1969) Chronic Neurotic Patients in General Practice. *Journal of the Royal College of General Practitioners* **17**: 162.

TALBOTT, J.A. (1979) Care of the Chronically Mentally

Ill – Still a National Disgrace. Editorial. *American Journal of Psychiatry* **136**, 5: 688–9.

TAYLOR, LORD and CHAVE, S. (1964) *Mental Health and Environment*. London: Longman.

TIDMARSH, D. (1974) Secure Hospital Units. Letter to *British Medical Journal*, November 3.

WALTON, H.J. (1966) Differences between Physically-Minded and Psychologically-Minded Medical Practitioners. *British Journal of Psychiatry* **112**: 1097–102.

WALTON, H.J., DREWERY, J., and CARSTAIRS, G.M. (1963) Interest of Graduating Medical Students in Social and Emotional Aspects of Illness. *British Medical Journal* **ii**: 588–92..

WHEATLEY, D. (1972) Evaluation of psychotropic drugs in general practice. *Proceedings of the Royal Society of Medicine* **65**: 317.

WILLIAMS, P. (1978) Physical ill-health and psychotropic drug prescription – a review. *Psychological Medicine* **8**: 683–93.

WING, J.K. and WING, L. (1970) Psychotherapy and the National Health Service. An Operational Study. *British Journal of Psychiatry* **116**: 51.

WORLD HEALTH ORGANISATION (1973) *Psychiatry and Primary Care*. Report on a Working Group. Copenhagen: WHO.

WORLD HEALTH ORGANISATION (1973) *Psychiatry and Primary Health Care*. Copenhagen.

Author
Index

Subject Index